PAUL

Paul O'Keeffe is a lecturer and writer [partly obscured] Liverpool. His acclaimed books include *Some Sort of Genius: A Life of Wyndham Lewis*, *Gaudier-Brzeska: An Absolute Case of Genius*, *A Genius for Failure: The Life of Benjamin Robert Haydon* and, most recently, *Waterloo: The Aftermath*.

ALSO BY PAUL O'KEEFFE

Some Sort of Genius:
A Life of Wyndham Lewis

Gaudier-Brzeska:
An Absolute Case of Genius

A Genius for Failure:
The Life of Benjamin Robert Haydon

Waterloo:
The Aftermath

PAUL O'KEEFFE

Culloden

Battle & Aftermath

VINTAGE

3 5 7 9 10 8 6 4 2

Vintage is part of the Penguin Random House group of companies whose addresses can be found at global.penguinrandomhouse.com

First published in Vintage in 2023
First published in hardback by The Bodley Head in 2021

penguin.co.uk/vintage

A CIP catalogue record for this book is available from the British Library

ISBN 9781784704452

Printed and bound in Great Britain by Clays Ltd, Elcograf S.p.A.

The authorised representative in the EEA is Penguin Random House Ireland, Morrison Chambers, 32 Nassau Street, Dublin D02 YH68

Penguin Random House is committed to a sustainable future for our business, our readers and our planet. This book is made from Forest Stewardship Council® certified paper.

For my ‘big’ brother Stephen O’Keeffe (1941–2018)
craftsman, historian, enthusiast.
Also for Robert O’Keeffe (1941–2019)
the brother I regret not having known better.

CONTENTS

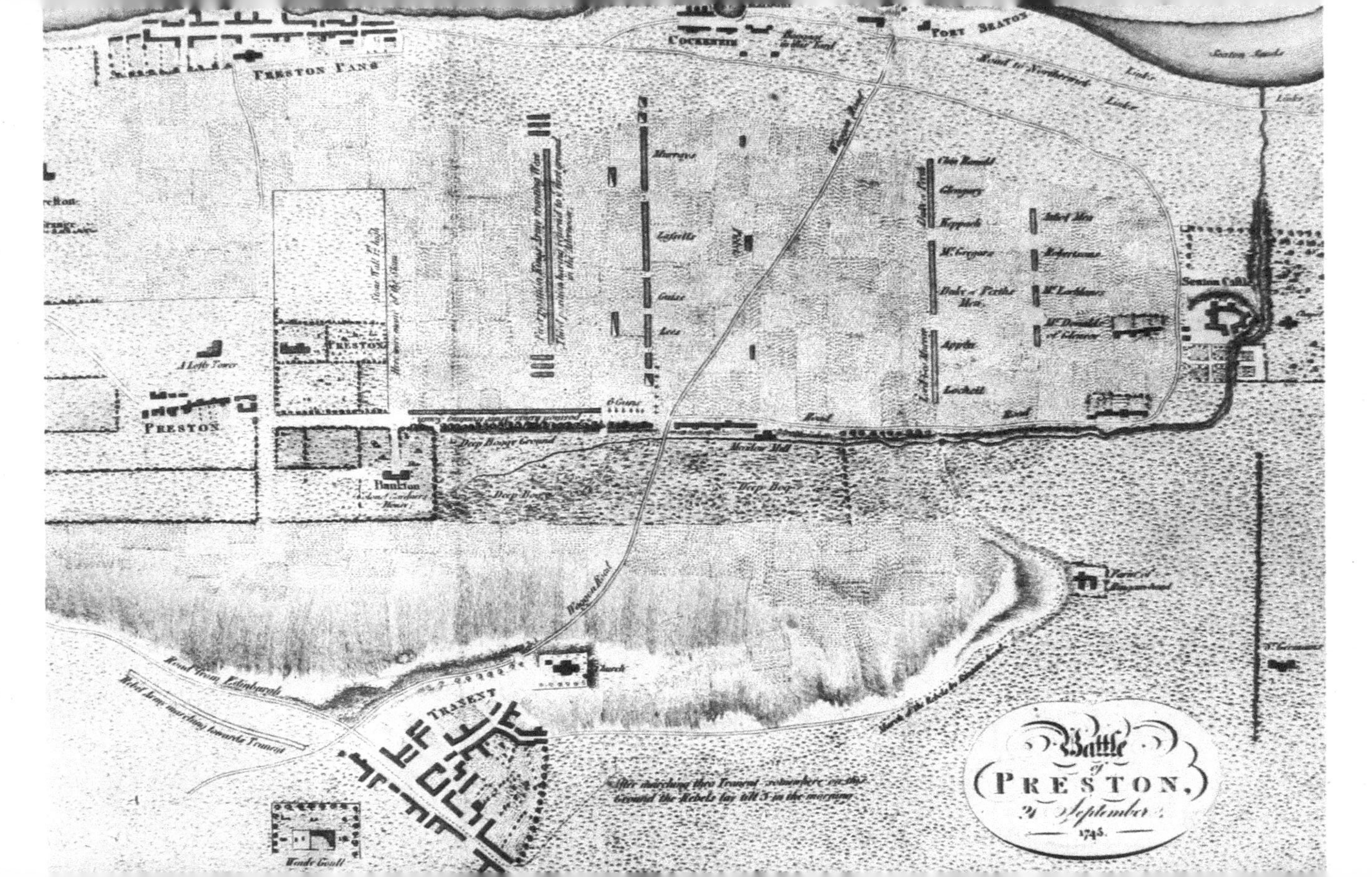

Battle of PRESTON, 21 September 1745.
PRESTON PANS
COCKENZIE
PORT SEATON
Road to Northberwick
Seaton Sands
Seaton Castle
PRESTON
TRANENT
Road from Edinburgh
Rebel Army marching towards Tranent
Waggon Road
Deep Bog
Deep Boggy Ground
Meadow Mill
Bankton
A Lofts Tower
Wende Gault
Farm of Ringanhead
Church
Chisholm
Glengary
Keppoch
Mc Gregors
Duke of Perths Men
Appin
Lochell
Athol Men
Robertsons
Mc Lachlanes
Mc Donalds of Glenco
Murrays
Lascelles
Guise
Lees
Road
After marching thro Tranent somewhere on this ground the Rebels lay till 3 in the morning

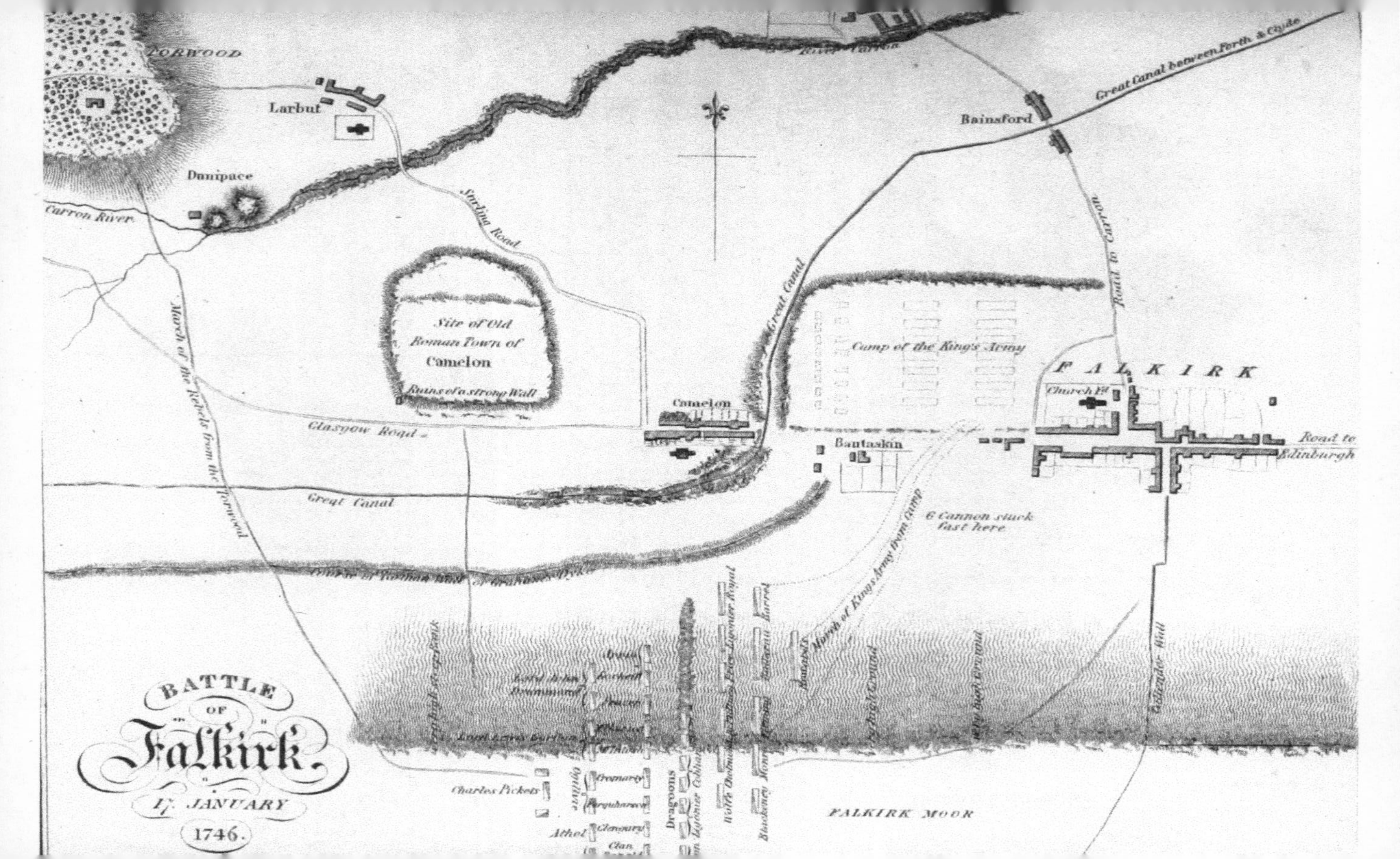
BATTLE
OF
Falkirk
17 JANUARY
1746.
TORWOOD
Larbut
Dunipace
Carron River
Stirling Road
Site of Old
Roman Town of
Camelon
Ruins of a strong Wall
River Carron
Great Canal between Forth & Clyde
Bainsford
Road to Carron
Great Canal
Camp of the King's Army
FALKIRK
Church Yd
Camelon
Glasgow Road
Bantaskin
Road to
Edinburgh
Great Canal
6 Cannon stuck
fast here
March of Kings Army from Camp
March of the Rebels from the Torwood
Charles Pickets
Ogilvie
Athol
Dragoons
FALKIRK MOOR

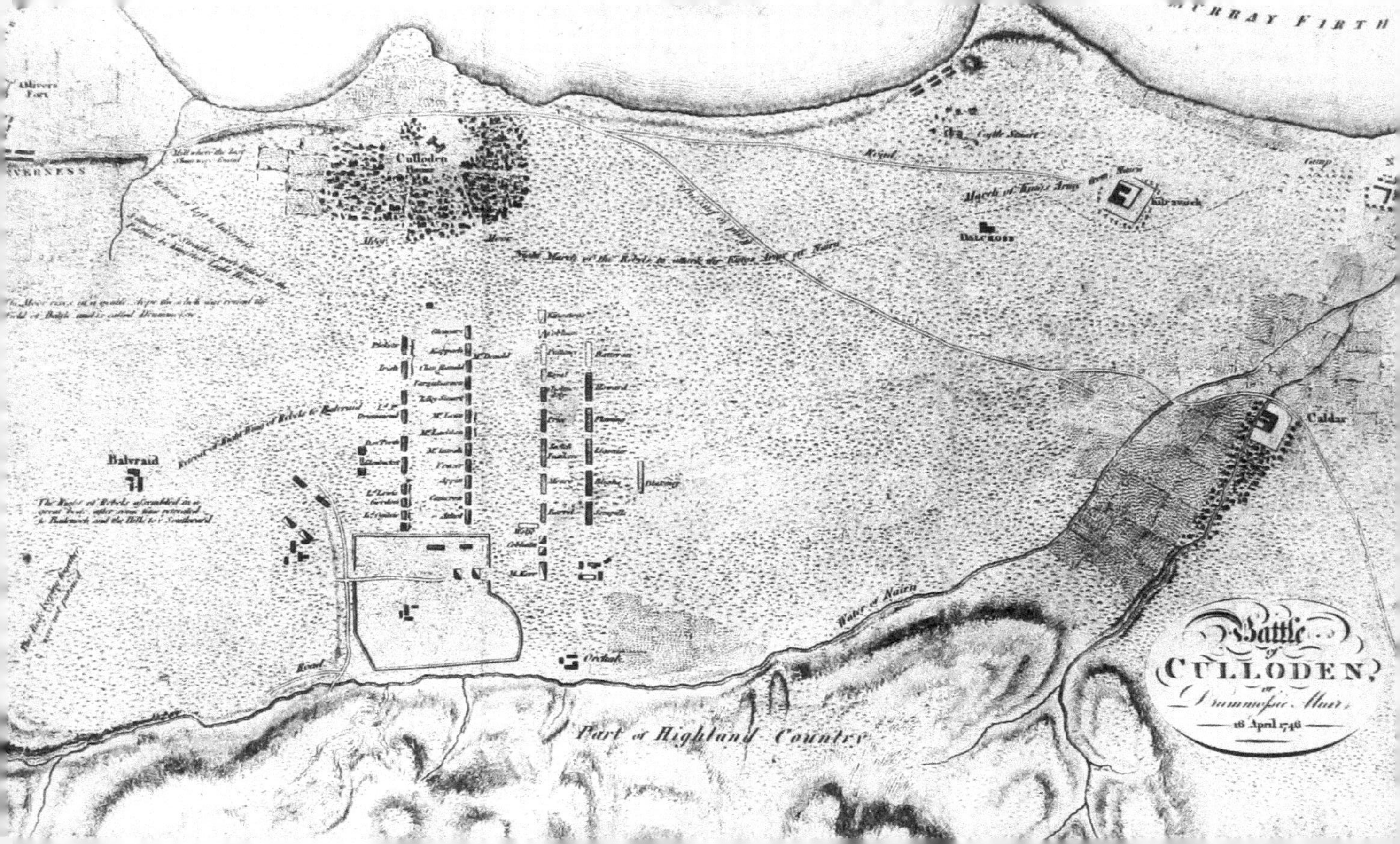
Battle of CULLODEN, or Drummossie Muir, 18 April 1746
MURRAY FIRTH
Culloden House
Castle Stuart
Kilravock
Dalcross
Caldar
Balvraid
Water of Nairn
Part of Highland Country
Ochak
Road
Camp
Night March of the Rebels to attack the Kings Army at Nairn
March of Kings Army from Nairn
Pickets
Drummond
Glengary
Keppoch
Clanranald
Farquharson
Appin
Cameron
Athol
Fraser
McDonald
Barrell
Munro
Royal
Price
Howard
Fleming
Blakeney
Bligh
Sempill
Kingston
Cobham
Balvraid

A likeness notwithstanding the Disguise that any Person who Secures the Son of the Pretender is Intitled to a Reward of 30 000 £.

PRELUDE: ADVICES

'RISING' or 'Rebellion'; 'King' or 'Pretender'; 'Usurper' or 'Rightful Sovereign': vocabulary of the 1745 insurgency has varied according to the political or religious persuasion – Tory or Whig, Episcopalian or Presbyterian – of those employing it. It has differed according to the perceived justice or injustice of the insurgents' cause, the legitimacy or otherwise of a Catholic Stuart over a Protestant Hanoverian succession, and of a parliament's right to legislate on the matter either way. From the Whig or Presbyterian perspective the insurgency's leader, born and raised in Rome – bringing arbitrary, absolutist monarchy and Papal tyranny in his wake – was 'the Italian', 'the Young Pretender', 'the Mock Prince', or 'the young Chevalier', derived from the title *Chevalier de St George* bestowed upon his father by Louis XIV of France.

Christened Charles Edward Louis John Casimir Silvester Severino Maria, his father called him Carluccio. His Highland supporters knew him as Teàrlach – the Scots Gaelic form of 'Charles', but pronounced 'Charloch' – its two syllables approximating phonetically to the informal familiarity of 'Charlie'. In a letter of September 1745 a sixteen-year-old girl described him to her cousin as the 'Bonny Prince',[1] but that epithet would not become inseparably applied in print until the first quarter of the nineteenth century.

From the Tory, Catholic, or Episcopalian perspective he was the Prince of Wales, eldest son of the anointed king and next in line to the throne by Divine Right, while its incumbent was the son of a German usurper and nothing more than 'Elector of Hanover'. From this perspective George II was king in name only, king by parliamentary statute, king according to the 1701 Act of Settlement, and his genealogical claim to rule Britain was more than fifty times removed from that of the man holding expatriate court in Rome: the true 'King Over the Water'. This putative King James III of England and VIII of Scotland, was, to the Whig party which disdained his claims, merely 'The Old Pretender', while the Latin form of his name – Jacobus – provided the doomed cause fighting to restore him with its particular designation: Jacobite.

*

'We have been alarmed with advices . . . of intended invasions' wrote the Lord President of the Court of Session, Scotland's supreme civil judiciary, 'and particularly of a visit which the Pretender's eldest son is about to make to us, if he has not already made it.' Duncan Forbes of Culloden – the name of his ancestral estate to the east of Inverness, still nine months from the infamy it would acquire the following Spring – was writing from Edinburgh to the Prime Minister, Henry Pelham, at the beginning of August 1745. He had previously given little credence to the rumours he mentioned and was still sceptical: 'This young gentleman's game seems at present to be very desperate in this country; and, so far as I can learn, there is not the apparatus for his reception, even amongst the few highlanders who are suspected to be in his interest.'

Nevertheless, as soon as his official duties would allow, Forbes intended travelling north, resolved, 'though my fighting days are over, [to] give some countenance to the friends of the government, and prevent the seduction of the unwary, if there be any truth in what is reported'.[2]

A day after the Lord President's letter, Norman MacLeod of MacLeod, Member of Parliament for Inverness-shire, was writing to Pelham from Dunvegan Castle on the island of Skye, confirming the reports: 'To my no small surprise, it is certain that the Pretended Prince of Wales is come on the Coast of South Uist and Barra, and has since been hovering on parts of the Coast of the main Land that lies betwixt the point of Airdnamurchan and Glenelg.'

Like Forbes, MacLeod saw little chance of success for the enterprise, convinced as he was 'that not one man of any consequence benorth the Grampians will give any sort of assistance to this mad rebellious attempt'. He deplored seeing 'any thing like disaffection to the Government . . . tho' ever so trivial', and equally was loath 'to march a single Company to quell it', given 'the present situation of Affairs in Europe'.[3]

The situation MacLeod referred to was a sprawling, intermittent struggle involving – at one time or another – not only most states and countries of Europe, but parts of North America and, in its latter stages, the Carnatic region of the Indian subcontinent. Its belligerents were ostensibly fighting to defend or oppose Archduchess Maria Theresa's right to the Habsburg throne following the death of her father, the Holy Roman Emperor Charles VI. The War of the Austrian Succession was, however, a power and land grab more than a dynastic dispute: Prussia invading Silesia, France Bohemia; Britain capturing the French-Canadian fortress of Louisburg, and France seizing Madras from the British East India Company. In addition, this wider conflict subsumed a more localised one in which the Royal Navy used the mutilation of a Welsh merchant ship's captain by Spanish coastguards as a pretext to enforce British rights to trade slaves in the Caribbean: the nine-year-long War of Jenkins' Ear.

Although European hostilities had broken out in 1740 it was not until June 1743 that a British army engaged with the French, at Dettingen, and George II became the last of his country's monarchs to command troops in battle. Following that victory, the army's next major encounter with French troops – this time commanded by the formidable Marshal Maurice de Saxe – ended in costly defeat at Fontenoy on 11 May 1745. In choosing this parlous juncture for the attempt to reclaim his father's throne – and coinciding with continued Spanish depredations to British slaving routes – Charles Edward Stuart might have expressed, *avant la lettre*, sentiments precipitating another insurrection at a time of European war, in Dublin at Easter 1916: 'England's difficulty is our opportunity.'

*

James Stuart's eldest son, heir and final hope of claiming the British crown had disembarked from the French frigate *Du Teillay* at Eriskay in the Outer Hebrides on 23 July.

Of the entourage that accompanied the Prince from France – known in Jacobite lore as 'the Seven Men of Moidart'* – only three had any degree of military experience. Colonel John William O'Sullivan, an Irish professional soldier in the French service, was appointed Adjutant General and Quartermaster General. Sir John MacDonald was another expatriate Irishman, veteran of the Fitzjames' Horse, a regiment originally raised by James II but incorporated into the French army in 1698. The Prince appointed Sir John Inspector of Cavalry. A not impartial witness described him as 'much subject to his bottle'.[4]

Then there was William Murray, Marquess of Tullibardine, eldest son of the late 1st Duke of Atholl. Convicted of high treason for taking part in the risings of 1715 and 1719, and subject to a Bill of Attainder deeming his bloodline corrupted and denying him all rights of property and nobility, William could neither inherit nor bequeath his father's title. This did not, however, deter his styling himself Duke, signing his corresponence 'Atholl', and exercising the feudal right of pressing his 'Vassalls, Tennants and Wadsetters' to the military service of King James, threatening disobedience with the 'hostile rigour that all Rebells

* From their point of disembarkation near Kinlochmoidart prior to raising the Stuart standard at Glenfinnan.

& disaffected people to their King & country deserve'.[5] He suffered from gout and was described on his arrival as 'still the old man as he was; he looks as if he were of greater age by ten years than he is'. He was fifty-six.[6]

The remaining four were Sir Thomas Sheridan, another trusted Irishman and the Prince's tutor, a Protestant Irish clergyman named George Kelly, Francis Strickland, an English Catholic hanger-on from the Jacobite court in Rome, and the Paris banker, Aeneas MacDonald, brother to Donald MacDonald of Kinlochmoidart.

An account published within months of his arrival has the Prince throwing himself down and kissing the Scottish ground, before being solemnly presented with a freshly cut piece of turf, a token of the land he had come to claim. His chaplain, the Abbé Butler,* then proceeded to invest him 'as Regent for . . . the most puissant James III with the Possession and Rule of the Kingdom of Great Britain . . . to hold at the Will and Pleasure of the Holy See'. The strident anti-Catholic bias of Henry Fielding's *History of the Present Rebellion in Scotland* is evident from the alleged oath sworn: that 'Possession and Rule' was granted 'on the Condition of fighting the Cause of our holy Mother the Church, to the utter Extirpation of the Persons of Hereticks . . . till [their] Blood . . . shall be washed away from the Face of the Earth.'[7]

To bring about this happy outcome, the *Du Teillay* contained arms, ammunition, and other essentials for the campaign: 1,500 muskets, 1,800 broadswords, and 'a good quantity of powder, balls, flints, Durks, Brandy etc.'[8] There were 'several cases of pistols',[9] about a hundred additional muskets, and more broadswords of indeterminate number, together with 'twenty small field pieces, two of which a mule [could] carry'. Finally, there was a war chest of 'near 4,000 lois d'or'.[10] Unfortunately, the enterprise had already lost another essential: men. A fortnight earlier, the frigate's escort *L'Elisabeth*, a much larger ship of sixty-four guns, had fought a British man-of-war off the Lizard, exchanging almost five hours' cannon fire to their mutual devastation. The *Du Teillay*

* Soon to return to France on board the *Du Taillay*.

escaped with her precious cargo and principal passenger but the *Elisabeth* – captain seriously injured and near two hundred men killed and wounded – had to struggle, severely disabled, back to her home port of Brest, taking with her seven hundred Irish troops in the service of France intended for the rising.

MacLeod of MacLeod's and Forbes's conviction that there would be little or no support in the Highlands for the 'mad rebellious attempt' seemed to be confirmed the day after the Prince's landing when he was visited by Alexander MacDonald of Boisdale, who implored him to return home. 'I am come home, sir' came the reply, 'and I will entertain no notion at all of returning to that place from whence I came; for that I am persuaded my faithful Highlanders will stand by me.'[11]

In another account of the conversation, Boisdale was asked whether a hundred men might join the cause, to which he replied: 'No doubt you'll get more than a hundred. But what then, though you get 500? what will that do?' And the Prince answered, 'Well then, if I can get only a hundred good stout, honest-hearted fellows to join me, I'll make a trial what I can do.'[12] Boisdale's influence was said to have prevented 'some hundreds of people from joining', a service to the government for which he was said to have received official thanks.[13]

Denied support from the MacDonalds of the Outer Hebrides, the Prince had more success with those on the mainland. The *Du Teillay* next made landfall on 25 July at Borrodale on the north shore of Lochnanuagh. Fourteen months later, and from the same place, Charles Edward Stuart would leave Scotland forever.

At Borrodale, young Ranald Macdonald of Clanranald, Boisdale's nephew, pledged his allegiance, as did Donald Cameron of Lochiel, effective chief of the widespread Clan Cameron. At first wary of committing to the venture, without the promise of considerable French military support, 'young Lochiel' reluctantly agreed to bring out his people on two conditions: that he would be given 'security for the full value of his estate in the event of the attempt proving abortive', and an assurance in writing that the MacDonells of Glengarry rise at the same time.[14] And so they did, along with the Grants of Glenmoriston from their neighbouring lands north of the seismic fault line of the Great Glen, the MacDonells of Keppoch from lands to the south, and the Appin Stewarts from theirs in the west.

Heads of clans set about recruiting men to the cause from the vassals and tenants under their sway as had always been done in times of war or insurrection. A hundred Camerons were led away from their homes on the banks of Loch Rannoch, having been warned that, should they refuse, the recruiting gang 'would that instant proceed to burn all their houses and hough [hamstring] their cattle', and the homes and livestock of MacDonells owing allegiance to Keppoch were threatened with the same.[15]

*

First blood of the rising was claimed by a group of eleven Keppoch MacDonells and their piper, who, on 16 August, routed two companies of new-levied Royal Scots on the way from Fort Augustus to Fort William. The encounter took place at General Wade's three-spanned bridge over the Spean gorge, just eight miles short of their destination. So unexpected was the attack that the troops 'were struck with such an unaccountable panick as with one consent to run of[f] without so much as taking time to observe the number or quality of their enemy'.[16] Had they done so they might easily have 'forced their way through this handful [and] soon . . . reached the fort, the road being plain and open'.[17] Instead they 'inadvisably' retreated the way they had come, towards Fort Augustus, eighteen miles distant. Donald MacDonell of Tirnadris led his men in pursuit, being careful not to follow too closely until they were reinforced by his cousin Keppoch, 'to about the number of forty-five or fifty att most'. Shots were exchanged, the redcoats firing as they fled, 'till their whole ammunition was exhausted'. Then Keppoch ran forward, sword in hand, and told them if they did not yield 'they should be cutt to pieces, upon which they immediatly laid down their arms'.[18] Captain John Scott, their commanding officer, had received a ball through his shoulder. A sergeant and three or four men were killed and about a dozen wounded. They had inflicted no injury on their opponents despite the final shots being fired at a distance of ten or twelve paces.

The Lord President, writing from Culloden House, did his best to make light of the affair, conceding that the Highlanders had 'begun the horse-play' with this exploit, and although expressing misgivings that it might 'be the occasion of farther folly', he suggested that the insurgents' victory was a meagre one. 'Two companies of the Royal[s] made prisoners, sounds pretty well,' he admitted, 'and will surely be passed for a notable achievement; but when it is considered that these companies were not half compleat; that they were lads picked up last season in the Low Country, without any thing of the Royal but the name, and that their officers were raw, the achievement is not by any means so important.'[19]

It was, nevertheless, an auspicious start to the campaign. Three days later, on 19 August, the captive redcoats were marched, under an escort of three hundred Keppoch MacDonells, to Glenfinnan at the head of Loch Shiel. Here, in the presence of around seven hundred Camerons, and a contingent of Clanranald Macdonalds bringing the total strength to an estimated 1,400,[20] the nervous prisoners witnessed the raising of the Royal Stuart standard, blue and white on a red silk ground, 'no motto at all'[21] and 'about twice the size of an ordinary pair of colours' carried by a British regiment.[22] While they would have understood little of James III's proclamation appointing his eldest son as Regent, intoned as it was in Gaelic, they might have recognised the 'very pretty gelding', formerly the property of their wounded Captain, that MacDonell of Tirnadris presented to the Prince, 'the first good horse he mounted in Scotland'.[23]

*

It was in Lochiel's house at Kinlochiel that Charles Edward, learned of the price on his head.

He had become an outlaw, in the eyes of the British government, in the spring of the previous year, while still living in Paris. Following intelligence that he had 'lately arrived in the *French* Dominions, and . . . been received and encouraged by the *French* King', an Act of Parliament was passed stating, in brief: 'if the eldest Son of the Pretender, shall after the first Day of *May* be found in *Great Britain* or *Ireland* he shall be adjudged attainted of High Treason and shall suffer and forfeit as Persons attainted of High Treason by the Laws of the Land ought to suffer and forfeit.'[24]

On 1 August 1745, as the alarming circumstances provided for by this legislation were realised, a proclamation was published, 'Offering a Reward of Thirty thousand Pounds to any Person who shall seize and secure the Eldest Son of the Pretender, in case He shall land, or attempt to land, in any of His Majesty's Dominions.'[25] Calculations of monetary equivalence between the eighteenth and the present century cannot be entirely reliable, but even at a cautious estimate, this fabulous sum would have amounted to around three and a half million pounds. At first the Prince intended ignoring this 'scandalous & malicious' attempt to apprehend him, treating it with deserved contempt as 'a mean, barbarous principle among princes, [that] must dishonour [the House of Hanover] in the eyes of all men of honour'. His outraged followers, however, insisted that honour could only be served by publishing a counter-proclamation. Against his will, therefore, he authorised a like reward offered 'to him or them who shall seize & secure, till our further orders, the person of the Elector of Hanover, whether landed or attempting to land'. George II was in fact enjoying a summer visit to his beloved Hanover at the time the proclamation was issued. 'Should any fatal accident happen from hence,' presumably to George's person, 'let the blame ly entirely at the door of those who first set the infamous example.'[26]

The prince's little army marched east along Loch Eil, moving inland to evade Fort William and the attentions of a warship patrolling Loch Linnhe. From Moy they benefitted from a fifteen-mile stretch of the military road built by General Wade to link

Fort William, Fort Augustus and Fort George at Inverness, running the entire length of the Great Glen, and known to the government army as 'The Chain'.

At Invergarry Castle, eight miles from Fort Augustus, the Prince was presented with a choice. A message of support from Simon Fraser, Lord Lovat, urged him to continue on that road as far as Inverness, raising the Frasers of Stratherrick on the way and with the possibility of MacLeods, MacKenzies, Grants and MacIntoshes rising into the bargain. However, the Marquess of Tullibardine pressed in favour of marching south to raise the Atholl country of Perthshire, then on to the prize of Edinburgh. The decision was forced by news that a government army under the command of General Sir John Cope was approaching from the south. Reinforced by 260 Appin Stewarts, 400 MacDonells of Glengarry, 120 MacDonalds of Glencoe, and an indeterminate number of Glenmoriston Grants, the Prince's growing army prepared to engage him.

On the same day that the Prince's standard was raised at Glenfinnan, General Cope had left Edinburgh to join his army at Stirling, and on 20 September he began his march north with the aim of 'crushing in the Bud, any Insurrection that had, or might happen'. His orders were to proceed, by way of Crieff and Dalnacardoch, to Fort Augustus, 'as it was from the adjacent Parts there, that the most Danger was to be apprehended'.[27] At Dalwhinnie on the 26th he received intelligence that if he continued on that road he would be marching into a trap, or at best a confrontation more to his enemies' advantage than to his own. 'We were informed,' wrote one of his officers, 'that the rebels were posted on and in . . . a noted pass, seventeen miles distant on our way to the Chain.'[28]

General Wade had judged the Corrieyairack Pass to be the only negotiable way across the range of Monadhliath mountains – between 2,500 and 3,000 feet high – through which he could take his road north to the Great Glen. At the steepest gradient it had necessitated no less than seventeen 'traverses' and hairpin bends to accommodate the final five-hundred-foot climb to the summit. Twenty-eight years later Dr Johnson and James Boswell would negotiate the Corrieyairack Pass on their way to the Western Isles. 'As we went upon a higher [traverse],' Johnson remarked, 'we saw the baggage following us below in a contrary direction.' And he marvelled at the tenacity of the men who had engineered it. 'To make this way, the rock has been hewn to a level with labour that might have broken the perseverance of a Roman legion.'[29] On the other side there was a sheltered area of flat ground that the soldiers who built the road called Snugburgh, or more literally, 'Snugburrow'. It was here, when the work was done, that their commander presided over an ox roast for them to celebrate the King's birthday on 30 October 1731. Wade must have regarded the road through Corrieyairack as his masterpiece and it appears – coiling off into the distance – in the landscape background of an oil portrait of him.*

However dazzling this roadbuilding feat, the Corrieyairack Pass could be murderously exploited by whichever army controlled its upper reaches. 'Each Traverse, in ascending, is commanded by that above it; so that even an unarmed Rabble, who were posted on the higher Ground, might without exposing themselves, extremely harrass the Troops in their March.'[30] In addition, the road was 'flanked [on the left] by a hollow water-course, where [the rebels] would be well covered, as likewise numbers of them might be among the rocks and on top of the hill'. And even supposing Cope's army could reach the top, their enemies 'proposed to break down the bridge at Snugburrow, which lifts the road over a steep precipice, and to place men in two hollow ways, which flank the road'.[31]

Realising that to proceed was utterly impracticable, while returning to Crieff 'would have had the Air of a Retreat, would . . . have dejected the Friends of the Government, and . . . increased the Insolence of its Opposers', Cope followed the sole course of action he believed open to him. 'His Orders being positive to march to the Chain of Forts', he abandoned Fort Augustus as destination and led his men instead along another of Wade's roads

* attributed to Johan van Diist (Scottish National Portrait Gallery).

to the right, following the Spey valley by way of Ruthven Barracks towards 'the only Part of the Chain to which [they] could proceed'.[32] The devastation of his army deferred, Cope marched to Inverness. Meanwhile the Jacobite army he was to face in little more than three weeks' time marched south, snaking down the Corrieyairack Pass, through Dalwhinnie, Dalnacardoch and Dunkeld, reaching Perth on 3 September. Here, during a stay of seven days, the Prince's general staff, together with his army's command structure, were considerably augmented.

William, Marquess of Tullibardine and titular 2nd Duke of Atholl, was reunited with his brother. Lord George Murray – as a younger son, the 'Lord' was no more than a courtesy title – had briefly served with the British Army as an ensign in the Royal Scots Guards during the latter stages of the War of the Spanish Succession. Although both brothers had been 'out' in the 1715 and 1719 Jacobite Risings, George was pardoned in 1724, returned from his French exile and swore an oath of loyalty to George II in 1739. Now, in 1745, aged 51, he had changed his allegiance definitively and for the last time, fully acknowledging that this course of action would 'very probably end in [his] utter ruen'. He was writing to James, his other brother, a staunch Whig, Member of Parliament for Perthshire, and Keeper of the Privy Seal of Scotland. James Murray was also the legitimate 2nd Duke of Atholl, having succeeded to their late father's title at the expense of William the attainted heir. 'My Life, my Fortune, my expectations, the Happyness of my wife & children, are all at stake', George told him, '& the chances are against me, & yet a principle of . . . Honour, & my Duty to King and Country, outweighs every thing.'[33] His correspondent can have been in no doubt as to the King he referred to. Few family divisions opened by the constitutional crisis of 1745 can have been so trenchant as this. And the division extended to George Murray's immediate family. His sixteen-year-old son deplored his father's decision. John Murray was then at Eton, his education being paid for by his uncle – and 'best friend' – James whose own two sons had died in infancy. Eager to take up a commission in the 54th Foot offered him by the Hanoverian king, John declared himself ready to 'lay down my Life and . . . spend the last drop of my Blood in his [Majesty's] service'.[34] Although he never bore arms against his father's espoused cause, it was not for want of inclination or capacity, being able to 'handle a broadsword or a musket well enough'. The following February, learning of a government army defeat, John, by then Captain Murray, would declare himself 'sorry to hear that the Rebles had the better of the Battle'. Writing to his uncle from London, he would make no mention of his father's part in the engagement: 'The only good which I can wish the Rebles is that they were all killed, which is the best thing that can happen to them.'[35]

Another recruit to the Prince's cause in September was James Drummond, eldest son of the attainted 2nd Duke of Perth who had fought against both William III at the Battle of the Boyne in 1690 and at Sheriffmuir in 1715 against the army of George I. On the death of his exiled father, James styled himself 3rd Duke of Perth, and was referred to as such in Jacobite correspondence, although the tainted line and title no longer had legitimacy in Hanoverian Britain. Despite having no title to his name, James maintained control and benefit of the family estate, his father having cannily signed it over to him in 1715 before the terms of the Attainder Act came into force. The two hundred tenants he brought from Crieff formed the nucleus of the so-called Duke of Perth's Regiment that would reach a maximum strength of 750 during the course of the Rising. James's brother, John Drummond, had long resided in France but later in the year would arrive at Montrose, on the east coast of Scotland, leading an 800-strong body of men composed of about 300 Irish Picquets, drawn from a brigade that had contributed to the French victory at Fontenoy, and the mercenary regiment Drummond himself had raised for the French king: the *Royal Ecossais*. As a younger son, John Drummond would, like George Murray, have been addressed with the courtesy title of Lord.

The titular Dukes of Atholl and Perth, and their brothers, George Murray and John Drummond respectively, were given the rank of Lieutenant General and together constituted the highest echelon in the Jacobite army, immediately below the Prince himself. In the first major engagement of the campaign, Perth would command the right wing and Murray the left.

*

The Prince's cause was enriched at Perth by £500 claimed from the town as Cess, or property tax. The sum was surrendered 'on the assurance that nothing else should be asked, and all supplies paid for'. Contrary to their prior apprehensions, it was noted that 'the towns people seem'd very well pleas'd that so good descpline had been keept, in so far as that non of them had the least reason to complean of any disorder.'[36]

And as the Jacobite army marched on Edinburgh, General Cope having – as one irascible citizen put it – 'give[n] up in a maner the key of North Brittan' by failing to engage and instead marching to Inverness, expectations were often confounded by their behaviour. Patrick Crichton, a Canongate saddler, ironmonger, and author of a journal, eccentrically spelled even by eighteenth-century standards, accorded them a grudging respect he often denied the 'infatwat'* policy of their opponents: 'The rebells approched with good disciplin for to give them there due never did . . . theiving naked ruffiens with uncowth wappons make so harmeless a march in a civilised plentifull cowntry, and the disciplin was so severe they hanged up one or two at Li[nli]thgow for pilfering.'[37]

*

At Coltbridge, a mile to the west of Edinburgh and marking the city's last line of defence, Colonel Gardiner's 13th Regiment of Dragoons 'was fatigwed having had long marches and watchings for three days befor [and] lookd very unlicke men [that] wowld stand to it'. The Colonel himself was not a well man either, had only recently returned from taking the waters at Scarborough,

* infatuated.

and was wont to say – with some justice as it transpired – that he 'had not long to live'.[38] The troopers of Hamilton's 14th 'looked better,' Crichton thought, 'but alace they were Irishmen!' Brigadier Thomas Fowke, newly arrived from London with a commission to take overall charge of the dragoons, cast a more professional eye over his new command. He 'found many of the Horses Backs not fit to receive the Riders', having recently been at grass in preparation for the winter. And the riders were in no better shape, especially those of the 13th. After three days in the saddle 'many of the Mens and some of the Officers Legs [were] so swelled, that they could not wear Boots', having had to cut through the leather to remove them.[39]

Supporting the dragoons at Coltbridge on 16 September, as the Jacobite army approached, were levies of a new Edinburgh Infantry Regiment that Crichton thought 'looked licke men for the purpose but they were a handful', together with a hundred Town Guards – watchmen and keepers of the peace – that the Lord Provost of Edinburgh had made available 'all the day Time; but by no Means could spare them in the Night'.[40] By mid afternoon that proviso was no longer relevant as Brigadier Fowke decided his men were not in a condition for further 'Night-Work'. Town Guards and Foot were ordered back to Edinburgh and at about three o'clock the dragoons, numbering over 550, began a withdrawal, provisionally to their barracks at Leith, but subsequently further. Fowke was later careful to emphasise that this tactical retreat had been conducted with exemplary military efficiency and no undue haste.

Orders had been given, he claimed, 'to retire slowly and without Confusion', he himself having 'march'd off slowly' with Colonel Gardiner at the head of the column, while those to the rear 'moved off in Order and without Hurry'.[41] Civilian witnesses reported a more frenetic progress, however. Walter Grossett, a Collector of Customs, said they 'quit their post at Coltbridge and retired in some haste'.[42] Crichton 'saw the dragowns mownt. They made 3 lowd huzaas and rod off to the northward and thane twrned east.' John Campbell, an Edinburgh banker, watched them 'run off along the north side of Edinburgh',[43] clearly visible on the crest of the 'Lang Dykes', the east–west ridge that would later be occupied by George Street. Another account explained the increased urgency of the withdrawal. A small rearguard of dragoons had been posted as pickets at Corstorphine, a mile or so along the road beyond Coltbridge. They were approached by a group of scouts from the Jacobite camp at Gray's Mill, two miles further back, 'young people, well mounted [and] ordered to go near, take a view of the dragoons, and bring back a report of their number'. These youths had overstepped the bounds of their reconnaissance mission, and ridden up close, fired pistols, and so intimidated the tired and inexperienced troopers that 'without firing a shot [they had] wheeled about, and rode off, carrying their fears into the main body'. Spurred by the contagious panic, the eight-mile ride of the 13th and 14th Dragoons became known as the Coltbridge Canter, and 'they did not draw brydle till they came to Musselburgh.'[44] Another three miles brought them to Prestonpans, close to Colonel Gardiner's home of Bankton, where he took to his bed, exhausted, leaving the men to encamp for the night in an adjacent field. The dragoons were still nervous, convinced, for no good reason, that their enemies were not far behind them. Then one of their number, foraging in the dark, blundered into a disused coal pit – a common hazard in that mining area – accidentally discharging his pistol as he fell, and caused the rest to take fright, thinking they were under attack. Scrambling to horse they galloped off in the opposite direction to the imagined threat, a trail of dropped and discarded small arms, swords and 'accoutrements of all kinds' marking the course of their eastward stampede. The detritus was later collected and sent after them in covered carts, 'so that the flight of the two regiments was very little known in the army'. When Colonel Gardiner rose the following morning, he found the camping ground deserted and, informed of what had happened, 'followed his men with a heavy heart'.[45]

*

In the meantime, Edinburgh had fallen to the insurgents 'without the least Bloodshed or Opposition'.[46]

Defence of the city had been ostensibly dependent on the hundred or so elderly watchmen of the Town Guard, together with the new Edinburgh Regiment – funded by public subscription to recruit a thousand men, but numbering to date only 120 – and a militia of four hundred volunteers, composed of enthusiastic university students and other Whig zealots. There was also a largely ceremonial body known as the 'Trained Bands', but they 'had not appeared in arms since the [Glorious] revolution, except on the King's birth-day'.[47]

Archibald Stuart, wine merchant and Lord Provost of the city, appeared loath to maintain even that degree of defensive strength, arguing that 'if a thousand Men had a Mind to get into this Town, he could not see how he could hinder them.'[48] His term of office at this critical period was characterised by vacillation, insisting on one occasion that the wording of a statement relating to the recruitment of volunteers be altered from 'this proposal was accepted by the Lord Provost' to read that he had merely 'acquiesced' in it.[49] He was said to be at best 'a secret jacobite'[50] and at worst treacherous. 'There was not a Whig in Town, who Did not suspect that he favour'd the Pretenders Cause; and . . . that his Backwardness and Coldness in the Measure of arming the People, was part of a plan to admitt the Pretender into the City.'[51]

On Monday morning, 16 September, the Provost received a message from the Jacobite camp at Gray's Mill, warning him 'that the City would be ill-treated unless it . . . be readily or speedily surrendred.' The messenger having imparted its contents to numerous bystanders on his way to and from the Provost, rumours of imminent 'Rapine and Plunder' spread. Disquiet increased later in the afternoon, as citizens had watched the last prospects of conventional military protection galloping away eastwards on the Lang Dykes. Towards dusk the Volunteers were ordered to surrender their weapons at the Castle garrison and disperse to their homes. Then, from Musselburgh, Brigadier Fowke sent a belated message, offering 'the whole, or any part of the two

Regiments of Dragoons' to assist in the defence of the city. Given the nervous state of men and horses, their effectiveness in that role would have been open to question. However, 'the Offer was not accepted of.'[52]

By this time the Provost had received a further ultimatum from the Prince, threatening undefined reprisals 'if [he] suffer any of the [Hanoverian] Usurper's Troops to enter the Town, or any of the Cannon, Arms or Ammunition now in it . . . to be carried off'. The Provost and his council dispatched two delegations to Gray's Mill that night. The first, requesting clarification, returned with a message from George Murray, demanding a final agreement to surrender the city by two o'clock in the morning. Unable to reach a decision, the council instructed the second delegation to request more time.

At five o'clock, the gates of the Netherbow Port – westernmost entrance to the city – opened, allowing a coach to pass through to livery stables on the Canongate. It was the same coach that had just deposited the second delegation at Mrs 'Luckie' Clarke's tavern in Writer's Close, off the High Street, where the Provost and other members of council were anxiously awaiting a reply to their plea for time. Before the gates could close again, thirty Highlanders led by Lochiel and O'Sullivan rushed through and overpowered the sentries. Then followed the remainder of the advance guard, from St Mary's Wynd and the Pleasance. A mathematician, Richard Jack, watching from a nearby window, counted with characteristic precision 468 of them, 'some ... altogether unarmed, others with a broadsword, some with corn forks, and many with muskets without locks, ... the number of guns that reasonably might be supposed to fire, did not exceed 200.'[53]

The Prince arrived with the rest of the army later in the morning, marching from the south-west to the King's Park and Holyrood. There, below the escarpment of Salisbury Crags, the army encamped, while their leader took up residence in the palace of his Stuart forebears.

Only the Castle – impregnable as the curtain of sheer basalt cliffs and half-moon battery could make it – remained under government control. Its garrison comprised just two hundred of Lascelles' Foot commanded by an octogenarian, Lieutenant General Joshua Guest. As though to make their presence felt by the Jacobite intruders, on the night of 18 September, they 'threw some bombs and c[u]lveren shells into ther camp and did some execution'.[54] It was sufficient to induce a removal of the army the following day, out of range, to Duddingston.

*

As he entered Edinburgh, the Prince received word that General Cope was arrived at Dunbar.

'Is he by God?' he replied.

It had taken Cope more than a fortnight to get the army from Inverness – a march of eleven days overland to Aberdeen, four days of waiting for naval transport and favourable winds, then two days at sea to the East Lothian coast – only to learn that his principal objective had that morning been captured. But his army had thus far behaved 'with so much Alacrity and Spirits' that he had 'all the Reason in the World to depend upon it, they would behave exceeding well in Action'.[55] He may also have been heartened by the reinforcement of Gardiner's and Hamilton's 560-odd dragoons, their recent erratic behaviour notwithstanding. Disembarkation of a further 1,500 foot soldiers, artillery, baggage and horses, was complete by the 18th and early the following day his army began its march west to liberate Edinburgh.

The Jacobite army that marched from camp on the eastern edge of the city to meet him numbered about 2,280. Patrick Crichton overestimated the numbers, but denigrated their quality: '1000 as good men as are in Europe, 1000 indiferent good and 1400 good for nothing old men, shepherds, and boys.'[56] It remained to be seen how they would fare against Cope's regulars.

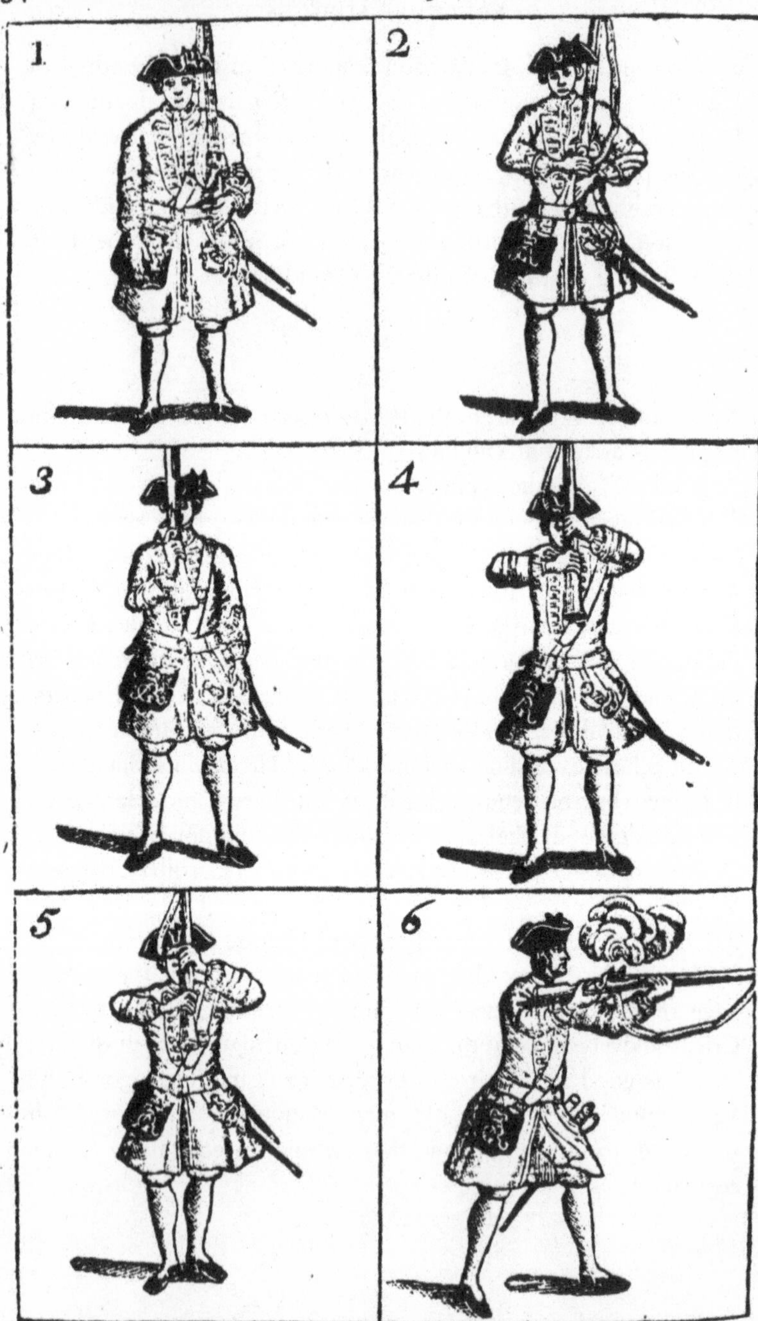

1 Take Care. 2 Join your Right-Hand to your Firelock. 3 Poise your Firelock. 4 Join your Left-Hand to your Firelock. 5 Cock your Firelock. 6 Present. Fire.

Tactics, Pox & 'Secrets'

A British Army infantry regiment was divided into platoons of between thirty and forty-eight men, drawn up in three lines one behind the other: standing, crouching and kneeling. Four or five platoons, 'distributed, or disposed into different Parts of the Regiment', fired in unison; another four or five, similarly distributed, began reloading, while a third completed reloading in unison, ready to fire in their turn. A concerted firing, or volley, along the entire front of a regiment – so as to 'extend [the] Fire in such a Manner, as to do Execution in different Parts of the opposite Regiment'[1] – was also known as a platoon. A disciplined regiment could maintain a near continuous and rapid sequence of volleys as platoon followed platoon with devastating collective effect. This went some way to compensate for the notorious inaccuracy of an individual weapon when fired at anything beyond close range.

The Highlanders' musketry tactic differed markedly from the regular army's system of platoon firing. They discharged their weapons into the enemy's ranks 'very near, being always sure that their one fire should do execution',[2] or as one put it, 'so near as that the colfin [wadding] of our shot might set their whiskers on fire'.[3] Once fired, the spent musket was discarded, and a circular, leather-faced, iron-studded shield – the target or targe – brought forward onto the left forearm, a dirk in the left fist, and the broadsword drawn in the right. Then, with 'a most frightful and hideous Shout',[4] they dashed on the enemy from the cloud of their own musket smoke. The extraordinary speed of the charge would have made all but the most seasoned, expertly drilled, and highly trained regular troops seem woefully sluggish by comparison. The relative inexperience of the government infantry during the first major engagement of the Scottish campaign was incidentally evident in that many, raising their muskets, fired high over their opponents' heads, while the length and weight of the Land Pattern musket's 46-inch barrel caused others to fire low, inflicting the majority of gunshot wounds on their attackers' legs.[5]

*

During the first months of national emergency a spate of amateur advice appeared in the public prints on how best to defeat the growing and immediate threat.

Suggestions ranged from the practical to the fanciful. In late November, 'A WELL-WISHER' wrote to the *Westminster Journal*, pointing out that 'the Rebels . . . are particularly fond of *exercising their Parts* on the Female Sex, and . . . commonly take up with whatever falls in their Way.' It was therefore proposed that the government provide:

> as many Ladies as we can *conveniently spare* out of the Hundreds of *Drury* [*lane*], and other parts of this great Metropolis, and see them safe convey'd to the Places that are likeliest to be visited by the *Highlanders*; who, pleased with such fine Lasses in Silk Gowns and large Hoop-petticoats, will . . . storm such illustrious Forts; whereby they'll contract a *Disease* which will effectually stop their Progress, disable them from defending themselves, and afford his Majesty's Forces an easy and cheap-bought Conquest.

Old Testament scriptural precedent was cited for this underhand strategy: the vengeance taken by Jacob's sons on the men of a 'Canaanite clan' for the rape of their sister Dinah. Offering them peace, provided they submit to circumcision, the brothers took the opportunity – when their enemies were most inflamed, sore and helpless – to attack and slaughter them wholesale.* The Well-Wisher urged that a committee be appointed to make the selection 'of such Girls . . . found to be *duly qualified* to answer the *intended Purpose*' and that a subscription might be opened 'to raise a Fund towards equipping them, and defraying their Expences to the Places where they may be . . . of infinite use to their Country'.[6] But by the time this plan was published, on 7 December, the threat to London had lifted and the patriotic contribution of its pox-ridden prostitutes rendered redundant.

Another, more conventional, suggestion was offered. A correspondent in the *London Evening Post* proposed combatting the Highland charge and the offensive capability of sword and shield – a style of fighting little changed since the Middle Ages – with a medieval defensive device, named after the northern Dutch province where it was said to have originated. The *cheval de frise*, or Friesland Horse, was a six- to nine-foot wooden beam studded along its length with rows of projecting spikes. A line of *chevaux de frise* would halt the charge and keep the attackers at bay while, behind the barrier, platoons of infantry, 'Kneeling, Stooping and Standing . . . loading and firing as fast as possible . . . will infallibly destroy Thousands of them in one Quarter of an Hour', forcing the survivors to retreat:

> Then our Horse may be let loose upon them from our Right and Left Wings, to trample and cut them down in their Flight . . . [Our Infantry] are then to rise up and pursue . . . in good Order with their Chevaux de Frise carried by Men before them, that if the Enemy should rally and face about, we may be ready to receive them as before, and an entire Victory over them must be the Consequence at a very cheap Rate.

While cheap victory and the stirring prospect of slaughter would have fired the imaginations of London Whigs, there is no record of *chevaux de frise* being used in combatting the insurgency.

* See Genesis 34.

The same correspondent offered a further recommendation: 'that every Man in the Army, both Horse and Foot, do wear an Iron Cap, or Horse-Shoe, under their Hats, to defend any Cut of the Broad-Sword of the Highlanders'.[7] While horseshoes might have afforded makeshift protection inside the tall mitre caps of the fusilier or grenadier, there is no reference to their having been used. However, defensive pieces of headgear – either of solid iron or composed of iron strips – had for some time been issued to cavalrymen to be worn with their tricorns on top. Such 'Skull Caps'[8] were among the equipment found scattered on the Dunbar road in the wake of the dragoons' flight following the Coltbridge Canter. They were colloquially known as 'secrets', the sense being to keep something under one's hat. They were effective against all but the most powerful sword stroke.

from Prefton Pans

For Gardiner's Dragoons.

PART I
ONSLAUGHT

I

PRINCE Charles Edward Stuart's military campaign to seize the British throne as Regent on behalf of his exiled father was punctuated by three of the shortest battles in history. It would end in April 1746 on a boggy moor above Culloden House with a catastrophic defeat, inflicted after less than three-quarters of an hour, by an army under the command of Charles Edward's distant cousin, William Augustus, Duke of Cumberland, the youngest son of King George II. Three months earlier, on another moor south of Falkirk, wind, rain and terrain as much as broadsword and musket baffled and beat a government force led by General Henry Hawley in under half an hour. And in the autumn of the previous year the first major confrontation took place. The Jacobites would call it Gladsmuir, after an East Lothian village that a thirteenth-century poet and seer, Thomas the Rhymer, prophesied would be the site of a great battle.[1] But it was on ground about four miles away from Gladsmuir, close to Prestonpans, that Charles Edward's army routed Sir John Cope's, in an engagement lasting little more than ten minutes.

On the eve of battle, Friday 20 September 1745, General Cope was expecting his enemy to advance from the direction of Edinburgh, nine miles to the west. The general deployed his troops accordingly: his right wing towards the Firth of Forth, with the coastal settlement of Prestonpans to the north-west, the village and harbour of Cockenzie to the north-east. His left was protected by a broad ditch and area of swamp at the foot of Falside Hill, which rose southward to the coal-mining town of Tranent. His rear was protected by the same ditch and swamp – bearing the bucolic name Tranent Meadows – which extended to the east and partway north to the village of Seton. His army faced the walls and dykes of Preston Park, Lord Grange's estate, and the adjacent grounds of Bankton House, home of Colonel James Gardiner, highest-ranking fatality in the brief spate of carnage that was to come at first light the following day. A narrow road divided the two properties, leading westwards to the village of Preston, with a broader defile to the north – between the Park and Prestonpans – through which the main attack was anticipated. Cope ordered parts of the Preston Park enclosure demolished, 'that if the Enemy should at any Time . . . line those Walls, (which were so high, . . . they could not be fired over) they might be dislodged'.[2]

The field was well chosen. 'There [was] not in the whole of the Ground between *Edinburgh* and *Dunbar*,' Cope was to tell the Board of General Officers enquiring into his conduct following the battle, 'a better Spot for both Horse and Foot to act upon.'[3] An eyewitness described it as 'about an English Mile Square . . . and very well Secur'd on all Sides to prevent any Surprize'.[4] But a secure position can leave limited avenues for escape should security fail, and a Jacobite officer would remark later that 'The strength of the enemy's camp became their destruction.'[5]

General Cope was 'a little, dressy, finical man'[6] and his 'furred nightgown'[7] would be one of the more exotic articles of plunder captured from his baggage train the following morning. According to a contemporary, he 'had already devoured the Rebels in his imagination',[8] and he is said to have primed his troops for the coming fight with a morale-boosting speech: 'Gentlemen, You are just now to Engage with a parcel of *Rable*; a parcel of *Brutes*; Being a small Number of *Scots Highlanders*.' He also gave them to understand that, although they could 'expect no Booty from such a poor despicable Pack', that the customary conquerors' bonus, motivating every private soldier preparing for battle, was assured following their inevitable victory: 'I have Authority to Declare, that you shall have Eight full Hours Liberty to Plunder and Pillage the City of *Edinburgh*, *Leith*, and *Suburbs*, at your Discretion, with Impunity.'[9] The speech was later published as a broadsheet and may well have been an invention of Jacobite propaganda, but the sacking of the city had been anticipated by its residents and seriously countenanced. 'I verily believe had Cope prevailed,' wrote Harry Guthrie some days later, 'the Town would have been plundered.'[10] The army General Cope was expecting to lead into Edinburgh may not have been one of benign liberation.

Early on Friday afternoon the Jacobite army made its appearance, not directly from the west as expected but along the slopes of Falside Hill to the south, and Cope wheeled his lines through ninety degrees to face the attack from that direction. The walls of Preston Park estate and Bankton House thereby lay against his right wing, his left towards Seton and his rear towards the Forth. From Falside Hill, within musket range of the government lines – as well as from closer, covert reconnaissance – the Jacobite commanders could see that this was 'not a proper Situation for highlanders for they must have nothing before them [that] can hinder them to run upon the enemy'.[11] Although the sloping ground would have provided admirable momentum for their preferred mode of attack – the terrifying headlong charge that would win them victory the following day and in all subsequent encounters, barring the last – the marsh and ditch at the foot of the hill would have stopped their charge dead in a fire trap, directly under the enemy's guns.

All afternoon Cope's men observed the Jacobites' activities, apparently 'marching and Countermarching in a Confus'd Manner'. Towards four o'clock a detachment of about fifty of them was seen moving forwards to occupy Tranent churchyard and a clump of trees: positions on either side of a heugh, or cutting, known as the Coak Road, which contained the wooden rails of a wagon way for transporting coal from the Tranent pits to the coast. Two gallopers – small manoeuvrable one-and-a-half-pounder cannon – were fired at close range from the government left wing and, according to one account, 'killed some of [the rebels], and soon dislodged them'.[12] Lieutenant General Lord George Murray, commanding one half of the Jacobite army, claimed that they only 'wounded a man or two', while others said the gallopers' bombardment had no effect whatsoever. Nevertheless, Cope's redcoats 'huzzaed at every discharge, thinking to frighten the Highlanders, who, they imagined, had never seen cannon'.[13] Coehorn mortar shells were also lobbed at the enemy but their fuses were 'damnified' from being badly stored and they failed to explode. One of these that 'fell short in a direct line where the Prince was'[14] might otherwise have stopped the course of the rising and all but extinguished the Stuart succession in a single burst of shrapnel. Cope gave orders that no more coehorns were to be fired lest they 'take off [the rebels'] Fear of them'.[15] Meanwhile the inhabitants of Tranent, together with their livestock and wildlife, spent the day in danger of being killed by superstitious Highlanders. No prosperity could attend a journey, it was believed, at the outset of which a pig or hare was encountered. Several of these creatures were shot from the Jacobite lines, 'to the great risk of Everybody that was near'.[16]

*

Alexander Carlyle – twenty-three-year-old son of the local Presbyterian minister – was watching developments from the steeple of his father's church in Prestonpans. A fervent Whig, he was one of the Edinburgh Volunteers relieved from defence of the city and was now assisting General Cope with the benefit of his local knowledge. Shortly after the enemy detachment had been flushed from the neighbourhood of Tranent churchyard, a much larger force of three or four hundred moved westwards and Carlyle could see them taking up positions beyond Lord Grange's estate, along what was called the Thorny Loan, a track between fields running from the village of Preston to Dolphingstone half a mile to the west. Anticipating an attack from that direction, Cope wheeled his army back ninety degrees to its original position. Then, at dusk, the Thorny Loan detachment unaccountably marched back the way they had come to the slopes of Falside Hill. The Earl of Home suspected them of 'marching and countermarching till it was dark, in order to deceive us',[17] and a Jacobite admitted later that they did it 'to amuse the enemy'.[18] As darkness fell, Cope wheeled his army back ninety degrees to face south yet again. His substantial baggage train was moved northwards inside the walled enclosure of Cockenzie House and placed under the protection of a 200-man guard, comprising the 'well-affected' Highlanders, raised by John Campbell, Earl of Loudoun, and the equally loyal Black Watch.[19] Cope himself spent part of the evening with the owner of Cockenzie House, a merchant by the name of Mathie.

Unable to see anything further from his post on the church steeple, young Carlyle went to find somewhere to sleep. His father's house being overcrowded with military men and excited clergy he found room with a neighbour and instructed a maidservant to wake him when the battle started.

Cope's army lay upon their arms all night. Three large fires were kept burning along their front line to ensure no enemy could approach unobserved from the direction of Tranent. This measure had unforeseen effects. It 'discovered to the rebels what was doing in [the government] camp, whereas in theirs not a word was heard, nor the least sign seen'.[20] Indeed, it must have made the darkness beyond the bonfires all the more impenetrable and intimidating to the waiting redcoats.

The evening remained quiet until a nervy crackle of musket fire broke out at eight o'clock near the south-eastern corner of Bankton House, where an ensign and some men of Colonel Lee's Regiment were stationed.[21] Then, an hour later, 'all the Dogs in the Village of *Tranent* began to bark with the utmost Fury.' Lieutenant Colonel Peregrine Lascelles of the 58th Foot visited the advanced guard of dragoons posted out in the darkness along the marsh towards Seton and 'found all very alert, but could see or hear nothing but the barking of Dogs'.[22] Ninety minutes later, about ten-thirty, the barking ceased. It had taken that time for the Prince's army to file through Tranent, disturbing the canine inhabitants in passing. On the opposite side of the town they waited in the darkness for several hours, 'observing the greatest silence, so that Cope did not perceive where [they] were'. Meanwhile, behind their fires, the government army 'made a great deal of noise, [and their enemies] could hear them talking and swearing'.[23] At around three o'clock the Jacobites began a stealthy outflanking march in the direction of Seton. 'There was not the least noise, and the officers with the horse were all afoot lest the neighing of the horse should discover the march.'[24] They were guided by a local man who knew the area well from wildfowling in the marshes. Robert Anderson took them eastwards, parallel with the treacherous Meadows, to a farm called Riggonhead, and 'the only pass betwixt Seaton and Tranent where it was possible to come at the Enemy'. Then they moved north. The Prince's Secretary of State, John Murray of Broughton, recalled that 'before we could get into the plain we past a bog which was so deep and Clay so Stiff that Some of the men left their shoes.'[25]

About five o'clock in the morning, according to an Edinburgh volunteer stationed with Cope's artillery train, 'the Rebels were discovered; moving like a Cloud, towards the Pass, between *Seaton* and the Morass . . . [having] stolen their March at about 100 Yards only from the Out-Posts of the Dragoons.'[26] One of the dragoons shouted: 'Who is there? Who is there?', then 'Cannons, cannons, get ready the cannons, cannoneers!'[27] The Jacobite army marched on rapidly through the dark, 'every step . . . sunk to the knee in mud'[28] until, clear of the swampy ground, they emerged onto the firm corn-stubbled plain: Clanranald, Glengarry and Keppoch men of the Clan Donald under the command of the Duke of Perth to the fore; MacGregors, Appin Stewarts and Camerons to the rear, commanded by Lord George Murray. Forming line from column in the same order of march, Perth's men comprised the right wing, Murray's the left. A less well-armed second line consisted of Atholl and MacLachlan men, and 'about 25 gentlemen, and their servants, a horse-back',[29] making a small reserve of cavalry. They faced west, early dawn lightening the sky behind them.

'It was not yet day,' recalled the Prince's Quartermaster General, John William O'Sullivan, 'so that we saw the enemy . . . before they cou'd see us; our dark cloaths was advantageous to us.'[30] It was said that when the order was given to attack, they 'pull[ed] off their bonnets and looking up to heaven, made a short prayer, and ran forward'.[31] To an officer in Cope's army, 'it was so dark when they came to attack us that I could only perceive them like a black hedge moving towards us.'[32]

*

Despite the Jacobites' stealth, the government army was not taken entirely by surprise. Cope had been kept informed by his sentries since three o'clock in the morning that 'the Rebells were moving', at first towards the east, then at about four o'clock 'Northwards, in order to Come and attacke [his] left Flank'.[33] It was at this moment – the alarm having been raised by the dragoon outpost towards Seaton and a galloper fired in response – that the General gave his troops the order to 'stand to arms' and wheel to the left, moving this time through forty-five degrees to face roughly north-east; all of which 'they Performed very Quickly and with great order'. The small battery of artillery – four coehorns and six gallopers – together with two squadrons of the 13th Regiment of Dragoons commanded by Colonel Gardiner, occupied the right wing; two of Hamilton's 14th Dragoons the left. In between the flanking horse there were three regiments of foot and, at the rear, a reserve force comprising a squadron each of Hamilton's and Gardiner's dragoons. At this time dragoons still served their original purpose in the army as mounted infantry, and were trained to fight on foot as well as on horseback. Each dragoon was therefore equipped not only with a basket-hilted broadsword and one or two pistols but also with a bayonet and a firelock carbine, its 42-inch barrel four inches shorter than the Land Pattern musket issued to the infantry.

The government troops, it was said, 'made a most gallant appearance both horse and foot, with the sun shining upon their arms'. Some Jacobite officers had doubts they could be beaten, fearing their own irregulars 'would be defeated in a moment and swept from the field'.[34] But the gallant appearance was deceptive and the strength of Cope's army fatally compromised.

Notwithstanding the General's later assertion that his army had not been taken by surprise, it was evidence of hurried manoeuvring that the artillery battery remained in its entirety on the right wing, instead of being more conventionally divided between the right and left. In addition, neither the gallopers nor the coehorns were manned by experienced gunners, but by Invalids rapidly recruited from Edinburgh Castle days earlier to fill the deficiency. These were men deemed fit for garrison duties but disqualified by age or infirmity from active service. The Invalids had been joined by half a dozen sailors detached from the *Fox* man-of-war anchored in the Firth. Since coming ashore they had been more often drunk than not. There was also the 'private Teacher of Mathematics', Richard Jack, who 'understood the Theory, but not the practical Part of Gunnery'. Requested to aim the gallopers at the enemy position in Tranent churchyard the previous afternoon, he had proved 'so awkward at levelling them [that he was] turned . . . off, and never suffered . . . to meddle with any of the Cannon afterwards'.[35] His only subsequent contribution was assisting the artillery train commander Major Eaglesfield Griffith to fit a new plummet on the pendulum of a quadrant used for elevating the coehorns.

The three infantry regiments – Lee's 55th, Murray's 57th, and Lascelles' 58th Foot – as signified by their high numerical designations, were newly raised and composed of raw recruits. None was at full strength. In addition Cope had effectively 'disarmed [them] of their most usefull wapon against Highlanders . . . [and] ordered all their swords to be laid up in Stirling Castle, so that at the time of ingaging not one of them had a sword'.[36] The reason given was 'that their Swords incumbered their March, and are of small Use in an Engagement, in comparison with the *Bayonet*'.[37] However, although each man carried a firelock musket on the morning of the battle, the bayonets remained sheathed in the leather scabbards at their belts.

Gardiner's and Hamilton's dragoons – fully armed though they were – had already shown their mettle five days earlier in the 'Coltbridge Canter'. Come from an extended period of garrison duty in Ireland, they had for the most part seen no action, and were mounted on horses that until recently had been at grass, accustomed neither to being ridden nor to the sound of gunfire.

Cope rode along the front of his hastily formed lines: 'Encouraging the Men, begging them to keep up their Fire, and keep their Ranks, and they would easily beat the Rebells'. He had made it his custom, on the march, to rally the troops in this way and, according to Lieutenant Colonel Charles Whitefoord, officer of Marines, 'had raised their Spirits to such a Degree, that all expressed the strongest Desire for Action; even the Dragoons breathed nothing but Revenge, and threatened the Rebels with nothing but Destruction'.[38] When he reached his left wing, however, Cope found Hamilton's Dragoons readying themselves in desultory fashion and, 'observing that their Swords were not Drawn, the General was very angry'.[39]

Meanwhile, preparations for the engagement were attracting considerable local interest. 'Early as was the hour, and notwithstanding the darkness, the walls of almost all the neighbouring fields around were covered by rustics and others, anxious to obtain, from a safe distance, a view of the impending conflict.'[40] One of the more eminent spectators, the fifty-five year old Senator of Edinburgh's Sessions Court, Hew Dalrymple, Lord Drummore, was 150 yards from Cope's left wing, having spent the previous night at Cockenzie. He sat his horse with no other weapon but a whip in his hand. With him was another 'near spectator', Robert Wightman,* who described their position as 'about a Muskett

* Treasurer of the City of Edinburgh 1716–17, First Bailie in 1719, Dean of Guild 1720–21. Confused in *Culloden Papers* with General Joseph Wightman who had fought at Glenshiel but had been dead 23 years by the time of Prestonpans. See Fergusson pp. 151–2.

shott' behind Hamilton's Dragoons, and would later dismiss what followed as a 'scuffle . . . for battle it was not'.

Cope's Adjutant General, Colonel John Campbell, Earl of Loudoun, was at the opposite end of the government lines from Wightman and Dalrymple, watching the Jacobite army advance at an oblique angle. '[They] were coming from our Left, running (not marching) towards our Right,' he recalled. 'When they had covered about two Thirds of our Front, there seemed to be a great Confusion among them; but still they kept on, and in a few Seconds were formed into five square Bodies or Columns – that on [their] Left the largest – and about twenty deep. I myself saw but three of those Bodies, from the Situation I happened to be in on the Right.'[41]

From his position on the left wing Dalrymple could see the other two. Unlike Loudoun, he was not a military man and struggled to explain what he witnessed. He was impressed by the densely packed, yet fluid formations, 'Columns, Clews, or Clumps': he did not know what to call them. 'I took particular Notice,' he wrote, 'that though I could see through the Files of the Line which was directly opposite me, and not above 200 Yards Distance . . . to my Astonishment every Front Man covered his Followers, there was no Man to be seen in the Open . . . in short, though their Motion was very quick, it was uniform and orderly, and I confess I was surprised at it.'

So much for the indiscipline of an irregular army – the 'parcel of *Rable*' – that Cope had anticipated.

Dalrymple was prevented from seeing what was happening on the government right wing by the camber of the ground, the intervening line of foot, and by the dense cloud of white smoke that blossomed from the artillery and hung in the still air. The guns 'made a great Shake among' the massed Jacobites, recalled Richard Jack, and he claimed to have seen 'several Files of the Rebels thrown down by this Fire'.[42] A Jacobite account noted only that it 'did no other Mischief than carrying off the Calf of a Gentleman's Leg'.[43] The government troops 'Huzza'd' at the cannon fire and, curiously, the attackers returned the cheer.[44] Dalrymple heard the artillery 'firing two, three, or four Shot'. In fact five of the gallopers were fired. The sixth, after it had been used to sound the alarm, remained idle because there was nobody to reload it, the Invalids and sailors having deserted at first sight of the enemy, and Richard Jack lacking competence. Colonel Whitefoord alone fired the remaining gallopers while Major Griffith fired the coehorns. The Invalids had carried off the powder horns when they fled so that the artillery could be neither charged nor primed, let alone fired again, even if there had been time enough to do so. As Whitefoord had touched the smouldering match to the last of his gallopers 'the [Jacobite] first Line opened in the Center, formed a Column to the Left, and advanced on [him] with a Swiftness not to be conceived.'[45]

Colonel Shugbrough Whitney commanded a squadron of Gardiner's Dragoons stationed between the guns and an *ad hoc* body of sentries recalled from outlying posts who had not had time to rejoin their regiments. As the Jacobite column advanced, Whitney was instructed by Lord Loudoun to wheel his dragoons to the right for the purpose of 'attacking these myrmidons in flank'. Whitney did so and at about two hundred yards from the enemy shouted the order to charge. A moment later there was a ragged burst of fire and his left arm was shattered by a musket round. His second in command came forward 'with great alacrity to the head of the Standard, but having a wild, unruly horse, he fell aplunging and never ceased till he threw the Lieutenant on his back on the ground'.[46]

The Jacobite musket fire frightened the 'raw and unmanaged' horses of the 13th Dragoons' forward squadron, and they in turn 'did the first execution and trod down and distressed and confused' the ranks of infantry next to them.[47] Then the hundred-strong guard of foot at the extreme right of the line that was supposed to protect the artillery 'fell into Confusion',[48] crowding and spreading the terror into another squadron of dragoons commanded by Colonel Gardiner himself and stationed behind the guns. As his men scattered in panic, the Colonel 'harangued them, begg'd and entreated them to stand to their Arms, and fight, like Men, for their King and Country'[49] – but to no avail.

*

The government horses that had not been panicked by the gunfire and shouting were stampeded by more direct assault. To overcome the foot soldiers' natural fear of cavalry, the Prince's army had been trained 'to aim at the noses of the horses with their swords . . . as the natural movement of a horse, wounded in the face, is to wheel round: and a few horses wounded in that manner, are sufficient to throw a whole squadron into such disorder, that it is impossible afterwards to rally it.'[50]

Even the riderless horses were attacked because 'a notion the Highlanders had that the horses fought as well as the men . . . made them kill a great many of them after their riders were dismounted.'[51] The ferocious long-hafted Lochaber axe and the improvised weapon of a scythe blade lashed to a seven- or eight-foot pole were particularly effective means 'to annoy the horse'. The Jacobite Captain James Johnstone recalled that the scythes especially 'did great execution. They cut the legs of the horses in two: and their riders through the middle of their bodies.'[52] According to one account Colonel Gardiner was brought down by such a weapon after his squadron deserted him. He had already received gunshot wounds to the breast and thigh when the scythe blade ripped open his right arm, and caused him to drop his sword. Dragged from his horse, the stroke of 'a broadsword or a Lochaber axe'[53] all but finished him. Another account had him fighting on foot, armed with a half-pike, when he received 'the mortal Stroke, in the hinder Part of his Head'.[54] An Edinburgh watchmaker would be executed at Carlisle accused of yet a third variant: 'the villain . . . shot Col. Gardiner behind his back and basely covered him with wounds after he was down.'[55]

The fracturing of Cope's right wing was mirrored, moments later, on the left, as the terrified horses of Hamilton's Dragoons reared into the adjacent infantry, then 'gave Way and went off', in the confusing words of Hew Dalrymple, 'not in a Body, but quite broke in two's or so'.[56] Wightman, from the same viewpoint, judged that '16 platoons were fired' along the right wing, but the dragoons on the left 'fled . . . upon the approach of the Edinburgh [rebel] Riff-Raff . . . without firing or being fired upon, and without drawing a sword'.[57] Dalrymple asserted that there had been some firing from his end of the line, but paltry and sporadic – an 'infamous Puff, Puff' – so that, while he could see nothing on the right wing for clouds of smoke discharged by cannon and musket, the troops nearest him were clearly visible, 'standing naked' and unprotected after the dragoons' flight.

His assailant closing at speed and with no time to reload his musket, an infantryman's only defence would have been his sword and bayonet. But because their swords had been left at Stirling and they 'had not there bayenets screwed when they were attacked, and non to give the word of command',[58] Cope's men were hopelessly vulnerable.

The Jacobites ploughed through the unresisting redcoat lines. 'Then the broadswords played their part,' said John O'Sullivan, 'for wth one stroke, armes, & legs were cout of, & heads split to the Shoulders, never such wounds were seen.'[59] This savagery would become the stuff of legend and nightmare: 'The strokes given by the Highlanders with their swords . . . evinced proofs of their strength; not only men's hands and feet were cut off, but even the legs of horses.' One instance – 'what many saw' and thereby 'affirmed for truth' – had a Highlander break through the front line of infantry on the government left and, 'fetching a blow at a grenadier, the poor fellow naturally got up his hand above his head, and not only had his hand lopped off, but also his scull cut above an inch deep, so that he expired on the spot.'[60]

The most ferocious sword stroke that day was inflicted by a Lochaber man, Duncan MacKenzie. He was 'six feet four inches high, thick and shapely in proportion' and accordingly known as 'Big Duncan'. Attacked by a dragoon, he aimed his first blow at the other's head, but the steel beneath the trooper's hat deflected the blade. 'Duncan jumped back and stood on an old dyke that was there. The Englishman came after him. Duncan sprang up, gave a stroke to him again and cleft the head to the chin through the helmet.' Afterwards, the two steel fragments of the skullcap were held up as proof of the deed, but it was the 'blunting of the edge of the sword corresponding to the split' that proved Big Duncan to be its author. 'Some of the [Jacobite] officers were very desirous of buying the sword and as many guineas as would cover the blade from one end to the other were offered for it.'[61] But Duncan refused to sell.

In face of the terrifying onslaught of broadsword, axe and scythe, whatever discipline had been drilled into the raw troops was forgotten in the spreading panic. Like Dalrymple, Major Talbot, observing from the government left wing, could see little of what was happening on the right. But he saw the effects: 'the Dragoons running off in great Confusion', out of the artillery smoke. Then as the infantry was attacked, a seemingly mechanical process of disintegration began: 'the breaking of the Foot come on regularly, as it were by Platoons, from the Right to the Left.'[62] It happened 'with so rapid a Motion, that the whole Line was broke in a few Minutes'.[63] In the midst of this debacle, General Cope, his command in ruins, could be heard attempting to halt and rally the terror-stricken troops: 'For Shame, Gentlemen, behave like Britons, give them another Fire, and you'll make them run . . . don't let us be beat by such a Set of Banditti.'[64]

As 'many an empty Horse' emerged from the smoke and galloped past Dalrymple, and since the dragoons remaining in the saddle made 'no Motion . . . towards the Enemy', the Sessions Court Senator assumed that the battle was lost. Reflecting that this was 'full time for a Pen-and-Ink Gentleman to provide for his Safety', along with Robert Wightman he rode west, comforting himself that they did so 'with more Discretion and Deliberation than the Dragoons did from the Line'.[65] Wightman was similarly scornful of the dragoons' conduct, and, in reference to their recent garrison duty, called them 'Irish dogs'.[66]

*

It was the cannon and not the maid that roused Alexander Carlyle. By the time he had thrown on his clothes and run, 'neither buckled nor gartered', the hundred yards to his father's house, the Reverend William Carlyle was descending from the steeple of his church with news that Cope's army was 'completely defeated'. Alexander hurried to the south-east corner of the clergyman's garden, where a mound afforded a view of the field close to where the government lines had been. 'The Whole Prospect was fill'd with Runaways, and Highlanders Pursueing them – Many had their Coats turned as prisoners, but were still trying to Reach the Town [of Prestonpans] in Hopes of Escaping. The Pursuing Highlanders, when they could not overtake, fir'd at them: and I saw two Fall in the Glebe.'[67]

But 'Twenty were killed by the Sword, for one who fell by a Bullet'[68] and Carlyle could not see, from where he stood, the area in which 'the great destruction was done after [the lines] were broke and scattered by the broadswords.'[69] The majority of injuries inflicted on the government troops were incurred as they fled, 'the private Men's Heads . . . almost cut through, the greater Number in the back Part'. Many of those who succeeded in reaching the park walls found themselves trapped, the narrow road between Bankton House and the Grange estate being already 'stopped up' by panicked dragoons, as were those breaches opened in the wall the previous day to prevent the enemy using the grounds for cover. Some fugitives tried to climb the twelve-foot-high walls only to be struck at from behind and 'killed without trouble'.[70] There was evidence of a killing frenzy, some of the dead having '7 or 8 wounds',[71] while 'the Field of battle presented a spectacle of horror, being covered with heads, legs, and arms, and mutilated bodies; for the killed all fell by the sword.'[72] Some of the wounded were 'desperately hacked', after they had fallen, 'by the Boys who followed the Rebels'.[73] A gentleman claimed to have found his friend 'among the Dead after all was over . . . so butcher'd and mangled, as scarce to be known; for his Hands were cut off, and his Head cleft to the Chin, and his Flesh almost strip'd from his Bones.'[74]

It was said that Charles Edward Stuart himself ordered a halt to the massacre. 'Make prisoners, spare them,' he shouted. 'Spare them, they are my father's subjects.'[75] Another account ascribed the cessation of killing not to the Prince but to others, and that the 'Slaughter was stopt by [Lord] *Perth* and [Cameron of] *Lochiel*.'[76] Testimony heard at the trial of a Jacobite officer, prior to his execution the following year, recounted the following exchange:

'Major,' shouted Perth, 'I am sorry to see so much English blood spilt, for God's sake give the men quarter.'

The reply, from Major Donald MacDonell of Tirnadris, had a remorseless but irrefutable logic: 'My Lord, if we do not kill them here, we shall have to do it in another place.'[77]

*

Lord Elcho, commander of the Prince's Lifeguard cavalry, estimated the battle 'did not last full a quarter of an hour'.[78] Alexander Carlyle claimed it lasted 'hardly . . . more than Ten or 15 Minutes after Firing the First Cannon'.[79] One witness gave it 'seven or eight minutes',[80] while another recorded that 'from the first fire 'till the whole was broken was but four minutes and a half.'[81] Robert Wightman declared that 'the scuffle' he witnessed 'lasted about 4 minutes, and no longer'.[82]

Each side predictably exaggerated its opponents' strength and understated its own, making victory the more creditable, defeat the less shameful. Witnesses called from Cope's army during the subsequent enquiry declared it to consist of only 'about 600 Horse and 1400 Foot'[83] and 'computed the Number of the Rebels to be about 5000'.[84] The more accurate testimony of the civilian Richard Jack – that he had observed the Prince's army 'at their Exercise' only two days before and claiming 'their Numbers to be 2740, whom he had counted to a Man' – was ignored.[85] According to the Jacobite account the government army, numbering 'above 4000 strong, besides Volunteers . . . &c. from Edinburgh', was defeated by '2000 Highland Foot, unsupported by Horse.'[86]

Some twenty miles south of the battlefield Sir John Cope, accompanied by Lord Loudoun, Lord Home, and about four hundred and fifty dragoons – all that could be mustered from the rout – paused in his flight at the town of Lauder and wrote to the Marquess of Tweeddale. He informed the Secretary of State for Scotland that, despite his best efforts, 'we lost the Day'. He admitted that the attack had been 'no Sort of Surprize'; that his troops had been 'in good Spirits Yesterday' and 'expected the Enemy'. He also intimated that 'the Men [had] been long warned' of their opponents' style of fighting. However nothing, it seemed, could have prepared them for the reality, and 'the manner in which the Enemy came on, which was quicker than can be described . . . was the Cause of our Men taking a most destructive Pannick.'[87]

Cope's insistence that his army had not been taken by surprise in the dawn attack was a necessary defence against the charge of incompetence. He would have been familiar with a significant passage in Major General Humphrey Bland's *Treatise of Military Discipline*, then in its fifth edition:

> There is not any thing in which an Officer shews the Want of Conduct so much, as in suffering himself to be surprized . . . without being prepared to make a proper Defence, and by not having taken the necessary Precautions to prevent it. When an Officer has had the Misfortune of being Beat, his Honour won't suffer by it, provided he has done his Duty, and acted like a Soldier. But if he is surprized by neglecting the common Methods used to prevent it, his Character is hardly Retrievable.[88]

Cope's own character and that of his officers would be exonerated and retrieved by ascribing blame for 'the Misfortune on the Day of Action' solely to 'the shameful Behaviour of the Private Men'.[89]

Cope reached the garrison of Berwick-upon-Tweed the following day with the remnants of his army. Lascelles and Brigadier Fowke had preceded him by some hours, having arrived there on the night of the battle. They, and not Cope, had broken the news to Lord Mark Kerr, who replied with the words: 'Good God! I have seen some Battles, heard of many, but never of the first news of a defeat being brought by the General Officers before.'[90] The exclamation inspired a couplet in Adam Skirving's derisive Jacobite ballad – with its refrain of 'Hey Johnnie Cope' – which would ever after cling to the hapless general's name:

> Troth now Johnny ye were nae blate*
> Tae come wi' the news o' yer ain defeat

While Cope had been at Lauder, writing his dispatch to the Marquess of Tweeddale, Charles Edward Stuart was an uninvited guest of that gentleman, having commandeered one of the Secretary of State's Scottish homes, Pinkie House in Musselburgh, as a field hospital. From there the Prince wrote to his father:

> This morning I have gained a most signal victory with little or no loss . . . If I had obtained this victory over foreigners, my joy would have been compleat; but as it is over Englishman, it has thrown a damp upon it that I little imagined. The men I have defeated were your Majesty's enemies, it is true, but they might have become your friends and dutiful subjects, when they had got their eyes opened to see the true interest of the country, which I am come to save, not to destroy.[91]

Damp notwithstanding, 'the Prince from this Battle entertained a mighty notion of the highlanders,' declared Lord Elcho, 'and ever after imagin'd they would beat four times their number of regular troops.'[92] Nevertheless, he forbade 'all publick rejoicing'[93] in Edinburgh over the victory, 'purchased at the expense of the blood of his [father's] subjects'.[94] No such scruple would be exercised eight months later by adherents of the Whig party when the Duke of Cumberland's army prevailed over his own father's subjects.

*

* Shy, bashful.

'A handfull of the Scum of the Highlands are Masters of Scotland without almost burning a pound weight of powder.' The Honourable John Maule, Member of Parliament for Aberdeen Burghs, confided his rage to Major General John Campbell, 4th Duke of Argyll, who was on campaign in Flanders supporting Maria Theresa's right to the throne of Austria. This foreign service seemed to Maule an inexplicable distraction from Britain's national interests: 'I hope we shall have you all over here immediately, for its folly to be fighting for others when the ship at home is in danger.'[95] As if in response to Maule's sentiments, William Augustus, Duke of Cumberland, arrived in London from Flanders on 19 October. At about the same time General Wade's 4th Regiment of Horse left Nottingham for the north 'with their Scull-Caps and Breast-Plates on, their Swords new grinded, and every Thing in Order, as if they were to have engaged the Rebels directly'.[96] In addition, sixteen transports moored in the Thames and bound for Newcastle were loaded with essential supplies 'for the Use of his Majesty's Forces in the North'. They included '1800 Tuns of Beer' and 'a great Number of Steel Caps . . . for the said Troops.'[97]

II

IN the weeks and months following the battle at Prestonpans – as Charles Edward Stuart's forces marched south from Edinburgh, and government troops from the Castle garrison repossessed that city in the name of King George only two days later; as the Jacobites crossed the river Esk into England, investing and capturing Carlisle before advancing through Lancaster, Preston, Wigan, Manchester, Macclesfield and Ashbourne; and as what had once seemed a remote disturbance affecting only Scotland arrived at Derby, within three day's march of London – apprehension, increasing to 'Pannic', spread through the capital. A run on the Bank of England was only averted, and the crisis ridden out, through an ingenious measure whereby the demands of anxious creditors were indefinitely deferred by employing a time-consuming string of agents to exchange notes for payment in sixpences.[1] The fear of Highlanders, sharpening their swords at Derby, was compounded by intelligence that a French invasion fleet was preparing to sail from Dunkirk. On what became known as 'Black Friday', 6 December, the threats from north and south 'struck such a Terror into several public spirited Persons', reported Henry Fielding, 'that, to prevent their Money, Jewels, Plate, &c. falling into Rebellious or French Hands, they immediately began to pack up and secure the same. And . . . they began to prepare for Journies into the Country; concluding, that the Plunder of what must remain in [the] City would satisfy the Victors, to prevent them at least for a long time from pursuing them.'

It was ironic that on the same Friday those faint-hearted citizens – 'fine Ladies' as Fielding called them, 'some of whom wear Breeches, and are vulgarly called Beaus'[2] – were preparing to quit the city in terror, the crisis was already ending and the Jacobite army beginning its retreat north.

A number of factors had contributed to the overruling of Charles Edward Stuart's determination to continue his march on London. The poor recruitment thus far of English adherents to the insurrection had left his forces severely outnumbered by those ranged against them: General Wade's army to the north-east at Doncaster, Cumberland's at Coventry to the south, and another expected in defence of London on Finchley Common. A successful assault on the capital seemed unlikely, if not impossible. There was an additional factor in favour of tactical retreat. Although Lord John Drummond, brother to the Duke of Perth, had recently arrived in Scotland from France with reinforcements to the cause – a force of 350 *Royal Ecossais* and 300 Irish Picquets in the service of Louis XV – no confirmation of the French king's promise of further assistance to support a campaign in the south of England had been received, and the Jacobite leaders were unaware of preparations at Dunkirk for imminent invasion.

While for the most part Londoners were relieved as the threat receded, in some sensation-loving quarters there was a feeling of anticlimax, even disappointment. The fascination of celebrity exerted a powerful influence regardless of political persuasion or personal safety. 'Three sensible middle-aged men [talked] of hiring a chaise to go to Caxton [sixty miles out from the city] to see the Pretender and Highlanders as they passed.' The late Prime Minister's son, Horace Walpole, likened the attitude to that of spectators cheering for both parties at a bear-baiting: 'Fight dog! Fight bear!'[3]

There was another London 'Pannic' a week later – on Friday the 13th – this time occasioned by a report that French transports were attempting to land on the Suffolk coast, though this was quickly dispelled by intelligence that the vessels were only 'some Smugglers and Fishing-boats of our own'.[4] The French invasion planned the previous week had in fact been abandoned when it became apparent that the Jacobite army had given up its advance on London and was in full retreat.

*

The engagement at Clifton in Westmorland on 18 December – notable as the last ever fought on English soil – was a skirmish rather than a battle, involving as it did only the Jacobite rearguard and an advance party of the Duke of Cumberland's army, with fatalities on each side numbering in the tens rather than hundreds. Following its retreat from Derby twelve days earlier, the main Jacobite army had arrived at Penrith. Two miles to the rear, Lord George Murray, delayed by the slower-moving artillery and ammunition waggons, held off the government pursuit from a position described by the Duke of Cumberland as 'one of the strongest posts I ever saw'.[5]

It was about five o'clock in the afternoon and – that late in the year – already dusk. The village of Clifton 'consisted of one street with poor houses'. The land to either side – criss-crossed by ditches, hedges and dry-stone walls – was unsuitable for horses, so 250 government dragoons were ordered to dismount and advance on foot: Bland's 3rd to the right, Cobham's 10th to the left, Kerr's 11th in the centre. The creak of heavy thigh-high riding boots was audible in the darkness, buff cross belts and the lace trim of tricorn hats clearly visible. The Glengarries – lining the walls of the road leading into the village – formed the Jacobite right wing; Appin Stewarts east of the road, the centre; and beyond them, the MacPhersons formed the left. All had the advantage of night 'and their dirty dress into the bargain', distinguishable from hedges and walls only in the momentary flash of their flintlocks. The dragoons directed their weapons at the fire of an otherwise invisible enemy. Taking cover in a ditch, Bland's men returned the Jacobite fire at a distance of 150 paces, a considerable range given the inaccuracy of their short-barrelled carbines. Nevertheless, Lord George Murray – who had lost his wig and bonnet while cutting his way through a hedge – recalled that the target he carried was stripped of paint in places by the shooting, 'and [the bullets] were so thick about me, that I felt them hot about my head, and I thought some of them went through my hair, which was about two inches long'.[6]

Murray shouted the order: 'CLAIDHEAMH-MÒR!' The Appin Stewarts and MacPhersons charged. As at Prestonpans the success of the tactic owed as much to speed as to surprise. 'The great hurry with which we went down towards the hollow upon them,' recalled Captain John MacPherson of Strathmashie, 'by which means they were so suddenly mistaken of us that much of their fire went over our heads, and [we] were at their muzles with our swords before they got all their fire given, which, thereafter they got noe time to give.'[7] It was claimed by the government side that when the Highlanders attacked, 'howling as they do', they cried out: 'Murder 'em, no Quarter.'[8] This reported detail became a staple of anti-Jacobite propaganda, and would be used to justify later retaliatory atrocities.

As the Appin Stewarts and MacPhersons hacked at the troopers cowering in their ditch, the *London Evening Post* correspondent might have smiled with satisfaction as 'noe less than 14 of [their swords] broke on the dragoons skull caps (which they all had).' One of the swords broken had been presented to its owner's father by James Stuart himself during the rising of 1715 and its blade bore the inscription:

With this good sword thy cause I will maintain,
And for thy sake, O James! I'll breathe each vein.

Necks and shoulders being unprotected, there were casualties despite the steel caps, as 'the better way of [the swords] doing their business was found out.'[9] As they fled, dragoons were also brought down by the Glengarries' enfilading fire from the road. 'On soft Ground, amongst Ditches',[10] their riding boots became a fatal encumbrance and a number tried to take them off that they might run faster. 'Some of them were killed with one boot off and another on, and some with a boot only half on.'[11]

Both commanders were able to claim victory: George Murray by being left in possession of the field for 'about half an hour after the enemy were gone';[12] the Duke of Cumberland by riding into Clifton when the Jacobites had withdrawn north by way of Penrith to Carlisle. He found a bed at the home of a local Quaker, while his army remained 'exposed on Clifton Moor . . . without cover . . . it being quite dark [and] rain[ing] very hard in the latter part of the night'.[13]

III

LIEUTENANT General Henry Hawley, newly appointed Commander-in-Chief of His Majesty's forces in North Britain, believed his enemies' fearsome reputation exaggerated. He had beaten Highlanders while commanding Evans's Dragoons at Sheriffmuir in 1715 and had every confidence of beating them again. He must, however, have had the baleful example of his predecessor, General Cope, in the forefront of his mind. He was aware that, since Prestonpans, regular troops were at a psychological disadvantage to the howling wild men wielding broadsword or axe; and that unless his troops were convinced otherwise, their enemies' notoriety alone would work like a superstition, unmanning them afresh and throwing them into confusion. Regarding the Jacobites' manner of fighting, there was 'nothing so easy to resist', he declared, 'if Officers and Men are not preposess'd with the Lyes and Accounts which are told of them'. Like General Cope, Hawley despised his adversaries: 'They Commonly form their Front rank of what they call their best men, or True Highlanders the number of which being allways but few . . . the rest being lowlanders and arrant scum.' And he was clear as to the most effective means of resisting those enemies and their Highland charge: black powder more than pointed steel. 'The sure way to demolish them is at 3 deep to fire by ranks diagonaly to the Centre when they come, the rear rank first, and even that rank not to fire till they are within 10 or 12 paces.' Timing was critical. If troops fired from too great a distance without effect – as the dismounted dragoons had done at Clifton – they would 'never get time to load a second Cartridge' and, if the line gave way, 'you may give your foot for dead', because a regular soldier laden with 'Arms, Accoutrements &c.' could not outrun men 'without a firelock or any load'. Nevertheless military discipline, he hoped, would outmatch Highland ferocity and speed. 'If you will but observe the above directions,' the general told his Field Officer, Major Willson, 'they are the most despicable Enimy that are.'[1]

Hawley's 'first Exploit' on arriving in Edinburgh illustrated his confidence in victory. He 'caus'd immediately two pair of Gallows to be set up,'[2] one in the Grassmarket, and the other on the road to Leith, 'to hang his prisoners upon'.[3] His failure to achieve that victory would inspire a thirst for vengeance and sharpen an already hearty appetite for brutal punishment. It would also re-affirm – with the execution of his own men on the Grassmarket gibbets for want of Jacobite prisoners – his longstanding soubriquet: 'Hangman Hawley'.

*

'It is not an easy task to describe a Batle,' wrote Lord George Murray after the engagement at Falkirk. 'Springs & motions escape the eye, & most officers are necessarly taken up with what is immediately near themselves, so that it is nixt to imposible for any one to observe the whole; add to this the confusion, the noise, & the concern that people are in whilest in the heat of the action.'[4]

Seventy years later, in a more elegant but no less violent age, the Duke of Wellington would liken the battle of Waterloo to a society ball, in which 'some individuals may recollect all the little events . . . but no individual can recollect the order in which, or the exact moment at which, they occurred, which makes all the difference as to their value and importance'.[5] Later still, Carl von

Clausewitz remarked that 'three quarters of the factors on which action in war is based are wrapped in a fog of greater or lesser uncertainty.'* From this observation a more succinct metaphor would be coined: 'the Fog of War'.

*

Weather and ground weighed against the government army on 17 January 1746.

Just before two o'clock in the afternoon General Hawley was informed that the enemy was approaching Falkirk Muir from the north-west. Earlier indications – the smoke of campfires, the white Stuart standard sighted beyond woodland to the north, and the advance of Lord John Drummond's cavalry from that direction – had been an elaborate Jacobite feint. Like General Cope after Prestonpans, Hawley would later protect his reputation by insisting that his army had not been taken by surprise.[6] Nevertheless, the speed with which his troops had been forced to mobilise – 'in less than half an hour'[7] – certainly indicated unpreparedness. According to one source, it was achieved 'in hurry and confusion . . . and the best dispersitions made . . . that time would allow'.[8] Hawley, like Cope, had expected the Jacobite force to advance from one direction and was made to face them approaching from another. 'The Generall,' reported a contemporary critic, 'thinking it dishonourable to be attacked in his camp, marched his troops towards a riseing ground . . . by which means he shortned the distance betwixt him and the rebells, and consequently lost so much time, which he greatly stood in need of, in order to form his army.'[9] Honourable it may have been; prudent it undoubtedly was not. The field of battle was 'certainly the most extraordinary that ever any general led his Troops to, when he was under no necessity,' reported one witness. 'They had a hill side to march up, the hardest part of which [the muddiest that

* *Vom Kriege*, Book 1, chapter 3. Published posthumously (1832); the first English translation, *On War*, was published in 1873.

is] took a man over the shoes, the Horses to the Knees, and the Cannons almost over the Wheels, which occasioned [the guns] sticking fast and never getting up.'[10]

Captain Archibald Cunningham, commander of the artillery, later testified in his defence that 'the Roads were so very bad and intricate that it was not only out of his power to keep up with the first Line [of Foot], but the rear Line also passed by the Train and were both forming [at the top] before he could possibly bring up the Artillery.' His two biggest guns in the front being immobilised in the mud, and another five stuck behind, made it impossible for him to bring forward any more than a 1½-pounder and two 4-pounders. Cunningham, like Colonel Whitefoord and Major Griffiths at Prestonpans, claimed to be disastrously ill-served by those under his command, having but one young Lieutenant, two Bombardiers, fourteen inexperienced matrosses – gunnery assistants – and twelve 'Country People he had hired'.[11]

Alongside the two columns of foot, 'marching up as hard as they could, running & quite out of breath with the fatigue', was a scholar occupying his time prior to taking up a university professorship. A volunteer in the Earl of Home's newly raised Glasgow Regiment of militia, William Corse had no idea what lay at the top of the hill: 'a large Moor . . . they say,' he wrote later, but for all he or Hawley knew it could have been anything, 'for neither of us saw it, at least before the action'.[12] Corse and his companions would see little during their ascent either, because a ferocious south-easterly gale was blowing torrential rain full in their faces, its strength intensifying the higher they climbed.

But Hawley put trust in his dragoons. 'In fact, he had boasted at White's Club not many weeks before, that with two regiments of dragoons he would drive the rebels from one end of the kingdom to the other.'[13] If this were so then how much more was to be expected from three: Cobham's 10th, Hamilton's 14th and Ligonier's – formerly Gardiner's – 13th. Following the death of Colonel Gardiner and the supposedly shameful conduct of his rank and file at Prestonpans, command of the 13th had been given to a 53-year-old veteran of the European war, Francis

Augustus Ligonier, 'an officer who should show them how to fight', the King is said to have remarked.[14] With this appointment, Ligonier had the rare distinction of holding two colonelcies simultaneously, the other being that of the 59th Foot. This infantry regiment would acquit itself with distinction on Falkirk Muir, unlike the incorrigible 13th Dragoons.

Hawley ordered the 1,300 horsemen, under Colonel Ligonier's overall command, up the north-facing slope ahead of the foot and artillery in a bid to secure the most advantageous ground to give battle: ground that none had even seen, let alone reconnoitred. 'The cavalry was a good way before the infantry, and for some time it seemed a sort of race between the Highlanders and the dragoons, which of them should get first to the top of the hill.'[15] The dragoons lost.

The undulating ground of Falkirk Muir rose gradually from west to east and it was at the highest point that the government cavalry arrived, fetlocks smeared with mud, to find Lord George Murray's front line – three Clan Donald regiments, Keppoch, Clanranald and Glengarry men – moving into position below them against an area of swamp known as Abbot's Moss to the south-east. Murray's choice of ground precluded any outflanking manoeuvre by the dragoons from that direction, leaving Ligonier the sole option of a frontal charge into the muzzles of the Jacobite muskets.

Having reached the moor ahead of the infantry the unsupported dragoons could only wait and watch as the rest of the Jacobite army marched into position. The Lowland Atholl Brigade formed the second line of Murray's right, while the Appin Stewarts and Camerons formed the centre; and – beyond the crown of the ridge – Farquharsons and Cromarties occupied the left. Lord Ogilvie's and Lord Gordon's regiments completed the second line, while the cavalry of Lords Elcho and Balmerino held the rear, though they were to take little part in the fighting.

The terrain was such – sloping from the central crown of the moor on either side to north and south and 'so very unequall',[16] – that it would be impossible for the right wing of either army to see what its own left wing was doing. Father Allan Macdonald of Clanranald rode along the Jacobite lines blessing the men before battle.[17]

As the government army 'enter[ed] the misty and storm-covered moor at the top of the hill'[18] spectators a mile away, watching from the church steeple in Falkirk, had their view obscured by the murky conditions. A second body of civilians, however, unwittingly found themselves much closer to the imminent action. Earlier in the day, assuming that the battle was to take place in the vicinity of the government army's camp on the low ground west of Falkirk, energetic sightseers had walked up onto the moor in large numbers to have a grandstand view of the contest. Among the curious were Presbyterian clergymen, longing to see the papist Pretender worsted. The Reverend Mr Simpson of Falla was there, as was Mr Muirhead, chaplain to Dr Doddridge, friend and biographer of the late Colonel Gardiner. There was also a 23-year-old minister from the living of Beith in Ayrshire. Eager to defend his country's 'religion and liberty, and in defence of [its] only rightful, and lawful Sovereign, King George',[19] the Reverend John Knox Witherspoon had raised a volunteer force of 150 men from his parish and marched them to Glasgow, only to be told by the military authorities there that the Beith Militia's services would not be required. Refusing to be discouraged, their commander, after dismissing his men, made his own way to Falkirk – unable to fight but determined to witness the proceedings. The Reverend Witherspoon was accompanied by his parish beadle, who carried a sword. Standing in the crowd of onlookers, the two men's excitement – if not dampened by the rain – turned to apprehension as the two armies, along with the prospect of battle, moved uncomfortably close.

Urging on his infantry and bareheaded in the driving rain, Hawley was still some way from the highest point of the moor – out of sight of the dragoons' position and that of the opposing Jacobite force – when he received a message from Ligonier, requesting instructions. Hawley's reply was carried back up to the dragoons' commander by an aide-de-camp, the Hon. James

Stuart-Mackenzie. Years later, Mackenzie was unsure whether Colonel Ligonier had actually said it was 'the most extraordinary order that ever was given', but he was certain that 'the Colonel *looked* as if he thought so'.[20] Whether he was unaware that supporting infantry necessary for such an action were still not in position, or confident in his boast that just two regiments of dragoons could 'ride over the whole Highland Army',[21] Hawley's order was to attack.

John Daniel, an ensign in Balmerino's cavalry, watched from behind the Jacobite right wing 'the moving cloud of horse, regularly disciplined, in full trot upon us down the summit, [and] doubted not but they would have ridden over us without opposition'.[22] But, as at Prestonpans, the dragoons' disciplined appearance was deceptive.

Lieutenant Colonel Whitney – his left arm, shattered at that battle four months earlier, proving no apparent handicap – rode at the head of the 13th Dragoons. He turned in his saddle and shouted to the men behind him 'that they should not heed for riding over him, should it be his fortune to fall'.[23] As the horses came within a pistol shot of the Jacobite front line, Lord George Murray – wig stuffed in his pocket and bonnet 'scrogged' firmly down on his head – gave the order to fire. According to one account no verbal command was given but Murray himself 'presented his piece' and fired, 'which was the signal'.[24]

Somewhere to the government rear, an Edinburgh Volunteer took out his pocket watch as the sound reached him: 'it wanted just ten minutes short of four o'clock.'[25] Those watching from the Falkirk church steeple saw the already cloud-laden moor 'thickened by a fast-rolling smoke' as the MacDonalds opened fire. A second later the sound of the detonations reached them.

Wind and rain at their backs, Murray's men had contrived to keep their powder dry and the explosion of close-range musketry that followed his order brought down a number of the advancing dragoons. 'For men and horse to field they brang,' wrote the hunchbacked poet and eyewitness Dougal Graham, 'And many in their saddles swang.'[26] Exactly how many varied between accounts. According to Captain Johnstone the MacDonalds' fire 'killed about eighty men, each of them having aimed at a rider'.[27] James Adolphus Oughton, a captain of Monro's Foot, just then reaching the crown of the moor with the rest of the government left wing, wrote that the 'very smart fire . . . dismounted & destroy'd so many of them as to make their breaking inevitable'. He also remarked, with hindsight, 'it is almost an Axiom in the Art of War that Cavalry cannot support the fire of unbroke Foot.'[28] The first official casualty figures compiled in the days following the action, listed only eighteen dragoons killed overall, thirty-three wounded and 114 missing.[29] Colonel Whitney was one of those killed and the men behind, attentive to his order, galloped across his body into the enemy ranks, 'throwing down every thing before them, and trampling the Highlanders under the feet of their horses'. If Johnstone's account is to be believed, the combat here was 'most singular and extraordinary'. Those brought down by the dragoons continued fighting, 'stretched on the ground, thrust[ing] their dirks into the bellies of the horses. Some seized the riders by their clothes, dragged them down, and stabbed them with their dirks; several again used their pistols; but few of them had sufficient space to handle their swords.'[30]

That night, in the lanes of Falkirk, riderless horses would be seen, girths having slipped and 'saddles turned round below their bellies, . . . many of them trailing their intestines on the ground'.[31]

Having 'march'd, all the way up hill, and Over very uneven Ground, greatly Blown',[32] the regiments of foot forming the government left wing were barely come to a panting halt – Wolfe's 8th, Cholmondeley's 34th, Pulteney's 13th to the fore, Blakeney's 27th, Monro's 37th and Flemming's 36th behind – when their lines were thrown into confusion by terrified horses and horsemen. Disordered by the point-blank musket fire, and 'incommoded with the smoke of [the] discharge' blown into their eyes by the wind, Hamilton's Dragoons – and those of Ligonier's not fighting for their lives among the Jacobite ranks – behaved as they had the previous September. 'The cravens of Preston[pans] rushed headlong over the left wing of their own foot, who lay upon their faces; bawling . . . "Dear brethren, we shall all be massacred this day!"'[33] Others took a clearer line of retreat, skirting the infantry lines, while the MacDonalds – ignoring Murray's orders to keep their ranks – went in pursuit. Some dragoons broke to the south, galloping into Abbots Moss and became stuck 'up to the saddle-laps in [the] bog, where the pursuing Highlanders cut them to pieces with so little trouble', it was said, 'that . . . the feat was as easy as slicing *bacon*'.[34]

The retreat of Cobham's Dragoons was also confused by the infantry support taking up positions behind. They 'broke upon [the] Foot, who fired too soon, by which some of the Dragoons were unsaddled'.[35] The rest jerked their horses' bridles to the right and dashed along the corridor between the two armies, in the words of John O'Sullivan, 'as if they run'd the gantellet, exposed to the fire of almost all the [Jacobite] ligne'. Highlanders on the left wing, having fired and thrown down their muskets, 'according to their usual custom, pursued them Sword in hand, & distroyed as many as they cou'd overtake'.[36]

Exposed by the flight of the dragoons – and with the Camerons and Appin Stewarts of the Jacobite centre 'in a thick Column 20 Men Deep' bearing down on them sword in hand[37] – the infantry at the government's left and centre 'gave way without . . . being attacked'.[38] It appeared to Brigadier General James Cholmondeley as if they broke and fled in a mockery of parade-ground drill, 'faced to the right about, as regularly as if they had had the word of Command, and cou'd not be rallied'. Pained by their conduct, his own regiment amongst them, Cholmondeley did not think 'they were pursued by two hundred men'.[39]

But the concerted disintegration was understandable. Their flintlocks rendered useless by the penetrating rain, a proportion of the government infantry found themselves effectively unarmed. They 'could not prime, nor their Pieces discharge'[40] and it was believed 'not above one in five [of the muskets] that were attempted to be fir'd, went off.'[41] Captain Oughton claimed six or eight of the officers on either flank of Monro's were killed, and described the leaderless platoons breaking their own regiment:

'they crouded down the Hill on the next Regiments to them, which encreased the Disorder, till the unhappy Contagion became almost general.' As the left wing broke so, 'like a catching Infection,' according to another report, 'the whole Front followed, and likewise the Rear.'[42] The regular Foot in turn broke the Argyllshire men, one of whom, when asked afterwards, had he fired his musket, replied he had not, 'nor none of them, for the foot of the Kings Army fell so close upon them, that unless they poured their shot in the face of the Redcoats they could not fire'.[43]

Abandoned by their men, Oughton and his brother officers were 'obliged to join in an ignomonious flight'. He himself, encumbered by boots and great coat, could not run and only narrowly escaped the attentions of Jacobite cavalry – 'their Scoundrel Hussars' – by the timely intervention of a servant on horseback. Several other officers, likewise hampered in their flight, 'were hack'd to pieces with a more than Indian Barbarity'.[44]

Captain George Fitzgerald was on the left of Monro's 37th, next to Blakeney's 27th, when the lines disintegrated. 'I was knocked down by a Musket ball which went thorow my hat & wig & graz'd my head but I rose again being only stunn'd by it and perceiv'd the left wings of both lines broke & retreateing down the Hill.'[45] He himself was preserved by an unlikely saviour. '[I] was surrounded . . . by a party of the Rebells who cut me in the head & knocked me down a 2nd time when they began to rob me & as I imagin'd would have afterwards murder'd me, but I call'd out to a French Soldier going by and desir'd he wou'd not suffer those Villains to kill me and he immediately came to my assistance & prevented their doing me any further mischief.'[46]

Nearby, the commander of the 37th Foot was battling for his life. Despite his obesity Colonel Sir Robert Monro was an agile and fearless fighter and the circumstances of his death were recounted by his son. 'After being deserted [by his men he] was attacked by six of Locheal's regt. & for some time defended himself with his half Pike. Two of the six, . . . he kill'd; a seventh, coming up, fired a Pistol into [his] Groin; upon which falling, the Highlander wt. his sword gave him two strokes in the face, one over the Eyes & another on the mouth.'

The Colonel's brother Duncan, a surgeon, was shot in the chest and 'terribly slashed' while tending him.[47]

What witnesses on Falkirk church steeple called the 'main event', occupied 'an amazingly brief space of time . . . From the commencement till . . . "the *break* of the battle," there did not intervene more than ten minutes.'[48] Immediately after the first Jacobite fire, they 'saw the discomfited troops burst wildly from the thunder-cloud . . . and rush, in far-spread disorder, over the spacious face of the hill'.[49]

*

Towards the bottom of the slope, Captain Cunningham had still not moved far beyond his bemired ordnance and was endeavouring to get the three cannon left to him past another bad piece of ground when he heard 'a Discharge of small Arms and looking round saw both Lines of the Army that went up the hill rushing down again with the greatest Precipitation and the Rebels pursuing'.[50] At this point all but one of his matrosses ran away, along with the dozen 'Country People'. Drivers cut the traces of those horses still attached to the seven abandoned artillery pieces and galloped off on them. 'In such a Situation,' Cunningham's defence continued, 'deserted by his Men and the Rebels within 200 paces of him, it was impossible for him to do any Service with [his] 3 Guns, he thought it most prudent therefore to order them down the Hill.'[51]

Up on the moor chaos was compounded by the 'numbers of by-Standers'[52] – one report described 'the cries and confusion of many thousands'[53] – fleeing among the horse and foot. These were 'country people whom curiosity to see the battle, and perhaps a design of striping the dead, had drawn together'.[54] Amongst them were the Presbyterian clergymen, Messrs Muirhead, Simpson and Witherspoon, who were taken prisoner by the Jacobites. John

Daniel, the Balmerino trooper, alleged that other men of the cloth were killed, but that – 'fired with holy zeal, [having] quitted their Bibles and [taken] their swords' – they deserved to be treated as any other combatants on a field of battle. An unnamed parson was said to have begged for his life, pleading 'I am a Minister of My Master Jesus Christ.' He was dispatched with the stroke of a broadsword and a possibly apocryphal rejoinder: 'If you are a good one, your Master has need of you; if not, it's fitting that you go and take your punishment elsewhere!'[55]

The Glasgow Militia had taken up its position to the rear of the government left, close to farm buildings and 'something more than two thirds up the Hill', when the fighting began 'out of sight' beyond the crest of the moor. They could hear the sounds of gunfire and screaming horses, and the future professor William Corse claimed to have seen 'day light . . . in several places' through the dragoons' ranks ahead and 'believe[d] they suffer'd a good deal' from the MacDonalds' first volley. Next, through the blinding wind and rain, 'about 60 Dragoons of Hamilton's [came] down the Hill in a body at the Gallop' straight at the hapless militia. They 'carry'd off about a Company of our people', wrote Corse, 'among whom I was, & would then have given my life for a shilling.'[56] Some were trampled, others ran, while a number of the Glasgow men retaliated: 'gave them a fire and brought down some of those Rascalls'.[57] When he got free of the stampede, Corse turned back up the hill but 'saw the Glasgow Regiment no more'. He was told later that a number of his comrades had regrouped and successfully engaged with seventy pursuing Highlanders. Then, attacked by 200 more, they 'fell into confusion, & finally ran away'. But with an officer and eighteen men killed, some wounded, and three officers and twenty-six rank and file taken prisoner, Corse was defensive: the regiment, he said, had acquitted themselves 'pretty well for Militia'.[58] Not so their patron, the Earl of Home. When the dragoons broke, he abandoned his command, put spurs to his own horse and was said to have been the first of Hawley's army to arrive in Linlithgow nearly eight miles to the east.

Meanwhile Captain Cunningham, with his remaining three cannon and the remnants of his gunnery crew, had reached the bottom of the hill. 'Perceiving every thing in Confusion, [and] the report running that the whole Army was broke, he retired with the Multitude to Falkirk whose Gates were so crowded with Officers and Soldiers, that he could scarce get Entrance.' With difficulty he made his way to his lodging where he retrieved from his baggage £120 of government money, 'which he thought it his Duity to secure lest it should fall into the Rebels hands'. In the subsequent enquiry, he recalled indignantly, 'grate stress [was] laid on this Circumstance as if it was a Crime, and the principal Motive of his leaving the Field.'[59]

At the town gate issuing onto the Linlithgow road, Cunningham heard that Major General John Huske was dead, and joined 'others of the Army' in marching east. Later he heard a contradictory report that General Huske had not been killed and, indeed, 'was keeping the Field with the Right wing of the Army.'

*

'About five minutes after [the] first fire' of the Jacobite guns had precipitated the rout of both horse and foot, the government army's reputation was saved from complete ignominy by a spirited if partial counterattack.[60] There were but two regiments of regulars, declared William Corse, 'that [had] any title to reproach' the Glasgow militia for a lack of resolve.[61] These exemplary troops – three regiments in fact and parts of two more – were on the right wing and initially protected from the onslaught of the Jacobite left by a ravine, cutting due north from the moor to the valley below. Ligonier's 59th Foot were in the front line and when the 1st Royals to their left broke and 'ran before they were engaged',[62] Barrell's 4th moved forwards from the second line to fill the space. General Cholmondeley – having just witnessed the disintegration of the rest of the army – took command. At the same time, Major General Huske brought forward a reserve of Howard's 3rd – the Old Buffs – and succeeded in rallying the fragments of Price's 14th Foot and Battereau's 62nd that had not given way to panic. Assembling his scratch command Cholmondeley 'got the men to be quite Cool, as Cool as ever [he] saw men at Exercise'.[63] They were drawn up at the head of the ravine and facing up the slope to the crown of the moor, front ranks kneeling, and the centre and rear ranks firing continuously into the flank of the Farquharsons and Cromarties racing in pursuit of the less steadfast government troops. So disciplined was the platoon drill of Cholmondeley's *ad hoc* company, and so punishing their enfilading fire, that John O'Sullivan mistook it for a more elaborate military formation: 'that accursed hollow square'.

Attacked in their turn, these men's coolness in the face of a Highland charge, the like of which had scattered the rest of the army, was recounted by a private soldier of Barrell's regiment. '[A] Party of [Rebels] came running upon us and fired, but at too great a Distance, and did us but little harm; they threw away their Guns . . . and advanced Sword in hand; we gave them a Volley of Shot . . . which caused them to halt and shake their Swords at us; we gave them three Huzzas and another Volley, which caused them to run.'[64]

It was a brief instance of professionalism prevailing over undisciplined zeal and prefigured what was to happen on Drummossie Moor three months later to the day. But according to Captain Johnstone – while he admitted the volleys 'greatly incommoded them' – the Jacobite left's retreat was occasioned as much by misunderstanding as by superior firepower. Hearing the huzzas and gunfire from their rear, 'Mr John Roy Stuart, an officer in the service of France', was convinced his men were being lured into an ambush. He shouted to them to stop their pursuit 'and the cry of stop flew immediately from rank to rank, and threw the whole army into disorder'.[65]

It was, reflected Johnstone, 'often more dangerous to stop the fire and impetuosity of soldiers, of whom the best are but machines . . . than to let them run all risks [and] carry all before them'. The alarm and resulting chaos presented 'a spectacle seldom seen in war . . . Part of the King's army, much the greater part, was flying to the eastward, and part of the rebel army was flying to the westward.'[66] It gave rise to a symmetry of phrase in Hawley's report of the battle the following morning: 'our left is beat, and their left is beat.' It accounted also for Major James Wolfe's dismissal of Falkirk as an 'encounter . . . not a battle, as neither side would fight'.[67]

With the Jacobite left in retreat, the tireless Cholmondeley left the resurgent government right wing with orders to hold their ground, and galloped downhill to recruit cavalry support. He was able to muster a hundred or so of Cobham's Dragoons who had regrouped following their dash between the armies. He told them he 'had repuls'd the Enemy, with two weak Battallions, and that if they would march up, [he] wou'd head them' and finish the work. The dragoons professed themselves 'greatly pleas'd . . . and with many Oaths and Irish Exclamations' agreed to follow Cholmondeley. Even so it was with difficulty that he got them back to the top of the hill and he had to 'fire a Pistol amongst them, before [he] could get them to do this'. To Cholmondeley's frustration – but perhaps to the dragoons' relief – 'Night was drawing on'[68] and General Huske ordered them to retire, along with the men of Barrell's, Ligonier's and the rest.

Barrell's Regiment gained the distinction of capturing the only Jacobite prisoner taken by the government army during the battle. It was Donald MacDonell of Tirnadris who had told Lord Perth at Prestonpans that if the opportunity to kill redcoats were not taken there then they would have to be killed elsewhere. At Falkirk he had been energetically furthering that resolve during the pursuit, the blade of his broadsword smeared with blood and matted hair. Trudging back up the hill in the gathering dark he approached a body of the 4th Foot, mistaking them for Lord John Drummond's men, and was taken.[69] Major MacDonell would not be hanged on an Edinburgh scaffold. Instead, a crueller death awaited him at Carlisle, where, following his trial for high treason, he endured the lingering retribution reserved for that offence alone.

The government right continued their march down the hill in good order. Passing Cunningham's abandoned artillery sunk in mud to the axles, a party of grenadiers tried to bring off one of the cannons 'by yoking themselves to it', while someone had the presence of mind to spike the rest. The guns were, however, 'so much in the Ground by the wetness of the Soil & Weather'[70] that any further attempt at recovery was found to be impossible.

It was while the last contingent of the army was on the road to Linlithgow that Cunningham himself claimed to have met them, having ridden back towards Falkirk, 'in hope he might have been usefull if the Artillery should have been regain'd'. He would be given no credit for his professed zeal, even were it believed. It was said that Hawley would have shot him, 'had [Cunningham] not, the night before it was to be done, with a penknife cut the arteries of his arm and bled to death'.[71] A later account said that, although he had 'cut himself desperately in both Arms [and] lost much Blood, he [was] not yet dead as was reported'.[72] In fact, he lived to be court-martialled at Montrose on 20 January. Found guilty, he was 'cashiered with infamy'[73] and suffered the ritual degradation proper to that verdict:

> The line being ordered out under arms, the prisoner was brought to the head of the oldest brigade, completely accoutred, when his sentence being read, his commission was cancelled, sword broken over his head, his sash cut in pieces and thrown into his face, and lastly, the provost-martial's servant giving him a kick on the posteriors, turned him out of the line.

Such was the preserve of officers, 'more terrible to a man of feeling than death itself'.[74] More straightforward examples were made of other ranks. 'Many of the private soldiers, who had displayed extraordinary cowardice, were severely whipped',[75] while four were hanged on Hawley's Grassmarket gibbet, 'a paper . . . pin'd upon the breast of each with the word Desertion in large letters'.[76]

By contrast, the proud private soldier of Barrell's Regiment wrote that, in their case, officers 'behaved exceeding well' after the battle, 'came to our Regiment to return us Thanks for our Courage, as they were pleased to express it, telling us we saved the Honour of the Field, besides many thousands of Lives'. Brigadier General Cholmondeley was particularly demonstrative, expressing his satisfaction 'by kissing our Men, and making us a Present of ten Guineas'.[77]

It was said that 'the interval between the first fire and the withdrawal of Barrell's Regiment did not exceed twenty minutes.'[78] William Corse pointed out that all actions against Jacobite irregulars, by their very nature, 'lasted but a short time'. Speed was all. The Highland charge either succeeded to devastating effect and rapidly swept the field; or it failed with equal rapidity and could not be attempted again. More remarkable, Corse observed, was 'why [the rebels] did not use their advantage, & enter where the Troops were broke, sword in hand, as is their way; & in the next place, why they did not pursue . . . when all fire-arms were useless; it is not to be comprehended. They cannot, in all human probability, ever have such another opportunity.'[79]

In his 150-page doggerel epic, *An Impartial History of the Rise, Progress, and Extinction of the Late Rebellion in Britain*, Dougal Graham summarised the lost opportunity in two couplets:

> It is well known by all about,
> The battle was not half fought out . . .
> On Janu'ry sixteenth, afternoon,
> This battle was fought, but never won.

An abiding memory among the Falkirk citizenry was of General Hawley riding through the town in the rain with the rabble of his army and pausing at the centre of the main street to express his 'rage and vexation by breaking his sword upon the market-cross'.[80]

The shivering of steel on stone can have done little to allay his mood. 'My heart is broke,' he wrote that night in Linlithgow.[81] Robert Wightman saw him there the following morning and reported that 'he looked most wretchedly; even worse than C[op]e did a few hours after his scuffle.' Here was a man who had 'reprobated the conduct of Mr Cope', repeating to brother officers his frequent assertion that 'Highlanders . . . could not stand against a charge of dragoons who attacked them well.'[82] And when news of the Falkirk disaster arrived in London, one man at least was predictably 'radiant with joy'. Comparisons between Prestonpans and Falkirk, between Generals Cope and Hawley were lost on few, least of all on Cope himself. It was said that he had 'offered bets, to the amount of ten thousand guineas, in the different coffeehouses in London, that the first general sent to command an army against [the Jacobites] in Scotland, would be beaten as he had been; and by the defeat of General Hawley he gained a considerable sum of money, and recovered his honour to a certain degree.'[83]

Wightman foresaw 'no bad consequence' arising from the defeat, 'unless H[awle]y's disgrace be reckoned one'. He even predicted benefits, chiefly 'our having an Army of 20,000 Men in this Country for some Months', together with 'the Duke [of Cumberland]'s coming hither'.[84]

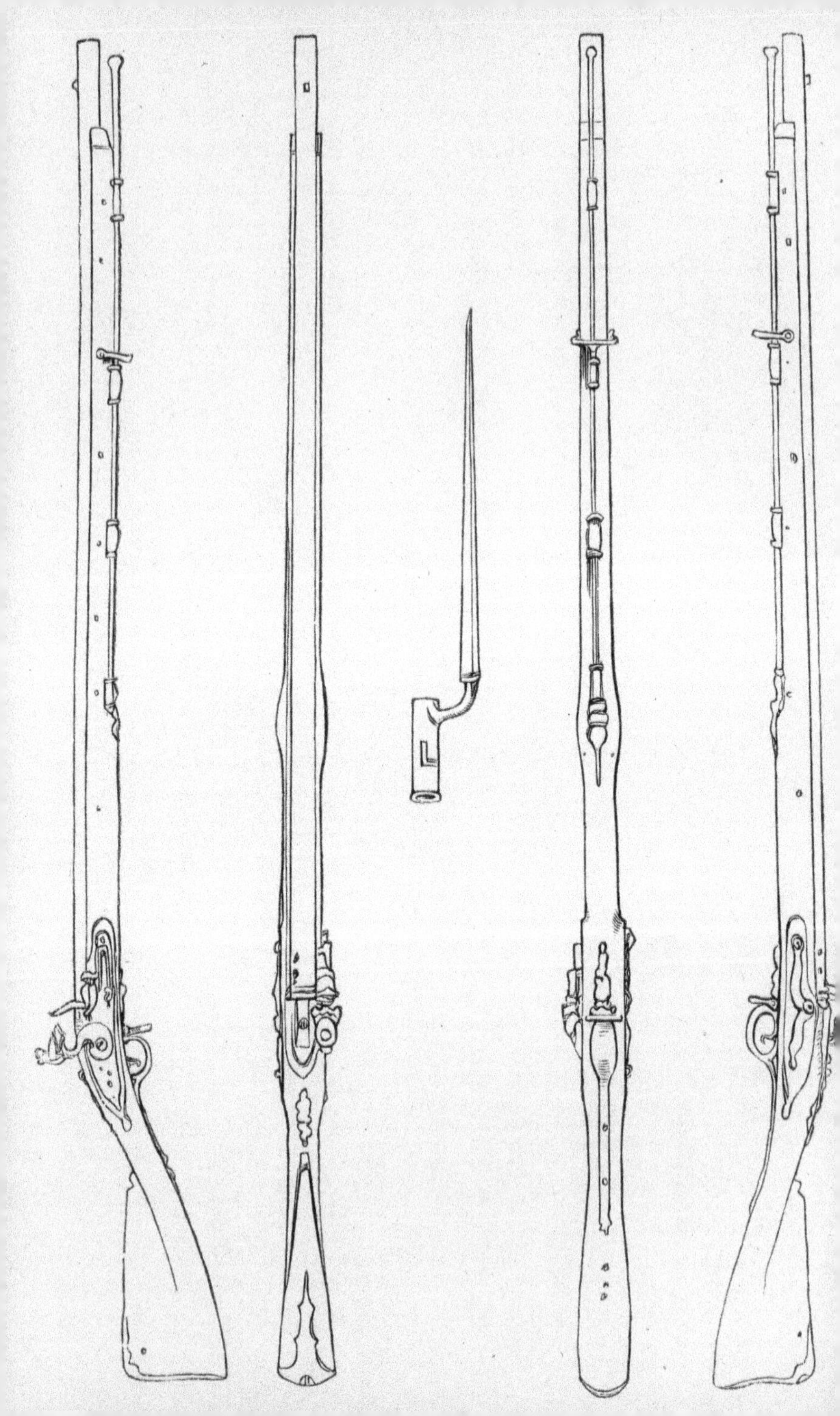

Bayonet & Broadsword

THE practical, tactical and lethal advantages of bayonet over basket-hilted broadsword – of horizontally thrust triangular point over downward slashing, gritstone-sharpened edge – had been pondered, following the disaster at Prestonpans, and before that of Falkirk, by an anonymous Whig gentleman from the comfort of his armchair: 'The Sword is managed by one Arm, the Musquet and Bayonet is thrust by both; the one may be escaped, the other is irresistible; the Blow of the former is slow, and must be perceiv'd, the Thrust of the latter is quick, and felt as soon as seen.'

However devastating the first sword stroke, the gentleman argued with mathematically elegant logic, time and strength were required to disengage and raise the weapon for a second. The push of the bayonet by comparison – palm of the right hand against the brass butt plate of the musket, left hand gripping the stock – expended minimal time, effort and motion, 'withdrawn and returned in a Moment'.[1] The gentleman further calculated that three bayonet thrusts might be driven home in the time a swordsman could complete a single stroke and ready himself for another. The empirical philosopher David Hume pointed out a further disadvantage of the broadsword, that it 'obliges each Combatant to occupy double the Ground that would suffice, did he employ the Pushing-Sword or the Bayonet'.[2] This consideration would prove critical in the congested struggle forming the climax of fighting at Culloden.

Until the close of the seventeenth century bayonets were of the plug type, with a hilt designed to be jammed inside the muzzle of the musket, its purpose being to convert a firearm into a pike for close-quarters combat. The obvious disadvantage was that the musket could not subsequently be loaded or fired so long as the plug bayonet was in place. In the first years of the eighteenth century the socket bayonet – attached by means of a collar that slipped over the outside of the muzzle – enabled the weapon to be fired while still doing deadly service as a pike. The blade, forged with a curved shank to the side of the collar, extended seventeen inches beyond the muzzle and at a slight angle from it. This angle prevented the soldier accidentally impaling his hand on the bayonet point when using a ramrod to tamp cartridge, ball and wadding down the barrel while loading.

In 1745 Thomas Hollier, proprietor of the Armoury Mills at Lewisham, Kent, manufactory of edged weapons for the Board of Ordnance, supplied the British army with 40,000 socket bayonets: more than in any previous year since the Land Pattern firelock musket was introduced in 1722.

The armchair tactician's intention in his sixpenny pamphlet was to counter the reputation for savage invincibility acquired by the Jacobite army in its early successes and to bolster confidence in the disciplined training and modern weaponry of an efficient regular fighting force. 'The Broad-Sword is dreadful,' he declared, 'but the Bayonet is deadly; it is the Edge of the Sword that cuts, but the Point of the Bayonet kills; a Man may live that has his Cheek cut off, but not with a Wound through the Vitals.' This heartening tract, published on 8 January 1746, was entitled *Seasonable Considerations on the Present War in Scotland, against the Rebels*.[3]

Bayonet drill, in Humphrey Bland's *Treatise of Military Discipline*, was to be accomplished with five commands: 'Draw your Bayonets', 'Fix your Bayonets', 'Rest your Bayonets', 'Charge your Bayonets', and 'Push your Bayonets'. The fourth command brought the soldier to 'Charge' position: weight fallen back 'a moderate pace' on the right foot, knee stiff and toe pointed to the right; left knee 'bent a little forward, with that Toe to the Front'; the firelock level, 'Stock lying between the Left Thumb and Fore-finger . . . the But-end in a full right Hand, the Thumb on the upper Part of it . . . and the Bayonet pointing directly to the Front and about Breast high.' The fifth command prompted the simulated kill and return to 'Charge' position:

> Push your Firelock with both Hands strait forward, without raising or sinking the Point of the Bayonet, bringing the But-end before the left Breast . . . and bring it back to its former Place.[4]

Modifications to this procedure were suggested by correspondents in the popular press as more effective means of combating the Highlanders' use of target and broadsword. It was pointed out that a forward thrust of the bayonet could be deflected by a targe held on the left forearm, leaving the soldier defenceless against the downward stroke of a broadsword held in his enemy's right hand. After the battle of Falkirk an essay, 'On regular and irregular Forces', appeared in the *Gentleman's Magazine* which sought to remedy this tactical disadvantage. It advocated training troops to fight with their muskets 'hanging at a balance' under the left arm, either slung from the left shoulder or, with a longer sling, from the right. This would allow the musket to be pushed by the left hand only, 'like a battering ram', evading the target and driving the bayonet under the opponent's raised sword arm into his right side.[5] And should defence prove necessary, this arrangement was supposed to free the soldier's right hand to parry with his own sword.

An alternative method was proposed by a person signing himself 'CITIZEN' in the *Penny London Post*. By the simple expedient of altering his grip on the weapon a soldier would change the direction of thrust. Instead of holding the stock or barrel in the left hand and pushing with the right: 'seize the Barrel with the Right Hand, and the Butt with the Left, and push from the Left

Side; if the Highlander lifts up his Arm to Strike with his Sword he exposes all that Side of his Body under the Sword Arm, to the Point of the Bayonet; if he offers to cover it with his Target he cannot make his Stroke and if he parries it with his Sword, he loses his Stroke.'[6]

Following the battle of Culloden much would be made of a specific bayonet drill employed in training during the nine weeks in which the government army was stationed at Aberdeen and the advance post of Strathbogie. The *Westminster Journal* reported that the Duke of Cumberland 'took the Pains to confer with every Battalion of Foot, on the proper Method of using the Musket and Bayonet to Advantage against the Sword and Target'. It went so far as to claim 'that the Success of the Engagement was unanimously ascribed to the seasonable Instructions of his Royal Highness'.[7] The divergence from standard practice 'was mighty little, but of the last consequence' and produced the same effect as that advocated by the 'Citizen' but without modifying the soldier's grip: 'Before this, the bayonet-man attacked the sword-man . . . fronting him; now the left-hand bayonet attacked the sword fronting his next right-hand man. He was then covered by the enemy's shield . . . on his left, and the enemy's right [lay] open to him.'[8]

It was an exercise in mutual defence; each man directing his bayonet thrust at the enemy attacking the man to his right, and relying on the man to his left doing the same for him.

This also marked a shift away from the reliance on platoon firing that had proved so inadequate at Prestonpans and – with some exceptions – during the 'tremendous storm of rain' at Falkirk. In preparation for Culloden, it was said, 'the Duke took care . . . to restore his army to that method of discipline, which led the troops to close with the enemy, and . . . to meet them hand to hand. The soldiers were instructed that the force of the bayonet consisted in order, and that the broad sword could in no instance claim any superiority, [except] where troops had disbanded themselves, and the individual had forgotten the protection that he derived from his comrades.'[9]

Daniel Hamilton, a Barrell's grenadier, had taken part in training at Strathbogie with the rest of the front line battalions. Divulging no details of the training, he was clear as to its nature and purpose: 'the grenadiers [were made to] attack the battalion, in exercising, with their broad swords, to convince the men of the superiority of the bayonets.'[10]

The *Gentleman's Magazine* predicted that the Duke's useful innovation would 'doubtless be enter'd in the books of discipline as proper against sword and target'.[11] Someone signing himself C.P.G. in his regular correspondence with the *Westminster Journal* – and on one occasion using the pseudonym 'Philo Britannicus'[12] – afterwards claimed to be 'the Inventor of [the] *new Method for pushing with the Bayonet in an Engagement*'. The *Journal*'s proprietor hoped 'that if the Fact be true, and proper Attestation be made of it, his grateful Countrymen, who have been so liberal to encourage and reward all who had any Share in the Suppression of this Rebellion, will not think barren Applause sufficient for the Author of this Invention.'[13]

Then, towards the end of 1746, a correspondent in the *Scots Magazine* cast doubt not only upon the authorship of the celebrated invention, but also on its implementation and even the training itself. Styling himself 'a lover of truth and liberty', this individual claimed that 'There is no foundation for what is said . . . of an alteration having been made in the manner of using the bayonet.'[14] Compounding the doubt – and contrary to the prediction in the *Gentleman's Magazine* – the alteration did not find a place in the 6th edition of Bland's *Treatise on Military Discipline*, published that same year, nor in the 7th edition of 1753.

However doubtful the provenance, it is unlikely that so rigid a tactic would have been effective anywhere other than the exercise yard. Amid the variables of terrain, visibility and weather prevailing on a Scottish battlefield, an oncoming enemy of irregular fighters could not have been expected to present itself, each in turn, to be conveniently skewered under the raised sword arm. But, at the very least, such training would have inspired the regular infantry with confidence – after the horrors of Prestonpans and Falkirk – that Highland savagery could be combatted with sound military discipline; it would have instilled trust in the individual soldier for his comrades in the line, especially the one to his left; and, during the intervening months of inaction at Aberdeen and Strathbogie, and the march westward, it would have served to occupy his mind with a positive focus, replacing the frightening uncertainties awaiting him in the inevitable confrontation to come.

Ruin'd & Defeated
4
3
Oh! Mercy Mercy
7
Oh Laird we're all Miscarri
8
6

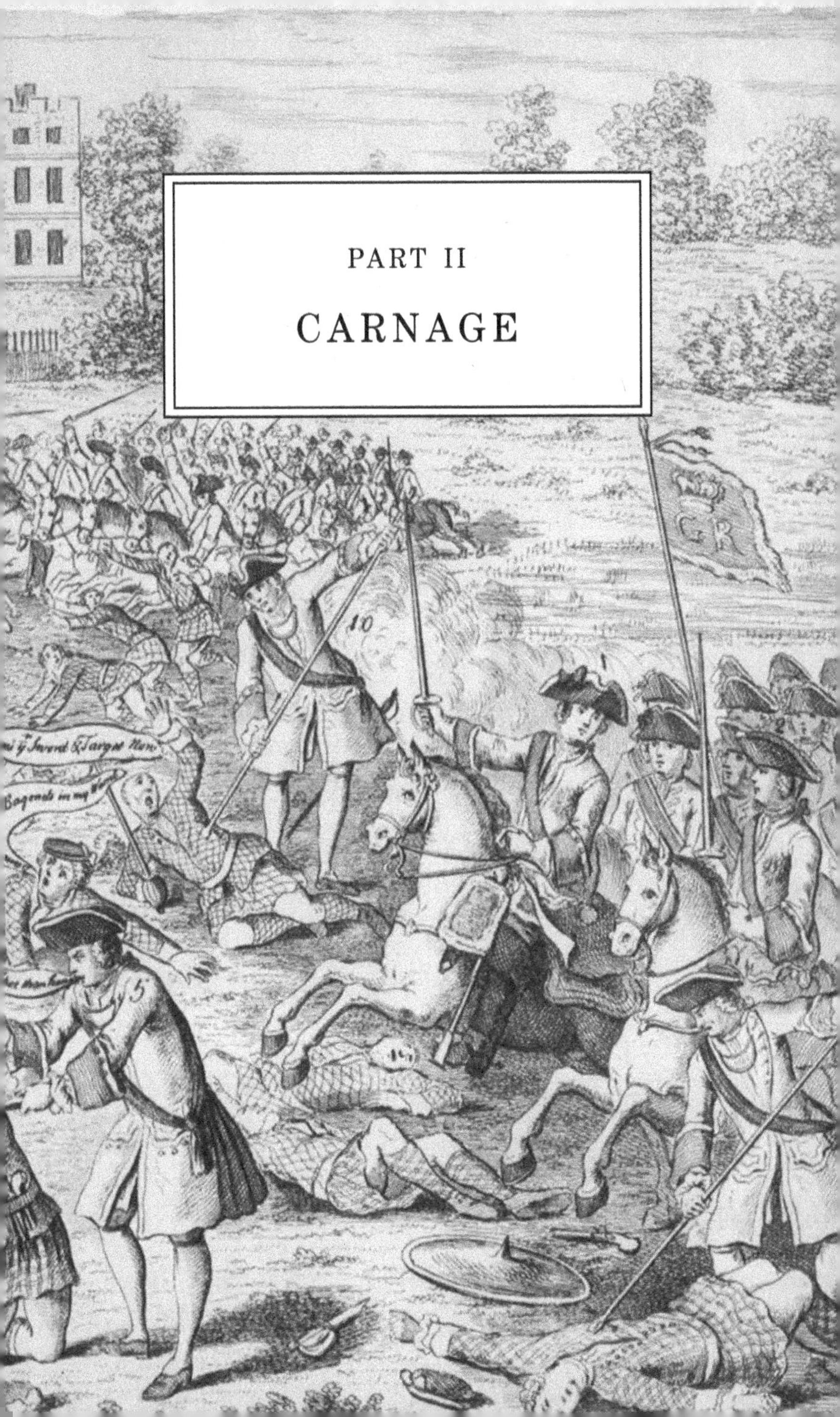

PART II

CARNAGE

I

THE eve of battle was the Duke of Cumberland's birthday. That night, as his soldiers enjoyed special rations at their Commander-in-Chief's expense, his enemies planned to mark the anniversary in different fashion.

Earlier in the day, eleven miles west of Nairn, the Jacobite army had assembled in battle order on Drummossie Moor. The Prince reviewed his men and was 'very well pleas'd to see them in so good spirits' despite many having eaten nothing for a day or two and that morning but 'one single biskit a man'. Nor had they received pay 'for a month past'.[1] As a result of these privations desertion was rife, the muster roll far from complete and Lord George Murray was having difficulty retaining the fighters he still had. After Falkirk 'Many of the men went home from all the different corps, and this evil was daily increasing.'[2] By April it was the demands of hearth and land that took some of them from soldiering. 'Many of our people, as it was seed time, had slipt home,' Murray complained, 'and . . . it was not an easy matter to keep them togither.'[3] Although professing confidence in the outcome of the imminent encounter, the order he signed on 14 April showed an attempt to instil the most rudimentary elements of military discipline into what forces were left him: 'That evry person attach themselves to some Corps of the Armie & to remain with that Corps night & day till the Batle & pirsute be finally over; This regards the Foot as well as the Horse. It is required & expected that each individual in the Armie as well officer as souldier keeps their posts that shall be allotted to them.'[4]

But discipline, morale and numbers were to diminish significantly before it was time to fight.

An issue of precedence in the order of battle arose that morning. The Clan Donald traditionally fought on the right. They had done so at Falkirk, at Clifton, at Prestonpans, and, in the words of a Clanranald officer, 'in all our battles and struggles in behalf of our Royall family since the battle of Bannockburn', when that honour was bestowed upon Angus MacDonald, Lord of the Isles, by Robert the Bruce.[5] So there was resentment on Drummossie Moor when they were assigned the left, and, at Lord Murray's insistence, his own Atholl Brigade were granted the prized right. The Duke of Perth did his best to placate the Clan Donald men under his command, telling them that 'they would make a right of the left' if they fought with their accustomed bravery.

As it became clear that the government army remained at Nairn and was making no move to give battle that day, a plan was made to take the battle to them in the early hours of the following morning. Murray stressed 'the advantages Highlanders have by Surprising their Enemy, and rather Attacking in the night time than in day Light'. His argument was simple: 'as regular troops depend intirely upon their discipline, and on the Contrary the Highlanders having none, the Night was the time to putt them most upon an Equality.'[6] They had a further advantage: their opponents, it was thought, would have spent the night celebrating Cumberland's birthday and 'they'l all be as drunk as beggers' when attacked.[7]

Fires were lit on the moor to deceive the watching spyglasses of Royal Navy ships anchored in the Moray Firth into thinking that the insurgents were still encamped.[8] The main road from Culloden to Nairn was to be avoided because of its proximity to places of habitation. Instead, guided by locals of the Clan MacIntosh, they were to follow the Moor road that 'had scarcely been ever trode by human foot'.[9] With the exception, when necessary, of a whispered password – *King James the Eighth* – the 'profoundest silence' was to be observed both on the march, and even during the anticipated slaughter in the government camp. 'We were . . . forbid in the attack to make any use of our firearms,' recalled Alexander MacDonald, 'but only of sword, dirk and bayonet, to cut the tent strings and pull down the poles, and where we observed a swelling or bulge in the fallen tent there to strick and push vigorously.'[10]

Murray estimated the night march would take six hours, and to have the benefit of darkness and surprise the attack had to be made by one o'clock in the morning, or two o'clock at the very latest. But, 'betwixt six and seven at night, a little before the march should have begun, the men went off on all hands, and in great numbers' – two thousand of them, Murray claimed – 'to shift for themselves, both for provisions and quarters: many officers were sent after them, but all to no purpose.' Prospects of success decreasing by the minute, Murray argued for abandoning the attempt. The Prince, however, 'continued bent on the thing', and the order was given to march. 'It was then eight at night, or past it.'[11]

Begun badly, the expedition continued worse. 'Such a road was never travelled', recalled Robert Strange, 'the men in general were frequently up to the ankles, and the horses in many places extricated themselves with difficulty.'[12] The road being narrow, they marched one column after another, not abreast, 'and in Consequence marched very Slow'.[13] The order of march replicated the battle order assumed earlier in the day and which would be repeated the day following. The right wing – Atholl Brigade, Camerons and Appin Stewarts, Lord George Murray commanding – formed the first column. The second, comprising what would form the centre, was led by Lord John Drummond. A third column, the unaccustomed and disgruntled left wing, led by Drummond's elder brother, the Duke of Perth, was made up of the regiments of Keppoch, Clanranald and Glengarry. Bringing up the rear, the Prince himself led the cavalry, the Irish Picquets, the *Royal*

Ecossais, Lord Ogilvie's and the other reserve regiments that would form the second line of battle.

After half a mile, Murray, in the vanguard, received a message that the rear columns had already fallen back by a considerable distance and requesting him to halt until they caught up. Instead of stopping he slowed the pace of march 'hoping that might do'. It did not. Over the next six miles he claimed to have received fifty such messages, brought by aides-de-camp and other officers from the struggling regiments behind. The woodland of Kilravock further impeded the rear of the army where a narrow gap in a wall had to be negotiated. Many of the exhausted, hungry, demoralised men wandered off into the trees to lie down and became lost in the darkness. When at last the van emerged from the woods a halt was called, an impromptu council held and the 'officers of distinction' consulted their timepieces; or as Murray put it, 'ten watches were looked'. They were still more than four miles from their objective, with barely a third of the army present, and 'it was found to be two o'clock in the morning.'

Murray was by then even more certain that the attack should be abandoned. The regiments under his command could cover at most two miles, even at a quick march, before sunrise. Then, for the next two miles, they would be in plain sight of the enemy 'before they could come at them.'[14] Cameron of Lochiel agreed. Others were for pressing on to attack regardless. Better that than retreat, it was reasoned. '[The enemy] will most certainly follow and oblige us to fight when we shall be in a much worse condition to fight them than we are now.' John O'Sullivan spoke for the Prince, still a mile or so behind with the cavalry and reserves. 'All his confidence is in yu,' he told Murray, 'the loss or the gain of the cause is in your hands & depends entirely on yu.' An already desperate position, he added, could not be improved by caution. 'If yu retire yu discourage your men who suffer enough already, you loose all yr advantages, & give all over to yr enemy.'[15]

A drum sounded from the government camp, as though settling the argument. The enemy was alarmed and could not be surprised.

That vital element lost and the number of fighters insufficient to prevail without it, their only course was retreat. O'Sullivan and the Duke of Perth rode back to inform the Prince what had been decided, while Murray led the head of the column to the left, 'and fell into the low road from Nairn to Inverness'.[16] The easier and shorter route was chosen 'as we had not the same reason for shuning houses in returning as we had in advancing.'[17]

During this march back many a famished and bone-weary clansman is said to have thrown away his cumbersome target – sole defence against bayonet and musket round – as though such warlike considerations had been entirely supplanted by those of rest and victuals.

When they passed the church at Croy, two miles from the place where they had turned round, the sun was up. It was confirmation of how exposed they would have been had they marched the remaining four miles from that place towards the government camp.

The most succinct account of this chaotic prelude to the battle is contained in the day book of James Stuart, a captain in Lord Ogilvie's Regiment: 'marched at night to surprise the enemys quarters, but returned *re infecta*, day coming on.'[18] *Re infecta*: 'without finishing the business'.

Wordier first-hand narratives of the night march and return contain striking disparities as to distance, time and topography. Four miles from the enemy camp by Murray's reckoning, contracted to three, two, even one mile by the reckoning of others. Likewise, if a time of two o'clock for the decision taken to retreat was arrived at by the consensus of 'ten watches looked', John Daniel would put it at three o'clock and Robert Strange at four. Admittedly, Strange and Daniel, marching with the cavalry at the rear, would have turned back at a considerably later time than those in the front columns. They may even have missed the place – 'a little to the eastward of Kilravock House' – where the rest of the army turned off to the left, and have marched on, oblivious, for a further two miles 'till . . . almost at a place call'd Killdrummie'.[19] From there the fires of the government camp could be seen and the sentries' exchanges heard. Suspicions would only then have dawned with the gathering light that something had gone wrong, Daniel and his companions realising that 'my Lord George Murray began to be missing'.[20]

The Jacobites' plan for a surprise attack had been not only ill executed, but ill conceived, and the assumption that their enemies would be 'drowned in Sleep, the Effect of that Day's Rejoicing', ill founded.[21] The 'half an Anchor'* of brandy issued to each regiment the day before, and 'divided equally between the men', would have amounted to somewhat less than a quarter pint apiece – by no means sufficient to stupefy.[22] Besides, according to the grenadier Daniel Hamilton, the government army was conscious of the need for habitual vigilance. At Strathbogie, General Bland had the front line battalions 'sit up in [their] accoutrements during the night . . . because [the rebels'] only hope of escaping destruction is their hope of surprising [us]'.[23] Also, four spies who had infiltrated the Jacobite army the day before, 'to gain intelligence of the Ennemy by H.R.H's Desire', were afterwards each paid a guinea for their services.[24] If these men – Messrs Brimner, Michell, Monroe and McIntosh – had mingled on the night march, before slipping away in the darkness to make their report, it would explain why 'the soldiers were ordered to lie down with their arms by them' when they rested.[25]

By four in the morning of the 16th the government army was striking tents and preparing to move, 'officers and soldiers in the Highest Spirits'.[26] Four day's cheese and biscuit had been loaded on the carts, each man being provided with half a pound of cheese 'to serve them on the March'.

Liberality was tempered with discipline, however. Lessons of earlier battles – the shameful conduct of Cunningham's men at Falkirk, and the panic there and at Prestonpans – would have been in men's minds as Orders of the Day were read aloud at the head of every company in the line: 'That if any Person, taking Care of the Trainhorses, or any other Horses loaded with Tents or General's Baggage, should abscond or run from them, He or

* An *anker* is equivalent to ten gallons, or around 38 litres.

They should be punished with immediate Death.' In addition, 'if any Officer or Soldier did not behave according to his Duty, in his Rank and Station during the Time of the Ingagement, [he] should be liable to the same Punishment.' Michael Hughes, a 'Voluntier from the City of London', serving in Bligh's Foot, applauded such sanctions. 'It was quite necessary and prudent to have a regular and strict Order preserved,' he declared, 'that a finishing Period might be put to the scandalous Progress of these rebellious Vermin.'[27]

On the Jacobite side, similarly harsh penalties had been threatened in the orders signed by Lord George Murray: 'if any man turn his back to Runaway the nixt behind each man is to shoot him.' Premature pillage was also deemed a capital offence: 'No body on Pain of Death to strip the slain or plunder till the Batle be over.'[28]

*

The government army marched in four columns: one on the left comprising six squadrons of Dragoons and two of Light Horse, then three columns of Foot, five battalions each, one behind the other and three men abreast. Each column was instructed to march about two hundred paces apart from the next 'when the Ground admits them'.[29] Artillery and baggage followed the column on the right. It was an arrangement, Lieutenant Colonel Whitefoord explained, capable of rapid deployment from column into line as circumstances dictated: 'If we were attaqued in flank, we had on faceing to the enemy 3 lines of 5 Bat[talion]s ready form'd with the Cavalry at liberty to post itself on either or both flanks, and if we were to be attack'd in front, we could form each Column, wheeling up into each line, and one into the reserve, the Dragoons forming two lines and the horse on the right and left of the reserve.'[30]

The army was preceded by 40 of Kingston's Light Horse and five companies of loyal Highlanders – mainly Argyll men – commanded by Lieutenant Colonel 'Jack' Campbell of Mamore.

Wind, rain and sleet were at their backs as they marched. Having been 'strictly ordered to secure [their] firelocks from the Rain' – the disaster of Falkirk fresh in mind – the men covered them with their coat laps to keep them dry.[31] After a march of five miles Campbell reported sighting enemy detachments ahead and the army formed in line of battle with an 'ease and alacrity as . . . gave the greatest hopes of future success'. The alarm proving false, line reverted to column and the march continued, only to be halted again three miles further on and battle formation made 'with equal skill and alacrity'.[32] One officer suggested that, far from being a waste of effort, these manoeuvres were intentional and served as psychological preparation: 'the Duke's Reason [being] to let the Men see they were to engage that Day and that the Lines, when there was Occasion, might the more readily form'.[33] Cumberland also took care that they would be fresh for the coming fight and 'made some short Stops to ease his Troops'.[34]

A mile and a half from their enemies, they 'drew up again in order of battle, and marched forward so formed' onto Drummossie Moor.[35] In the front line of six battalions commanded by Lord Albemarle, Barrell's Foot were to the left of Monro's; Scots Fusiliers to the left of Price's Foot; Cholmondeley's to the left of the Royals. Each battalion in Major General Huske's second line covered the gaps between those of the first: Colonel Edward Wolfe's Regiment to the left of Ligonier's; Sempill's to the left of Bligh's; and Flemming's to the left of Howard's. Daniel Hamilton claimed it was because Barrell's 'had behaved so creditably at Falkirk, [that it] was, in the order of battle, advanced from the right of the second line to the left of the first'.[36] It was to suffer more losses in that position during the coming battle than any other regiment.

Commanded by Brigadier General Mordaunt, a reserve of three battalions – Blakeney's, Battereau's and Pulteney's – occupied the third line, flanked by a squadron of Kingston's Light Horse to the right and left.

In each interval between the front-line battalions was a brace of three-pounder cannon, and between the first and second lines a row of six coehorn mortars. Finally, in the second line, 'three Pieces of Cannon [were] placed between the first and second Battalion, on the Right and Left . . . that if the Enemy either broke through the Center, or out-flank'd either the Right or Left of the Front, they might conveniently play upon them.'*

At Prestonpans and Falkirk, when part of the front line broke, so broke the whole. But lessons had been learned and the government army disposed accordingly. The new arrangement – 'as just as the mind of man was capable of contriving' – was intended as proof against the terrible onslaught of the Highland charge. Just as the celebrated bayonet training was designed for the mutual defence of individuals, so with regiments and artillery. 'If one failed, a second supported; and if that failed, a third. The enemy could no way take two pieces of cannon, but three must play directly upon them; nor break one regiment, but two were ready to supply the place [and] if any Part of the king's Army broke, they rallied and were supported.'[37]

Following the calamitous showing of the dragoons at Prestonpans, and their equally disastrous contribution to the chaos at Falkirk, a rumour had circulated in February that 'the Duke

---

*James Maxwell mentions that 'They had sixteen pieces of cannon placed in the intervals of the battalions of the first and second line.' (p.150) Lord Elcho gives 'two pieces of Cannon betwixt Every Battalion in the first line, and three on the right, & three on the left of the Second.' (p.425) However, the deployment of six cannon in the government second line is contentious. They are shown in the plan of the order of battle reproduced in the May 1746 issues of the *Scots Magazine* and *Gentleman's Magazine*, and in Elcho's sketch map but on no other contemporary map or plan. It might be argued that Maxwell and the author of the account printed in both magazines confused the six coehorn mortars deployed between the first and second lines with cannon. These coehorns were undoubtedly used in the battle, as proved by recent archaeological finds of mortar shell fragments. They also appear on two other contemporary maps: a schematic plan of the battle in Colonel Joseph Yorke's orderly book (Hardwicke Papers BL, Add. MS 36257, f.100) and one drawn by Lord Cathcart (Cumberland Papers, Royal Archive, Main/14/4,1746, 16 April-13 May), albeit in no others. Coehorn mortars, however, with their high trajectory, could not have been used – as the account in the *Scots Magazine* and *Gentleman's Magazine* described – to 'conveniently play upon' the enemy at close range, should they break through the front line or outflank it. See also the footnote on p.103, below.

has alter'd the method of fighting with Dragoons on the flanks; & in his line of Battle he has thrown them with the Irregulars into the Rear.'[38] As it was, in the disposition on Drummossie Moor, the two dragoon regiments – comprising the six troops of Mark Kerr's 11th and all but two of Cobham's 10th, ten troops, or five squadrons, in total – were placed some way to the left of the government lines, for no other reason than it was 'where the ground was firmest' for them.[39] A less sympathetic explanation might have been that there at least they could not trample the adjacent ranks of infantry. They were supported by about 140 loyal Scots, most of them Campbells, under the command of Captain Colin Campbell of Ballimore – regulars drawn from the 43rd and 64th Highlanders, together with irregulars of the Argyll Militia. From this position – drawn up along the six-foot-high wall which formed the eastern boundary of the Culwhiniac enclosure – General Hawley's dragoons would at last perform according to expectations, serving a decisive role in both the final stage of the battle, and in the murderous pursuit that followed it.

*

The Jacobite ranks had roared their defiance as Cumberland's army marched into view but elicited no response from the enemy as it came on – in the words of John Daniel – 'like a deep sullen river'.[40] From side to side of the government force, instead of huzzas and bravado, the thunder of 250 drummers carried on the driving wind and sleet across the intervening space. The Prince asked a French officer on his staff for an opinion of the day's prospects. The answer was not encouraging. 'He believed it lost, for he had observed the Duke's Army narrowly, and never saw Men advance in a more cool and regular Manner.'[41]

The Prince's army, by sorry contrast, was unrested, underfed, and under strength. 'We had not been joined by a considerable number of our men,' recalled Robert Strange: 'the whole of the Macphersons, a considerable body of the Frasers, some few of the Mackintoshes, in general all the Mackenzies, and several other bodies of men who had been raised in the more northern counties.'[42] There had been desertions both before and during the ruinous night march, and many of those who returned exhausted to Drummossie Moor that morning had since dispersed to Inverness and the surrounding areas in search of food. Cattle and sheep found in the immediate locality had been slaughtered, but slaughtered in vain as there was no time to butcher, let alone cook, the meat 'before the Alarm came of the Enemy being on their March, and approaching'.[43] Men who had fallen asleep on the road from Nairn were only then wandering onto the moor to join what was more like a loitering, lacklustre crowd than an army. 'No line was as yet formed; the men were standing in clusters; and stragglers in small numbers were coming up from all quarters.'[44] Another witness, however, gave a surprisingly sprightly account of the deployment that followed: 'In less time than one could have imagined, the best part of the army was assembled . . . every corps knew its post, and went straight to it, without waiting for fresh orders.' The order of battle was the same as that of the previous day: Atholl Brigade, Camerons and Appin Stewarts of Murray's right abutted the north-west corner of the Culwhiniac enclosure; Clanranalds, Glengarries and Keppochs of Perth's left, the north-east corner of the Culloden park; the remaining Highland regiments – Lord Lovat's, Lady Mackintosh's, Farquharson of Monaltrie's Battalion, the Macleans, MacLachlans and Chisholms – were ranged between. This front line numbered about 3,800 men. Three-pounder artillery pieces were placed, three to the right, three to the left and five in the centre. All eleven would be inventoried captured after the battle. A twelfth – described as a Swedish four-pounder – was positioned on the extreme left of the line at the corner of the Culloden park. It would be destroyed by government fire.

A 'corps de reserve – so called because there was no other', constituted what passed for a second line.[45] Numbering some 1,900 men, it was composed of units formed in column to be marched forward as needed: Lord Perth's Regiment, Glenbucket's, John Roy Stuart's Edinburgh Regiment, Kilmarnock's recently formed Footguards and Lord Ogilvie's Regiment. Two bodies of regular troops – 300 Irish Picquets commanded by Colonel Walter Stapleton, and Lord John Drummond's 350 *Royal Ecossais* – were placed on the left and right respectively.

The 160 or so cavalry were in the rear: Hussars and Strathallan's Horse on the left, Lord Elcho's Lifeguards, and the Irish unit of Fitzjames' Horse, commanded by Colonel Robert O'Shea, on the right.

Charles Edward moved among the ranks of his heavily outnumbered army, talking to officers and soldiers alike, reminding them of recent glories: 'Here they are coming, my lads, we'll soon be with them. They don't forget Gladsmuir, nor Falkirk, and you have the same arms and swords.' He told his men how much depended upon them; the obligations he would owe them; that in serving King James, they served their country; that they would all be happy at the end; that victory depended upon a bold stroke; that they were not to be distracted by the firing but march directly towards the enemy. 'Go on my lads,' he told them, 'the day will be ours and we'll want for nothing after.' He told them 'all [that] cou'd be imagined to set them in Sperits', wrote O'Sullivan, who suspected however that 'the Prince in bottom had no great hopes.' At one point in the line he reached for a man's sword: 'Let me see yours,' he said, taking hold of the weapon and flourishing it, 'I'll answer this will cut off some heads and arms to-day.'[46]

A quarter of a mile away, the Duke of Cumberland also encouraged his men as he rode along the government front line, and 'desired [them] not to be Affraid'.[47] Even if he had not personally initiated the bayonet tactic of 'mutual defence', he nevertheless urged complete confidence in that weapon: 'Depend . . . depend, my lads, on your bayonets. Let [the rebels] mingle with you; let them know the men they have to deal with.'[48] And in like manner Major General Huske instructed the men of the second line, as Michael Hughes, recorded, 'That if we had Time to load, so to do; and if not, to make no Delay, but to drive our Bayonets into their Bodies and make sure Work.'[49] Cumberland is supposed to have delivered a longer speech, similar in substance to Henry V's amnesty before Agincourt to those with 'no stomach for this fight'.[50] It should perhaps be treated with scepticism:

> If there be any amongst you, who thro' Timidity, are diffident of their Courage or Behaviour . . . it is my Desire that all such would immediately retire; and . . . they shall have my Pardon for so doing; for I had much rather be at the Head of One Thousand brave and resolute Men, than Ten Thousand amongst whom there are some, who, by Cowardice or Misbehaviour [would] bring Dishonour and Disgrace on an Army under my Command.[51]

*

From where he stood on the right of the Jacobite line Lord George Murray could see that the anticipated forward advance of his Atholl Brigade would be seriously compromised by the protruding curve of a turf-wall between the north-east corner of the Culwhiniac enclosure and the government left wing. To bring his men clear of the enclosure wall on their immediate right and give them an unrestricted run at the enemy, he effectively narrowed the frontage of the Brigade's three battalions by re-forming them from line into column and from three ranks deep to six. What O'Sullivan referred to as Murray's 'changement' had a number of consequences. It brought the right wing some two hundred yards forward from its original position so that, as the other regiments further along the line adjusted to compensate – and as the left wing stayed contiguous to the south-east corner of the Culloden park to avoid being outflanked – the line was no longer parallel with the government's but skewed at an angle of twenty degrees to it. This lack of symmetry would affect the coordination of the Jacobite attack and even the capability of parts of the army to engage at all.

In addition, as the front line stretched, gaps opened: the first O'Sullivan heard of what Murray had done on the right were shouts of 'Close! Close!' from further along. Going to investigate he found 'intervals that he had not seen before'. To remedy this disintegration, the Edinburgh Regiment was brought forward from the reserve between the Camerons and the Appin Stewarts, on the right of centre, while the Duke of Perth's Regiment and Glenbucket's moved between the Glengarries and the Culloden park wall. 'The McDonels by this had no more the left,' observed O'Sullivan, 'they were almost in the Center.'[52]

Murray's 'changement' had the additional consequence of altering the government order of battle. Levelling his spyglass and observing the two regiments being marched forward apparently to reinforce the Jacobite left, the Duke of Cumberland assumed that the main attack would come from that direction. He accordingly gave orders to strengthen his own right by bringing forward two regiments from the rear: Pulteney's to fight alongside the Royals in the front line, Battereau's alongside Howard's in the second. He also reinforced Kingston's Light Horse on the wing with a squadron of Cobham's Dragoons that had been patrolling to the north.

Meanwhile, Campbell of Ballimore's Highland battalion on the extremity of the government left had broken down part of the eastern wall of the Culwhiniac enclosure where it sloped from the moor to the river Nairn. Through this breach passed the 450 officers and men of Cobham's and Kerr's dragoons, General Hawley in command. One of the five squadrons dismounted and joined the Campbells along the northern wall flanking the Jacobite right, while the rest rode on across the enclosure and through another gap broken in the far wall to threaten the Jacobite rear. Such an outflanking manoeuvre had been anticipated, however, and when they had cleared the second breach and turned north they were confronted – from the opposite side of what was variously described as a 'ditch' or 'hollow way' – by two battalions of Lord Ogilvie's Regiment and one of Lord Lewis Gordon's, together with the seventy troopers of Fitzjames' Horse and the thirty of Lord Elcho's Lifeguards. 'The ascent was somewhat steep on both sides, so that neither could pass safely in presence of the other.'[53] Without infantry support – Ballimore's men having been left inside the enclosure – Hawley's dragoons could only await developments on their own side of the gulley.

*

Notwithstanding the clamour of assembly in the Jacobite army – the shouted commands, the drums, the pipes – still 'men were scattered among the woods of Culloden, the greatest part fast asleep. There were several hundreds absent from the battle though within a mile of it.' Lord Elcho estimated 'near two thousand of them that was not at the Battle', while Robert Strange lowered the figure to a thousand, 'who knew nothing of the action till awakened by the noise of the cannon'. The sounder sleepers, it was said, 'never waken'd till they found the enemy cutting their throats'.[54]

II

THE firing began shortly after one o'clock.

It was the Jacobite artillery that opened, 'twice from right to left', at which Kingston's Horse on the government right 'were observed to reel a little'.[1] A corporal in Monro's Regiment on the left declared that 'they began to play their Cannon very briskly upon us, but as soon as we saw them pointed, we stoop'd down, and the Balls flew over our Heads.'[2] One round found a mark in the ranks behind, however, and 'took a man full below the abdomen, and shot his body off' at the pelvis.[3] It was thought that the guns' principal target – observed and identified by spyglass – was the Duke of Cumberland himself, conspicuous on the right wing by his girth, but as they were 'extremely ill served and ill pointed' they fired 'to very little purpose'.[4] Some came close, nevertheless: 'several shots nearly missed him, and one shot took off two men exactly before him.'[5] These would have been two of only three losses suffered by Cholmondeley's 34th Foot. It can be inferred that, because this regiment did not engage with the enemy hand to hand, the one man killed outright and two others later dying of their wounds could only have been casualties of artillery fire. By the same token it was probably Jacobite cannon that accounted for a dozen more: from Howard's Regiment one man killed, one dying of wounds and another, Charles Appleton, surviving 'disabled in [the] right hand'; six from Flemming's

Regiment were fatally wounded, while Captain Thomas Carter of Battereau's survived along with two private men: William Mathews, 'wounded in his right side', and Daniel McIntosh who 'lost his left leg.'[6] All were on the right wing in the general neighbourhood of the Duke of Cumberland.

When the ten guns punctuating the government front line opened fire in response, Major Belford's crews, like their opponents, had initial difficulty gauging range and trajectory in that 'many of the balls went quite over the Highland lines.'[7] Thereafter, John Daniel reckoned that they too were attempting the expedient of killing the enemy's commander-in-chief, given 'the number of balls that fell about [the Prince]'[8] and amongst the horsemen in his vicinity. One hit the ground close enough to splash his face with dirt, and another decapitated a groom called Thomas Ca, 'scarcely thirty yards behind him'.[9] Daniel saw the dead bodies of a number of Hussars covering the ground nearby, and an aide-de-camp, Captain Lachlan MacLachlan, was killed by a round shot while riding to the right with the Prince's order to Lord George Murray to advance. The only other specified Jacobite casualty documented at this first stage of the bombardment was a horse. Robert Strange told of a man called Austin, a cavalryman in Lord Elcho's Lifeguards, 'a very worthy, pleasant fellow', who rode an especially prized mare. As they came under fire from the government guns he felt the horse 'give a sudden shrink' and, looking down, said to Strange, 'Alas! I have lost my lady!' One hind leg had been hit and was hanging by a shred of skin. Without another word, Austin dismounted and pushed the animal out of the line where it collapsed. He took his carbine and pistols from their saddle holsters. If he used one of them to put the creature out of its suffering, it is not recorded, only that he walked forward to join the infantry ranks and 'was never more heard of'.[10]

Round shot is most effective on hard ground when it can ricochet or skitter into the enemy ranks, killing and maiming in its passage. In the boggy conditions of Drummossie Moor a cannonball was as likely to bury itself harmlessly as it was to find an unfortunate target like Thomas Ca or Austin's 'lady'. But had the ball which spattered the Prince with mud bounced, it might have taken him apart like his groom.

Reports vary as to how long the Jacobite lines came under artillery fire before they charged. Major James Wolfe, aide-de-camp to General Hawley, put it at 'a quarter of an hour'.[11] When Alexander Taylor, a government soldier in the Royals, told his wife that 'cannonading . . . continued for half an hour or more with great guns',[12] he was probably referring to the duration of artillery fire throughout the entire action. The most precise timing came from Captain Campbell of Airds – who must have consulted a pocket watch and claimed that 'the Cannonading continued about Nine Minutes & the whole was over in less than an hour.'[13] Other witnesses' testimony suggests that the preliminary artillery fire may have been of even shorter duration. Time, in this and any battle, could contract as well as expand. One of the Duke of Cumberland's aides-de-camp, Colonel Joseph Yorke, observing from the government left, declared that the ten cannon had only fired 'about two rounds' apiece when, 'two or three minutes' later, the Jacobite lines 'broke from the centre in 3 large bodies, like wedges, and moved forward'.[14] To Colonel Whitefoord it seemed that '[the rebels] broke into Columns from the moment our cannon began to play.'[15]

*

An officer in the Jacobite cavalry, James Maxwell of Kirkconnell, believed that 'the only chance the Prince had for a victory that day, was a general shock of the whole line at once', and had that happened 'it [was] more than probable that the first line of the enemy would have been routed, whatever might have been the consequences afterwards.'[16] But because of Murray's 'changement' the Jacobite right wing was only some three hundred yards from the government lines, while the left was as much as five hundred. Also, the Duke of Perth's division, in addition to having a greater distance to advance, was faced with 'marshy [ground] covered with water, which reached half way up the leg'.[17] While it was to their advantage that this was unsuitable ground for enemy cavalry, it was equally unsuitable for advancing on foot. The result was that the MacDonalds' forward progress was so slow and hesitant that it appeared to Colonel Yorke, watching from the opposite end of the field, to be no more than a 'feint' towards the government right. However, two of the 'wedges' – the centre and right – had firmer ground in front of them and 'Like Wildcats their Men came down in Swarms upon [us]',[18] recalled the volunteer Michael Hughes, while Alexander Taylor likened them to 'troops of hungry wolves'.[19]

As those in the centre came within range of three hundred yards, government artillery crews loaded grape and canister instead of round shot, 'to make more Dispatch and completer Execution'.[20] A type of projectile ordinarily employed in naval gunnery, grapeshot was a bundle of nine three-and-a-half-ounce lead balls tightly wrapped in canvas and deriving the name from its knobbly likeness to a bunch of fruit. When fired the canvas burst apart, sweeping the deck of an enemy ship with a spread of missiles capable of inflicting multiple casualties. Canister shot – also known as case, cartridge or cartouche – was the land army equivalent. A cylindrical tin container packed with musket balls was designed to disintegrate as it left the cannon, scattering a wide fan of devastation into oncoming cavalry or foot. Especially effective at close range, it was said to have been put to particularly vicious use at Fontenoy the previous year – producing ragged wounds to frustrate the most skilled of surgeons – when French gun crews filled the tins with 'rusty Nails, broken Glass, and such irremediable Missiles as the Laws of War disavow'.[21] An equally sinister cache of 'warlike stores' destined for use by the King's enemies in Scotland had recently been found on a captured French transport: 'white Iron Cartridges . . . filled with old rusty Nails, old broken Iron and Flints,' a newspaper report noted, 'which shows the inhuman Treatment they design for us.'[22] Clearly the use of conventional canister against Jacobites gave at least the lower slopes of moral high ground to the Royal Artillery.

It has been calculated that the six guns firing into the centre and right of the advancing insurgents were killing or maiming between sixty and eighty men every twenty seconds.[23] Such was the efficacy of grape and canister. The clan chief, Donald Cameron of Lochiel, was among the first to fall, both ankles shattered. Michael Hughes watched from Bligh's Regiment as the artillery did its work. 'Their Lines were formed so thick and deep, that the Grapeshot made open Lanes quite through them, the Men dropping down by Wholesale.'[24] Another account called the swathes of carnage 'Avenues'.[25]

Every musket primed, charged, and fully cocked, bayonet locked by an anticlockwise twist on the iron lug of the gunsight, government infantry had been instructed 'by positive Order to reserve their Fire' until the enemy came 'near close upon them'. As they got within pistol range 'and a sure Mark' – about fifty yards – 'the King's Men discharged a complete running Fire, that dropt [the Rebels] down as fast as they came on.'[26] They fired, 'first by order, and afterwards as fast as they could load, with good effect, three or four times'.[27] O'Sullivan called it 'as regular & as nurrished a fire as any troops cou'd',[28] while a government soldier, veteran of three field battles in the previous year, described it as 'the warmest fire given . . . that ever I saw for the time it lasted'.[29]

Unlike at Falkirk, the prevailing wind on Drummossie Moor was from the east, blowing dense smoke from government cannon and musket directly into the Jacobites' faces. And this time it was 'more detrimental, as there was much more firing,' observed Maxwell. 'They were buried in a cloud of smoke.'[30] One man remembered running forward and seeing the government line for the first time only from about twenty yards – a 'long row of white gaiters' – through a fleeting break in the smoke.[31]

The devastating barrage of fire and resulting obscurity may have contributed to the unevenness of the Jacobite advance, causing the centre to veer to the right and, unable to see but a few feet in front of them, to follow the clear and firmer ground of the Moor road running aslant the field directly towards the

Monro and Barrell battalions at the end of the government line. This brought parts of the Jacobite centre into collision with the right, mingling Atholl men, Camerons, Ardshiels, Frasers and MacIntoshes in an undifferentiated pack,[32] 'a Sort of mob, without any order or distinction of Corps, mixt together'[33] and 'in such confusion, that they could make no use of their fire-arms'. Blinded, 'their nostrils filled with sulphur . . . faces burnt with wadding'[34] from the close-range musket fire, the foremost insurgents dashed into the government left determined 'to cut and hack in their own natural Way'.[35] But some would have glimpsed the glitter of bayonets in the murk seconds before engaging, while others – transfixed on the points of steel – 'felt their enemies without seeing them'.[36] And as the muskets of the rear second and third ranks of the government front line fired again at close range into the faces of the enemy, the bayonet men immediately to the fore were 'bespattered with their blood and brains'.[37]

Meanwhile, the advancing Atholl Brigade on the Jacobite right wing 'received a most terrible fire, not only in front, but also in flank',[38] from Ballimore's Highland battalion in the north-east corner of the Culwhiniac enclosure. James Maxwell wrote of an 'advanced battery' on the government left, 'which flanked the Athol men, as did likewise the Campbells from behind the walls'.[39] Johnstone claimed this battery comprised four artillery pieces and that the grapeshot it fired from inside the enclosure 'being quite close . . . was so terrible that it literally swept away, at once, whole ranks'.*[40] Under this deadly enfilade, the Atholl men charged on through the smoke towards Barrell's men. 'Those in front were spitted with the bayonets,' Lieutenant Colonel Whitefoord wrote succinctly, 'those in Flank . . . tore in pieces by the musquetry and grape shot.'[41]

* Tony Pollard casts doubt on the presence of artillery in the Culwhiniac enclosure and also on the deployment of cannon in the government second line. See his 'Capturing the Moment: the Archaeology of the Culloden Battlefield', in *Culloden, the History and Archaeology of the Last Clan Battle*, pp. 159–61.

It seemed to Colonel Yorke, from the rear of the government left, that 'the violence of the shock' with which the attackers came on, 'a little staggered' Barrell's battalion, but Major General Huske, riding up behind from the second line, and 'bidding the men push home with their bayonets, was so well obeyed . . . that hundreds perished on their points'.[42] And as for the bayonet drill supposed to counter the highlander's principal article of defence, Lord Elcho claimed the killing was made 'the more easy as they had no targetts, for they would not be at the pains upon a march to carry them'.[43]

It was said afterwards that Barrell's battalion – 373 officers and men – 'kill[ed] almost their own number' in the fight.[44] The Duke of Cumberland reported that 'there was neither Soldier nor Officer . . . who did not kill . . . one or two Men',[45] while a letter to the *Gentleman's Magazine* graphically stated that there was 'not a Bayonet in this regiment but was either bloody or bent'.[46] Michael Hughes joined the chorus extolling their quota of killing: 'scarce one Soldier in *Barryl's* Regiment who did not each kill several Men,' he declared, 'and they of *Monro*'s which ingaged did the same, beside what the Officers killed with their Spontoons.'[47]

A variant of the half-pike – with which both Colonel Gardiner and Sir Robert Monro are said to have fought in their final moments – the 'spontoon' served officers in ceremonial capacity on the parade ground, and in lethal fashion during close-quarters combat. Together with 'a longer and larger blade at the end of the staff' it had one simple advantage over the half-pike: a short steel crosspiece at the base of the blade was designed to stop its forward progress, rendering the weapon 'easily recovered when thrust into the enemy'. It allowed ample penetration of the vital organs to kill but without running 'so far [through] as to be often lost or broken'.[48] Axe head and hook either side its blade, the sergeant's halberd killed with similar convenience. A visceral account of the fighting on the government left recorded the means of piercing flesh with pointed steel peculiar to each rank in its turn: 'the Officers of the Army . . . pushing with their Spontoons, the Serjeants running their Halberts into the Throats of the Enemy, [and] the Soldiers ... ramming their fixed Bayonets up to the Socket'.[49]

And owing to the mutually defensive mode of hand-to-hand fighting purportedly introduced by the Duke, the ratio of killing was greatly in favour of the government side: 'Our soldiers, by [the] new practice,' wrote a captain of Monro's, 'became much too hard for the swords; and the rebels, as they pushed forward, fell on certain death. Ours at least killed ten men to their one in this kind of fighting, besides what fell by the musketry and cannon.'[50]

The two cannon between Monro's battalion and Barrell's had 'made a dreadful havoc' as they discharged their last rounds of canister within six feet of the attackers, before being overrun and silenced, with Sergeant Edward Bristoe and five of his gun crew slaughtered. Barrell's and the left fringe of Monro's wavered, were pushed back, and broke apart, their assailants pouring through the gap roaring 'Run, ye dogs!'[51] But this time they did not run. The Barrell's commander, Lieutenant Colonel Robert Rich, received a deep cut to his right elbow, 'six in his head, one or two very bad ones', and a regimental colour was taken from him, his severed left hand with it.[52] The fate of Lord Robert Kerr – a Captain in Barrell's Foot, and the only aristocratic government fatality of the battle – was a cautionary lesson in the difficulty of retrieving a half-pike. When the line moved back, he was left exposed. 'He had struck his pike into the body of a Highland officer; but before he could disengage himself, was surrounded.'[53] His body, wrote Andrew Henderson, 'was covered with Wounds; his Head was cut . . . from the Crown to the Collar Bone . . . he was in a Manner hashed in Pieces.'[54]

But with this penetration into the left wing, Cumberland's tactical disposition proved its worth. As two front line battalions gave way, forming an angle either side of the breach, General Huske ordered forward two more from the second – Sempill's and Bligh's – who opened fire with their muskets. Lord George Murray claimed he and his men also came under cannon fire from the same quarter. In his memoir of the campaign he wrote little of the last 'so fatal' battle, but that little included reference to this incident and his reason for remembering the direction of fire. 'Our men broke in upon some regiments on the enemy's left; but others came quickly up to their relief. Upon a fire from these last, and some cannon, charged with cartouch shot, that they had, I think, at their second line, (for we had passed two that were on their front) my horse plunged and reared so much, that I thought he was wounded; so quitted my stirrups, and was thrown.'[55]

In addition to his horse Murray lost 'his periwig and bonnet', just as he had at Clifton. Bearing 'several cuts with broadswords in his coat, . . . covered with blood and dirt',[56] but otherwise unscathed, he made his way back up the field and led two second-line regiments – Kilmarnock's Footguards and the *Royal Ecossais* – forward to the support of his beleaguered right wing.

Those who had broken beyond Barrell's and Monro's battalions 'were now between two Lines,' Hughes observed, 'and . . . severely handled both Ways, for those who escaped the Fire of *Bligh*'s and *Sempill*'s Regiments, met a worse Destruction from the Bayonets of our first Line.'[57] Daniel Hamilton remembered the attackers – seemingly undiminished by musket round and grape – as a dense mass pressing forward, which by sheer weight 'bore its opponents from their ranks, and intermixing with them every where . . . both sides at last formed a sort of mass themselves.' Another account confirmed this: 'the ranks were so tightly packed that even those the Highlanders had cut to pieces did not fall, and the living, the wounded and the dead formed so solid a body' as made further advance impossible.[58] Hamilton estimated that this macabre deadlock continued for half an hour before support arrived from the government rear to tip the balance. 'No man turned his back, the contest never ceased, and the struggle (strokes on the head, and stabs to the body) was violent and personal, with now and then a shot.'

Fiercely loyal to his regiment and unwilling to admit even that it had given way – 'unless being pressed back a few yards . . . can be so interpreted' – the Barrell's grenadier was at a loss to know 'why Wolfe's regiment marched so late to the succour of the front'.[59] But march they did, and the intervention was decisive. On General Huske's orders, Ligonier's Regiment moved forward to join Sempill's and Bligh's, while Wolfe's moved to the left, outflanking the compacted press of insurgents, then wheeled inwards to form at roughly ninety degrees to the original line, effectively trapping them in a salient exposed on three sides. From this position 'the whole then gave them 5 or 6 fires with vast execution.'[60] It was this gunfire that wounded David Lotty, John Low and George Webb, and killed other Barrell's men engaged hand to hand in the melee. The friendly fire probably accounted also for John Tovey having his 'jaw shot away', for six other gunshot-wounded of Monro's, and for Archibald Smith of Bligh's, who was 'shot in the mouth'.[61] Such was the density of congestion and the concentration of fire that musket balls have been found nearly sheared in two by impact on a raised broadsword blade, 'a form of deformation . . . unique to Culloden'.[62]

Captain James Ashe Lee, of Wolfe's, admitted that those in front 'had nothing left to oppose us but their pistols and broadswords' while on the opposite flank Hamilton noted that the fire fell 'principally [on the rebels] who had not got into the contest'. And from the rear and centre of the twenty- or thirty-deep struggling mass, came Jacobite fire, 'vastly more fatal to themselves,' Lee observed, 'than to us'.[63] Firing from the rear may have come from the two second-line regiments Murray had brought forward – Kilmarnock's Footguards and Lord John Drummond's *Royal Ecossais* – discharging their muskets blindly into the smoke. 'But nothing could be done,' Murray wrote later; 'all was lost.'[64] Those able to escape the terrible crossfire turned and ran.

A government officer remarked on the futile carnage of the Jacobite right: 'their great Effort was there, but it was vain, they could not penetrate, and lay in Heaps.'[65]

*

The Duke of Cumberland had taken his position on the government right wing, thinking 'the greatest Push would be there'. He could not have been more mistaken. Perth's Regiment, Glenbucket's and the MacDonalds of the Jacobite left, 'advances but slolly', wrote O'Sullivan, in the urgent historic present he so often adopted in his account of the battle, '& really it is not possible that any troops that cant answer such a fire as the enemy kept can do otherwise'. In vain did the Duke of Perth grasp the Clanranald colours '& tells them from that day forth he'l call himself McDonel if they gain the day'.[66] But the difficulty lay not so much in the enemy's fire but in the field. The left had much further to advance than the right, and they were in places knee-deep in waterlogged ground. Clans that had initiated havoc among government horse and foot at Falkirk, and prevailed with the deadly rapidity of the headlong charge at Prestonpans, found themselves condemned to a leaden nightmare in which, far from charging to engage the enemy, they could only with difficulty set one foot in front of the other. 'They came down three several Times within a Hundred Yards of Our Men, firing their Pistols & brandishing their Swords,' wrote the Duke of Cumberland. This account agrees with Colonel Yorke's observation from the other side of the field, that the northernmost 'wedge' of Highlanders 'at first . . . made a feint, as if they would come down upon our right'.[67] If they were attempting to draw the nervous government troops into opening fire so as to overwhelm them, sword in hand, before they reloaded, the tactic did not work. Colonel Whitefoord was specific as to the wary restraint from both sides at this part of the line and that 'the Battalions there never fir'd a shot' while their would-be opponents 'thought proper not to come too near'.[68] The verse of Dougal Graham makes it sound like a game:

The Duke right stood, and saw the fun,
Some reg'ments never fir'd a gun;
They only twice or thrice presented,
But seeing them run it was prevented:
For the order was, that fire they don't,
Till within few paces of their front.

So when they see'd them so present,
Back they fled with one consent.[69]

As though on a drill field, awaiting the command to bring their slung weapons from the left shoulder, through the seven motions prescribed by Bland, to 'Present' position and 'Fire', the Royals and Pulteney's 'hardly took their Firelocks from their Shoulders'.[70] They waited, motionless, until the Duke himself, observing through his spyglass the first Jacobite fugitives from the government left exclaimed, 'They run! They run!'

Then, 'Rise up Pulteney's and shoulder!'

His right wing moved forward a few paces, raised their muskets 'and gave their fire in so close and so full a manner, that the ground was soon covered with the dead and wounded'.[71]

Captain Johnstone, advancing with the Glengarries, was 'not twenty paces from the enemy', when the command 'Fire' was given, and the resulting volley cut down Donald MacDonell of Scotus at his side. Alexander MacDonell, 17th clan chief of Keppoch, together with his brother, was also killed. The chief had advanced ahead of his men with pistol and drawn broadsword. Shot once, rising and shot again, he was shot for the last time in the back while being carried from the field. To the right of Keppoch's regiment, all the officers of the Chisholms of Strathglass were killed or wounded, as were many of the Macleans and MacLachlans. The Farquharsons of Monaltrie lost at least thirteen officers dead.

The fire of Pulteney's and the Royals coincided with the Jacobite rout becoming general, starting with survivors staggering from the smoke-enveloped slaughter ground on the right, and spreading 'to the left of [the] army with the rapidity of lightning'. That left was thereby dangerously isolated, 'abandoned on the right, and exposed to be flanked by enemies that had nothing to oppose them in front'.[72] No sooner had Scotus fallen than Johnstone found himself surrounded by panic. 'What a spectacle of horror!' he recalled. 'The same highlanders, who had advanced to the charge like lions . . . were, in an instant, seen fleeing like trembling cowards, in the greatest disorder.'[73] Enraged, he fired his blunderbuss and both pistols at the enemy before he also turned and fled with the rest. Some, according to Dougal Graham, 'threw their durks and then retired'. Others were 'expressing their rage by hewing up the heather with their swords'.[74] The Duke of Cumberland remarked of his beaten adversaries that, in impotent frustration when they 'could not make any Impression upon the Battalions, they threw Stones at them for at least a Minute or two, before their total Route began'.[75] True or not, the fact that neither the Royals nor Pulteney's suffered any casualties whatsoever testified to the inequality of the contest. 'The cannon being again loaded, these fired in the midst of the fugitives, and made a frightful carnage.'[76]

Johnstone, on foot and in riding boots, was in a similar plight to the hapless dragoons at Clifton and Captain Oughton at Falkirk. 'So overcome by the marshy ground, the water on which reached to the middle of the leg . . . instead of running [he] could scarcely walk.' He was fortunate to find a riderless horse and – by 'menaces' and a pistol barrel to the head – persuaded the servant holding the animal to let go of its bridle, and made his escape.[77]

As the Jacobite left joined the general retreat the squadron of sixty Cobham's Dragoons on the government right closed for the kill. They were spurred on by the Duke of Cumberland himself, slapping some on the shoulder and shouting, 'One Brush, my Lads, for the Honour of Old Cobham!' Swampy ground notwithstanding, 'rather like Devils than Men they broke through the Enemy's Flank, and a total Rout followed.'[78] Andrew Henderson described how they 'rode in among the fugitives, and hacked them terribly with their broad swords; some had their brains beat out by the horses.'[79] They did not go entirely unchallenged. Commanded by Colonel Walter Stapleton, the Irish Picquets, last of the Prince's infantry reserves in that sector, 'fires at the Dragons & oblidges them to retir', O'Sullivan wrote. 'This gives time to the McDonels to make their way . . . the Piquets throws themselfs into the Park that was at our left, continues their fire where

Stapleton was wounded, & are at last oblidged to give themselfs up prisoners of War.'[80] By then a hundred of them had been killed or wounded. The dragoons emerged lightly from the encounter. Enoch Bradshaw, a Cobham's trooper, wrote to his brother in Cirencester: 'we lost but one man; tho I fear I shall lose my horse, he having at this moment of writing a ball in his left buttock. 'Twas pritty near Enoch that time, but thank God, a miss is as good as a mile, as we say in Gloustershire.'[81]

*

While the Irish Picquets were engaged in support of the retreating MacDonells, on the other side of the moor the *Royal Ecossais* were withdrawing their unavailing support of the embattled Jacobite right. The other reserve regiment, Kilmarnock's Footguards, had disintegrated and were mingled and fleeing with those they had been brought forward to relieve. Drummond's regulars, however, were marching back in good order along the Culwhiniac enclosure when they were fired on by Ballimore's men from behind the boundary wall. The *Royal Ecossais* gave back as good as they got. Colin Campbell of Ballimore himself was shot dead passing a 'slap', or breach, in the wall, and John Campbell of Achnaba died of wounds the following day. In addition three rank and file were wounded and six killed. When they were disinterred during the nineteenth century, it was found that most had been shot through the head as they appeared above the parapet.[82]

Further up the field, the stand-off across the steep 'ditch' or 'hollow way' to the west of the enclosure was broken when Hawley ordered General Bland to charge with the three squadrons of Kerr's Dragoons, and two of Cobham's in support. By this stage the defenders on the opposite edge had thinned, the insurgents were in full retreat, and the crackle of government musketry had slackened, obviating the risk of injury from friendly fire. Nevertheless, in crossing the ditch, three of the Kerr's troopers were wounded and three killed, along with nineteen horses.

Hawley's orders were carried out, wrote his aide-de-camp, James Wolfe, 'with wonderful spirit and completed the victory with great slaughter'.[83]

As he left the moor with Lord Elcho's Lifeguards, Robert Strange saw 'a body of horse . . . from the Duke's left . . . advancing with an incredible rapidity, picking up the stragglers, and, as they gave no quarter, were levelling them to the ground'. The government artillery, he recalled, was still firing, 'though not a soul on the field'.[84]

Captain Johnstone recounts an extraordinary incident during the Jacobite right's retreat towards the river Nairn, the authenticity of which can neither be entirely confirmed nor wholly discounted. A body of Highlanders was confronted by government cavalry whose English commander gave orders, allowing them 'to pass at the distance of a pistol-shot, without attempting to molest them or to take prisoners'. Only one officer disobeyed the order, attempted to seize one of the fugitives and was cut down by the intended prisoner's broadsword and killed on the spot. The Highlander, with admirable *sang froid*, 'stopt long enough to take possession of his watch, and then decamped with the booty'. This, according to Johnstone, was watched by the English commander who 'renewed his orders to his men not to quit their ranks, and could not help smiling and secretly wishing the Highlander might escape, on account of his boldness, without appearing to lament the fate of the officer.' Considering the massacre of fugitives on the road to Inverness that would be conducted by Kingston's Horse and Cobham's Dragoons in the aftermath of the battle, this commander's apparent magnanimity seems improbable. But the coda to Johnstone's account could explain his restraint: 'If this body of cavalry had not acted so prudently, they would instantly have been cut to pieces. It is extremely dangerous in a defeat to attempt to cut off the vanquished from all means of escape.'[85] Another incident also gives credence to Johnstone's story. John Mackenzie of Torridon, nephew to MacDonell of Keppoch, led a remnant of his uncle's regiment from the field following the death of their chief. 'Keep together men', he told them, as a party of dragoons approached. 'If we stand shoulder to shoulder these men will be far more frightened at us than we can be of them. But remember, if you scatter, they have four legs to each of your two, and you will stand singly but small chance against them.'[86]

Torridon's reasoning agreed with Maxwell of Kirkconnell's assertion that the government cavalry 'made no attack where there was any body of the Prince's men together, but contented themselves with sabering such unfortunate people as fell in their way single and disarmed,' and that 'the fury of the enemy . . . increased as the opposition and danger diminished.'[87]

*

Writing home to his 'Loving Spouse', Edward Linn, a Royal Scots Fusilier who had been in the front line next to Monro's, told her he 'never Saw a Small field thicker of Dead'.[88] There on the government left lay the most concentrated shambles of the Jacobite assault, 'their bodies . . . *in layers three or four deep*; so many, it would appear, having in succession mounted over a prostrate friend, to share in the same inevitable fate'.[89] The authors of the slaughter, bayonets 'stain'd and clotted with the Blood of the Rebels up to the Muzzles of their Muskets', manifested exhilaration, survivor relief, and hysteria in perhaps equal measure.[90] They were 'full of ardour and noise . . . boasting of their exploits'.[91] A letter written from Inverness a day or so later carried the incidental postscript: 'I have a Broad Sword wash'd in the Blood of Rebels.'[92] It was a cult of blood, celebrants participating with the playfulness of children: 'the moor was covered with blood; and our men, what with killing the enemy, dabbling their feet in the blood, and splashing it about one another, looked like so many butchers.'[93] Barrell's officers began barking orders to 'dress ranks', putting the gruesome scarecrows into a semblance of military order. The Duke of Cumberland rode along the excited, chattering lines 'exhorting them to be silent as they were brave'.[94] Three months earlier, after accepting the surrender of Carlisle without putting its defenders to the sword, he had expressed the wish he 'could have blooded the Soldiers with these Villains' as he would a pack of young hunting dogs.[95] Now they were blooded indeed. Praising both officers and men, he 'Said he never Seed better ordered or better done'.[96]

In less time than a written account of it takes to read, the Battle of Culloden, or Drummossie Moor, was over. The battle, as a reciprocally opposed and defended conflict, that is. What followed for the rest of the afternoon would be unopposed, defenceless slaughter. The City of London volunteer Michael Hughes made the demarcation clear, albeit allowing for the great disparities of time and duration observable in other accounts: 'the Battel begun at Twelve a Clock, and the Runaway at One.' The latter phase belonged to the Light Horse, to the dragoons, and to the Argyllshire Campbells, who 'were the only Foot who pursued'.[97]

*

The Lord President of the Court of Session, and proprietor of Culloden House and estate, was away from his home at the time of the battle, but within four days was fully briefed as to all that had occurred, by 'a Boy who saw the action . . . and the Examination of Some Persons who Fled [and were] apprehended'. Duncan Forbes was told that some fugitives from the Jacobite left wing escaped into his enclosures and that 'the walls and Thickets Prevented the Immediate Pursuit', but between that temporary haven and Inverness, 'the Dragoons Pursued them, over took and Cut Severall to Pieces on the Road, and made a Considerable Slaughter of them in the Town, and on the Bridge as they were passing it.' There were others who did not follow the road but for several miles westward of the battlefield, the moor lying flat and featureless, and Kingston's Horse being 'very nimble, . . . many could not escape', while those that did 'Describe[d] the Slaughter as Dreadful'. As late as four in the afternoon a body of horse could be seen 'Pursuing very quickly towards Loch Ness, the Road where many supposed the Young Pretender had taken'.[98]

An account that reached Edinburgh some days later told that they pursued 'for above three miles, with great execution',[99] and the *Extraordinary Gazette* of 24 April added that they 'did it with so good effect, that a very considerable number was killed in the pursuit'. According to Michael Hughes, it was 'the Duke of *Kingston*'s Light Horse [that] pursued vigorously, and killed great Numbers . . . without Distinction'. This 'nobleman's regiment' of volunteers had the enthusiasm of raw recruits, 'being new raised Men . . . more willing to exert themselves' than regulars and, as a result, 'the Road leading to *Inverness* was covered with dead Bodies.' James Ray, an equally zealous volunteer from Whitehaven in Cumberland, rode with Cobham's Dragoons that day and said 'there was much knapping of Noddles, [and] above 500 were killed in the Pursuit.' As at Falkirk, spectators suffered collateral harm and 'many . . . who came out of Curiosity to see the Action, or perhaps to get Plunder, never went home again to tell the Story; for they being mixt with their own People, [pursuers] could not know one from the other.'[100]

Sword wounds inflicted from horseback upon those fleeing on foot were most commonly to the shoulders and head, and such was the case, observed south of Kings Mills, of 'a boy betwixt 10 and 12 years of age and his head cloven to his teeth'.'[101] No sooner killed, those who fell were relieved by the camp followers of anything that could be sold on. In Kings Mills itself – a mile outside Inverness – there were twelve or fourteen corpses 'lying all stript, and some of them laid in undecent postures'. There were other instances of this vindictive refinement, with 'carnage made on both sexes'. Near Stoneyfield on the coast, a woman was also 'stript and laid in a very undecent posture' and men, mutilated, 'their privities placed in their hands'. Elsewhere was 'ane old beggar . . . his fingers chopt off, and severall cutts in his head, lying dead unstript, because all the cloaths he hade were not worth twopence for any use, and . . . he was upwards of fourscore.'[102] Five miles from the field, Elspeth McPhail, 'ane honest poor woman' carrying a three-day-old child was attacked by four dragoons 'who gave her seven wounds in the head . . . and one in the arm'. A dragoon took hold of the baby by its thigh, swung it about and threw it to the ground. Elspeth's husband was chased into a morass until – the pursuing horse unable to follow – he was shot dead at a distance.[103] Both Elspeth and her baby survived. As Kingston's men galloped through Lady Inches' estate about a mile from the field, one of her tenants, Alexander Young, and his nine-year-old son came out of a cottage to see what was happening and both were shot in passing, the boy dying instantly, his father lingering two days.[104] The troopers entered another house 'where a poor beggar woman was spinning, and . . . shot her dead upon the spot,' it was alleged. 'They were really mad,' Lady Inches recalled, 'they were furious, and no check was given them in the least.' Quite how out of control some of them were was shown by another incident recounted by the same witness. On the Friday after the battle she was approached by a group of soldiers who called her 'a rebel-bitch' and took delight in showing her two bodies covered by a curtain. The faces, uncovered, were 'so cut and mangled that they could not be discerned to be faces'. In addition, they had been 'given . . . a fire to their hinder-end[s] . . . roasted and smoked . . . to death'. Lady Inches saw 'the ashes and remains of the extinguished fire.'[105]

The anonymous 'Impartial Hand' that penned *A full and authentic history of the Rebellion* discounted all but three instances of indiscriminate slaughter and declared that none 'but such as were in Arms suffer[ed] that Day'. If this was to be believed, only a man named Noble, 'peeping out of a Door, received a Ball in the temple' intended for a legitimate fugitive target, while similar accidents accounted for the deaths of 'the other two; these being old Weavers'. As a result of a few isolated misfortunes, the defence continued, 'their Friends loudly complain'd and Fame magnify'd "the Barbarities" beyond the Strength of Imagination itself.' Yet even the 'Impartial Hand' admitted that victorious troops, 'when near *Inverness* . . . appeared somewhat concerned at the Case of the miserable People whose Carcases lay strewed in the Way'.[106] Some days later, when a command was sent to Moy Hall – their drummers sounding 'the dead-beat' – to arrest Lady Mackintosh with maximum intimidation, 'the horses trode many corpses under foot' on the road from Inverness, and trampled them again as they returned, to the mortification of their 'generous hearted' captive.[107] Robert Chambers, the last historian to collect first-hand accounts, described the road from the battlefield as 'a broad pavement of carnage marking four of the five miles intervening'.[108]

A report in the *Gentleman's Magazine* that 'the pursuit . . . had been continued quite thro' the town of Inverness, where the streets ran with blood' might be dismissed as hyperbole but for two documented incidents, suggesting bloodlust had not been fully sated on the road from Drummossie Moor.[109] In the first a merchant, James Aberdeen, was 'highly distressed with a fever, not able to stur from his bed', in the house of a widow, Mrs Davidson. Her servant – from stupidity or malice – told some dragoons that 'there was a rebell above stairs' and they slit his throat where he lay. This was confirmed by Mrs Davidson's neighbour, 'an honest woman . . . who went to the room and saw the gentleman after his throat was cut'.[110] The names of the dragoons could not be verified.

The other incident concerned a man, 'in the habit of a dragoon', called Rea, who would later describe himself as a volunteer from the County of Cumberland, 'come out to feight for his religion and liberty'. Among the first to enter the town, he had galloped down a close in pursuit of two Lowlanders, dismounted and accosted a servant girl, Margaret Grant, ordering her to hold his horse. He then followed the unarmed men into a house 'where he hash'd them with his broad sword to death'. Frightened by the 'lamentable cryes', Margaret let go of the horse and ran away to a distance where she watched him emerge from the house. 'He was all blood.'[111]

Identification of this individual, 'Rea', with the author of *A compleat history of the Rebellion*, James Ray, is open to conjecture. There are certainly coincidental parallels: both were volunteers, both attached to regiments of dragoons and both native to Cumberland – Ray specifically to the port of Whitehaven. That no reference was made in his memoir to the ignominious killings in Inverness would be unsurprising, while the callous phrasing concerning 'knapping of Noddles' during the pursuit suggests he was not of an overly sensitive or squeamish temperament. Whatever his activities during that day, they had not impaired his appetite. 'The Rebels had ordered the Inhabitants of *Inverness* to . . . bake Bannocks for their Suppers, against their Return from the Victory,' he wrote gleefully; 'but their Disappointment was very pleasing to us, who camed to eat it in their Staed; many of them having lost Their Stomachs, and gone to-bed Supperless.'[112] He might have been referring to the gut-shot and bayonetted dead and wounded lying that night on Drummossie Moor.

The LYON in Mourning:

Or,

A Collection (as exactly made as the Iniquity of the Times would permit) of Speeches, Letters, Journals, &c. relative to the Affairs, but more particularly the Dangers & Distresses, of

---

Vol: 3d.

Cui modo parebat subjecta Britannia Regi,
Jactatus terris, orbe vagatur inops!

— — — — — — — —

1747.

The Lyon in Mourning

'A very honest old gentleman, of the name of McLeod', was pursued by two horsemen to a place near Inverness called Barnhill, where, despite his entreaties for quarter, they 'shot him through the head'. It was said that several inhabitants of Inverness were witnesses to the incident. Another man was shot dead as he walked towards the river past a house in Bridge Street belonging to the Widow McLean.[1]

An assiduous correspondence conducted by the Reverend Robert Forbes with a number of informants and eyewitnesses, meticulously transcribed, is the primary source for most anecdotes of atrocity committed by government forces in the days and months following the battle.

In common with most Episcopalians of his day, Forbes was a staunch Jacobite and, upon receiving news that Charles Edward Stuart had arrived in Scotland, set out from his living at Leith to join him. His active participation in the cause was brief, however, ending with his arrest on suspicion in early September at St Ninians and confinement for the next five months in Stirling Castle, then in Edinburgh Castle for another four. Widowed in 1750, he was married for a second time the following year, to a lady who shared his political sympathies and on occasion sent seed cake to the exiled Prince. He was appointed Bishop of Ross and Caithness in 1762, but when a majority of local clergy elected him to the Bishopric of Aberdeen five years later, the College of Bishops – ingratiating themselves with the Hanoverian state – disallowed the election and substituted a more loyal candidate in his stead.

It has been suggested that conversations during his imprisonment in Stirling and Edinburgh, and the narratives of fellow prisoners, inspired the task that would consume him for the rest of his life. For nearly thirty years – from late 1746 until October 1775, a month before his death – Forbes compiled, in close-written manuscript, a body of work that he called 'The Lyon in Mourning'. Despite its wilfully archaic spelling of Scotland's heraldic beast, this was a chronicle of contemporary reportage. Each black-bordered title page – of ten black-edged volumes bound in black leather – bore the identical description, 'A Collection (as exactly made as the Iniquity of the Times would permit) of Speeches, Letters, Journals, &c. relative to the Affairs, but more particularly the Dangers and Distresses of . . .'

The ellipsis, replacing Prince Charles Edward Stuart's name, must have seemed a necessary precaution considering the 'Iniquity of the Times'. While some of the enormities recounted in the Bishop's black archive might invite scepticism – slaughter of pregnant mothers, babes and the aged being a staple of propaganda against any tyranny – he was far from credulously accepting of everything told him to the government army's discredit. 'I never chuse to take matters of fact at second-hand if I can by any means have them from those who were immediately interested in them,' he told one correspondent. 'I love a precise nicety in all narratives of facts,' he told another, 'as indeed one cannot observe too much exactness in these things . . . I love truth, let who will be either justified or condemned by it.'[2]

Wherever possible the conscientious Bishop would give credence to an incident by supplying a name – for witness, victim or perpetrator – in order to 'fix the facts against all contradiction and cavilling'.[3] Told of an attack by government troops on a woman three days after the battle and four miles distant from it, he wished to know 'the name of the said woman' and 'to what regiment did the sogers belong, and by what officer or officers commanded when they so cut said woman'. He received the reply that 'Jean Clerk had her nose slit and head cut, out of which came severall bones' but that it was 'impossible to get the officers or sogers names, for none durst ask them questions'.[4]

PART III:

AFTERMATH

I

TWO to three thousand of the Jacobite army, with their commanders, Lord George Murray, the Duke of Perth, Lord John Drummond and Lord Ogilvie, retreated nine miles south-east of the battlefield, assembling in and about the ruins of Ruthven barracks, a former government stronghold – perched on an outcrop of rock in the Spey valley – that had been captured and burned in February. Here they waited for their leader. Captain Johnstone found them 'cheerful, and full of spirits to a degree perhaps never before witnessed in an army so recently beaten . . . all in the best possible dispositions for renewing hostilities and taking their revenge'.[1] There was talk of rallying; of recruiting formerly neutral clans to the cause; of turning defeat into victory. In a few days it was said, their Prince might count on an army of eight or nine thousand men. Then the message arrived. Their leader had given up the fight and his last instruction to them was terse: 'Let every man seek his own safety in the best way he can.'

*

On Drummossie Moor 'a beautiful young man' of eighteen years lay naked, shin bones splintered by grape shot. Around him were between 1,500 and 2,000 dead and wounded, the carnage of Charles Edward Stuart's army. After the victorious government troops had marched north-west to make camp outside Inverness, the young man saw a coach and six approaching on the road that crossed the carrion-strewn field from the direction of Nairn. '[They were] driving . . . so near the spot where I was lying that I begun to be afraid they would drive over my naked body,' he recalled, 'and then in their passing I saw ladies in the coach.'[2] The Countess of Findlater, whose home at Cullen on the Banffshire coast had been ransacked by Jacobites only a week earlier, was following the Duke of Cumberland to offer congratulations. As her carriage rattled past, its wheels cleared the youth's shattered limbs by inches.

Chilled successively by rain, sleet and frost, as the afternoon and night following the battle gave way to morning, the young man – Captain MacDonald of Bellfinlay – was able to crawl for a time until the skin had been scraped from his knees and hands by the frozen ground.

*

It had always been customary in the aftermath of a conflict to strip the slain, together with the unresisting wounded, like crippled Bellfinlay, if opportunity offered. Achilles stripped the corpse of vanquished Hector, just as the Trojan champion had earlier stripped Patroclus. Naked bodies on the field at Hastings are pictured towards the end of the Bayeux Tapestry and two cadavers shown having tunics of chain mail stripped from them by vassals. A pen drawing of 1521 by the Swiss goldsmith, printmaker and mercenary, Urs Graf, depicting the recent engagement at Marignano, shows a foreground strewn with hacked and stripped corpses, discarded weapons, a severed hand, while the battle rages beyond. During the Thirty Years' War, of 1618 to 1648, Flemish painter Sebastiaen Vrancx enlisted the landscape genius of Jan Bruegel II for the backgrounds to panoramic battle scenes in which precise delineation of nude and partly clothed slain recorded the gradations of victorious spoliation. Vrancx perfected a clearly defined subgenre in Netherlandish art: '*plunderingstaferelen*', or plunder scenes.[3] Following the sack of a German town during the same war, Hans Jakob Christoffel von Grimmelshausen described in his *Adventures of Simplicius Simplicissimus* 'Dead bodies . . . strewn down streets to left and right, some stripped naked, some in their undershirts.'[4]

At Prestonpans between eleven o'clock and noon, only a few hours after the cessation of fighting, as Alexander Carlyle and his father rode across the field, 'the Dead Bodies still lay', about two hundred they thought, and 'mostly Stript'.[5] This office had been performed, it was said, 'by the women who followed the English army'.[6] These same camp followers – whores, soldier's sweethearts, wives now widows – had previously irritated young Carlyle with their 'Howlings, and Cries, and Lamentations' over the dead and wounded. It was behaviour, he judged, which 'Suppressed Manhood and Created Despondency'.[7] That they recovered so quickly to engage in the hard-nosed pursuit of plunder showed this to be a commonplace of military life.

After Falkirk, it was said that Hawley's men – because of the greater marketability of their clothing – were as 'easily distinguished by their comparative nudity' as by 'the deep gashes which seamed their shoulders and breasts, the dreadful work of the broad-sword'.[8] Highland dead by contrast – not so comprehensively stripped – were recognised by their curious habit of slinging bannocks or other comestibles under the left oxter for safekeeping during combat, allowing the sword arm free play. Dougal Graham's poetic account ignored such distinctions in referring to the efficiency of pillage:

> For by their clothes no man could tell,
> They stripped were as fast's they fell.[9]

The work of scavengers had been so thorough that, seen from a distance next morning, the corpse-scattered field presented a strangely bucolic illusion to one Falkirk citizen, who 'could compare [it] to nothing but a large flock of white sheep at rest on the face of the hill'.[10] And during the following night when

Captain Johnstone led a detachment of twenty men and a sergeant to locate and secure the abandoned enemy cannon, the pallid flesh of stripped slain lent a macabre luminescence to their search; the sergeant's lantern had been early extinguished by wind and driving rain and 'we lost our way . . . among heaps of dead bodies, which their whiteness rendered visible, notwithstanding the obscurity of the very dark night.' The eerie proximity of death was disturbing to man and beast alike, and Johnstone 'remarked a trembling and strong agitation in [his] horse, which constantly shook when it was forced to put its feet on the . . . bodies, and to climb over them'.[11]

Between friend and foe, officer and man, nowhere was the grim democracy of naked and dead more marked than in the most noted government fatality of that battle. Lieutenant Colonel Sir Robert Monro, 6th Baronet of Foulis, was found stripped of clothing, side by side with his younger brother in a pool of rain-water. His carcass – pistol-shot to the groin and facially disfigured – was identified only by its bulk.[12]

*

Looting began at Prestonpans while the brief battle was still in progress. No sooner had Cope's army broken than the Jacobite front line itself fell 'into the Greatest Confusion, some pursuing their Enemy wherever they saw them running, others . . . pilladging the dead'.[13] It was later suggested that 'could [the] Dragoons have been brought to rally again, and to have charged the Highlanders, while intent on Plunder, it would have entirely changed the Fortune of the Day.'[14] Hew Dalrymple had even offered to escort them back, 'with assurance of Victory when the Highlanders were busy with the Booty'.[15] But no such attempt was made and the pillage went uninterrupted. Colonel Gardiner was still alive, though mortally wounded, when he was 'plundered of his Watch and other Things of Value . . . also stripped of his upper Garments and Boots'.[16] Boys who followed the Jacobite army appropriated gold-laced tricorn hats, bandoliers and breeches too big for them, while 'rough old Highlanders were seen going with the fine shirts of the English officers over the rest of their clothes.'[17] Among the prisoners, officers were relieved 'both of their Money and Watches', as were servants, many of whom would as a matter of course have been entrusted with their masters' valuables for safekeeping. Local spectators, 'Country Gentlemen, who were not in Arms, were treated in the same manner.' Inquisitive folk from nearby towns 'were stript, by the Conquerors, of their Clothes, Shoes, Buckles, &c'; likewise sightseers come from Edinburgh to view the field.[18] A ballad penned by the Haddingtonshire farmer Adam Skirving recalled the penalties of curiosity:

At Afternoon, when a' was done,
  I gade to see the Fray, Man,
But had I wist what after past,
  I had better stay'd away, Man.
On *Seaton* Sands, wi' nimble Hands,
  They pick'd my Pouches bare Man.[19]

For so comparatively small an army Cope's had 'made a great show' on the march from Dunbar, 'occupying at once several miles of road'.[20] A great part of that traffic comprised the baggage train which yielded the most substantial plunder. Wagons, carts and carriages containing the officers' luggage, provisions, tents, arms, ammunition, and other equipment, had been parked on a field in front of Cockenzie House, with some of the most valuable baggage inside the walled enclosure of that residence. The guard of Black Watch and Lord Loudoun's 'well-affected Highlanders' surrendered it after the battle, following a brief negotiation and the firing of a token volley from the walls.

Among the luxurious items found in the general's carriage was 'a quantity of chocolate'. The looters, ignorant of its use, mistook it for medicinal ointment and it was later sold in the streets of Perth as 'Johnnie Cope's saw', or salve. Likewise, 'wigs and other ordinary appurtenances of the toilette, were . . . the subject of wonder and curiosity.'[21] The carriage itself was presented to

Alexander Robertson of Struan, the 75-year-old poet and clan chief who had brought 140 men to the Prince's cause, and was perhaps the only individual to have borne arms in the Jacobite risings of 1689, 1715 and 1745. This veteran of Killiecrankie, Sherriffmuir and Prestonpans was carried home in triumph to Kinloch Rannoch, wearing Cope's furred nightgown.

The greatest prize was found in the house of the merchant, Mr Mathie, where the general had spent part of the previous evening. 'Hid under a Stair . . . amongst a parcel of old broken barrels and other lumber', was a military chest containing, by various accounts, 1,500, 2,500, 'betwixt two and three thousand', or 4,000 pounds sterling.[22]

The philosopher David Hume pointed out that it was a characteristic of irregular Highland troops of the Jacobite army that 'they become weaker by their Victories; while they disperse to their Homes, in order to secure the Plunder they have acquired.'[23] So it was after Prestonpans, although anecdotes suggest that not all the loot secured was of equal use or value. 'Out of the great numbers which deserted . . . more than one were seen hurrying [away], with nothing but a great military saddle upon their backs.'[24]

*

The torrential rain that lashed Falkirk Muir both during and after the fighting did nothing to deter looters. Even some of the retreating government troops picked up what they could, and it was reported that 'many of Ligonier's foot . . . got a deal of money in plundering the enemy.'[25] Whoever composed these rapacious crews – camp followers, surviving rank and file, or local opportunists seeking profit from a battle fought in their neighbourhood – had both the dead and the living for their prey, if Dougal Graham's doggerel is to be believed:

The plundering wives, and savage boy
Did many wounded men destroy . . .

Some of the brutish commons too,
I saw them run the wounded thro'!

The extensive killing and stripping of officers devalued the market rate of plunder following the battle, and 'Gold watches were at a chape rate.'[26] Enoch Bradshaw of Cobham's Dragoons had sold his watch a short time before, and 'the dear lad who bought it was kill'd the first fire, so that he and all he had fell to these inhumane dogs.'[27] Footwear was an especially prized commodity. One determined Highlander was seen stripping an expensively dressed English officer. Planting his foot into the fork of the corpse's spread legs he tugged with all his strength at the boots, grunting in Gaelic with each exertion: 'Brod Brògan! Brod Brògan!' Excellent shoes! Excellent shoes!*

Attempts were made to prevent civilian plunder. 'As I was agoing towards the Town,' a local resident recalled, 'I heard & saw several Gunns go off round the Field of Battle . . . I was told it was the Rebell Huzzars firing at the Country people that were carrying off the Arms.'[28] Where weaponry was concerned, not surprisingly, private enterprise was discouraged, especially after the Prince had issued all regiments orders 'to Advertise the Soldiers that those that Brings in Gunns, Swords or Pistols shall be Rewarded for them'.[29] The abandoned government camp yielded much more plunder, although not before local scavengers had the first pickings 'immediately on ascertaining the fortune of the day'. There had been an attempt by the retreating government army to burn the tents, but the continuing rain prevented them from catching fire. The total booty seized by the Jacobite army from field and camp comprised '7 cannon, 3 mortars, 1 pair of kettle-drums, 2 pair of colours, 3 standards, about 600 muskets, a large quantity of granadoes, 4000 weight of powder, 28 waggons laden with all kinds of military stores, tents for 5000 men, and all the baggage that escaped the flames.'[30]

* Chambers, vol. 2, p. 303 gives the phonetic 'Praw proichin! praw proichin!' ('Fine brogues, fine brogues').

At the same time the Prince's rank and file 'enriched themselves with a variety of articles which the people of Falkirk had not previously abstracted'.[31]

An entry in the government army's order book for 24 January suggests that at least two officers cherished hopes of retrieving personal property 'Lost in the Field of Battle' and looted by men of their own side. One, from Barrell's, offered five shillings reward for 'a Brown Camlet Cloak lined with Bays', while Lieutenant Colonel George Stanhope, commanding Ligonier's 59th Foot, promised a guinea for the return of a valued 'Blue Great Coat [with] Brass Buttons [and] Velvet Cape'.[32]

II

ACCORDING to the *Newcastle Journal*, around 150 government troops had been killed at Prestonpans. The wounded numbered seventeen officers and 368 other ranks. Jacobite casualties were light by comparison: just five officers and about thirty men killed; between seventy and eighty wounded. The Prince sent orders 'to the neighboring villedges, upon peine of milletary execution that houses & every thing necessary shou'd be provided for the wounded'. Surgeons were sent for to Edinburgh and instructed 'first to dresse the highlanders, & afterwards to neglect nothing for the others'.[1] A Jacobite surgeon, James Murray, afterwards taken prisoner and tried at Carlisle, would be acquitted 'on account of attending the King's wounded at Preston Pans'.[2] It was even claimed, by one of the Prince's staff, that provision for the government wounded took precedence, 'to the great loss of the wounded of [our] own army, who from being neglected till most of the troops were taken care of, their wounds festered, being all gun Shott and mostly in the legs and thighs.'[3]

Conversely it was said,when the still-breathing Colonel Gardiner was recovered from the field by his servant he was carried to the minister's residence in Tranent, because his own Bankton House – which was nearer – had been 'made an hospital for the Highlanders'.[4] In the Reverend Jenkinson's manse the Colonel died, 'having rather breathed than lived a few hours'.[5] An empty house in the locality – Mr Cheape the revenue collector being away from home – was commandeered for the injured government officers, and it was there that young Carlyle offered his services, 'tho' no surgeon, [but having] better hands than a Common Servant'. He found twenty-three men being tended by two dragoons surgeons, Alexander Cunningham and William Trotter, both having surrendered 'that they might attend the Officers'. One of the wounded, Captain Robert Blake of Murray's Foot, lay in an easy chair, a portion of skull sheared off by a broadsword stroke and his brain exposed. Carlyle was shown the cranial bone fragment, 'about 2 Fingers Breadth and an Inch and an Half Long', lying on a chest of drawers.

'This Gentleman must Die', he said.

'No', replied Cunningham, 'the Brain is not affected, nor any vital part; he has Youth and a fine Constitution on his Side; and could I but get my Instruments, there would be no Fear of him.'[6]

Carlyle was dispatched to Cockenzie House with permission from the Jacobite command to search the captured baggage train for a medicine chest, but without success, and Captain Blake was eventually trepanned by Cunningham with the aid of instruments borrowed from a local surgeon and made a full recovery. James Clarke, a captain in Hamilton's Dragoons, received a similar injury and spent the rest of a long life with a silver plate in the back of his skull.

Surgeons brought from Edinburgh tended the 368 wounded rank and file. Of these only 197 survived to be admitted as pensioners to the Royal Hospital, Chelsea. Broadsword injuries were the most common. One of Captain Blake's men, Alex Mill, also 'lost . . . a piece of his Scull', together with the use of his right hand. Most lost the use of one or both hands, arms or legs, suggesting severe ligament trauma. Thomas Moore was described specifically in the Royal Hospital admissions register as 'Cut and Hamstringed'. Others lost hands or limbs altogether. Another high proportion of wounds were to the head, face and shoulders. William Cuthbert had 'His Nose Cut off and his Eyes hurt by Wounds'. John Johnston of Lascelles's had 'His right eye cut out,

[and] lost both his hands'. Richard Malpous was 'Cut a Cross [the] left side of his face and stabd in the right cheek'. George Tullock was 'Cut in [the] head' and 'lost eyesight' as a result.[7]

Notwithstanding the severed limbs littering the field, Alexander Carlyle claimed that 'as almost all . . . Wounds were with the Broad Sword, [the injured] had Suffer'd little', because easily healed.[8] By the same logic, David Hume once remarked blithely that a broadsword 'gives not one Wound in ten that is mortal'.[9]

Two of Hamilton's Dragoons were injured by their own horses falling on them. A Sligo man had 'His left leg quite disabled [and] Several bones taken out', and a trooper called Farel was 'Bruized' in the ordeal which later 'brought Convulsions on him'. At the other end of the field Anthony Wells of Lee's Regiment of Foot, a casualty of the breaking government right, was 'Disabled by Six broken Ribbs, being Rid over by the Dragoons'.

The Chelsea Hospital admissions register ascribed relatively few injuries explicitly to gunfire, although Thomas Fleckfield's 'shattered' left leg may have fallen into that category. David Singlewood was 'Shot in left leg and thigh', James Chapman 'through left foot', Edward Butcher of Lascelles' 'through left Hipp' and James Miller was 'Wounded in right shoulder and right leg' and 'shot in left leg'. Two of Gardiner's Dragoons, John Brereton and a man named Blytie, were shot 'in the Groin' and 'thro' the body' respectively. John Ford of Murray's, aged 33 and with six years' service in the army, had the distinction of suffering, and surviving, the highest number of single injuries that day. When admitted to the Royal Hospital on 17 August 1747 it was recorded he had 'Received Two Hundred & Sixty five Wounds at Preston Pans'.[10] Such comprehensive damage could only have been inflicted by a blunderbuss, the weapon favoured by Major James Stewart, Captain James Johnstone, his Sergeant John Dickson, and probably others of Lord Perth's Regiment on the Jacobite right, as they bore down on Ford and his comrades of the 46th Foot.

*

Just as care and accommodation for the wounded was enforced on the local populace, so they were ordered to 'come with speads & other instruments to bury the Dead'.[11] The Prince had written to his father from Pinkie House recounting his difficulty in managing the operation. 'Those, who should bury the dead, are run away as if it was no business of theirs. My Highlanders think it beneath them to do it, and the country people are fled away.' He contemplated offering payment to undertake the work, 'for I cannot bear the thoughts of suffering Englishmen to rot above ground'.[12]

While the friends of Colonel Gardiner gave him a dignified burial alongside eight of his children in Tranent churchyard, the rest of the government dead received indiscriminate interment near to where they fell, the majority stripped and thrown into mass graves close by the north-east corner of the park wall. For many years after, the ground here was 'perceptibly elevated in consequence'. A map of the battlefield drawn by John Elphinstone shows six such 'Graves of the Soldiers'.[13] Another grave was dug near to a thorn tree – at the centre of what had been the government line – in which 'a considerable number were buried'. There may have been another, towards Tranent Meadows, and those who had failed to escape from the Jacobite onslaught against Cope's right wing were consigned to it, including 'a small party of dragoons'. According to local legend a few were not only fully dressed, when tossed into the pit, but fully shod, and one of the Prince's army, in pursuit of a fine pair of boots, jumped down to retrieve them. A disgruntled grave-digger – whether paid for his labour or pressed – stove in the Highlander's head with a spade and buried him among the corpses of his enemies.[14]

*

After the fighting at Clifton, Jacobite swords broken on government-issue iron skullcaps were readily replaced from the field by plunder, and 'in place of 14,' wrote Captain MacPherson, 'our men took noe less than 50 from the dead dragoons.'[15] The correlation of government dead with swords collected was probably an exaggeration. According to the Parish Register, only ten dragoons – six from Bland's, three from Kerr's and one from Cobham's – were consigned to a communal grave in St Cuthbert's churchyard. An eleventh, from Bland's, Robert Akins by name, survived three weeks to be buried on 8 January. Along with twenty-one rank and file there were four officers injured: two Cornets, Owen and Hamilton, 'almost cut to Pieces', Captain East with 'a large Wound in his Neck, and some on his Head', and the Colonel who had led the attack.[16] A veteran of the European war, Sir Philip Honeywood had been wounded five times at the battle of Dettingen three years earlier. At Clifton he received four more injuries, all to the head, 'by neglect of putting on his scull capp'.[17]

Casualty figures on the Jacobite side are unreliable. There were only 'five left kill'd on the Spot',[18] but it was said that, following the withdrawal from Clifton, there were many others 'whom the Rebels had thrown into [the River Eamont], that the Number of their Slain might not be known'.[19] The stripped bodies had been dropped off Eamont Bridge and there was a suspicion some had entered the river alive as 'great Groanings and Complaints' had been heard by passers-by. 'Between forty and fifty were [later] cast up by the Water, opposite *Brougham* Castle', a mile away to the east.[20]

A dragoon, shot through the right shoulder and index finger, probably exaggerated when writing home to his wife in Manchester that 'we killed upon the Spot, and drove into the River *Lowder* 122, and took Prisoners about 100'. Many of these prisoners, left behind when Murray's force moved on, were captured the following day both by government patrols and the loyal local populace. Some of the captives were from the Manchester Regiment and the wounded dragoon gloated over the plight of his renegade townsmen: 'I am perswaded, [they] had rather chose to have been at the Looms or Grinding of Corn, than to be driven from Place to Place with their Hands ty'd, . . . without Shoes, Stockings or Breeches . . . their Companions are Dirt and Lice, and their Reward for so great a Fatigue a Halter.'[21] The so-called 'Rebel Tree' on the southern edge of Clifton village is supposed to mark the place where the small number of Jacobite dead left behind were interred, after the Duke of Cumberland's men had had their sport with at least one of them. 'Some frolicksom Soldiers dug a deep Hole in the Ground, and put [him] into it with his Feet downwards, and so filled the earth about his Body, that nothing but his Head and Shoulders were above the Earth, and in that Position left him.'[22]

*

After Falkirk, statistics of killed and wounded varied from source to source, and between Jacobite and government estimates. Hawley at first gave out that his army had lost twelve officers and fifty-five men killed, with 213 either wounded or missing.[23] Three or four days later he submitted a fuller, but still by no means complete, tally of 290 missing, eighty-two wounded, and eighty-nine killed, twenty-three of whom were officers. Falkirk was remarkable for the high proportion of government officers killed compared to other ranks, thought to be a consequence of having been deserted by their men, as Colonel Gardiner had been at Prestonpans. The majority of fatalities, both of officers and other ranks, came from the four broken infantry regiments on the extreme left wing: Wolfe's, Cholmondeley's, Blakeney's and Monro's.[24]

The official Jacobite account of the battle* conceded 'not above forty Men killed on our Side [and] near double that Number wounded', whilst enemy losses were put at 'above six hundred . . . killed in the Field of Battle, besides what we are told were drowned in fording the River *Carron*'.[25] According to local tradition it was not only government men who perished thus. Forty years later a woman was still spoken of who had waded barefoot

* Printed at the Prince's headquarters in Bannockburn House, on a press 'prudently stole[n] from *Glasgow*', for dissemination of propaganda in Paris, Madrid and Rome.

across the river some weeks after the battle and 'gone deranged by treading upon the . . . face of a dead Highlander'.[26]

Individual Jacobite sources were generally in agreement as to the proportion if not the number of losses: James Maxwell of Kirkconnell putting them at 'betwixt four and five hundred [government] men killed upon the spot', the Prince's 'not exceed[ing] forty killed . . . and about sixty wounded';[27] while Lord Elcho estimated 'between 500 & 600 kill'd' on the one side, and 'about fifty kill'd & Sixty wounded' on the other.[28] Lord George Murray supplied no figures for Jacobite casualties, claiming only that '500 [of the enemy] are kill'd.'[29]

Press reports erred in favour of the government side, the *London Magazine* declaring that 'the Rebels, by all Accounts, lost many more Men than the King's Forces.'[30] The *Glasgow Courant* was more specific: 'Loss of the Regular Troops, by the best Computation, does not exceed 200; and by all Accounts the Rebels have at least lost double that Number.'[31]

Captain James Wolfe – who maintained that Falkirk fell short of being a battle at all – was even-handed in understatement: 'The loss of either side is inconsiderable.'[32]

To the variable number of government fatalities might have been added Colonel Francis Ligonier whose death from pleurisy in Edinburgh six days later was deemed a direct consequence of the battle. The harsh weather conditions on Falkirk Muir aggravated a chest infection and the memorial raised by his brother on the south side of Westminster Abbey cloister states that 'a Distemper could not confine him to his Bed when Duty called him into the Field, where he Chose to meet Death, rather than in the Arms of his Friends. But the Disease proved more victorious than the Enemy.'

Another fatality, on the Jacobite side, was entirely peripheral to the battle. In a room giving on to Falkirk High Street, a private soldier of the Clanranald regiment was cleaning a musket he had claimed as plunder from the field. Finding it to be still loaded he first extracted wadding and round from the barrel, then, believing he had made the weapon safe, pointed it through the window and pulled the trigger to clear the powder charge. But before going into action the former owner had 'double shotted' his musket to enhance its killing power and instead of producing a harmless flash in the pan and puff of smoke, the charge propelled a second ball into the street, mortally wounding Colonel Aeneas MacDonell, son of the clan chief of Glengarry. He was a 'modest, brave, & advisable lad [and] vastly regreated,' George Murray told his wife; 'it is more loss to us than all we suffer'd at the Batle.'[33]

Other versions of the story assign greater culpability to the anonymous 'miserable fellow' who fired the shot. It was said that he had been 'working with his Gun, Carelesly, which the highlanders are too apt to do';[34] that 'Highlanders were eternally handling their fire-arms, and frequently discharging them; [and] no prohibition [having] hitherto been able to prevent that abuse it was unlucky that a young gentleman of merit and consequence should be the first to suffer by it.'[35] Old Alexander Robertson of Struan was unconvinced even that his nephew's death was an accident. 'His Enemys are . . . authors of the murder [and his] growing worth made him envyd by Beggers and hated by Traytors.'[36] Whatever the circumstances – and despite a plea for clemency from the stricken Colonel before he died – 'the fellow was order'd immediately to be Shot . . . to prevent mischeif happing between the two Clans.'[37] As a gesture to impartiality, and 'to make his death as instantaneous as possible', the condemned man's father joined the firing squad.[38]

Neither clan enmity nor mistrust was entirely assuaged by the speedily settled score. 'When Glengarrie died,' it was said, 'a 1000 MacDonalds went off at once.'[39] Donald MacDonell of Lochgarry was less specific as to the effect of his kinsman's death, saying only that 'during this time there was a generall desertion in the whole army.'[40]

*

Only officers, when identifiable as such, were interred in the consecrated ground of Falkirk churchyard. Rank and file were buried *en masse*. Heavy rain had softened the ground, allowing easier excavation of grave pits and, as at Prestonpans, local labour was assigned the task, its only mitigation that those digging and burying might claim whatever scraps of value still attached to the dead. Two pits were dug close to the highest concentrations of slain. One was at the foot of the hill below the abandoned cannon where, wrote Johnstone, 'the corn-fields were thickly strewed with dead bodies.'[41] The other was to the north-east at a place where many fugitives from the broken government left wing were overtaken and cut down. The first of these pits was partially uncovered by workmen in February 1839, tunnelling the approach to Falkirk High Railway Station, although only a single skeleton and two skulls, one of them 'of large dimensions', were found.[42] While yielding no human remains of any sort, delineation of the other site, on a housing estate at the junction of Craighorn, and Dumyat Drive, can still be clearly seen. Over the intervening two and a half centuries, the compacted mass of bodies decayed and disintegrated, causing the ground above to subside. The resulting 'considerable hollow'– exposing tree roots and dragging the earth away from a low boundary wall – is known locally as the 'English graves'.[43]

Rumour circulated that the Prince had given orders for all the dead to be buried, with the exception of eight Presbyterian ministers, 'whose corps[es] he would not allow the honour of burial till he should know their names and from whence they came'.[44] A popish atrocity was suspected by detractors, that 'their naked bodies [would] be exposed to dogs, the fashion in France with the dead Protestants'.[45] The Reverend Étienne Abel Laval's recently published four-volume epic of anti-Catholic propaganda, *A Compendious History of the Reformation in France and of the Reformed Churches in that Kingdom*, had encouraged such suspicion, haunting Presbyterian nightmares with anecdotes of state persecution in general and accounts of those who died refusing the sacraments in particular. One concerned a gentlewoman of Alençon, 'her Corpse . . . thrown out at the Window into the Street stark naked, . . . put a-cross upon a Horse, . . . carried in that Condition without the City, amidst the Insults of a brutish Mob, and thrown upon a Dunghill'. And there were others at Vitré, 'their Corpses . . . open'd, and thrown into the City Ditches, where Dogs and Birds of Prey fed upon them'.[46] No such post-mortem outrages were known to have been visited upon the non-combatant ministers who perished at Falkirk, and the Prince's supposed reluctance to bury them with the rest would seem inexplicable – unless he intended sparing them indiscriminate interment by returning the bodies to their respective parishes.

*

A list of government army prisoners taken at Prestonpans comprised 73 officers, 114 dragoons, and 1,212 other ranks, inclusive of wounded.[47] 'Then saw I human Nature in its most Despicable abject form,' remarked Alexander Carlyle of captured officers gathered on the foreshore, 'for all most every aspect bore in it Shame, and Dejection and Despair.'[48]

Corporal John Louden, a dragoon in Hamilton's Regiment was confined overnight in the yard of Colonel Gardiner's house and, with about 200 others, the following night in Musselburgh. On the next day they were marched to Edinburgh and lodged in the Canongate Kirk.

Rank and file prisoners were given the option of enlistment in the Jacobite army, their captors 'promis[ing] them all Commissions, and their arrears fully paid them'. Admittedly those rewards were dependent upon London falling to the Prince and 'their getting to St. James's'. A witness in Edinburgh told of seeing 'about 200 soldiers with the livery of H.M. King George go down under guard to the Abby [at Hollyrood], and shortly after saw about 40 carried away under guard . . . and the remainder were set at liberty . . . many going about at large with white cockades along with the rebells.'[49]

About fourteen of Hamilton's dragoons were recruited into the Edinburgh Regiment raised by Colonel John Roy Stuart. 'Gentlemen . . . you certainly know the business we are upon,' he addressed them in St Anne's Yards behind Holyroodhouse, 'there is no force or compulsion upon you; pray lay your hands to your heart. If you join us, you shall be well paid; but if you endeavour to deceive us, you can expect no mercy if ever you should fall [again] into our hands.'[50]

They were allowed time to digest the implications of this momentous choice. It was one which would result in court martial and probable execution for desertion if they were subsequently captured by the government army. The oath sworn was of abjuration as well as of allegiance:

> I solemnly promise and swear in the presence of Almighty God, That I shall faithfully and dilligently serve James the Eighth, King of Scotland, England, France,* and Ireland, against all his Enemies, forreign or domestick And shall not desert or leave his service without leave asked and given by my officer. And hereby pass from all former alledgeance given by me to George Ellector of Hanover. So help me God.[51]

A sergeant who had witnessed Roy Stuart's speech to the dragoons 'gave out, that he was sick, and desired to be excused', and later testified against those who enlisted. In due course all were hanged.[52]

*

The numbers of government men reported as taken prisoner at Falkirk varied. A statement from Bannockburn House put it at 'above seven hundred', Lord Elcho at 600, Murray 'about 300', and Maxwell 'some hundreds'. Another Jacobite source claimed that more government prisoners could have been captured by better mounted cavalry, and that 'in a flight in which 5 or 6000 . . . might have been taken, we did not make above 600, only 250 of which were regular troops.'[53] The rest were militia,

* Stuart claimants to the British throne also laid nominal claim to that of France as had every English and British monarch since Edward III.

volunteers, 'and Country People . . . present at the Action out of Curiosity'.[54] The diversity was reflected in prisoners incarcerated at Doune Castle, a late-fourteenth-century stronghold, once the seat of Robert Stewart, 1st Duke of Albany, and by 1746 'in a most ruinous condition'. There were 'above 100 soldiers of the King's army, a good many Argyleshire men . . . some men of the Glasgow regiment,' and two officers and three men of the Edinburgh Volunteers. A further eleven civilians included two citizens of Aberdeen held on suspicion of espionage, and the Reverend John Knox Witherspoon, spared the fate of his co-religionists on the Muir. When the Volunteers devised a plan of escape from the battlements by a rope of knotted blankets, the two civilian spies elected to join them. 'Mr Witherspoon said that he would go to the battlements and see what happened, [and] that if they succeeded, he would probably follow their example.' On 31 January the two officers, one of their men and one of the spies descended safely. But as the second spy – a 'very tall and big' man – succeeded in joining them the rope snapped twenty feet clear of the ground. Then the fifth man reached the extremity of the shortened rope and let go. Despite those below impeding his fall, he 'dislocated one of his ancles, and broke several of his ribs' but, being 'slender and not very tall', was able to get clear of the castle, carried and supported by his companions. On the battlements the last of the Volunteers retrieved the truncated rope and added more blankets, restoring it to the requisite length and strength before making his own descent. However, in strengthening the rope he made it considerably thicker and, reaching the point at which it had been repaired, was unable to keep a grip on its girth and fell the same distance as the other man. With no one to break his fall the unfortunate Volunteer 'was so grievously hurt, bruised and maimed, that he languished and died soon afterwards'.[55]

Meanwhile the Reverend John Knox Witherspoon, having assessed the dangers of escape, chose to avoid further risk and await his deliverance patiently. Released some days later, within a fortnight he was back in his parish endorsing a committee which pledged support to the Duke of Cumberland, assuring him 'how joyful it is to the presbytery that His Grace is come to our country to oppose the present Rebellion.' The clergyman never fully recovered from his adventure and for some years 'had a nervous affection of the most distressing kind which sometimes took the form of a sudden and overwhelming presentiment in the midst of a service that he would not live to finish his task'.[56] His condition, however, did not prevent him living a further half century. Thirty years after Witherspoon's first encounter with insurrection, he would – following another, successful, rebellion against the House of Hanover – append his signature, with fifty-five others, to the American Declaration of Independence.

III

SOME three hundred yards behind the government lines on Drummossie Moor a gargantuan erratic boulder, abandoned by a melting glacier following the last Ice Age, is known as the 'Cumberland Stone'. The inscription carved into its upper surface – deep enough to harbour an infill of pine needles all year round – alleges it to be the 'Position of the Duke of Cumberland during the Battle of Culloden'. While this claim is contradicted by eyewitness accounts placing him in the forefront of the government right wing throughout the fighting, another connection between Duke and boulder lies in the tradition that he sat on top of it to eat dinner after the battle. It may have been a conscious echo of his late opponent's meal following the fighting at Prestonpans. A table had on that occasion been laid close to the captured government guns and, following 'a long blessing' by a Scots Minister, Charles Edward Stuart ate breakfast.[1] A guard of the Clan Gregor stood around, 'each receiving a glass of wine and a little bread'.[2] The scene was described by the historian Andrew Henderson who provided a characteristically jaundiced gloss to the Prince's meal. 'With the utmost Composure [he] eat a Piece of cold Beef, and drank a Glass of Wine, amidst the deep and piercing Groans of the wounded and dying, who had fallen a Sacrifice to his Ambition.'[3]

If Cumberland did indeed take refreshment on top of the stone that now bears his name, he would have been out of earshot of all but the most carrying screams from the main slaughter ground of the battle and able to eat relatively undisturbed. Shortly afterwards he is supposed to have visited that part of the field where Barrell's, Monro's, Bligh's and Sempill's men had met the compacted assault of the Jacobite right. 'Lord! what am I!' he is said to have mused, 'that I should be spared, when so many brave men be dead upon the spot.' His remark was widely reported as an 'expression of *deep humility* towards God, and compassion towards his fellow man . . . worthy the greatest man alive'.[4]

*

Cumberland gave orders that each regiment was to send a detachment from the camp at Inverness comprising a subaltern and twenty men, with carts, to bring the government wounded off the field. Making the task more congenial, discarded weapons were also to be collected and a cash premium offered as reward. A shilling would be paid for every broadsword, and half a crown for every firelock. 'The same price [was offered] for Swords and Firelocks . . . brought in by the Country People.'[5] Any man fortunate enough to find a Jacobite colour or standard was promised the extraordinary bounty of sixteen guineas for his trouble. The search for lucrative plunder may even have taken precedence over the recovery of wounded, because that humanitarian operation was far from complete by nightfall on the 16th and another order was issued the following day 'to bring off all our wounded men that could not be found last night'. As late as Saturday the 19th, between fifteen and twenty additional carts were to be sent 'as soon as possible to the houses in the Neighbourhood of the Field of Battle in order to bring to the Hospital . . . the poor wounded Soldiers who . . . were left there without Care'. The negligence of officers and – perhaps unjustly – surgeons was blamed for the delay.[6]

In addition to weapons, 'all Dragoons or Troopers Cloaks' found and given up would be paid for at two shillings apiece, while a seeming connoisseur's interest in French military decorations was evinced by Lord Albemarle. 'If any Cross of the Order of St Lewis is found by any of the men, they are to bring them to [his Lordship] who will give them the value of them.'[7] Established by Louis XIV in 1693, and named after the canonised thirteenth-century King Louis IX, the Order's medal on its scarlet ribbon might have been worn by any Catholic officer in the French Service fighting for the Jacobite cause.

Another collector was less discriminating. 'If any Soldier or Soldiers wife have found in the late Action any plate or Rings, Gold or Silver watches, Horse Furniture or any thing of that kind, they are to bring them to Mr Bruce who wants to look at them and will fully satisfy them for any thing he purchases.'[8] This avid procurer of looted valuables was David Bruce, the army's Judge Advocate, a civilian barrister responsible for overseeing and giving legal advice in courts martial.

Although the *Gentleman's Magazine* reported that plunder gained from stripping the dead and wounded 'was not very considerable',[9] the great number of Highland chiefs killed was gauged 'by the Appearance of our Soldiers, who are strutting about in rich laced Waistcoats, Hats, &c'.[10]

Ten days after the battle, a public auction 'of things Taken from the Rebells' was announced as taking place at ten in the morning at the Weigh House in Inverness's market square. But captured horses 'taken in the Field' had already been sold at the Mercat Cross, presumably to prevent their contaminating the army's animals. Glanders, affecting horses, mules and donkeys – and causing lesions on the lungs and ulceration of the windpipe – was the farriers' principal concern. The acute form of the disease manifested as fever, coughing, an infectious nasal discharge, septicaemia and death. Any that recovered acted as carriers. An order issued on 23 April stated 'that all the Soldiers and Womens horses pick'd up in the country [were] to be dispos'd off in 48 Hours, those which are not dispos'd of in the time . . . to be Knock'd on the Head'. To ensure that contamination had not already occurred, the horses of every regiment, those of the artillery train 'and Bread Waggon Horses' were to be inspected and 'if any of them are found to be Glanderd they will be Shott immediately.'

The collected 'Firelocks of different Kinds' numbered 2,320, while only 190 'Broad Swords and Blades' were recovered. This disparity was consistent with the Highlanders' practice – despite orders to the contrary – of discarding their muskets after firing so as to engage with their swords unencumbered. Some weaponry was of superior quality to others and Cumberland ordered that 'French or Spanish Firelocks and Bayonets and Cartridge Boxes' were to be distributed among the government soldiers released from Jacobite captivity.[11] The Duke's first act on reaching Inverness – 'all bespattered with dirt, covered with dust and with sweat, and with his sword in his hand' – had been to demand the keys to the Tollbooth prison. He is said to have personally liberated the government army prisoners, clapping them on the shoulder, saying, 'Brother Soldiers you are free!'[12] Along with full arrears of pay owed since their capture, a guinea was given to each for refusing to enlist with the enemy.[13]

John Hay, 4th Marquess of Tweeddale, Earl of Gifford, Secretary of State and Master of the Ordnance for Scotland, claimed most of the swords. Many bore the mark of Andrea Ferara, virtuoso swordsmith and 'a magic name to the Highlander.'[14] In a spirit of whimsical desecration, Tweeddale had the points sawn off, the hilts removed, and the blades fashioned into a dainty garden fence at the rear of his newly acquired property, Twickenham House.

Captured colours of the defeated army – paid for handsomely by the Duke – would in the wake of any other victory have been carried in triumph to London. But deeming it 'no Honour' to flaunt the standards of so despised an enemy, the liberal outlay of reward money bought Cumberland only the grim satisfaction of ordering these silk and linen spoils destroyed. In Edinburgh, on 4 June, they were paraded downhill from the Castle to the

Mercat Cross on the High Street. Escorted by a detachment of Lee's 55th Foot, the procession was led by the public hangman, Mr John Dalgleish, bearing the white silk standard emblazoned with Prince Charles Edward Stuart's coat of arms and the motto 'God Save the King'. Colours of the Farquharsons, the Chisholms, Lord Lovat, and ten others followed, red and blue saltires, silk and linen, each in the soot-soiled hands of a chimney sweep. Nothing was neglected to the detriment and degradation of these treasured symbols of clan and Stuart pride. At the Cross a bonfire had been lit, 'the Honourable Sherriffs' assembled, 'the Heralds in their Robes, and the Constables with their Battons'.[15] As three trumpet fanfares blared out, Dalgleish lowered the Prince's colours into the fire to the 'Acclamations of an innumerable company of Spectators'.[16] One by one the sweeps stepped forward with their colours, 'the Heralds always proclaiming the Names of the traitors to whom they belong'd', and the hangman burnt each in turn to 'the Sound of Trumpet and loud Huzzas from the Populace'.[17] Lord Lovat's camp colour was the last destroyed, 'with equal and repeated Huzzas'.[18] Lieutenant Colonel Whitefoord called the ceremony 'a burnt offering . . . made to Pluto . . . where Jack Ketch acted the part of high Priest'.[19]

Three weeks later, a fifteenth standard was consigned to the flames 'with like solemnity', and at Glasgow, during 'the principal weekly Market', the colours of 'the Rebel Macdonald of Keppoch' were consumed 'amidst the Huzzas and Acclamations of many Thousands of Spectators, and to the infinite Joy of the whole Inhabitants of this City'.[20]

*

An army surgeon had 'counted all the bodies that lay on [Drummossie Moor] as exactly as he cou'd, and [said] that the kill'd on both sides amounted to about 750, of which he did not doubt but the one-half were of the regular troops'. He also believed 'the number of the slain, both in the field and in the pursuit' was no more than twelve hundred.[21]

The official tally of government dead – officers and men – came to about fifty killed outright. In addition there were some 233 wounded, although of these many would subsequently die of wounds because only eighty-one figure in the Chelsea Hospital admission records as having survived. John Pringle, Physician General of the army, estimated the government wounded to number 270 and an Inverness Charity School and two malt barns had been requisitioned to receive them. Many had suffered broadsword wounds which – while less common in the military hospitals of the time than gunshot injuries – were more 'easily healed', according to Pringle. While the blade could lay open a gruesome trench of raw tissue, the relative shallowness of the gash and the irrigating haemorrhage as it 'bled much at first', cleansed it of dirt and prevented lingering infection. These factors aided what Pringle called 'a good digestion' – or healing – of the wound.[22] Gunshot injuries, by contrast, invited complication: 'from being small at first [they] grow dayly larger from a large suppuration of the bruised parts, and are tedious of curing.' Such wounds, remarked a surgeon during the Flanders campaign, 'when seemingly healed often breake out again from part of the cloathes being forced in with the bullet & not extracted'.[23]

The Physician General was less concerned about the condition of the wounded than about the deadlier spread of disease. He had first encountered what he termed 'malignant, or hospital-fever' in Flanders three years earlier. 'Attended with a sunk pulse and a constant *stupor* . . . it appeared to arise from the foul air of some of the wards crouded with sick; and especially of one room, in which a man lay with a mortified limb.'[24]

This led Pringle to preface his *Observations of the Diseases of the Army, in Camp and Garrison* with the stark declaration that 'among the chief causes of sickness and death in an army . . . I should rank, what is intended for its health and preservation, the *Hospitals* themselves.'[25] At Inverness, in the aftermath of Culloden, he recognised the perfect conditions for a major epidemic. The town was small and harboured 'a morbid state of air, from the measles and smallpox' that had prevailed even before the arrival of the army. But by the end of April, the jails being filled to capacity with Jacobite prisoners and wounded, there was 'the prospect of a long encampment and camp-diseases', exacerbated by 'the crouds and filth' – animal waste and blood – 'of a place where the markets of an army were kept'. Pringle apprehended the worst. He tried to remedy the problem by providing 'two well-aired houses' as accommodation for the sick, and by instructing regimental surgeons to 'send to the general hospital such a proportion of the worst cases, as might lessen their labour, without crouding these houses'. Apart from segregation, the only known – but entirely futile – treatment for this and indeed for any feverish or inflammatory condition, was copious extravasation. 'Dr Pringle recommends to the Regimental Surgeons timely Bleeding,' the Duke of Cumberland wrote in his daily orders for 22 April. Furthermore, 'If for the future such patients are sent to the Hospital without bleeding, Complaints will be made of the Surgeons.'[26] For the rest of his life the Duke followed this recommendation, having himself heavily bled at the onset of every minor complaint. It was a practice suspected of hastening his death at the age of 45.

The disease that had so alarmed Pringle was caused by rickettsial bacteria. It was borne by lice and fleas – not 'foul air' – and no amount of bleeding would have done any more than weaken the patient. It was later to be designated typhus, as would the identical scourge incubated by the overcrowded, insanitary and foetid conditions on the 'Common' side of prisons.

Notwithstanding all of Pringle's precautionary instructions at Inverness – to keep the wards clean, 'likewise . . . to clean the jails every day, to remove speedily the bodies of those who died, and to prevent crouding' – all such measures were set at nought when an epidemic of typhus broke out by 'unforeseen accident'. Towards the end of May a transport arrived at Nairn bringing Houghton's 24th Regiment of Foot to reinforce the pacification of the western Highlands. In the same ship were thirty-six British Army deserters – captured some months earlier while in the service of France – on their way from English prisons to courts martial in Scotland. These captives carried with them the contagion of so-called gaol fever. Within days of disembarkation a dozen of Houghton's men were in hospital with the infection despite being 'blooded largely upon admission'. Then six officers succumbed and by the time the regiment marched west a total of eighty men were left behind sick. During the following ten days in Inverness a further 120 were hospitalised with the same fever, the disease also spreading 'among the inhabitants of the town'.

It was estimated that from mid February when Cumberland's army crossed the Forth until the campaign ended in mid August 'there had been in hospitals upwards of 2,000, including the wounded; of which number near 300 died, and mostly of this malignant fever.'[27] The number of civilian deaths is not known, but as many as 684 Jacobite prisoners – 'about 19 per cent of the whole' – may have perished from typhus before they could be brought to trial.[28]

*

'A Captain and 50 Foot to March directly and visit all the Cottages in the Neighbourhood . . . to search for rebells'. The Duke's morning order for 17 April gave no instruction as to what should be done with them when found, but the sentence that followed left little scope for ambiguity: 'The Officer and Men will take Notice that the public orders of the Rebells Yesterday was to give us no Quarters.'[29] An order by Lord Murray had been discovered in the pocket of a prisoner, which allegedly contained the injunction 'to give no Quarter to the Elector's Troops, on no Account whatsoever'.[30] Despite the contentious sentence appearing only in a 'Copy of Rebel Orders' preserved in the Duke of Cumberland's papers – while the original in Murray's hand contained nothing of the kind – the forgery received widespread quotation in the propaganda arsenal of the popular press, and generated rumours throughout the army to justify acts of reciprocal brutality. The Cobham's dragoon, Enoch Bradshaw, was told that 'we were to have been every soul of us cut off . . . and for the Duke he was to have been cut as small as herbs for the pot.'[31] Another, in Lord Kerr's regiment, heard that Murray's order had been 'To kill men, women, and children of their enemies without distinction, for eight days after the battle, in case victory should declare for them.' This same dragoon – Garnet by name, a printer's son from Sheffield and 'a discreet and ingenuous man' – claimed to have witnessed firing parties of government soldiers, each commanded by an officer, scouring the field and shooting any wounded insurgents who had survived the night. So zealously was this operation carried out that sometimes as many as six or eight muskets were aimed and fired to dispatch a single man. This was done without a word of command, although the officers 'stood by and watched the service performed'. It was apparent that some of the wounded 'seemed pleased to be relieved of their pain by death'.[32] Others begged in vain to be spared. This was corroborated by Captain MacDonald of Bellfinlay who, maimed and naked, witnessed 'that cruell command coming to execute their bloody orders, and saw many of his unhappy companions putt to death in cold blood'.[33] A number of wounded, discovered by troops in a nearby barn, were taken out, propped against a park wall 'as so many marks to be sported with, and . . . shot dead upon the spot'.[34]

It was suggested that these measures could be excused on the grounds that 'it was not proper to load or crowd this little town [of Inverness] with a multitude of wounded and incurable men of our enemys.' The firing squads, it was argued, were 'performing the greatest act of humanity, as it put an end to many miserable lives remaining in the outmost torture without any hopes of relief'.[35] One officer disputed Garnet's and other reports of atrocity because of the 'praemium . . . given for every gun and sword brought to the king's camp'. He claimed that the men under his command 'were so busied in carrying guns and swords' as to have neither time nor inclination for gratuitous slaughter. He also reasoned that such cold-blooded killing, 'being a thing very uncommon . . . his men could not miss to observe and to tell him of it'. As for the notorious Jacobite order forbidding quarter, he doubted its very existence. 'A particular serjeant in a certain regiment was said to have it; [but when asked for it] answered he heard another serjeant had it, and went two or three thus, and always found less reason to believe there ever was any such order.'[36]

But, cumulative testimony compiled by the Reverend Robert Forbes recorded that the killing continued. A young captain in the government army claimed to have seen seventy-two 'knocked in the head' and killed on the Friday alone.[37] And the following day, as carts were sent to fetch in the remaining government wounded from the field, others trundled more enemy wounded to summary execution. Eighteen or nineteen officers had been held captive, 'wallowing in their blood and in great torture', in the cellars of Culloden House when the carts arrived, 'which they imagined were to carry them to Inverness to be dressed of their wounds'. Instead they were driven half a mile from the house to the site of another gigantic glacial boulder, which, like the 'Cumberland Stone', was to acquire a sinister notoriety. The captives were dragged from the carts, made to kneel and shot at close range, the mute witness to this shambles known thereafter as the 'Prisoners' Stone'.[38] For the *coup de grâce*, the firing party were ordered to club their muskets and beat out the brains of those yet alive. Among the dead and dying was an ensign in Lovat's regiment, John Alexander Fraser, sole survivor of the massacre. A soldier brought the brass-bound butt of his weapon down onto Fraser's face and 'dashed out one of his eyes, . . . beat down his nose flat and shattered . . . his cheek', then left him for dead.[39] That he lived to report the ordeal was due to his having been helped into hiding by a local gentleman. A long and painful convalescence left him half blind, with a paralysed arm and lame in both legs, but still able to 'step about upon crutches'.[40]

Captain Bellfinlay also had a fortunate escape. He was about to suffer the same fate as those he saw killed, the soldiers 'presenting their firelocks to his own breast', when Lieutenant James Hamilton of Cholmondeley's 34th Foot, interceded and had him taken as prisoner to Inverness, along with wounded redcoats who abused him 'all the way for a damn'd rebellious rascal', but did him no further harm. He would count himself lucky in the three years remaining to him that, although both left and right tibia had been smashed, the two fibulae were unbroken, 'preserv[ing] his legs from shrinking up and growing shorter'.[41] Instead, the fractures knitted following the removal of no fewer than twenty-four bone fragments and a piece of iron shot.

Mercy was shown – albeit for profit – when Alexander MacIntosh of Issich 'being much wounded in the battle . . . did save himself by crawling [through] the night immediately after'. Passing between two sentries he was able to offer each a shilling, which they accepted 'saying that the money was better to them than the taking of his life'.[42]

Such forbearance was uncommon, however. At a small distance from the field was a hut used for sheltering sheep and goats in stormy weather. Wounded men had been carried, or crawled there during the night only to be found by soldiers in the morning. Their captors did not trouble to take them outside for execution but instead 'made sure the door, and set fire to several parts of the hut, so that all within it perished in the flames, to the number of between thirty and forty persons'. This total was said to have included some beggars, 'spectators of the battle, in hopes of sharing in the plunder'. It may not have been an isolated incident. There are other accounts of neighbouring barns or houses sheltering wounded being burnt and those trying to escape forced back into the flames at bayonet point. As local people viewed 'the smothered and scorched bodies' among the ashes, a circumstantial detail was noted: clearly discernible 'ruffels' on the clothing of incinerated corpses which crumbled when touched.[43]

*

Government regiments 'who had any men killed in the Battle' were ordered the following day 'to send a small detachment to bury them either there or in the nearest Church yard'. Niceties of consecrated interment disregarded, a mass grave was dug, filled and covered close to the main concentration of slain, a place that became known as the 'Field of the English'. A local boy, drawn there by curiosity, was witness to this grim activity. As an old man, he would tell his granddaughter that one of the burial party had picked up 'a man's dissevered arm', slapped him across the face with it and sent him about his business. The government dead did not rest peacefully in this arable ground and for years afterwards there were 'bones again and again turned up by the plough'.[44]

The dead Campbells of Ballimore's battalion – those killed with their commander under fire from the retreating *Royal Ecossais* – were buried close to where they fell, along the north wall of the Culwhiniac enclosure. Nearly a century later, in 1834, 'a large skeleton' was dug up there, 'the skull of which had a musket-bullet in it'. Further to the east ploughing brought to the surface 'seven skulls at one time'.[45] However, the only known human relic of the battle surviving to the present day is a skull acquired by the nineteenth-century surgeon Sir Charles Bell.* A musket ball had entered close to the crown, crashing out at the posterior base of the cranium. The alignment of holes and implied trajectory of the round suggests that the victim's head was lowered when hit. He might have been running headlong towards the fire; or bending over his own weapon reloading; or else already wounded and slumped forward on his knees. With no record as to where on the field the skull had been found, it is not known on which side the man fought.

*

After Prestonpans Charles Edward Stuart had expressed abhorrence at leaving the dead of Cope's army 'to rot above ground'.[46] But for the Duke of Cumberland, burying his enemies did not seem a priority. Lady Inches wrote that the local people 'durst not venture upon burying the dead . . . till particular orders should have been given for that purpose' and such orders were not immediately forthcoming.[47] By contrast, on 2 May John

* Now in the museum of the Surgeons' Hall, Edinburgh.

Fraser, Provost of Inverness, was instructed 'that all dead Horses and Carrion near the Camp be buried this day'. It was just over a week since the glandered horses had been shot or 'Knock'd on the Head', and the close proximity of festering decomposition was considered a nuisance if not a danger to health. But the late battlefield was over five miles away and neither reference nor instruction appeared in the Duke's orders regarding the disposal of bloated carrion on Drummossie Moor. The Reverend George Innes, one of Robert Forbes's informants, could 'not . . . precisely remember how many days the dead bodies lay upon the field to glut the eyes of the merciless conqueror'. Certain it was, however, 'that there they lay till the stench oblig'd him to cause bury them'.[48] If Cumberland did so, he departed from standard practice in neglecting to issue a written order to that effect. Nevertheless, according to local tradition 'country people were employed in the work of interment'. A series of long trenches was dug and some smaller pits, into which the bodies were thrown. Over a century later they were still discernible, 'slightly raised above the surface of the ground, and . . . distinguished by their vivid green turf amid the brown heather'.[49] The historian Robert Chambers, writing in the 1820s, noted the 'little eminences . . . displaying a lively verdure' as well as other graves – of runaway and arbitrary victim alike – fringing the 'unimproved secondary road' to Inverness.[50]

Over time Drummossie Muir attracted tourists, generating in turn a demand for souvenirs. Walter Scott possessed a musket ball, in addition to a morsel of oatcake he was told had been found on the field. 'Bullets, and fragments of armour,' according to a record of 1798, 'picked up by people in the neighbourhood, [were] anxiously sought after, and carefully preserved, by the virtuosi, as curiosities and valuable relics.'[51] Inevitably, souvenir hunters were drawn to probe those 'distinct and well defined' areas of fertilised green, a practice deplored by Chambers, who remarked that 'modern curiosity has, in some cases, violated these sanctuaries, for the purpose of procuring some relic of the ill-fated warriors, to show as a wonder in the halls of the Sassenach.'[52]

A guidebook of 1920 'particularly requested that parties visiting the field of battle will not in any way destroy or dig up the graves. Too much of this has been done; and it is hoped that . . . proper respect may be henceforth shown to the last rest-place of many a brave Highlander.'[53]

IV

A venerable gentleman encountered in the Highlands – 'an honest Whig' and loyal supporter of King George – enquired disingenuously of his companion whether the Duke of Cumberland was a Jacobite? Asked to explain such an apparently absurd question he replied: 'Sure, the warmest zealot in the interest of the [Pretender] could not possibly devise more proper methods for sowing the seeds of Jacobitism and disaffection than the Duke of Cumberland did.'[1] The same argument had been put to the Duke himself, albeit nuanced and at greater length, by Duncan Forbes, Lord President of the Court of Session. 'No Severity that is *necessary* ought to be dispensed with' – the ten page memorandum began belligerently enough – 'the omitting such Severity, is Cruelty to the King & to the Kingdom.' But by emphasising 'necessary' in his first sentence he anticipated the even-handed antithesis of his second: 'Unnecessary Severitys create Pity; & Pity from unnecessary Severitys is the most dangerous Nurse to Dissaffection.' Had all the insurgents present at Culloden perished or been captured, he declared, 'their Fate would neither have moved Pity, nor . . . sower[ed] Minds against the Government'. However, if those who escaped were to be hunted down '& to a Man, destroy'd' – even though it would result in the same loss to the Jacobite cause – 'the Complaints . . . and the Compassion . . . naturaly arising, in the Minds of weak Persons that are not at present disaffected, may . . . furnish a much stronger Recruit[ment] to that villainous Cause, in a short Time.' And he urged the Duke to 'restrain merited Punishment' and 'extend unmerited Mercy', so as to preserve 'the future Tranquillity of the Kingdom'.[2] Thereafter, whenever the Duke spoke of Forbes, he dismissed him as '*that old woman that talked to me about humanity*'.[3]

Other advocates of humanitarian restraint received harsher treatment than scorn at the hands of the military authorities. When Alderman Hossack, former Provost of Inverness, suggested to a group of senior officers that 'As his Majesty's troops have been happily successful against the rebels . . . [their] excellencies [might] be so good as to mingle mercy with judgement', he was kicked headlong downstairs on the orders of General Hawley. Hossack's successor, Provost John Fraser, for some similar interference, was forced up to his ankles in manure to oversee the cleansing of a regimental stable. The unfortunate officials became famous to local urchins as Kick-Provost and Muck-Provost respectively.[4]

And wherever else troops were garrisoned the local population was subject to arbitrary violence. At Stirling, a periwig-maker's apprentice by the name of William Maiben was thrashed for insolence in his master's workshop by Lieutenant Stoyt of the Old Buffs. The unfortunate Maiben was 'struck . . . over the head, once and again, with a staff, till it broke', and beaten in the face 'to the effusion of his blood'. He was then dragged before Stoyt's superior officer who ordered him stripped, tied spreadeagled against crossed halberts in the market place and whipped 'till his back was severely cut by the stripes'. Local magistrates protested, bringing charges of 'hamesucken' – in Scots law, the assaulting of a person in his dwelling place – for the first beating, and 'a most barbarous and cruel abuse . . . of the rights and liberties of the subject', for the second.[5] However, no further action could be taken as the following day the regiment marched to Glasgow where its officers received lavish entertainment and were honoured with the freedom of that loyal city.

After a riot which resulted in £130 worth of damage to property, Aberdeen magistrates complained that soldiers responsible for the wanton destruction did 'not hesitate to tell [us], That we are yet under military Power, and that they are not lyable to the Civil Government'.[6] And when Duncan Forbes ventured to speak to the Duke of Cumberland about legal matters – 'as it well became his character and station' as Scotland's senior legislative officer – the reply he received left little doubt that the land was indeed effectively under martial law: 'The laws of the Country, my Lord!', said the Duke, 'I'll make a brigade give laws, by God!'[7] Parliament was to provide him with ample scope to do so.

Towards the end of 1746, legislation was passed for 'the more effectual disarming [of] the Highlands', making it an offence 'to have, use, or bear, Broad Sword or Target, Poignard, Whinger, or Durk, Side Pistol, Gun, or other warlike Weapon'. All arms were to be delivered up 'at a certain Day . . . and at a certain Place . . . unto such . . . Person or Persons appointed by His Majesty'. Failure to comply, and the concealing of weapons, was punishable by a £15 fine, six months' imprisonment or forcible enlistment as a soldier in His Majesty's forces in America. Extrajudicial penalties were imposed by proclamation. An advertisement posted in the city and environs of Aberdeen warned 'That where-ever arms of any kind are found, that the house, and all houses belonging to the proprietor or his tenants, shall be immediately burnt to ashes,' and in the event of arms being found buried underground, 'the adjacent houses and fields shall be immediately laid waste and destroyed.'[8] A revival of the 1716 and 1725 Disarming Acts – introduced in the wake of earlier risings – that of 1746 contained other clauses having more to do with subjugation than with weaponry.

Highland dress was proscribed for the civilian population. 'No Man or Boy . . . on any Pretence whatsoever, [was to] wear or put on . . . the Plaid, Philebeg or little Kilt, Trowse, Shoulder Belts . . . and . . . no Tartan or party-coloured Plaid or Stuff . . . used for Great Coats, or for Upper Coats.' The penalty for contravention was six months' imprisonment for a first offence and, for a second, seven years' forced labour in 'his Majesty's Plantations beyond the Seas'.

Six clauses dealt with measures 'to prevent the rising Generation being educated in disaffected and rebellious Principles'. All teachers in Scottish private schools were to 'give Evidence of their good Affection to his Majesty's Person and Government' and be required, 'as often as Prayers shall be said in such School, to pray, or cause to be prayed for, in express Words, his Majesty, his Heirs and Successors, by Name, and for all the Royal Family'. Failure to do so would result in the customary six months' imprisonment, but a second offence would incur transportation to the American plantations for life.

A sinister provision of the Act was contained in Clause XVIII. It clarified a piece of legislation from earlier in the year intended 'to indemnify such Persons as have acted in Defence of his Majesty's Person and Government . . . during the Time of the present unnatural Rebellion'. Shorn of its legal qualifications, conditions and equivocation, the gist of this indemnity clause was that any personal prosecution brought against members of the armed forces was rendered impotent – 'discharged and made void' – when countered by a defence of acting 'to suppress the said unnatural Rebellion', or 'for the Preservation of the publick Peace', or 'for the Service or Safety of the Government'. Plunder, assault, even execution without trial, was thereby deemed to be justified by Act of Parliament, even though 'not justifiable by the strict Forms of Law'. And to further discourage troublesome legal action being brought against those operating 'in Defence of his Majesty's Person and Government', punitive 'double Costs' would be awarded against plaintiffs on the inevitable collapse of their suit.[9]

*

The Duke of Cumberland set out from Inverness on 23 May, travelling south-west along General Wade's military road through the Great Glen to Fort Augustus at the far end of Loch Ness. He rode at the head of Kingston's Regiment of Horse and eight regiments of foot, all – with the exception of Houghton's 24th and Skelton's 12th – blooded veterans of Culloden. A powerful presence at Fort Augustus was necessary, both 'to keep the Country in Awe' and to have troops 'ready to move where ever there may be Occasion', and particularly in the neighbourhood of the Frasers, Camerons, MacDonalds, MacKenzies and MacPhersons. The Duke's professed intention was 'to pursue and hunt out these vermin amongst their lurking holes'.[10]

Howard's Old Buffs, Price's and Cholmondeley's Foot, and eighteen companies of Highland militia, had taken the same route a week earlier, and already occupied the fortress that would serve as headquarters for pacifying the western Highlands. Built between 1729 and 1742 by General Wade, and named on completion in the Duke's honour, Fort Augustus had fallen into Jacobite hands in early March following a two-day siege and a mortar-shell explosion in the powder magazine which demolished part of the north-west bastion wall. Nineteen barrels of gunpowder had been subsequently used to raze the hated edifice of Hanoverian power, leaving only fire-gutted buildings and heaps of rubble for the advance guard of troops who arrived in May. As an extensive military camp grew outside the ruins a grim discovery was made in the shell of the old Kiliwhimen barracks nearby. Floating at the bottom of a cistern or well were the bloated corpses of nine government soldiers, 'drowned by the rebels', it was said, 'after having been made prisoner'.[11] The revelation can have done little to soften the men's feelings towards the insurgents they were being sent to hunt.

On the eve of Cumberland's departure from Inverness, his aide-de-camp Colonel Joseph Yorke wrote of the enemies awaiting them in the wilds of Lochaber; deluded by their clan chiefs into believing 'there would be no further search after their persons, that it would be impossible for the troops to get after 'em and that . . . the glorious Duke would be ordered to Flanders and think no more about 'em.'[12] And he anticipated, with relish, their dismay 'when our Red Coats appear in the heart of their country [and] our bayonets glitter in their eyes, or are buried in their bodies'.[13]

The Duke's first daily orders at Fort Augustus contained the apparently unequivocal injunction, 'No Plundering or Marauding on any acco[un]te'.[14] But a later court martial sentence of 1,500 lashes with a cat-o'-nine-tails was inflicted, not for plundering as such but for 'plundering under pretended orders from HRH'. There was no perceived contradiction that other entries in the Order Book dealt with the distribution – amongst sergeants, corporals and private men – of money accrued from selling the livestock they had brought in as officially sanctioned plunder. A 'Sale of plate at the Old Barracks', disposed of more luxurious looted goods.[15] While the disarming and pacification of the Highlands were Cumberland's principal objectives, punishment of the pacified and profit were concomitant concerns.

'This country begins to feel a little the consequences of entering into an unprovoked rebellion,' wrote Colonel Yorke, '[and] that the King can, whenever he thinks proper, march his troops into the remotest parts of the mountains and punish 'em as he sees fit.'[16] An anonymous officer, writing to the *Gentleman's Magazine*, boasted of 'carrying fire and sword thro' their country, and driving off their cattle, which we bring to our camp in great quantities, sometimes 2,000 in a drove'.[17] Houses left vacant were 'plundered and burnt . . . their ploughs and other tackle destroyed',[18] every article essential to subsistence wrecked, 'pots, pans, and all household furniture, not excepting the stone quarns, with which they grind their corn, breaking them to pieces'.[19] These people, remarked the officer, 'are deservedly in a most deplorable way, and must perish either by sword or famine.' It was, he concluded, '*A just reward for traitors*'.[20]

*

Lord George Sackville led a detachment of five hundred volunteers, 'well shode & good Marchers',[21] the forty miles from Fort Augustus through Knoydart to the westernmost barracks of

Bernera in Glenelg, with orders 'to scour that Country & along the Sea Coast' before turning inland 'over against the head of Loch Arkaig'.[22] At the same time Lieutenant Colonel Edward Cornwallis was to approach that location more directly from the east with a second detachment comprising three hundred men. Sackville and Cornwallis between them, 'with full Commission to plunder, burn and destroy',[23] were expected 'to clear every thing down to the River Lochy'. They were instructed to prepare for rough country, and 'those who have a spare pair of Shoes will take them.'[24]

Meanwhile, the garrison commander of Fort William, further to the south, advanced with another three hundred men along the right and left sides of Loch Eil. Honoured for his successful defence the previous March and April, of that stronghold commemorating William III – unlike his counterpart at Fort Augustus, cashiered for surrendering – Captain, soon to be Major, Caroline Frederick Scott was the godchild and namesake of the Duke of Cumberland's mother, Caroline of Ansbach. He would acquire a ferocious notoriety in the western Highlands to compensate for his appellation.

'And that no Part of the Country may pass unexamined', the tripartite advance into Lochaber by Sackville, Cornwallis and Scott was complemented from the south by Major General John Campbell of Mamore who, with two detachments of Argyllshire Militia, totalling a further three hundred men, was to patrol both sides of Loch Shiel, and 'to sweep in every thing that lyes in Sunart and Morvern'.[25] Campbell had assured the Duke of Cumberland that he could 'depend on my taking care to distress and disarm those parts recommended to me'.[26] However, encountering a surprising willingness among the inhabitants to surrender their arms and submit to the King's mercy, he also declared, 'I have used no violence having that Country in my power at any time.' His restraint would be more than balanced by the excesses of others. Depredations came from the seaward side of Morvern, if not the landward, and no fewer than fifteen coastal towns and settlements were set ablaze along the Sound of Mull and the coast of Ardnamurchan, by men from a Royal Navy squadron that included the aptly named *Furnace*, and the bomb ship *Terror*.[27]

*

Those surrendering their weapons in accordance with the Disarming Act were given certificates and allowed to 'return unmolested to their homes'. Unmolested that is, 'till his Majesties further pleasure [was] known',[28] and even then 'without any promise or intimation given 'em that mercy is designed 'em'.[29] Clan members were expected to take collective responsibility, 'the one for the others', each subscribing to a document pledging 'to send in all the Arms we can find in the Cuntry', with the proviso 'that the Consequence of any arms being taken there [subsequently] will be forfeiting any good Intentions . . . towards us.' Names were signed – or crosses marked – in two columns headed 'Those not in Rebellion', and 'Those that was in Rebellion'.[30]

Weapons brought in were of varying quality. In Lochaber Major General Campbell wrote of one submission as 'the best Arms I have seen, some belonging to His Majesty's Troops, and some Spanish'.[31] Conversely, it was reported towards the end of the year that 'they [still] have plenty of small arms [in the west], for what they deliver'd up was such as was good for nothing.'[32] In other areas of Scotland it was the same story. Seven out of thirty-seven muskets surrendered at Aberdeen had broken stocks, the firelocks missing from another ten, and two of the fifteen pistols damaged.

'Such as do not submit,' reported Yorke, 'are pursued and put to the sword as rebels in arms, their cottages and husbandry gear burnt and all their cattle drove away and disposed of.' Compliance with the Act, however, was no guarantee of being left in peace. Military execution was enforced if the deadline for submission was missed, as happened in the case of John MacDonell of Glengarry, whose 'Castle [was] blown up and his estate laid waste;

and [was then] forced to comply with the surrender of arms notwithstanding'.[33]

Sometimes retribution was entirely arbitrary. Two men who surrendered themselves and their loaded firelocks in Cornwallis's camp were shot after half an hour's questioning. 'They absolutely refused to kneel, or to have Caps over their Faces', and the firing party was obliged to carry out the sentence as they stood.[34] Captain Caroline Frederick Scott ordered three men hanged from the wooden spout of a watermill in Glen Nevis using rope from a salmon net. They had been on the way to surrender their weapons at Fort William when apprehended. Thinking themselves safe, and the Captain merely sporting with them, they grinned as the halters were put around their necks. The bodies were left hanging for two days. On the Island of Barra Scott hanged a man, 'considered one of the handsomest in the Highlands', in the presence of his mother and from the roof of her house. 'He was found dressed in the Highland garb, and had been in the battle of Culloden.'[35]

*

On 10 June Sackville's detachment returned from its foray into Knoydart with 'upwards of 2,400 black cattle, besides a great number of goats and sheep', together with eight prisoners albeit 'none of them of note'.[36] The expedition's success had been marred only by a rare occurrence of retaliation: the looting of Lord Sackville's baggage train in the rear by a dozen local bandits, the 'plundering [of] his servants' and theft of 'all his horses, bedding, linen, [and] provisions'. Nevertheless, the camp at Fort Augustus celebrated the captured livestock the following day with bareback races on Galloway ponies. These creatures were 'little larger than a good tup, and . . . excellent sport', and the Duke himself awarded prizes to the winners. A week later there were other competitions. General Hawley raced Colonel Howard for a wager of twenty guineas, the 'Hangman' winning 'by about four inches'. Eight soldiers' wives competed, on the same diminutive mounts, 'also bare backed, and riding with their limbs on each side the horse, like men'. The prize, of 'a fine holland smock' – offered by His Royal Highness – was won 'with great difficulty, by one of the Old Buffs Ladies'. The Reverend Robert Forbes heard it 'frequently reported' although with 'no account of the certainty', that the women's races were run 'having no cloaths but their shirts' or 'quite naked . . . sometimes on foot, and sometimes mounted astraddle . . . for the entertainment of Cumberland and his officers'.[37]

*

Cameron of Lochiel was rumoured to be 'skulking'* on the shores of Loch Shiel and a reward of £50 was offered for information leading to his capture. Wounded at Culloden, the clan chief in fact remained in hiding until his eventual escape to France in September. Devastating vengeance, however, had been wrought by Cornwallis's troops upon his estate at Achnacarry. 'Fine Chairs, Tables, and all his Cabinet Goods were set a fire and burnt with his House,' recalled the London Volunteer Michael Hughes, betraying, perhaps, a flicker of sensitivity as a 'fine Fruitgarden above a Mile long, was pulled to Pieces and laid waste [and a] beautiful Summerhouse . . . set on Fire, and every thing valuable burnt or destroyd'. It was believed that the best of Lochiel's 'Moveables' were carried off and hidden before the soldiers arrived, a belief that led to Captain Scott having the estate gardener whipped to death for failing to divulge where the family plate had been secreted.

Scott's detachment from Fort William would later burn six towns in their march through the Appin country on the south side of Loch Linnhe between Ballachulish and Keil, mansions and tenants' houses alike destroyed and not even the hovels of the poor being spared. He also carried out the most meticulously vindictive instance of plunder on record, the dismantling of Ardsheal House on Kentallen Bay, home of Charles James Stewart,

* The word meant 'hiding' but lacked the disparaging connotation it has today.

fifth clan chief of the Appin Stewarts. Frustrated at failing to capture the chief himself, Scott first evicted his pregnant wife – allowing her a small amount of her own meal to feed herself and children – before turning his attention to the ancestral home. Not only the slates, but also the sarking boards, were removed from the roof. The whole house, together with the outlying buildings, was gutted of its internal wooden beams 'with the least possible damage even to the drawing of the nails'. The walls were then taken down, free stone carefully separated from lintels and rabats. Finally, the entire estate's planting, 'which chiefly consisted of many large ash trees', was chopped down, and with the slate, the internal timber and stone, loaded onto carts and taken to Fort William to be 'disposed of [for] above £400 Stir[ling]'.[38]

In late November, two government agents, travelling from Glenelg to Fort Augustus, by way of Glen Shiel and Glen Moriston, reported twenty villages 'all burnt', the inhabitants 'much incens'd against Major Lockhart, who burnt their houses and carried off their cattle'. Operating to the north of Lord Sackville and towards the end of June, James Lockhart and a detachment of Cholmondeley's 34th Foot had been responsible for a number of well-documented atrocities in the area. John MacDonald, Hugh Fraser and his son, harrowing a field 'and expecting no harm', were shot and their corpses hung by the feet from a gallows. Another Fraser, fording a river and waving a letter of safe conduct, or 'protection', from a Presbyterian schoolteacher, was also shot dead by Lockhart. The Major later threatened the schoolteacher himself with the same treatment.[39] 'When any Protection was shewn him,' declared Michael Hughes, 'his Answer was . . . if they were to shew him a Warrant from Heaven, it should not hinder him from following his Orders.'[40]

In Glenmoriston, a gentlewoman, Isobel MacDonald, was raped by Lockhart's men in full view of her husband who was in hiding, and a number of her tenants' wives were 'ravished at the same time . . . by all the party'.[41] Isobel and another victim 'formed a resolution not to allow their husbands to lie with them till nine months should be expired, lest they should have been with child

. . . But they happened (luckily) not to fall with child by the ravishing, nor to contract any bad disease.'[42]

There are comparatively few explicit instances of rape – including that of 'a woman big with child' and of 'a poor girl that was blind' – recorded by Robert Forbes in his 'black register', although numerous anecdotes of women and girls stripped naked by soldiers.[43] The bishop's reserve on this subject was likely due more to delicacy than to infrequency of occurrence. Of those cases he did mention, however, most implicate Lockhart or Scott and the troops under their command.

*

Lieutenant Colonel Whitefoord basked in the satisfaction of a mission all but accomplished. 'We . . . have entirely swept Lochaber,' he declared, 'in which at present there are but very few houses standing.' Further north, Ross, Sutherland, Strathnaver and Caithness 'are quiet and we have put it out of the power of the others to give us any disturbance'.[44] Within ten days of his arrival at Fort Augustus, Colonel Yorke had also anticipated that the army's work would be 'pretty soon finished', while at the same time conceding 'that these rascals die hard'.[45] Captain Scott is said to have hanged eight men 'without any form of trial, because they would not give him information about the Prince, although they had none'. He also tortured a man fruitlessly for three successive days to elicit the same intelligence.[46] But the fugitive remained at large, and the £30,000 bounty promised for his capture lay still unclaimed in the Treasury's coffers.

*

'God knows where or when this will find you,' began a father's letter from his country residence, the Palazzo Savelli, at Albano:

> but still I cannot but write to you in the great anxiety & pain I am in for you from what the publick news mentions from Scotland.

> I know nothing else, & I doubt not but those accounts are exaggerated . . . But still it is but too plain to see that affairs with you don't go as I could wish; I am tho' still in hopes you may be able to keep your ground in Scotland . . . But if you really cannot maintain yourself . . . Do not for Gods sake drive things too far, but think of your own safety . . . you should really have no temptation to pursue rash or desperate measures at this time . . . Enfin, My Dear Child, never separate prudence & courage.

Underneath his secretary's copperplate script the father added in his own hand a more intimate benediction: 'Adieu my dearest Child I tenderly embrace you & am all yours, once more God bless you & protect you.' He signed the single sheet, 'James R.'[47] It was 6 June 1746 and for three weeks Charles Edward Stuart had been skulking in a forester's cottage at Corodale on the Hebridean island of South Uist. But that day, warned of approaching government troops, he escaped north to the smaller island of Wiay.

He had intended making his escape from Scotland shortly after the army's defeat at Culloden, and explained his long-term strategy in a circular letter to the clan chiefs, written some time between 22 and 25 April at Borrodale on the west coast. There was little he could do, he told them, 'on this side of the water'. But by 'going into France instantly' he would be able 'to engage the French court . . . to assist [the cause] effectually and powerfully'. This would also, he believed, stiffen the French king's half-hearted commitment to the Jacobite succession:

> It is thought to be politick [or policy], though a false one, of the French court not to restore our master, but to keep continual civil war in this country, which renders the English government less powerful, and of consequence themselves more.

That policy, he reasoned, would be 'absolutely destroyed' by his leaving Scotland and would persuade the French that 'this play cannot last'. With Britain at peace, 'the Elector will soon be as despotick as the French king' and oblige Louis to take more decisive action and launch a full-scale invasion, 'to strike the great stroke, which is always in their power, however averse they may have been to it for the time past'.[48]

On 26 April he embarked for the Western Isles in the company of Colonel Sullivan, Captain O'Neil, Allan MacDonald, Donald MacLeod and eight oarsmen. His objective was to reach Stornoway, on Lewis, where he hoped to take ship for France. But foul weather, and the opposition of residents – alarmed he was come to plunder the town and cost them 'both their cattle and their lives'[49] – frustrated the initial plan, while the dogged pursuit by government patrols on sea and land would further delay his departure until 20 September.

The Prince's wanderings during those intervening five months created a legend and in time a heritage industry to market it. His every resting place was to become a stop on some future tour guide's itinerary: north and south on the broken spine of the Outer Hebrides – known as the 'Long Island' – from Benbecula to Arnish, and from Scalpay to Kyle Stuley. Four 'Prince Charlie's Caves' on Skye are reputed to have sheltered him during the few days he spent on that island, and another six, so named, on the mainland in North and South Morar, on Loch Arkaig, and on the eastern slope of Ben Alder, overlooking Loch Ericht.

Associated objects immediately acquired the status of treasured relics: a shortened clay pipe or 'cuttie' that had scorched the Prince's cheek, was kept 'as a valuable rarity', while even an emptied brandy bottle was 'preserve[d] as a curious piece'.[50] Three teenaged girls in a crofter's cottage came to blows over who should possess a stool he had sat on; the youngest, who lost two teeth in the battle, was awarded the prize for 'having fought so valiantly and suffered so much in the Prince's cause'.[51] An elderly lady, after he left her house, 'took the sheets in which he had lain, folded them carefully, and charged her daughter that they should be kept unwashed, and that, when she died, her body should be wrapped in them as a winding sheet.' The story was recounted by James Boswell, who added: 'Her will was religiously observed.'[52]

In December 1748, the Reverend Robert Forbes acquired two little splinters of wood which he attached inside the backboard of 'The Lyon in Mourning', Volume Four. The smaller of the two fragments was subsequently lost – leaving behind only the crust of black sealing wax that had secured it – but the provenance written underneath identified both as 'pieces of that identical eight-oar'd Boat, on Board of which . . . the Prince set out from Boradale for Benbecula in the Long Isle'. Forbes must have received them with the awed veneration of a medieval divine receiving fragments of the True Cross.

A number of other quasi-sacred artefacts are fixed inside the front and back boards of the third volume, and the back board of the fifth. The majority of these disparate objects relate to that most celebrated incident of a familiar, often-told story: the fugitive's escape by boat from North Uist to Skye in company with the legendary Flora MacDonald. One was a swatch of 'stamped linen with a purple sprig', cut from the gown worn by Charles in his disguise as the heroine's Irish maidservant, Betty Burke. Its pattern would later be copied and marketed, becoming a popular dress fabric in fashionable Jacobite circles, Scottish and English alike. The fragment of a single blue garter – of French design – backed with white silk was another treasure, while a short length of 'Apron string, which the Prince wore about him' with the same ensemble, was presented to Forbes 'out of Miss Flora Macdonald's own Hands'. He was shown the whole apron by that lady in Edinburgh and was even permitted to put it on. Two bits of a leather lug from one of the Prince's brogues were lovingly mounted at the rear of Volume Five. He later acquired the shoes themselves, near intact, that he 'sacredly preserv'd . . . and made friends drink [loyal toasts] out of them'.[53] Finally, a piece of tartan, 'as much as would . . . cover little more than One's Loof' – or palm – and a scrap of scarlet lining, were all that remained, unrotted, of a waistcoat worn briefly by the Prince after doffing his female attire on the island of Skye.

*

'I heartily wish you success in your Chace,' the Duke of Cumberland's secretary, Sir Everard Fawkener, wrote to Major General Campbell. 'If you can keep your Game upon the Island I dont see how it can escape.'[54] But at the time Fawkener penned his letter on 13 July, Campbell's quarry was no longer to be found on Skye or upon any other island, having crossed to Mallaig harbour at the mouth of Loch Nevis, on the Scottish mainland, just over a week before. Following reports to that effect, 1,500 men marched from Fort Augustus to scour the western coast and by 20 July there were reported to be two thousand regular troops out, besides Highland irregulars, and 'a chain of centries, . . . from Inverness to Fort Augustus, and from Fort William to Inverary . . . and stronger guards at important passes; so that it was thought almost impossible he could escape.'[55]

Two months later, shortly after midnight on 20 September, Charles Edward Stuart embarked for France, never to return.

'Nothing is to me a more convincing proof,' wrote Lord Albemarle, now Commander-in-Chief in Scotland, 'of the disaffection of that . . . part of the Country than that of [the Pretender's] lying so long concealed amongst those people, and that he should be able to elude our narrowest and most exact searches, and at last make his escape notwithstanding the great reward offered to apprehend him.'[56]

Robert Forbes thought it particularly remarkable considering the villainous reputation of those who had protected him during his wanderings through Morar, Glengarry and Glen Moriston: 'The Glenmoriston men . . . were such infamous thieves and noted lifters of cattle . . . that the country people who knew them would not drink with them . . . These very men . . . that could at any time risque both body and soul for less than the value of a single shilling, were found proof of *thirty thousand pounds sterling*, and generously despised the tempting bait.'[57]

Leaving aside the undoubted loyalty of the Prince's adherents, Forbes quoted an opinion – afterwards current in Edinburgh among 'people of no mean sense and discretion in the common affairs of life' – to the effect that 'the Duke of Cumberland and his army were not willing to take him, but, on the contrary, avoided laying hands on him when they might have done it.'[58] As a prisoner he would have become a more dangerous focus of disaffection than as either a fugitive or an exile. And certainly his escape spared the British government the constitutional complications of trying him for treason, not to mention having to behead a second scion of the House of Stuart in less than a century. To avoid such embarrassments, claimed Captain Johnstone, 'the Duke . . . never failed, in his instructions to the commanders, to enjoin them not to take him a prisoner, but to put him to instant death.'[59]

Such an unequivocal injunction to murder would be scarcely credible – even from a more reliable source – but a passing reference by Robert Forbes offers a basis for conjecture. 'The Duke of Cumberland gave orders in writing sealed up and not to be opened till they should happen to catch the Pretender, and if they should miss him, to return the orders unopened.'[60] If such sealed orders ever existed, they would have been duly returned with the seals unbroken, the contents unread, the instructions unexecuted. The Duke's intentions regarding the person of his distant cousin cannot be known, but a musket round in the back and verdict of 'killed while attempting to escape' might have offered the simplest solution to a complicated problem.

Wine, Punch & Patriotism

IT was to curb scurrilous lampoons on the popular stage at his administration's expense that the late Sir Robert Walpole had introduced legislation in 1737 which brought 'common players of interludes' acting 'for hire, gain, or reward' under the proscribed category of 'rogues, vagabonds, sturdy beggars and vagrants'. Theatres operating without benefit of Royal Patent, or a licence from the Lord Chamberlain, were prohibited from producing 'any interlude, tragedy, comedy, opera, play, farce or other entertainment' in front of a paying audience. However, this legislation might be circumvented by a playhouse if such entertainment was 'given Gratis' during a concert of music, or else performed before an audience that had paid for refreshment only, 'Each Person [being] admitted for a Pint of WINE or PUNCH'.

One such establishment was the New Wells Theatre in Clerkenwell. It lay close to the Fountain Inn, noted as much for its health-giving waters as for its ale, and known in contemporary spelling as the 'London Spaw'. The New Wells was distinct from Sadler's Wells, a short distance to the north in Islington, and likewise deriving its name from the mineral springs found in the area. Confusingly there was another New Wells Theatre adjacent to Goodman's Fields in Whitechapel, the site of yet another ancient water source. All three of these unlicensed playhouses provided diversions, including rope dancing, tumbling, and ladder dancing.

All three offered pantomimes 'in Grotesque Characters' such as *The AUKWARD SQUIRE; or Harlequin Philosopher*, and *HARLEQUIN a CAPTIVE in FRANCE; or, The Frenchman Trapt at Last*. All three advertised admittance for the customary purchase of wine or punch. Discerning patrons of the New Wells, Clerkenwell were given an additional inducement and assurance: 'Care will be taken that the Wine shall be Neat.'

A further consequence of the 1737 Licensing Act – the necessity that all new plays be vetted for offensive content by the Lord Chamberlain – meant that revivals of old plays were favoured by theatre managements. Ironically, John Gay's *The Beggar's Opera* – first produced in 1728 – fell outside the 1737 jurisdiction despite its scabrous satire on establishment corruption being the very type of material the legislation had been enacted to prevent. And it was in keeping with the preoccupations of the time that such permissable works as George Farquhar's forty-year-old comedy, *The Recruiting Officer*, or Thomas Shadwell's *The Humours of the Army* – 'Not Acted these Thirty Years' – also had a military theme. Even *The Beggar's Opera* had for its central character Captain Macheath, who sports a red coat and 'looks upon himself in the Military Capacity'.[1]

*

In October 1745, performances at both of London's licensed playhouses, the Theatre Royal, Drury Lane and Theatre Royal, Covent Garden, concluded in identical fashion. Twenty men appeared at the end of the play, and one stepping forward from the rest, 'with uplifted hands and eyes', began singing:

God save great GEORGE our King
Long live our no-ble King
God save the King.
Send him vic-to-ri-ous,
Happy and glo-ri-ous,
Long to reign o-ver us,
God save the King.[2]

The future National Anthem – lyricist and composer unknown* – is said to have originated in the 1680s and been sung in praise of James II. Its appropriation from the Jacobite to the Hanoverian cause in 1745 was the work of Thomas Arne, whose own 'Rule Britannia'† has run it close as a patriotic staple ever since. 'The Music is within the Compass of most Voices,' remarked a newspaper correspondent of the time, 'and the Subject of the Words suited to the Inclination of most Hearts. The *Air* is easy, grave, and elegant, and admirably well connected in its Parts.'[3] Arne – in his capacity as house composer at the Theatre Royal, Drury Lane – had orchestrated 'the old anthem tune' and set it to two voices, although its first rendering 'by the Gentlemen belonging to that House' on Saturday 28 September was in chorus. 'The universal Applause it met with, being encored with repeated Huzzas, sufficiently denoted in how just an Abhorrence [the audience] hold the arbitrary Schemes of our invidious Enemies, and detest the despotick Attempts of Papal Power.'[4] It was only four days since news of General Cope's defeat at Prestonpans reached London and a suitably urgent middle verse reflected the heightened state of national emergency:

O Lord, our God arise,
Scatter his enemies,
And make them fall;
Confound their politics,
Frustrate their knavish tricks,
On him our hopes we fix,
O save us all.[5]

Evidence of a growing popularity and frequent repetition over the following months, a number of attempts were made to improve

* Although the air has been attributed to Henry Purcell. See *Gentleman's Magazine*, Aug 1814 and October 1836.

† From the masque *The Distresses of Alfred the Great, King of England, with his Conquest of the Danes*. It was first performed in the royal palace at Cliveden in 1740, but received its first London performance on 20 March 1745.

its lyrics, and these variants appeared from time to time in the correspondence sections of the popular press. However, no contemporary published reference exists of a notorious extra verse calling on divine assistance for Field Marshal George Wade to 'Victory bring / . . . sedition hush, / And like a torrent rush / Rebellious Scots to crush'. If this variant was ever sung, it can have been 'of temporary application only [and] but short-lived',[6] given that the septuagenarian Wade had resigned command of the army to General Hawley by late December 1745.

*

While officially countenanced spoken drama was confined by royal patent to Drury Lane and Covent Garden, opera was the preserve of the King's Theatre in Haymarket alone. Opera, in London, was 'Italian opera' by definition. Sung in Italian by Italian performers, it had flourished as fashionable entertainment since 1711 and the first performance of Handel's *Rinaldo*, featuring virtuoso harpsichord improvisations by the composer himself, a flock of live sparrows released into the auditorium for an effect of birdsong, and two extravagantly expensive *castrati* in the principal roles. And despite the curious anomaly – observed by Joseph Addison – that London citizens, 'like an audience of foreigners in their own country', chose to be entertained 'in a tongue which they did not understand',[7] Italian opera had remained fashionable until late 1745 when its patronage began to seem disloyal. 'At a time when we are engaged in a war with *France* and *Spain*, and under the necessity of stemming a rebellion at home', an indignant correspondent wrote in November, 'I cannot but be surprised to see some men . . . more anxious about securing the performances of operas . . . than they are to secure the repose of the nation.' At war with two Catholic countries and the civil peace threatened by a Catholic pretender to the throne, paying to hear Catholic singers and musicians appeared an act of mild treachery. Those who did so, the patriot went on, 'will incur the imputation of men of levity, and of men who neglect all that is valuable and laudable for what is in itself greatly pernicious to this country'.[8]

Henry Fielding told of a fashionable lady, her 'public Spirit . . . as amiable as her private Character', who refused a subscription to the opera season on the grounds that, 'had [she] any Money to spare in this Time of Distress, it should be given to buy Gin to comfort those brave Fellows . . . forced . . . to lie on the cold Ground, in the Service of their Country, and not lavished on Foreigners, who first plunder and then laugh at us.'[9]

So the customary winter programme of Italian opera in the Haymarket was cancelled because of 'popular prejudice against the performers . . . being foreigners [and] chiefly Roman Catholics'.

Sung in English but without a full theatrical staging, the oratorio form provided London audiences with a viable and patriotic alternative. Unlike Italian opera, English oratorio was not confined by regulation to the Haymarket. It was also to be enjoyed at the Theatre Royal, Covent Garden.

*

Whether performed in licensed or in unlicensed establishments, through the medium of forty-year-old plays, Italian opera, English oratorio, musical drama, harlequinade or anthem, as the time approached for the final suppression of 'unnatural Rebellion' the patriotic fervour that swept through London and the wider country was as much in adulation of one overweight young man as in loyalty to his father.

Even conventionally idealised portraits of the Duke of Cumberland presented him as obese. 'From his childhood he was healthful,' noted his physician, Sir John Pringle, euphemistically; 'from the age of puberty he was of a full habit, but on his advance to manhood he grew plump & from about the age 20 he began to grow fat, & in a few years became extremely corpulent.' Pringle continued, 'He ate heartily & of nourishing foods, but was always temperate in liquor . . . For a person of his bulk he [was] always active, & [took] a good deal of exercise on horseback.' He was also subject to violent headaches and an incidental disability may have been a concomitant. 'About the age of 23 he found that he had the sight of one eye only, but as there was no visible blemish in the other, nor that any ophthalmic complaint had preceded this discovery, it was uncertain how long he had been deprived of the use of that eye. It is probable that whatever was the cause of the cephalalgia [or headaches] had likewise occasioned the paralysis of one of his optic nerves.'[10]

He had been injured at the battle of Dettingen in June 1743, when a piece of grapeshot passed through the ample flesh and muscle of his calf. Its entry caused 'so exceedingly wide [an] orifice [as] might have very well admitted a large hen-egg' and another '[not] a jot less considerable' by its exit. The wound healed slowly 'owing to his being constantly on his legs, and scarce ever without his boots on'.[11]

Britons, *behold presented to your View*,
In Contrast, *the* Mock Hero, *and the* true!
Stealing from Rome to Caledonian *Lands*,
The young Italian *trains his slavish Bands*,
But less on these Banditti *builds his Hope*,
Than Beads & Bulls & Blessings *from the* Pope:

His Standard Death, *or* Victory *proclaims*,
His Ensigns Slav'ry, *threat*, & Smithfield Fla
Religion Laws, and Liberty must dye,
But *at* Culloden *see the* Blust'rer *fly*!
Trembling at Distance he the Onset view
Then scuds away, for CUMBERLAND *pursu*

Published according to Act of Parliament, October 16. 1749. by J. Gibson Engraver; in

PART IV: CELEBRATION

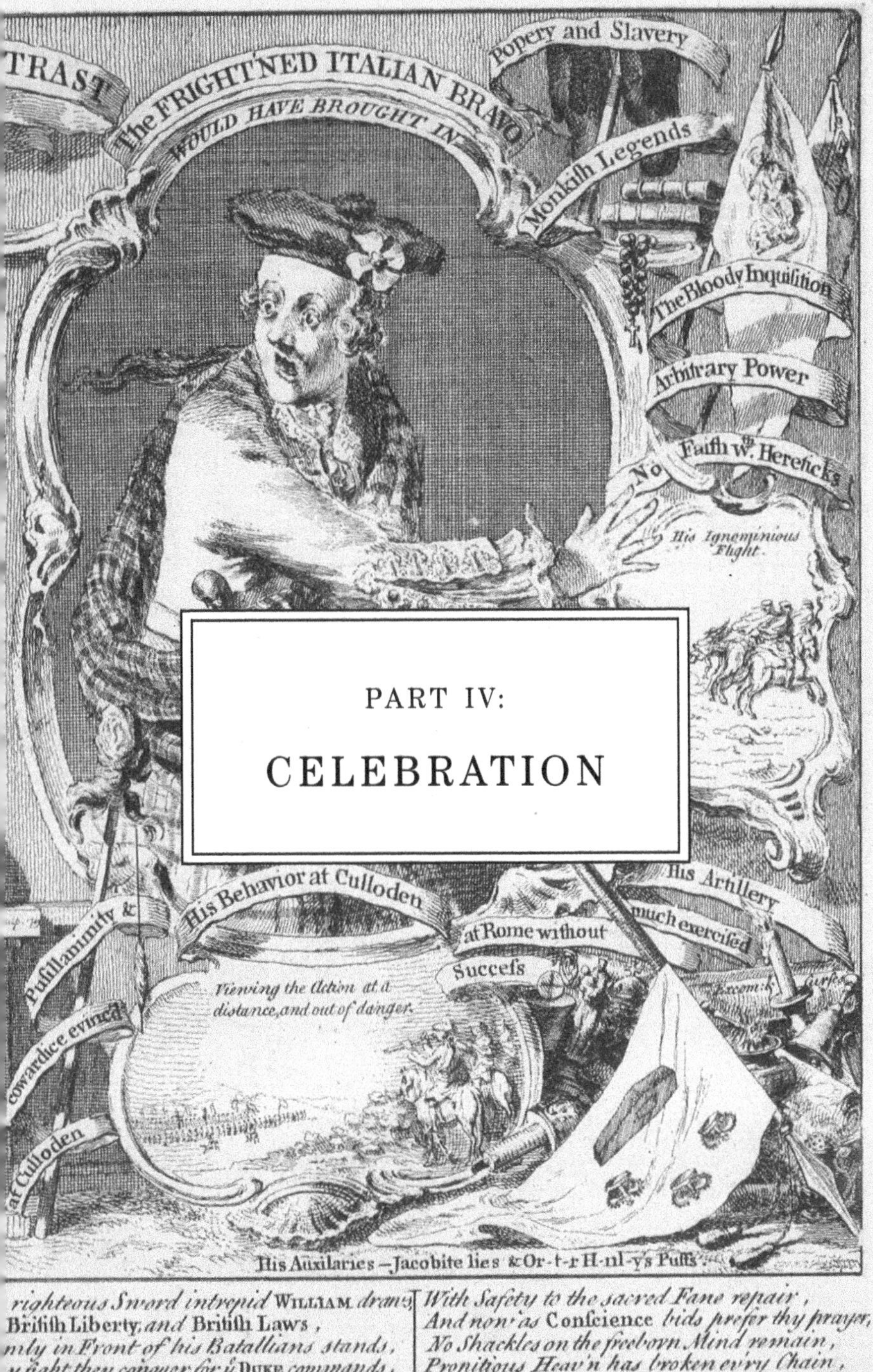

righteous Sword intrepid WILLIAM draws,
British Liberty, and British Laws,
nly in Front of his Batallians stands,
y fight, they conquer, for y[e] DUKE commands,
v, Britain, full Security is thine,
w cultivate the Olive, plant the Vine,

With Safety to the sacred Fane repair,
And now as Conscience bids prefer thy prayer,
No Shackles on the freeborn Mind remain,
Propitious Heav'n has broken ev'ry Chain,
Nor doubts Britannia to maintain her Rights,
Long as a BRUNSWICK rules or WILLIAM fights.

eet near Red Lion Street, Clerkennell. Price Sixpence.

I

THE evening of 15 April 1746 had been one of celebration in the government camp at Nairn. To toast their Royal commander's twenty-fifth birthday 'every Man had a sufficient Quantity of Bisquit, Cheese and Brandy allowed him at the sole Expense of the Duke.'

Earlier in the day a seventeen-year-old civilian, accused of being a Jacobite spy, was hanged. The local Presbyterian minister, Mr Rose, pleaded for clemency, claiming him to be 'but a poor simple Youth . . . deluded away' by the rebels. His Royal Highness, in magnanimous mood, scribbled a reprieve. The condemned was fortunate that execution by hanging more often entailed lingering strangulation than a quick fracture of the neck, and he had been squirming at the end of the rope for ten minutes when his pardon arrived. The executioner cut him down carelessly and he dropped, unconscious, a considerable distance to the ground. A surgeon was on hand to bleed him and being 'young and strong, [the lad] . . . came to Life, though much disordered in his Senses'.[1]

William Augustus, Duke of Cumberland, and sponsor of this act of mercy, was just three and a half months younger than the remote kinsman whose army he was going to destroy the following afternoon.

His Royal Highness's natal day was an anniversary not publicly observed previously. But as he entered 'the 26th year of his age', it was marked by celebrations far beyond his military camp, 'solemnised in a very distinguished manner', and toasted with more varied fare than brandy, biscuit and cheese.[2] Edinburgh – no longer occupied by Prince Charles and his 'Highland bandits'[3], and consequently predominantly Whig in complexion – celebrated 'with the utmost Demonstrations of Joy and Gladness by all Ranks'.[4] It was said that 'the whole Companies of this City have joined to present him with his Freedom in their several Corporations in a Gold Box . . . valued at 150 Guineas.'[5] Bells rang out at eleven o'clock in the morning. At midday there was a discharge of guns from the Castle and platoon firing from Colonel Lee's Regiment drawn up in the Abbey Court. Men-of-war anchored at Leith, and beyond in the roadstead of the Forth, thundered their response. A Grand Ball was held in the Assembly Hall, 'at which a great many Gentlemen and Ladies of Distinction were present', and in taverns across the city the gentlemen of Merchants', Constables' and Crafts' Societies met and 'chearfully drank to his Majesty [the King]'s Health, the Prince and Princess of Wales, the Duke, and all the Royal Family, with many other loyal Healths'. Buildings were illuminated with candles burning in every window, 'very splendid and surpassing'. In the windows of several houses the name *William, Duke of Cumberland* appeared on waxed paper, and 'being curiously illuminate, made a beautiful Appearance'. No lingering Jacobite sympathy was apparent, 'owing chiefly to the Vigilance of the Constables, who caused a Picquet Guard of the Edinburgh Regiment [to] patrole . . . till late at Night . . . by which the Peace of the City was secured, and all Manner of Disorders prevented'. Bonfires proliferated in the streets, the Abbey Court and Castle, and far into the surrounding countryside, 'the Parishes of Ratho and Currie particularly distinguish[ing] themselves'.[6]

In fiercely loyal Glasgow, 'the Musick Bells [of the High Kirk] played two Hours at Noon [and] in the Evening they were again rung.' At the Town Hall toasts were drunk to the Duke, 'Success to his Majesty's Arms, and Disappointment to his Enemies'. University students assembled in the Great Hall of the college.

'Healths were drank; afterwards they repaired to the Balconys, where the Royal Healths were repeated.'[7]

There was more festivity in Newcastle, bells rung, cockades worn, tar barrels burnt, illuminations lit, healths drunk, and 'an uncommon Cheerfulness appear'd in every Countenance.' The 71st Foot 'Leicester Blues', garrisoned in the town, 'fir'd with great Applause in Honour of the Day'. Raised by the Marquess of Granby the previous November, this regiment was destined to see no more belligerent action than this before their disbandment the following August. Ships anchored in the Tyne responded to the Blues' salvoes with firing of their own, 'having all their Flags display'd . . . and drinking loyal Healths'. In the evening there was a Ball that attracted a 'very grand Appearance of Gentlemen and Ladies, [who] were elegantly entertain'd at the Expense of the Military Officers in Town'. Twenty miles away to the west, at Hexham, Lancelot Allgood, High Sheriff of Northumberland, gave a lavish dinner to the local gentry and afterwards repaired to the market cross where he dispensed 'a great Quantity of Liquor to the Populace [and] all loyal Healths were drank'. The evening concluded with 'Ringing of Bells, Bonfires, Illuminations, &c.'[8]

Celebration of the Royal birthday was the more fervent for knowing that its object was on campaign in defence not only of his father's throne, but of what many perceived to be the threatened Protestant faith. In the Irish town of Derry – memories of earlier sectarian struggle, then as now, fresh – the local militia marched, carrying the Duke's picture before them 'in Order to rouse up their minds by the Image of him who is hazarding his Person for their Religion and Liberties'. Following a revival of *The Distressed Mother** in Dublin, David Garrick declaimed an Epilogue in honour of the royal birthday. Written by a 'person stiling himself the FARMER',[9] it made specific reference to the national crisis, and concluded with the lines:

This Day is sacred to the Martial Boy;
The Morrow shall a diff'rent Strain require,

* A translation, by Ambrose Phillips, of Racine's *Andromaque*.

When . . . all Delights retire,
And (a long Polar Night of Grief begun)
Thy Soul shall sigh for its returning Sun.[10]

Neither Garrick nor his Irish audience at the Theatre Royal in Smock Alley could have known that in little more than twelve hours 'the Martial Boy' would indeed engage his troops in the decisive battle of that crisis, bringing widespread civilian depredation across the Highlands – if not quite the predicted 'long Polar Night of Grief' – in its aftermath.

II

FOUR months earlier, the insurgency in retreat from its abortive attempt on London – hounded by the armies of Cumberland and Wade – it was only a matter of time before the denouement. And as His Majesty's troops marched north a 'veteran Scheme' raised funds to supply them with flannel waistcoats, woollen socks and other comforts. On 9 December the entire takings of a performance of *The Recruiting Officer* at Drury Lane were donated to that end, and a Prologue, specially written for the occasion, reminded the audience of a soldier's claim to their generosity:

For you his unremitted Zeal defies
The changeful Seasons, and inclement Skies;
With painful Steps the tedious March endures,
And gives his own Repose to purchase yours.

The final couplets expressed soon to be familiar sentiments of prayer and praise for the King's youngest son:

O! thou, who dost o'er human Acts preside,
If Britain is thy Care, be WILLIAM's Guide;
The noble Youth, whom ev'ry eye approves
Each tongue applauds, and ev'ry Soldier loves;
In the dire Conflict may thy Power afford

Strength to his Arm, and Vict'ry to his Sword:
On Freedom's Basis may he fix the Throne,
And add new Lustre to his Father's Crown.[1]

Not to be outdone in generosity by its rival, the Theatre Royal, Covent Garden presented the fund with 'the whole Receipt' from John Gay's *The Beggar's Opera* on the 14th, 16th and 17th December. The perennially popular entertainment took in the highly respectable sum of £602 7s. 'Every Comedian play'd Gratis,' the public was assured afterwards, 'and the Tallow-Chandler that furnishes the House, gave all the Candles used the three Nights' without charge.[2]

Songwriters and composers, meanwhile, had already been at work providing suitably melodic accompaniment to the looked-for victory. George Frideric Handel had stiffened the resolve of Michael Hughes, and other Gentlemen Volunteers raised by the City of London, with a spritely and bellicose 'Chorus Song' to words by John Lockman:

Stand round, my brave boys, with heart, and with voice
And all in full chorus agree;
We'll fight for our King, and as loyally sing,
And let the world know we'll be free.
The rebels shall fly, as with shouts we draw nigh,
And echo shall victory ring;
Then safe from alarms, we'll rest on our arms,
And chorus it long live the King . . .
With hearts firm and stout, we'll repel the bold rout,
And follow fair Liberty's call;
We'll rush on the foe, and deal death in each blow,
Till conquest and honour crown all.

The third verse was a reminder of why the City merchants had raised their militia: the rewards expected, in town and country, when this emergency and its disruption to trade had been brought to an end by force of arms:

Then commerce once more, shall bring wealth to our shore,
And plenty and peace bless the isle;
The peasant shall quaff off his bowl with a laugh,
And reap the sweet fruits of his toil.

'Stand Round My Brave Boys' ended in the sentimental tradition of pastoral poetry – blushing shepherdess reunited with faithful swain:

Kind love shall repay the fatigues of the day,
And melt us to softer alarms;
Coy *Phillis* shall burn, at her soldier's return,
And bless the brave youth in her arms.

The song had been given its first performance 'by Mr. LOWE and others' at the Theatre Royal, Drury Lane on 14 November, following a revival of Vanbrugh's *The Relapse*, partly compensating for that fifty-year-old comedy's deficiency of military interest. It was greeted 'with universal Applause' and reprised the following night, 'By particular Desire'.[3]

The following month, at the rival playhouse in Covent Garden, principal singer John Beard performed 'A LOYAL SONG' to a traditional air and refrain:

From barren *Caledonian* lands,
Where famine, uncontroul'd commands;
The rebel Clans, in search of prey,
Come over the hills and far away.[4]

The predictable targets of its propaganda were, 'perjur'd traitors, dupes to Rome', the 'Popish priests', and the 'weak, deceiv'd, believing fool' ruled by them, as well as the predatory Highlanders in retreat. The unknown librettist denied the Jacobite cause even a vestige of honour or integrity:

Regardless, whether wrong or right,
For booty not for fame they fight,

Banditti like, they storm, they slay,
They plunder, rob, and run away.

On 8 January, Mr Beard gave the first performance of another 'new English Ballad', accompanied by seven named singers – including the composer's wife – and others from the Covent Garden company.[5] It can be assumed that this was a catchpenny attempt to field a song to rival the popularity of 'God Save the King', by then being sung as often in the streets as from the stage. However, despite four subsequent performances, it achieved no lasting fame, and neither the lyrics to 'The English Hero's Welcome Home' nor John Frederick Lampe's music have survived.

Topical songs were written and published that received no widespread public performance on the stage. A notable example was yet another 'Loyal SONG' – to the tune of *Lilliburlero* – advertised as 'proper to be sung at all merry Meetings'. Its six rhyming couplets carried a mischievous irony developed through a series of paradoxes:

O Brother Sawney, hear you the News,
An Army's just coming without any Shoes
The Pope sends us over a bonny brisk Lad,
Who to court English Favour wears a Scotch Plad.
A Protestant Church from Rome doth advance,
And what is more rare, he brings Freedom from France.
If this should surprize, there is News stranger yet,
He brings Highland Money to pay England's Debt.
You must take it in Coin which the Country affords,
Instead of broad Pieces, he pays with broad Swords.
And sure this is paying you in the best Ore,
For who once is thus paid will never want more.

Although its cleverness may have been at odds with the more straightforward sentiments expected from such productions, the wit was more than blunted by a thumping choral refrain, orchestrated for the accompaniment of pewter tankard on tavern table:

Twang 'em, we'll bang 'em, and hang 'em up all.
To Arms, to Arms,
Brave Boys, to Arms!
A true English Cause for your Courage doth call,
Court, Country and City,
Against a Banditti.
Twang'em, we'll bang 'em, and hang 'em up all.

Printed in the first issue of *The True Patriot* on 5 November 1745 it was written – along with the rest of that weekly paper – by Henry Fielding. Journalist, satirist, novelist and Whig, Fielding can also be credited with the first, albeit necessarily incomplete, '*History of the present Rebellion in SCOTLAND*.' The forty-seven page pamphlet, priced at one shilling, provided a record of the insurrection 'From the Departure of the Pretender's Son from Rome, down to the present Time [with] a full Account of the Conduct of this Invader, from his first Arrival in Scotland; with . . . a very particular Relation of the Battle of Preston[pans].'[6]

The *History* was published a fortnight after that battle and in the final paragraph Fielding issued a direct call to arms. Cope's regular army having been found wanting in the recent debacle, 'every Man in this Kingdom is to exert himself . . . as far as Health, Strength, and Age will permit.' It was an appeal to men like Alexander Carlyle, William Corse and Michael Hughes – volunteers and militiamen – even to such as John Knox Witherspoon and his parish beadle, that 'however foreign his Way of Life may have been to the Exercise of Arms, to take them up, and enure himself to them'. The national emergency was not a matter of party political allegiance – of Whig versus Tory – nor was it a cause concerning the King only:

> Your Religion, my Countrymen, your Laws, your Liberties, your Lives, the Safety of your Wives and Children; THE WHOLE is in Danger, and for God Almighty's Sake! Lose not a Moment in ARMING YOURSELVES for their Preservation.

Fielding assured the loyal and patriotic Briton in suitably emphatic capitals, that nothing less than 'HIS ALL IS AT STAKE'.[7]

On 28 September the *General Advertiser*'s front page made plain the paper's political and religious affiliation in the current crisis. Down the right and left margins ran three slogans: 'No Pretender', 'No Popery', and 'No Slavery'. Along the bottom of the page were two more. 'No Arbitrary Power' reflected widespread fear of an autocratic Catholic monarchy – like that of France – unchecked by Parliament. Finally, the spectre of British subjects reduced to the level of a downtrodden, *sabot*-wearing, Gallic underclass was raised by the slogan 'No Wooden Shoes'.

Towards 5 November, the failure of an earlier attempt to impose a Catholic monarch on the English throne was celebrated in Deptford with elaborate topicality. Organised by 'a Gentleman . . . remarkable for the generous and ingenious Diversion he gives his Neighbours upon all loyal Occasions', it consisted of a procession led by 'A Highlander, in his proper Dress, carrying on a Pole a Pair of Wooden Shoes, with [the] Motto, *The newest Make from Paris.*' Next came 'A Jesuit . . . carrying on the Point of a flaming Sword, a Banner [reading] *Inquisition, Flames and Damnation*'. He was followed by two flagellant monks with knotted ropes, beads and crucifixes. 'One of them bore on a high Pole, a Bell, Mass-book, and Candle, to curse the British Nation with.' The other carried a bill of fare for remitting sins:

> INDULGENCIES *cheap as Dirt.*
> Murder, ——— Nine Pence.
> Adultery, ——— Nine Pence Halfpenny.
> Reading the Bible, — A Thousand Pounds.
> Fornication, ——- Four Pence Halfpenny Farthing.
> Perjury, ——— Nothing at all.
> Rebellion, ——- A Reward . . . of thirteen Pence Halfpenny Scots Money.

An effigy of 'The Pretender' came next, 'with a green Ribbon, Nosegay of Thistles . . . riding upon an Ass, supported by a

Frenchman on the Right and a Spaniard on the Left, each dressed to the Height of the newest Modes from Paris and Madrid'. The Pope, in effigy, brought up the rear, 'riding upon his Bull'. The procession moved through the Deptford streets accompanied by 'all sorts of rough Music', the 'several Actors play'd their Parts with great Drollery', and the monks rattled their money boxes as they took collections from spectators. In the evening 'Pope and Pretender' were burnt 'according to Custom', having been first 'confess'd, absolv'd, and purged with Holy-Water, by the Jesuit'. As the bonfire blazed, the troubling irony might have occurred to onlookers that a Stuart claimant to the throne was being burned in effigy to celebrate his direct Royal Stuart forebear's preservation from the gunpowder conspiracy of 1605. But if it did their gaiety was undiminished, and the night's entertainment ended with 'Illuminations, and grand Fireworks, and the Song of *God save the King*'.[8]

*

As the tide turned against the insurgency and the Jacobite army retreated to a safe distance across the Scottish border, Italian opera became again admissible in London, if harnessed to the patriotic cause by a morally uplifting fable. The King's Theatre's new house composer Christoph Willibald Gluck obliged on 7 January 1746 with a setting of five arias and a duet by the librettist Francesco Vanneschi.

The main action concerned an insurrection of titans or giants to wrest control of heaven from the Olympian gods. A four-sided romantic intrigue involving Jupiter, Mars and two goddesses formed the subplot, 'Juno's Jealousy, and Jupiter's Amour with Iris [being] introduc'd merely as Episodes'. The part of Jupiter was taken by the castrato Monticelli, damned with faint praise by the contemporary music historian Charles Burney, as having 'a style of singing . . . suitable to his voice and powers'. Giuseppe Jozzi, another castrato – 'a good musician with little voice' – appeared as Mars. La Signora Pompeati, with 'such a masculine and violent manner of singing that few female symptoms were perceptible', took the role of Iris, while Signora Imer, who 'never surpassed mediocrity in voice, taste, or action', sang Juno. Advertisements promised 'DANCES and other Decorations Entirely New'. Mr Burney recalled that the dances, performed by the 'charming Violetta', later to become the wife of David Garrick, 'were much more applauded than the songs'.[9]

The piece was entitled *La caduta de' giganti* – Downfall of the Giants – and ran for six performances, on Tuesdays and Saturdays throughout January. On one occasion the Duke of Cumberland, 'to whom the whole was written and composed', was in attendance.[10] He had recently returned to London from Carlisle 'in perfect Health to the general Joy of all true Englishmen', and would shortly depart again for the north to take overall command of his father's army from General Hawley, following that gentleman's worsting at Falkirk. Neither Cumberland nor the rest of the audience would have been left in doubt as to the allegorical significance of the action on stage – subtitled *La ribellione punita* – Rebellion Punished – and what was confidently expected of him in the forthcoming military campaign. Those without Italian might have read the 'Argument' in the bilingual libretto, on sale for a shilling:

> The Giants having rebell'd in order to dethrone Jupiter, in the Skies, and deprive the other Gods of their Freedom; whilst they are piling Mountain upon Mountain, Jupiter darts Thunder from Olympus, and takes due Vengeance on their daring Attempt; by burying them under the ruins of the Mountains they had rais'd.[11]

During the first part of the opera, Mars sang deploring the threatened consequences to the gods of the giants' rebellion, consequences familiar to those fearful of a Catholic Stuart king regaining the throne:

> For should [the] rebel-foes (avert it fate!)
> Succeed, our privileges soon were lost:

Jove drove from his bright throne, th'ethereal Essence
Wou'd sink to slavery, and rise no more.[12]

And if a conflict between giants and gods still seemed remote from the current state of British affairs, Sig. Vanneschi's text of the final chorus* was very loosely translated in the printed libretto, making the connection explicit for the King's Theatre audience:

Hail, Liberty! Without thy charms,
The Brightest regions are unblest. —
O! keep thine ALBION from alarms,
And lull her pangs to balmy rest.

On the night that the hoped-for deliverer of this happy state attended, applause would have been directed more loudly at Cumberland's box than at the singers on stage. Notwithstanding his army's defeat by the French at Fontenoy the previous May, and the indecisive engagement at Clifton more recently, he was by year's end the nation's darling.

On 30 December, following a ten-day siege, he had recaptured Carlisle Castle from a Jacobite garrison comprising a hundred and thirteen of the so-called 'Manchester Regiment', and about 250 Lowland Scots. Despite a report that 'the Musket-Balls flew like Hailstones', Cumberland's army had suffered only four men wounded, although he had reciprocated by having four Jacobite captives hanged within sight of the walls.[13] When the garrison showed a white flag of capitulation, he refused them any concession for their surrender beyond an assurance 'That they shall not be put to the Sword but be reserv'd for the King's Pleasure'.[14] That pleasure would prove to entail particularly ferocious treatment towards the predominantly English – and therefore deemed doubly treacherous – Manchester Regiment. Most officers and sergeants were executed for treason and a high proportion of

* Non vi è piacer perfetto
Non vi è grandeza, onore
Che alletti, o piaccia al Core,
Senza la Libertà.

other ranks either transported as 'indentured servants' to the West Indies or presumed dead of disease in captivity. On his first night in Carlisle the conqueror wrote that 'we may have the happiness to say that this part of the kingdom is clear of all the rebels.'[15] This as yet solitary, unequivocal military achievement of the Duke's would be lauded in late February with an elaborate panegyric, its Pindaric verse form befitting a subject of exceptional heroism.

Hailing his 'martial Prowess' at the battle of Dettingen – nominally his father's victory – and without mention of Fontenoy, which no degree of hyperbole could raise to anything more than an honourable defeat, the poem reached the meat of its subject in the seventh stanza. If the form owed a debt to Pindar, the anonymous poet's apocalyptic evocation of the forces of insurrection bore comparison with Milton:

REBELLION from her native Realms of Night
Disclos'd her baleful Head to mortal View,
And, winging upwards her impetuous Flight,
On *Scotia*'s Hills her *Stygian* Trumpet blew . . .
OBSERVANT of her Call, disgusted PRIDE,
RAGE, RASHNESS, RAPINE in her Van appear,
Fell SUPERSTITION glitters at her Side,
And PERSECUTION thunders in the Rear.

Five stanzas later – the 'plund'ring Host' having been put to flight, 'scared by WILLIAM's thund'ring Arm' – the Duke's victory was told in a single couplet:

To thee, *Carlisle!* long exercis'd in Woe,
He brought the wish'd Relief, and freed thee from the Foe.

More lines were devoted to the celebration than to the success:

The Victor then this generous Labour o'er,
Comes crown'd with Laurels thro' the grateful Land
While Crouds, oppress'd by Lawless Pow'r before,
With deaf'ning Shouts confess his saving Hand.[16]

His journey to London was anticipated by the citizens of Manchester, eager to celebrate the relief of Carlisle, to demonstrate their 'Zeal, Respect and Loyalty' and to hoot the 'Pretender burnt in effigy with target and sword'.[17] The fate of the unfortunate Manchester Regiment disregarded, the welcome given to the Jacobite army as it marched south only a month earlier was apparently forgotten.

Two months prior to the bloody victory that would define him, *Ode on the Success of His Royal Highness, the Duke of Cumberland* ended, perforce, with only anticipated triumph:

For him the Fair shall weave the laureate Wreath:
For him the Swains in festive Accents sing:
For him the Canvas shall be taught to breathe:
For him each Artist wake the vocal String.
But chief the Poets in harmonious Verse,
That lifts the Patriot to the realms above,
His god-like Acts, and Triumphs shall rehearse.

An enterprising manufacturer was already advertising the minting of a medal in his honour and inviting orders from 'Gentlemen and Ladies desirous of the first Impression', at £2 10s for gold, five shillings for silver and 'some in Metal', though a later announcement in the same newspaper carried a qualification that 'The Price of the Gold ones, as mentioned . . . was a Mistake.'[18]

Medals of varying quality commemorated the fall of Carlisle. One, embossed DUKE OF CUMBER for want of space, pictured the hero as a sprightly sword-wielding figure on a rearing horse. The reverse showed a body being cut down from a gallows, two figures kneeling below, MORE REBELS A COMEING at the rim. Another had three tartan-clad captives doffing their hats to a similar horseman pointing with his sword as if to prison ship, gaol or gibbet: REBELION JUSTLY REWARDED AT CARLILE DEC 1745. Yet another featured a warrior in classical helmet and armour bearing a shield embossed with the King's profile, putting the seven-headed hydra to flight: FOR MY

FATHER AND COUNTRY, and CARLILE REDUCED AND REBELS FLEW.

*

A week after the *General Advertiser* reported the imminent departure of the Duke to 'quell the present unnatural Rebellion'[19] it published a poem on the subject by Thomas Gibbons, author of a foaming anti-Papist diatribe called *Britannia's Alarm*.[20] His latest effort was similarly vindictive. Having caused the Jacobite army's retreat by dint of his 'dreaded Sight' alone, the 'Illustrious Youth' was urged north to consolidate its defeat in battle:

> Thither, O! thither, bend thy Glorious Way,
> On *Scotia*'s Hills let *British* Standards play,
> Unlock the Cannons, bid the Bombs be hurl'd,
> To crush the Scoundrel Rabble of the World.

That end accomplished, the 'murd'rous Imp of *France* and *Rome*', their leader, was to be either forced back into exile, perish in battle, or else – condemned to a traitor's death – 'stain the Crimson Ax, and drench the thirsty Block'.[21]

Celebrations accompanied the Duke north. Approaching Newcastle he saw how readily passionate acclamation could turn to violence. Earlier in the evening a large building on the southern outskirts known to contain a Catholic place of worship had attracted an enraged mob who 'destroy'd and broke every Thing' in both chapel and house, gutting them of 'Pictures, Images and Furniture', before setting the whole establishment on fire. 'House and Appurtenances,' a witness reported, 'being vastly large, it was a terrible Sight, and was very near the Height of the Blaze, when the Duke pass'd by.'[22] More conventionally illuminated, Newcastle itself received him 'with the greatest Demonstrations of Joy and Loyalty imaginable', although even there the rule of the mob was observed 'and every House that had not Candles lighted was sure to have its Windows broke'. When the Duke departed six hours later, all 115 of the town's guns thundering in salute, and the charred ruins of the 'Mass-House' still smoking, he left orders with the commander of troops quartered nearby 'to suppress immediately any Tumults or Mobbing if there should be occasion'.[23]

The conflagration south of Newcastle was not an isolated incident. Only a week before, on 22 January, a 'Popish Mass-House' in Sunderland was attacked by 'a Number of People, consisting chiefly of Sailors'. It was ten o'clock on a Wednesday morning and there were 'several People at Prayers, and a Couple to be married'. All fled with Father Hankins, their priest. 'The Sailors immediately pull'd down their Altar and crucifix, together with all the Seats, the Priest's Robes, all their [prayer] Books, the Furniture, and every individual Thing in the Room, and burnt them in a Fire in the Street made for that Purpose; and also a large Library of Books and papers belonging to the Priest.'[24]

A month earlier, what began as casual vandalism escalated to similarly comprehensive destruction in the North Yorkshire town of Stokesley. When a group of local youths pulled some tiles off the roof of a Catholic chapel – damage it was said amounting to about eleven shillings – the minister complained to the Constable and on Christmas Day an arrest was made 'of one of the Boys (a Sailor) who had been the most active in the Affair'. The boy's acquaintances, grown to a mob of over two hundred, 'march'd in Order (with Drums beating, and Colours flying)' to demand his release. Mr Skottowe, the Constable, discharged his prisoner with 'a gentle Reprimand' and the company marched to the village of Ayton where, 'beating up for Volunteers for his Majesty's Service', about thirty or forty more were recruited. Returning to Stokesley they fixed their colours to the market cross and lit several large fires in preparation for what was to follow. They then dealt with the chapel. Climbing onto the roof they stripped off all the tiles, broke down the ceiling and descended inside, 'pull'd it all to Pieces, and toss'd the Things out of the Windows into the Yard'. When it was completely gutted – altar, seats, pews, even the doors removed and the wainscotting ripped away – they bore the combustible wreckage back to the cross and proceeded to burn it. The entire operation was carried out with the utmost efficiency and, bizarrely, in its latter stages, a sense of theatre. One of the plunderers, who had dressed himself in the priest's vestments and cap, and carried a bishop's mitre in his hand, mounted the cross and addressed the flamelit assembly: 'In Consideration of the great Service they had done to their king and Country, in destroying the Mass-House that Day, he presum'd from the great Authority he was then invested with, to absolve them from all their past Sins, but exhorted them for the future to lead a peaceable and godly Life.'

Acclaimed with 'a great Huzza, God save King George, and down with the Mass', he descended, threw off the vestment and cap and tossed them, with the mitre, into the fire. When everything that had been dragged from the chapel had been consumed, the crowd 'dispersed, and went to their respective Homes'.[25]

*

When the Duke arrived in Edinburgh on 30 January the city greeted him as it had greeted General Hawley's army earlier in the month. 'It was illuminated, the Streets crowded with Flambeaux, and lined with Militia, the Windows with Women, the Mob huzzaing, and destroying the Windows that would not afford light, the Cannon-Gate, Cow-Gate, High-Street, the Lawn Market, Bow and Grass-Market . . . fill'd with Lights, and the Bells ringing.'[26]

Candles were lit in the windows of both Whig and Jacobite, of Protestant and Catholic alike, dissenting households deeming it safer to do so than otherwise. But the mob smashed those of known Jacobites and Catholics regardless of their illuminations and, as a result, 'not a Foot of Glass [was] to be had at any Price; so that many Families [were] starving of Cold.'

At Holyroodhouse – it being his custom to occupy any headquarters previously occupied by his enemy* – the Duke had a

* He had done so at Penrith and would again in the Dowager Lady MacIntosh's home at Inverness, and in Culloden House.

conference with Generals Hawley and Huske and the rest of his principal officers, 'who all appeared in Boots' as befitted a council of war. He later received a delegation of clergy and gave a speech thanking them for their 'Zeal and Loyalty'. The loyal ladies of the town also presented their compliments, 'richly dress'd'. One young woman, a Miss Car or Keir, had taken considerable trouble and 'made a very fine Appearance' when introduced. At the top of her stays, drawing his eye to that part of the bodice covering her breasts, was a lavishly embroidered crown, and beneath it, 'in Letters extremely plain to be seen', WILLIAM DUKE OF CUMBERLAND. To left and right of the crown were the words 'Britain's Hero'.[27]

Two months after Cumberland's departure from Edinburgh he was belatedly honoured in absentia by the 'Chirurgeon [or Surgeon] Apothecaries' of that city. 'As the Best evidence . . . of their Dutiful Respect and sincere Acknowledgement for his coming to this part of the Kingdom, to maintain, protect and Defend our Valuable Constitution of Church and State most unjustly and unreasonably attacked by the present Rebellion, [he was admitted as] a free Surgeon Apothecary of their Corporation, To Enjoy all the Rights and Priveleges thereof.'

Three weeks before the battle that would consign him to posterity as 'Butcher Cumberland', therefore, he was inducted as an honorary member of another bloody trade, and that recognition, on vellum, was 'inclosed in a Gold box properly Ornamented'.[28]

*

As the Duke of Cumberland began his expedition into Scotland, and as *La caduta de' giganti* was receiving its final performances at the King's Theatre, Handel was preparing to catch the national mood with a three-part oratorio for the Theatre Royal, Covent Garden.

A fast-working musical journeyman, Handel was not averse to plundering previously applauded tunes – his own as well as others'

– to fill the programme, and the text by Newburgh Hamilton, compiled from Milton's psalm translations and Spenser's 'Hymne of Heavenly Beautie', was likewise variegated. Indeed, it was 'an inconceivable jumble', declared Charles Jennens, Handel's former librettist and a not entirely disinterested critic of his successor, 'a Chaos extracted from Order by the most absurd of all Blockheads, who like the Devil takes delight in defacing the Beauties of Creation. The difference is that one does it from malice, the other from pure Stupidity.[29]

The combined efforts of composer and collaborator ensured this 'Oratorio of Shreds and Patches' made rapid progress and seemed likely to precede the anticipated outcome of Cumberland's Scottish campaign that it was intended to honour. ''Tis a triumph for a Victory not yet gain'd', Jennens remarked in a letter of 3 February, '& if the Duke does not make haste, it may not be gain'd at the time of performance.' Since word of the government army's defeat at Falkirk had arrived in the capital only ten days earlier, His Royal Highness's victory must have seemed considerably overdue and the oratorio more a truculent bolstering of morale in time of crisis than a celebration. 'Fly from the threat'ning vengeance, fly!' one chorus exhorts the enemy:

E'er 'tis too late,
Avoid your fate:
The bolt once launch'd, ye surely die.[30]

A clergyman who attended one of the rehearsals wrote that the libretto was 'expressive of the rebels' flight and our pursuit of them',[31] but marking no other specifically decisive occasion at the time of its premiere on 14 February the piece would be billed generically and without further commitment: *A New Occasional Oratorio*.

As with Handel's earlier oratorios, *Deborah*, *Israel in Egypt*, *Samson*,[32] – all derived from Old Testament scriptural narrative and all pillaged for this his latest – the Israelites' struggle against their variously Canaanite, Egyptian or Philistine oppressors was to be interpreted as a struggle against Papist tyranny. And so for loyal Whigs in the Theatre-Royal's audience, God's chosen people were British and Jehovah a Protestant god – as well as a defender of the Hanoverian dynasty:

May God, from whom all mercies spring,
Bless the true church, and save the king![33]

Following the first two parts, comprising defiant chorus, aria and recitative, urging divine vengeance on the King's enemies, national salvation was heralded in the third by the German-born bass, Henry Reinhold:

The sword that's drawn in virtue's cause
To guard our country and its laws;
Friend, parent, children dear,
To guide its edge we Heaven invoke;
Rebellion falls beneath the stroke,
And joy succeeds the fear.
Millions unborn shall bless the hand
That gave deliv'rance to the land.[34]

The audience left the theatre roused by music taken from 'Zadok the Priest', the anthem Handel had written for George II's coronation of 1727:

Blessed are all they that fear the Lord.
God save the King, long live the King,
May the King live forever!
Amen, Alleluia.[35]

*

On 3 March – one month after the *Occasional Oratorio*'s first performance and with the national emergency still far from resolved – a less elevated entertainment was staged at London's other licensed playhouse, in Drury Lane. The pantomime *Harlequin Incendiary, or Columbine Cameron* was the first theatrical work which overtly referred to, and ridiculed, the Jacobite insurgency, in other than allegorical terms. Accompanied by Thomas Arne's musical score – which has not survived – its action concerned the farcical chaos wrought by a demon sent into Scotland, disguised as Harlequin, with orders from both Pope and Devil, to 'Bid Faction and Rebellion grow [and] spread contagious Evil'. The demon's infernal title – 'Prince of Mischief' – invited comparison with the incendiary of rebellion himself, Prince Charles Edward Stuart, and, dressed in Harlequin's chequered costume, more explicitly with the tartan clad 'Pretender' of crude satirical prints.

By *commedia dell'arte* tradition, Harlequin's fixed purpose was his pursuit of the apple-cheeked Columbine. 'Court the Fair to thy Arms', he is told by the Devil:

They are ever to Folly inclin'd;
Since first they were made,
It has still been their Trade,
To help us in cheating Mankind.

Harlequin's arrival in Edinburgh and encounter with his Columbine – Cameron by name – gave the pantomime its subtitle and provided the knowing audience with a further connection to the Jacobite leader. Jennie, or Jeannie, Cameron is said to have been present when the Prince raised his standard at Glenfinnan. She was described then as 'a widow nearer 50 than 40 years of age . . . a genteel, well-look'd, handsome woman, with a pair of pretty eyes, and hair as black as jet . . . of a very sprightly genius, and . . . very agreeable in conversation.'[36] However, she acquired unwanted notoriety through a single – probably spurious – anecdote published by the *General Evening Post* in mid December. She was, by this account, 'the Niece of a Person of some Fashion in the Highlands, . . . sent by her Uncle to pay his Compliments to the young Pretender, on his March from Lochaber to Perth.' She brought with her 'a considerable Quantity of Cattle, some Usquebaugh [whisky], and other little Presents'. When she arrived in the Jacobite camp, 'She jumped off her Horse, and told [the Prince] with great Frankness, that she came like the Queen of Sheba, to partake of the Wisdom of Solomon: He answered, and thou shalt, my Dear, partake of all that Solomon is Master of. – He took her in his Arms, and retired with her into his Tent, and were there some Time alone; the rest . . . we are to guess.'[37]

That whiff of sexual scandal proved irresistible to the popular press and its readership. Later she was said to have 'very assiduously ministered unto [the Prince]' when he was sick during the retreat from Derby, and in subsequent references variously described as 'the young Pretender's Favorite', 'the celebrated Jenny Cameron', or 'that Jenny Cameron, who has been of late so much talked of'.[38]

An allegorical scene in the published text of *Harlequin Incendiary,* had Britannia extolling past practitioners of the Arts and Sciences – Wren, Newton, Pope and Purcell – while anticipating 'The Glories [yet] to record of George's Reign'. She is interrupted by the 'Genius of England', with news of conspiracy hatched by 'Rebellious *Scots* . . . treach'rous *Rome* . . . *Spanish* Pride, and *Gallic* Perfidy'. Undaunted, arrayed in 'a small pasteboard helmet, silvered, with a plume or feather, . . . the hair long and flowing, a large full silk robe, either white or red, and a spear',[39] Britannia would have moved to the front of the stage, promising salvation and rallying support from gallery, box and pit:

Ye Friends to Freedom, swiftly take Alarm,
And bravely for your glorious Monarch arm;
To lead you on, behold a *Royal Youth*
Burns to employ you in the Cause of truth;
His virtuous Labour Victory secures,
Danger and Glory his, Protection yours.

The Drury Lane audience, however, was denied this evocation of the Duke of Cumberland and stirring appeal to its patriotism, the entire scene being 'left out on account of the Length of the Entertainment'. The management no doubt assumed its patrons would be impatient for the comic business of pantomime to begin. This derived from Harlequin's courtship of Columbine by frustrating a trio of her suitors through a series of tricks and theatrical 'transformations'. A fashionable beau was changed to a swineherd, an elderly miser to a suckling infant, and a Scottish laird entering a *bagnio* – or bathhouse-cum-brothel – to keep an assignation, only to have it burst into flames and himself drenched by water from a bookseller's stall transformed into a fire engine. All three rivals were swindled of money and goods by the mercenary Columbine. Harlequin's campaign to win her is only challenged when 'The Pretender and his Party' enter and she, 'with all the affection of *Jenny Cameron*, embraces and receives him'. The slighted Harlequin prepares his final revenge by promising the other suitors that all will be restored to them 'provided they'll join the Pretender's Cause'. At this moment a Standard rises – recalling Glenfinnan – emblazoned with the three crowns, of England, Ireland and Scotland, and a coffin.

A pastoral scene – for the sole purpose of carrying a romantic duet, and barely related to anything that had gone before or that was to follow – had the shepherdess Amoret bidding farewell to her lover Thirsis as he departs for the war,

> To drive Invaders from our injur'd Shore,
> And make Rebellion to [our] Valour yield.

The decisive confrontation – promised by the Duke of Cumberland, anticipated with such eagerness and anxiety by the nation – was passed over in a single tableau showing the victory won: 'A Noise of a Battle. Several English Soldiers plundering a Waggon belonging to *Glenbucket*'s Regiment.' A final magical transformation was needed to resolve the action, give rebellion its just desert and return the Harlequin to hell. This stage direction, like the last, promised more spectacle in production than appeared in perfunctory print:

> Scene: An *English Palace.*
> A Party of Scotch, headed by the Pretender, rush in, Sword in Hand; the Palace immediately changes into a Prison, where *Harlequin* leaves them, and sinks.

Before the audience left the theatre, they were roused by a finale in which the entire company, including Britannia, Fame and Victory, appeared in 'a beautiful Garden'. The band struck up an air by the house composer, Mr Arne, and Britannia sang:

> To *William's* Name
> The Trump of Fame
> Her sprightly Sounds shall raise,
> Whilst all around
> The Hills resound,
> And Echo tells his Praise.

With so many songs in his honour much was expected of the Duke of Cumberland. Final victory could not be long coming; but until then all anyone could do was join in the chorus and sing:

> With George our Defender we ever will join,
> For the Voice of the People's the true Right divine;
> Thro' Dangers to Safety brave William shall guide,
> And our Hearts, Swords, and Fortunes be still on his Side.

*

On 31 March 1746, the patrons of the New Wells, Clerkenwell, witnessed the first performance of 'a New Entertainment of Musick' reflecting the national emergency rapidly approaching its crisis: an allegorical Masque entitled *Britannia Rediviva; or Courage and Liberty*.

After the acrobatic 'USUAL DIVERSIONS', singing by various members of the company, and 'MR BATT PLATT, the Original Mad Tom', the curtain rose on 'a desolate Part of the Island of *Britain*, full of Rocks and dismal Caverns', a setting no one in the audience could mistake for anywhere but Scotland. Costumed as the Genius of England, Miss Vaux came forward 'in a dejected Manner' and bemoaned the state of her northern province in solemn recitative:

Unaw'd *Rebellion*, with audacious Heat,
Attempts to seize fair *Freedom*'s last Retreat;
And furious *Rapine*, broke from Hell, again
With wolfish *Rage* affrights the Village Swain.

The mood lightened with a change of scene to 'the Prospect of a delightful Country' as – accompanied by Mr Brett's Courage – Miss Lincoln made her entrance in the role of Liberty. Urging England to 'droop no more', she reviled 'The wretched, mean, enervate Race' of Scots and promised to 'lash with Terror and Affright / These pilf'ring Dastards to the Realms of Night'. An aria from Mr Brett followed:

Come, ye Sons of *Liberty*,
Come in haste, and follow me;
My nimble Spirits all rejoice
To hear the sprightly Trumpets Voice.
I come, I come;
Strike the Drum.
Hence, Intruders! hence! begone!
Courage leads the Britons on.

Following a 'Grand MARTIAL DANCE' there was an interval during which *The Fortunate Volunteer; or, the Amours of Harlequin* was performed, 'Scenes, Machines, Musick and Dresses, being entirely New', and Miss Lincoln making a swift costume change from *Liberty* to appear as Columbine. No script for this pantomime has survived and the narrative content is unknown, although its title suggests that the plot made topical reference to the belligerent Gentlemen Volunteers raised by the City of London.

The second half of *Britannia Rediviva* opened with the Genius of England enthroned in 'a magnificent Palace', abject Rebellion dragged before her in chains, and Courage, in triumph, singing:

Peace and *Plenty*, Hand in Hand
Come and reassume the Land . . .
Anguish, *Sorrow*, *Grief* and *Care*
Vanish with the Toils of War

The versatile Miss Lincoln now reassumed the role of Liberty, and pointed up the anti-Papist, Hanoverian moral:

Britons, from strong Example wise,
My various Treasures learn to prize;
Since first I left the faithless Land,
And monkish *Slav'ry* bore Command,
See what vile Wretches are become
My once much boasted Sons of *Rome*.
With steady *Truth* support my Cause,
And guard your Liberties and Laws;
Let honest *Loyalty* impart
Unerring *Faith* to ev'ry Heart;
So shall you always, always see
A Monarch fit to guide the Free.

An aria by Mr Brett's Courage continued the theme, extolling constitutional rule over the supposed tyranny of a Catholic king:

Let other Monarchs, meanly Great,
By cruel Penalties and Pains,
Toil to preserve despotick State,

And hold a Herd of Slaves in Chains.
Great *GEORGE* enjoys a pow'rful Part
In ev'ry willing Subject's Heart.

The rousing final chorus owed something – in lyric and spirit if not in Mr John Dunn's notation – to Handel's coronation anthem:

May the King live for ever – the shrill Trumpet sounds;
May the King live for ever – each Briton rebounds
Repeat the glad Sound; oh, repeat it again;
May the King live for ever – *Amen* and *Amen*.[40]

Few among the New Wells' patrons would have been aware that the glorification of Hanoverian power they were applauding shared its Latin title with a long poem of 1688 penned by the then Poet Laureate, John Dryden. Nor would they have known that it commemorated the birth of the Prince of Wales, claimant to the titles James III and VIII, a Roman Catholic dismissed by them as the 'Old Pretender'. Would have known, or even have cared. Instead, flushed with punch, with unadulterated wine, and with patriotic fervour, they rose from their seats cheering another premature celebration; another triumph without as yet a victory.

III

AN exclusive club was founded at Inverness on the night following the battle. The inaugural meeting of the Cumberland Society agreed that its membership at any one time 'shall not exceed the number of years of His Royal Highness the Duke's Age'. Having just entered his twenty-sixth year, this was the full complement of members at the Society's inception. It would meet annually on 15 April in celebration of his birthday, keep pace with his age by electing one further member, and commemorate his greatest and – as became clear with time – only, military victory. An oval medal 'of ten Guineas price' would be struck in gold bearing Cumberland's portrait and, on the reverse, a naked Apollo leaning nonchalantly on his bow and indicating the arrow embedded in a dead dragon. The Latin inscription, ACTUM EST ILICET PERIIT translated loosely as 'The deed is done, it is over, he has perished.' It derived from a shorter legal term ACTUM EST ILICET – the procedural formula for bringing a Roman trial to an end: 'case is complete, all may disperse'. The medal was to be worn suspended round the neck from a pink and green ribbon. According to Rule 12 of their constitution, the majority of members – though by no means all – being military men, were enjoined 'to wear their medals openly in . . . action and should any member . . . lose his medal by falling into the enemy's hands, the Society to present him with another at their expense'.[1] This contingency proved necessary on only one occasion, in July 1755, when Major William Sparkes lost his to French and native American forces at the disastrous battle of Monongahela River, Pennsylvania.

*

In Edinburgh on 17 April 1746 – with news of the previous day's battle yet to arrive – 'solemn Fasting and Humiliation' was observed in the city and Presbytery, 'to implore Success on his Majesty's Arms against the Rebels'. The day was also marked by a sentence of 300 lashes carried out on one of the castle gunners, before he was drummed out of the garrison. His offence had been 'drinking the Pretender's health'.[2] On Saturday the 19th some in the city who shared the gunner's allegiance 'impudently promoted a story of the Dukes being surprised and defeated and himself taken prisoner, for which there were . . . rejoicing amongst them'. Whether wishful thinking or wilful misinformation, they had 'an unpleasant awakening . . . out of their first sleep' when the thunderous detonations of the Castle cannon – 'answered by the ships of war in Leith road'[3] – broadcast news of the victory at two o'clock the following morning.[4] This first intelligence had arrived the previous night in an express letter from the Duke of Atholl at Perth, giving little more than the bare facts, that 'there had been an Engagement' and that 'the Rebels . . . had been defeat.'[5]

By noon on the Sunday news had reached Stirling, prompting 'a whole Round of their Guns', a bonfire by six in the evening, 'Illuminations all over the Town, ringing of Bells, and all other imaginable Demonstrations of Joy'.[6]

Celebration in Glasgow was deferred to avoid disturbing the quiet of the Sabbath, but on the following day a correspondent reported: 'we had here the greatest Rejoicing, has been known these 30 Years past.' The 'Musick Bells' of the High Kirk were played at ten o'clock, 'and other Bells set a ringing'. At noon 'a very great Number of Bonfires were lighted at the Cross, before the College Gate and in every Street.' At six o'clock in the evening all the bells were rung again, as the Magistrates, Masters of the University, 'several Persons of Distinction . . . and principal Inhabitants of this Loyal City' gathered on the steps leading to the Great Hall and drank healths to the King and his family, while a large detachment of the Glasgow Militia discharged volleys of small-arms fire over their heads. That night all the windows fronting the streets were illuminated – and even those giving backwards into the closes. Many of them 'were prettily decorated with emblematical Figures, and proper Devices'. One ground floor window attracted particular attention with a verse by Isaac Watts displayed before its flickering candle. Written forty years earlier in praise of Queen Anne, but rephrased and tailored to the hero of the hour, it served just as well:

Great CUMBERLAND! The Rebels dread thy Name:
Go mount the Chariot of Immortal Fame.
The Vengeance of thy Rod, with general Joy,
Shall scourge Rebellion and the Rival boy;
Thy sounding Arms his Gallic Patron hears,
And speeds his Flight, nor overtakes his Fears;
Till hard Despair wring from the Tyrant's Soul
The Iron Tears which he cannot controul.
WILLIAM, a generous Soul, who scorns his Ease,
Tempting the Winter, and the faithless Seas,
And pays an Annual Tribute of his Life,
To guard poor Scotland from a Popish Knife.
When we saw Tyranny and Rome
Portending Blood and Night to come,
CUMBERLAND diffus'd a Vital Ray,
And gave the dying Nation Day.

Their Guard of Honour duty done on the steps of the Great Hall, companies of the Glasgow Militia – basking in Cumberland's reflected glory and recalling their own service at Falkirk – swaggered from bonfire to bonfire, 'drinking all the Royal Healths' and firing a small-arms volley at every halt. At one such a firelock burst as it discharged and the owner 'was miserably hurt in the Hand', while his companion standing beside him – Alexander Marshal, a journeyman dyer – was killed instantly by a wooden splinter from the stock 'which pierced into his Brains'.

Meanwhile, the Presbytery of Glasgow, their prayers answered sooner than expected, altered devotional plans for the coming week and 'a Day of Solemn Fasting and Humiliation for the Sins of the Land, and to implore GOD for Success to his Majesty's Arms', long since scheduled for Thursday the 24th, was at short notice ordained as a day of equally solemn Thanksgiving, 'devoutly observed by Persons of all Ranks both in City and Country'.

That same Thursday, as confirmation and further details of the 'glorious Victory' reached Edinburgh, there was another 'compleat round of 31 Guns' from the Castle, and the garrison troops 'return'd the Fire by regular Discharges of their small Arms'. Throughout the day the Union Flag flew, 'the Musick Bells play'd proper Tunes', gentlemen repaired to the Assembly Rooms 'to drink the Duke's Health', and night promised 'the most splendid Illuminations and Bonfires known in this Place'.[7]

On the following Sunday sermons were delivered from texts 'suitable for the happy Occasion'. A favourite was from the Second Book of Samuel:

> And Ahimaaz called, and said unto the king, All is well. And he fell down to the earth upon his face before the king, and said Blessed be the Lord thy God which hath delivered up the men that lifted up their hand against my lord the king.[8]

Perhaps the farthest-flung thanksgiving sermon preached in George II's dominions was that given at the South Church in Boston, New England, on 14 August. The Reverend Thomas Prince MA took his inspiration from Exodus:

> I will sing unto the LORD, for He hath triumphed gloriously: – Thy right Hand, O LORD, is become glorious in Power: Thy right Hand, O LORD, hath dashed in Pieces the Enemy, and in the

> Greatness of thine Excellency Thou hast overthrown them that rose up against thee.[9]

*

One of the Duke's aides-de-camp, George Keppel, Lord Bury, entrusted with a letter to the King conveying news of the battle, had left Inverness at seven o'clock in the evening of the 16th aboard the sloop *Shark* bound for Newcastle. 'With all our victory,' observed Horace Walpole, 'it was not thought safe to send him through the heart of Scotland.'[10] By the following Monday, 'the Wind proving contrary' and the *Shark* 'kept beating at sea for five days', he made landfall at North Berwick, well short of his intended destination.[11] It took nearly three more days, riding post 'with a fever upon him' to reach London, where he arrived in the early hours of Thursday the 24th, a week after he had set out.[12] Unofficial news of the victory had anticipated him the previous noon by express from Edinburgh. Nevertheless, Lord Bury received a thousand guineas from the King for his pains and it was rumoured would have a Regiment of Foot as an additional perquisite 'for bringing the agreeable News'.[13] He was later given the yet greater honour of a commission as aide-de-camp to His Majesty.

The windows of George Bubb Dodington, Treasurer to the Navy, were among the earliest to be lighted on Wednesday evening following 'the first report' when he displayed 'a very pretty illumination'. It was so pretty, and so prompt, that Walpole suspected he must have 'had it by him, ready for *any* occasion'. At noon on Thursday the guns in Hyde Park and the Tower were fired and immediately afterwards the bells began to ring. That night Mr Dodington's example was followed and 'there were more Illuminations and greater Rejoicings throughout the Cities of London and Westminster, and Borough of Southwark, than has been known in the Memory of Man.'[14] At his home in Arlington Street, Walpole wrote that 'the town is all blazing round me . . . with fireworks and illuminations' and he had 'some inclination to lap up half a dozen skyrockets' himself. Around the corner from Walpole's house, Stephen Poyntz – governor and steward of the Duke of Cumberland's household – was watching the 'Bonfires, Illuminations and Fireworks' from his apartment in St James's Palace and noted that the King himself was at that moment taking advantage of a window in the Duke's private quarters to watch the spectacle his son's efforts had inspired.[15]

The nearby Gloucester Tavern hosted 'a Grand Entertainment . . . and the House [was] illuminated in a very extraordinary manner'.[16] Elsewhere, private homes were no less demonstrative: 'Persons of Distinction . . . had their Iron Rails stuck full of Flambeaux, some of which were of white Wax; and others illuminated the outside of their Windows with Wax-Candles; many adorn'd the Roofs and Eaves of their Houses with Candles; and others set their Lamps, or Candles, in the most pleasing Figures: The very Garrets and Cellars were lighted up, and even the Chairmen's Vehicles.'

The effect was 'like that of the Lanthorn-Feast in China' and 'it seem'd to change Night into Day'. The metaphor of light overcoming darkness was not lost upon the newspaper correspondent as he continued: 'this infamous Rebellion, hatch'd in Obscurity, [was] being hooted off in so much Splendour, that none of those Birds of evil Omen (the Jacobites) dar'd . . . to face it . . . and not a Malcontent was seen in the Streets.'[17]

Even back in October, it had been said, 'The mob in London [were] high against the Pretender, and a Scotchman is lookt ill on, because of [the] rebellion, and no wonder.'[18] With the insurgency crushed, the streets were hazardous for anyone overheard speaking with a Scots brogue, regardless of political affiliation. Even in the 'British', a coffee house on the corner of Cockspur Street, much frequented by Scotsmen, it was best to be careful. Former Edinburgh volunteer Alexander Carlyle and Tobias Smollett, ship's surgeon and aspiring novelist and poet – yet to pen his first published work, *The Tears of Scotland* – were there in company when news of the victory arrived. A young man by the name of John Stuart turned pale, and 'Murmuring many Curses, Left the Room in a Rage, and slap'd the Door behind him with much Violence'. Everyone knew why he was upset. His father, Archibald Stuart, former Lord Provost of Edinburgh and suspected 'secret jacobite' was at that time confined in the Tower awaiting trial for 'Neglect of Duty' in surrendering the city. Carlyle turned back to his companions: 'That Lad . . . is either a Madman or a Fool to Discover himself in this Manner.'*

By nightfall, 'London all over was in a perfect uproar of Joy.' At 9 o'clock Carlyle was anxious to get home to his lodgings near New Bond Street and Smollett, who lived in Mayfair, had agreed to guide him. Notwithstanding Carlyle was a Whig, and his companion, 'tho' a Tory, was not a Jacobite', a degree of circumspection was required when they got outside the coffee house. 'The Mob was so Riotous, and the Squibs so Numerous and Incessant', that they took precautions. Turning down an alleyway, they stuffed their wigs into their coat pockets so as not to lose them in a fight – just as George Murray had done prior to Falkirk – and drew their swords before stepping back out into the street. 'John Bull . . . is as Haughty and Valiant to-night,' remarked Smollett, 'as he was abject and cowardly . . . when the Highlanders were at Derby.' He further advised Carlyle not to open his mouth 'Lest the Mob should Discover [our] Country and become Insolent'. From Cockspur Street they reached the end of the Haymarket 'thro' Incessant Fire' and from thence to their respective destinations 'by narrow Lanes' where they encountered nothing more intimidating than 'a few Boys at a Pitiful Bone Fire, who very civilly ask'd us for 6d'.[19] Elsewhere, however, failure to participate in the 'general Spirit of Good-Humour and Benevolence' was met with customary punishment: 'The Mob were so inrag'd at those that did not light up Candles . . . that they broke all the Windows of empty Houses, and of those who were in the Country, all over the City and Liberty of Westminster.[20]

On the following Sunday the King, the Prince and Princess of Wales and the Princess Amelia attended holy worship at the Chapel Royal, St James, 'and heard Te Deum sung for our

* Archibald Stuart was brought before the High Court of Judiciary in Scotland on 24 March 1747. He was finally acquitted on 2 November.

Successes over the Rebels', together with 'a fine new Anthem compos'd for the Occasion'.[21]

*

News spread through the country, and, wherever it reached, windows were illuminated, bells rung and bonfires lit. Celebration, as ever, often led to wanton destruction. At Liverpool a mob of 'tradesmen and sailors' set fire to a widow's house that contained a Catholic chapel. In another part of town they burnt down not only a chapel but four adjoining houses. It was reported that 'furniture, papers, bonds and valuables were consumed in the flames', along with caged songbirds, poultry, 'and a monkey'.[22]

One of the most extravagant celebrations, and certainly one of the noisiest, was mounted by the Member of Parliament for Yorkshire, Mr Cholmley Turner, on his estate in Kirkleatham. A large union standard flew from the church tower as the bells started ringing at nine o'clock in the morning. At the same time, on the summit of a nearby hill, another flag was hoisted and a battery of seven cannon fired. At ten o'clock Mr Turner marched, 'with several Companies under Arms, the Drums beating and colours flying', into his park where he was met by 'several neighbouring Gentlemen and Volunteers, and a very numerous Appearance of People of good Rank'. All dined 'in a very splendid and generous Manner' at the Honourable Member's expense, from an 'elegant Cold Entertainment, of One hundred and forty Dishes . . . provided for the Ladies in the Summer-House, [and] for the Gentlemen in a large Tent'. Officers and Volunteers ate at 'six Tables of Green Turf' specially erected for the occasion.

After dinner, a series of ten clamorous and carefully calibrated healths were proposed and drunk. The King's was accompanied by all seven cannon firing from the hilltop; that of the Prince and Princess of Wales by five; the wider Royal Family, another five; while the health of 'The Ever Glorious Duke of Cumberland, with Thanks to him for his Heroick Behaviour, and Excellent Conduct in the late Battle near Inverness', warranted a discharge of five cannon to himself. Three guns were fired for 'Success to his Majesty's Forces by Sea and Land, particularly the brave Men that fought the Battle'; another three for the Archbishop of Canterbury, Lord Hardwicke the Lord Chancellor, the Duke of Newcastle, and his brother Mr Pelham, the Prime Minister; three more to the Archbishop of York, 'and all Mr Turners Fast Friends'. The ordnance falling silent for the time being, a toast to the 'Glorious and Immortal Memory' of the man who ousted James II nearly sixty years earlier, 'our Great Deliverer, King William', was drunk to a volley of small arms from the assembled Volunteers, as was another wishing 'Everlasting Disappointment to the Popish Pretender, and all his Adherents'.

Following the tenth specific toast – to Great Britain's continued maintenance of the European balance of power – there were several more, all accompanied by loud huzzas from the assembled populace, 'computed to be no less than two thousand', their patriotism fuelled by the several hogsheads of punch and strong beer that Mr Turner had supplied. Festivities continued into the evening with more bell-ringing, cannon fire, musketry and fireworks, 'a very large Bonfire, and burning the Pope and Pretender in Effigy'. And beyond Kirkleatham, across the entire Wapentake or Hundred, 'not only the Market-towns, but every little Village and Grange, or Farm-house' celebrated in like manner, so that for five nights in succession, 'the whole Country seemed in a Blaze'.[23]

*

On 29 April, during a performance of *Britannia Rediviva* at the New Wells in Clerkenwell, seating was wrecked by the patriotic enthusiasm of its audience. The instant Mr Brett – costumed as the Duke of Cumberland – appeared on stage to sing the role of Courage, 'several hearty Britons' pounded their walking canes 'in such a Torrent of Satisfaction, as . . . render'd [the] Damage far from inconsiderable'. The proprietor, Mr Yeates, while thankfully acknowledging the applause, hoped that his patrons would not in future be so transported 'as to prove of such Detriment to his Benches'.[24]

Having at last an unequivocal victory to celebrate, theatre managers put their companies to work devising suitable, up-to-date spectacles to awe and gratify a receptive public. Less than a week after news of the victory arrived, the proprietor of the New Wells in Goodman's Fields reported he had 'been at a great Expence . . . in representing the Battle near Culloden House and defeating the Rebels, that it has given universal Pleasure to all that have seen it'. It attracted 'such a crouded Audience . . . that Numbers were oblig'd to go away for want of Places'.[25]

On 7 May, at Clerkenwell, *Britannia Rediviva* – now billed as 'Being in Praise of his Royal Highness' – was followed by another tableau to surpass even that in Goodman's Fields: 'the exact View of the Battle fought under the Command of our Glorious Hero the Duke of CUMBERLAND . . . with the Horse in Pursuit of the Rebels, and the compleat Victory over them.' One promised element in the spectacle – 'Cannonading the Walls of Culloden-House'[26] – implied a not entirely accurate representation.

Sadler's Wells was slower off the mark, opening five days later with yet another 'grand Representation of the compleat Victory'. Management defended the delay, explaining that 'it is impossible to do Justice to an Affair of this Consequence without sufficient Deliberation', and was confident that 'every Person of Judgement will excuse its being a while deferr'd'. The curious were promised 'every particular Incident correspond[ing] with the latest Intelligence . . . of a furious Battle [presented] with the greatest Caution, and executed with the greatest Vigour that a Stage is capable of'. Rival efforts 'exhibited in other Places' were dismissed as 'little irregular Skirmishes' by comparison. The public was nonetheless complimented on its 'prevailing Spirit of Loyalty', in that even these inferior efforts had 'delighted the politest Audiences, in the severest Weather'.

Mr Yeates in Clerkenwell retaliated with a claim of 'such universal Applause from Crowded Audiences' for his presentation 'as every one . . . is pleased to say it is done far beyond all other trifling Attempts'. No other theatre, he asserted, had 'a Stage sufficient to shew such a Distance of the Hills, the River Spey, and the Number of Horse and Foot that must be engag'd in the Battle, and in pursuit of the Rebels'.[27]

*

'This town has been in a Blaze these two days.' Sir John Ligonier had written to the Duke of Cumberland from London on 25 April. Celebrations were at their height and he urged the hero to take full advantage of the erotic opportunities: 'Return as soon as you Please, no Lady who Prides in the name of an English woman will Refuse you.'[28] And by succumbing to the warrior's sexual advances – Ligonier added in French – 'Glory touches them as well as Pleasure.'* But such amorous adventures would have to wait. Throughout May, June and most of July the Duke was fully occupied consolidating his success in the Highlands.

In the meantime, London found additional excuses for jubilation. On 29 May – Oak Apple Day – there was another spate of bell-ringing, cannons, bonfires, illuminations 'and other publick Demonstrations of Joy, and Loyalty, throughout the Cities of London and Westminster'.[29] Ironically, these celebrations commemorated an event that had so recently come within 126 miles of being re-enacted. It was eighty-six years since Charles II – last legitimate Protestant King of his line – returned from exile and entered London to reclaim the Stuart throne. The Duke of Cumberland's long-awaited return from Scotland, by contrast, almost took the capital unawares.

He had arrived in Edinburgh from Fort Augustus at half past eight on the evening of Monday 21 July. Celebration was denied the loyal elements of the populace 'by his Highness's Pleasure . . . that no such Thing should be done'. He did, however, express satisfaction at 'a very pretty Company of Boys in Grenadier Caps, made of Paper and Pasteboard, and Drums beating', assembled at the West Port to greet him. Staying at Holyrood House long

* 'que la Gloire les touche aussi bien que le Plaisir'.

enough to accept the freedoms of 'several Corporations of Trades' – including that of the Surgeon Apothecaries – he set off again at four the following morning. He reached Newcastle shortly after midnight on Wednesday the 23rd, departing at three in the morning when freedom of the city had been bestowed in the customary gold box, and a like honour from 'the Company of Malters, Mariners, &c.' contained in another. Both were said to be 'of curious Workmanship'. Following his departure, the citizens of Newcastle gave themselves up to the revelry Edinburgh had been forbidden, and 'had great Illuminations, Bonfires, and other Rejoicings; and Mock Pretenders . . . burnt in different Places'.[30]

On 25 July, seemingly shunning display, as he had at Edinburgh, the Duke entered London by the least public route – his post-chaise took 'the Back Roads from Barnet to Kensington Gravel-Pits' – reaching Kensington Palace at about two o'clock in the afternoon, 'before the Messenger . . . sent to give Notice of his coming'.[31] However, when the news became known, celebrations took their customary form, as the hero's return was greeted with 'the grandest Illuminations that had been known [and] never was greater Loyalty and Affection shewn in the Memory of Man'.[32]

*

In Scotland meanwhile, celebration was understandably contentious. The first day of August, being the thirty-second anniversary of the late King George's accession to the British throne and establishment of the Hanoverian dynasty, the Earl of Ancram, commander of government forces on the eastern coast, had ordered 'a day of rejoicing . . . by ringing of Bells and Illuminations'. It had not previously been customary in Scotland to mark the occasion, but to humour him the Aberdeen magistrates gave instructions that the first part of His Lordship's injunction only be observed, 'and the Flag display'd'. For the most part, however, the town remained unlit and it was later pointed out that at this time of year 'the day was . . . so long [that candlelit windows] would make no shew untill so late as the Inhabitants ought rather to be at rest.' The practice of illumination had also been discouraged on the grounds that it generally 'occasioned Noise and Confusion upon the Street'.[33]

Officers belonging to the five companies of Flemming's 36th Foot stationed in the town met that night in a tavern and drank loyal toasts, while a party of soldiers was drawn up outside discharging volleys of small arms fire into the air. At about ten o'clock, Captain Hugh Morgan dismissed the men, gave them 'a 36 shilling piece' to drink the King's health, and whispered instructions to their sergeant.[34] Between ten and eleven – allegedly in response to those instructions – Sergeant Wilson and his men ran amok. 'Wee can scarcely Describ,' protested the magistrates afterwards, 'the atrociousness of the Ryot and the great Disturbance it was in the Town in the night time, by throwing of the stones and breaking of the windows, wounding the Inhabitants in their beds with the Stones, and intimidating all of them, as if the whole town had been to be destroyed.'[35]

The inventory of damage ran to fifteen pages, itemised necessary repairs to two hundred and thirteen separate properties, and the total cost calculated at 129 pounds, three shillings and a halfpenny. 140 panes of glass were broken in the Town House alone, Sergeant Wilson being heard to say it should not be spared because 'the Magistrates ought to have given good example to others'. The merchant George Forbes suffered the greatest financial loss when his warehouse and shop was attacked. Apart from nearly sixty window panes, broken frames and damage to the slated shade above his sign, he lost an estimated seventeen pounds, five shillings and sixpence in smashed mirrors. After the rampage Captain Morgan – identified by witnesses as wearing a white frock coat – was seen in the company of two other officers strolling along a shard-glittering street, 'Pointing up to the Windows that were broke and laughing heartily at them'.[36]

Captain Morgan was arrested the following day but promptly freed on bail put up by his commander. Lieutenant Colonel Jackson maintained the officer's innocence, claiming the mob of perpetrators had been composed primarily of townspeople and that the Captain had 'actually endeavoured . . . to save the windows, but to no purpose'. Accusations by 'several of the meaner sort', that he had not only instigated the destruction but 'threw stones' himself were provoked, Jackson declared, by resentment of his recent military duties: 'Morgan was on Command with me in the hills and very active in Ferritting Gentlemen who were and are lurking, some of whom are of this Neighbourhood. I take this to be one of their reasons of spleen.'[37]

It was left to the Lord Justice Clerk, Andrew Fletcher, to respond in emollient fashion to the Aberdeen magistrates' closely written 'Precognition' – or witness testimony – and demands for compensation. 'This Ryot,' he conceded, 'had its rise from an ill tim'd zeal for the Royal Family, inflamed perhaps with a little too much liquor.' He gave assurance, however unconvincing, that 'next morning when the Officers cooled they repented of what they had done.' Finally, he appealed to a sense of civic duty, to patriotism, and to indulgence:

> You must be sensible of what importance it is to His Majesty's Government and to the peace and happiness of this Country . . . that the Civil Magistrates shall as far as possible maintain and Cultivate a good understanding with the Gentlemen of the Army, That differences between them be as much as possible prevented, and when they happen, that they be accomodated in the softest and easiest way that may be.[38]

Four weeks after the riot, the magistrates wrote again to the Lord Justice Clerk, explaining that, with elections at hand, their constituents were 'insisting to have their Damages Repaired and such Satisfaction given to the Town as the Insult done deserves'. They also pointed out that 'a great many of the Sufferers are so poor that they have not wherewith to repair their Damage, and their Windows do continue in ruins.'[39]

A contrary anniversary to that of 1 August had been observed about two months earlier. On 10 June in Edinburgh 'great Numbers of Ladies appeared with Bunches of White Ribbons', marking the birthday of the exiled 'Old Pretender', and on the same night the citizens of Montrose had illuminated their houses 'in as grand a manner as they could'.[40] This town, some thirty-five miles down the coast from Aberdeen, was occupied by the remaining five companies of Flemming's Foot, but unlike their comrades to the north, civilian loyalty or lack of it did not on that occasion appear to concern them. The Duke of Cumberland, however, writing from his headquarters at Fort Augustus, was not so tolerant. He was particularly exercised when told of 'a Number of Boys' who had built a bonfire, and upon being questioned had the impudence to say it was for 'King James'. Concerned that 'pernicious principles . . . instilled into youth [were] sewing the seed of [a] dangerous & destructive . . . Harvest', the Duke determined that 'it should, by Punishment, be choaked before it came to Maturity'. He ordered the Montrose magistrates to have the boys arrested, and 'whiped through the Town, their Parents or Guardians assisting, & the cryer proclaiming at proper Places, what it is for'. The garrison commander Major Chabane was 'to see that this correction be given properly, & in a manner suitable to the age of the boys, and likewise to take care to place proper Guards, if he should have Reason to apprehend any sort of ill Behaviour of the People.'

The implied threat with which Cumberland ended his letter raised before the secular authorities of Montrose the image of a judgemental and retributive Old Testament God:

> It will . . . be incumbent on the magistrates, & all who wish the Welfare of the Town, to be more than ordinary diligent to wipe off this stain, . . . for after all, the Supreme Magistrate beareth not the Sword in vain, [if] the Peace & Security of the whole, must be provided for.[41]

On 20 December, the last significant date in the Jacobite calendar, anticipation of treasonous demonstrations provoked the military authorities in Edinburgh to farcical overreaction. The birthday of Charles Edward Stuart fell on a Saturday, and during the previous week rumours spread: 'dinners were bespoke at Leith with an intent to have Balls afterwards, and several Societies were to meet in Town.' Women were to 'distinguish . . . themselves by wearing Tartan Gowns with Shoes and Stockings of the same kind, and White Ribbands on their heads and breasts'. Believing this 'surprising, audacious and impudent' marking of the son's natal day to be more difficult to ignore than the father's six months earlier, the Earl of Albemarle – Commander-in-Chief of His Majesty's Forces in Scotland following the departure of the Duke of Cumberland – spoke to the Lord Justice Clerk, the Lord Advocate and several Lords of Session, urging preventive action; but none of those worthies 'could give credit to [the reports], not thinking it possible that such a spirit of rebellion should continue to reign amongst the inhabitants of Edinburgh'. Reassured, his lordship had accepted a dinner engagement on the 20th, four miles outside the city, only to be called back by news that an arrest warrant had, after all, been issued by the Lord Justice Clerk and that Major General John Huske had ordered five companies of Fusiliers to be under arms at four o'clock and all available Dragoons dispatched to the Leith Links, to deal with the emergency. By nightfall guards had been posted in every avenue between Edinburgh and Leith 'to stop all Coaches and apprehend such women as were cloathed in Tartan', while troop detachments accompanied Civil Magistrates to 'disaffected and suspected houses'. But Albemarle had missed his dinner for nothing. Prior warning had been given and before any arrests could be made the Jacobite revellers had dispersed, 'the women had undressed themselves', and by one o'clock in the morning 'every thing was quiet', and the troops returned to barracks.[42]

*

Performance of Handel's definitive celebration of Cumberland's victory – the oratorio *Judas Maccabaeus* – was deferred until 1 April the following year, just a fortnight short of the battle's first anniversary. The Reverend Thomas Morell's libretto, however, had been written, at the composer's instigation, some months before Culloden in early 1746, before even the *Occasional Oratorio* had been completed, itself a celebration well in advance of anything to celebrate. Indeed, his text for the aria 'Oh Liberty' was, according to Morell, 'design'd, and wrote' for the later work 'but it got, I know not how, into the [earlier] and was there incomparably Set, and as finely executed'.

Handel's music to Morell's words was composed in the main during July and August while London was erupting with fireworks, flambeaux and illuminations honouring the Duke's return. As with previous oratorios, the Chosen People in *Judas Maccabaeus* were cyphers for loyal Hanoverian Britain, while to their earlier Philistine, Egyptian, and Canaanite antagonists were added Samarian and Syrian armies, routed in turn by the eponymous warrior. The libretto's dedication made explicit comparison between 'this faint portraiture' of its Jewish hero, 'a Truly Wise, Valiant, and Virtuous Commander' and Cumberland, 'the Possessor of like Noble Qualities'.[43] And the Duke reciprocated, instructing his steward to make Morrel 'a handsome present'.[44]

At the beginning of Act II, with a phrase that might have recalled reports of slaughter at Culloden to her London audience, Caterina Galli sang of the victorious general pursuing his enemies 'Through hills of carnage and a sea of blood'. Morrel claimed to have 'introduced several Incidents more *apropos*' into his text, 'but it was thought they would make it too long, and were therefore omitted'.[45] Handel may also have felt that more overt topicality would stale the oratorio for future revivals.

The success of that first performance was repeated two nights later, and on four subsequent occasions – each advertised '*with* ADDITIONS' – over the following fortnight. One such addition was a march with military kettledrums, hired for that purpose from the Tower of London. But what has become the oratorio's best-known item of choral music would not be added to the score for some years. It originally formed part of a further collaboration with Morrel, composed by Handel over a four-week period in July and August 1747. *Joshua* was yet another biblically disguised celebration of Hanoverian triumph over Popish idolatry, in which the liberated Jewish people subjugate and destroy the cities of Canaan, the land promised them by God. In Act III, following the fall of Jericho and Ai, a chorus of Israelite Youths and Virgins greet the young warrior Othniel returning from his victory over Debir:

See the conqu'ring hero comes!
Sound the trumpets, beat the drums.
Sports prepare, the laurel bring.
Songs of triumph to him sing.

See the godlike youth advance!
Breathe the flutes, and lead the dance;
Myrtle wreaths, and roses twine.
To deck the hero's brow divine.

This would henceforth be the standard musical accompaniment to heroic achievement of any kind. In 1773, following General William Dalrymple's campaign against the 'Black Carib' inhabitants of St Vincent, someone suggested that 'whenever his Excellency . . . is pleased to walk out, he ought to be preceded by Post Horns or by two Pair of Bagpipes, sounding out the Tune of "See the conquering Hero comes".'[46] In 1775 it greeted General Thomas Gage's return to London following the battles of Lexington, Concord and Bunker Hill.[47] It was played in February 1779 when a Naval Court Martial acquitted Admiral Augustus Keppel of misconduct and neglect of duty.[48] It sounded in Admiral Rodney's ears as he was presented with the freedom of Huntingdon for beating the French at the battle of the Saintes in 1782,[49] and it honoured Admiral Howe twelve years later, after he beat them again in the engagement known as 'The Glorious First of June'.[50] Following his bare-knuckle match against Sam Martin in the summer of 1787, the Jewish prize fighter Dan Mendoza was brought in triumph from Barnet to Leadenhall Street, 'attended by the principal Israelites, who had witnessed the dreadful conflict, with lighted torches and martial music, the principal voices belonging to the synagogue, resounding in full chorus, "See the Conquering Hero comes".'[51] It was an impromptu addition to the musical programme at Vauxhall Gardens on the night of 21 June 1815 as the dispatch arrived in London bringing news of the victory at Waterloo and it subsequently accompanied the Duke of Wellington's every public appearance for the rest of his days.[52] Throughout the 19th century it would invariably be struck up by provincial brass bands across the country praising victors of parliamentary election and sporting event alike.

But long before the opening night of *Joshua*, 9 March 1748, informed opinion had been turning against the conquering hero of 1746. Writing only three months after Culloden, in early August, Horace Walpole remarked that when 'it was lately proposed in the City to present [Cumberland] with the freedom of some company; one of the aldermen said aloud, "Then let it be of the *Butchers!*"'[53]

Dr. Cameron drawn on a Sledge to Tyburn

'A publick, cruel & barbarous Death'

THE sentence passed upon seventy-four Jacobites, at courts in London, York and Carlisle during the latter part of 1746, was substantially identical to that suffered more than four centuries earlier, in 1305, by the Scottish insurgent William Wallace: to be 'drawn, hanged, beheaded, his entrails burned, and his body quartered'.[1]

Three months after the battle of Culloden, Sir William Lee, Lord Chief Justice to the Court of King's Bench, addressed the first group of condemned and shackled men brought before him in Southwark. He spoke of the gravity of their offences, the unlikelihood of reprieve, the certain prospect of damnation to come:

> The crime you stand convicted of is the most atrocious that mankind can commit. As you have so greatly offended the government by which you were protected, you can expect no protection or clemency from that government which you have endeavoured to subvert and overturn. You have murdered many of his Majesty's liege subjects . . . whose blood cries for vengeance against you. And unless you repent sincerely in this world, you will inevitably be doomed to everlasting torments in the next.[2]

The crime for which they had been tried – and for which they would shortly be put to death in the manner peculiar to it – was not, however, the murder of subjects regardless of their number. Offences constituting High Treason, and defined as such by a statute of 1350, were to 'compass or imagine* the death of our Lord the King' and to 'levy War against our Lord the King in his Realm'.[3] According to the indictment read at the beginning of their trial, the accused, 'Not having the fear of God in their hearts . . . but being moved and seduced by the instigation of the devil, as false traitors and rebels' were charged with 'devising . . . most wickedly and traitrously intending to change and subvert the rule and government of this Kingdom, and also to put and bring our said present Lord and King to death and destruction'.[4]

The seventeen men having been found guilty of High Treason in the Court House on St Margaret's Hill, Southwark, Sir William Lee pronounced sentence:

> Let the several prisoners . . . return to the gaol of the County of Surrey, from whence they came; and from thence they must be drawn to the place of execution; and when they come there, they must be severally hanged by the neck; but not till they be dead; for they must be cut down alive; then their bowels must be taken out, and burnt before their faces; then their heads must be severed from their bodies, and their bodies severally divided into four quarters; and these must be at the King's disposal.[5]

It was a customary, and degrading, part of the sentence that the condemned be denied the meagre dignity of cart or carriage, but instead were dragged or 'drawn' on sledges to meet their death. Six of these low contraptions, each accommodating three prisoners, were 'to be new built at the Expense of the County'.[6] However, notwithstanding the Lord Chief Justice's remarks on the unlikelihood of clemency, only nine of the seventeen were executed and just three of the sledges used. The other eight prisoners were reprieved for three weeks, although one was to die

* i.e. to design or intend.

in gaol during this period. Two were eventually pardoned and the rest either banished or transported. It was by reason of their youth that the jury recommended seventeen-year-old Ensign Charles Deacon and James Wilding for mercy. Deacon was permitted to visit his less fortunate elder brother Thomas on the morning of his execution, and was so distressed by the meeting that 'he had much ado to keep upon his legs'.

Colonel Francis Towneley occupied the first sledge, alongside Captain Andrew Blood and Lieutenant John Berwick, formerly a linen draper. Their arms pinioned and each with a halter round his neck, they sat with their backs to the horse pulling the sledge, while the executioner crouched in the rear facing his charges 'with a drawn scymeter'. The second sledge contained Lieutenant Thomas Theodorus Deacon, the Welshman Captain David Morgan and Adjutant Thomas Syddall, a barber by trade, who was observed 'to tremble very much' as the halter touched his throat, but bolstered himself 'by taking a pinch of snuff'. Finally, Lieutenant Thomas Chadwick, a tallow chandler, Captain George Fletcher – another linen draper – and Captain James Dawson, a student before joining the Prince's cause at that hotbed of Jacobite support St John's College, Cambridge, were drawn in the third sledge. Each of them was 'genteelly dressed', despite their mean mode of transport.

All nine were officers in the Manchester Regiment, left behind by the Prince to defend Carlisle as the rest of the army retreated over the border, and captured when the city fell to the Duke of Cumberland. Never numbering more than 300 men, its strength at the end was just 113. Composed principally of English adherents to the Jacobite cause it was deemed especially treasonous and, of all units of the insurgent army, was proportionally the most savagely treated by the Hanoverian state. Even before they were convicted, 'in passing to and from their trials, the prisoners were very rudely treated by the spectators, who were exceedingly numerous, and whose resentment was so great, that had not the soldiers kept them off, it is probable they would have pulled the prisoners out of the coaches, and torn them to pieces.'[7]

A further seventeen officers, sergeants and other ranks would suffer the gruesome penalty for High Treason before the end of the year, on execution sites at York and in the county of Cumberland. Five of the twenty-four executed at York were from the Manchester Regiment, as were twelve of the thirty-three prisoners condemned at Carlisle.

Foot guards and a party of dragoons to the fore, foot guards in flank and to the rear, set the funereal pace of the procession from the New Surrey Gaol, down Borough High Street, Blackman Street and Newington Butts. 'It was observed that the mob offered no insults to any of the prisoners this day.'[8] A carriage followed the sledges, under heavy guard, taking Charles Deacon to watch his brother die.

Reaching the execution site on Kennington Common, the nine men were helped from the sledges and, their arms untied, they mounted a cart drawn up under the gallows. A wooden block and pile of faggots – essential instruments in the ritual to come – were placed nearby. For over half an hour, in the absence of a priest, the bespectacled David Morgan, being the eldest of the condemned and a practicing barrister, 'read prayers and other pious meditations to them, out of a book of devotion; to which the rest seemed very attentive, [joining] devoutly in all the prayers and ejaculations with a great deal of seriousness'. Meanwhile the faggots had been set on fire. Each man then scattered among the spectators written papers containing declarations 'that they died in a just cause; that they did not repent of what they had done; that they doubted not but their deaths would be revenged; and several other treasonable expressions'. They threw their prayer books also into the crowd along with their hats, 'six of which were trimmed with gold'.

The executioner set about his work. Each man's hands were again tied and his halter fastened to the crossbeam of the gibbet, a cap placed on his head and pulled down to cover his eyes. Then the cart was drawn away from under their feet, dropping off each in succession. After about three minutes guards below pulled off the shoes, stockings and breeches of the still strangling men while the executioner mounted a ladder and stripped off the rest of their clothes. Towneley's body was the first to be cut down and laid naked on the block.

In deference to an enlightened, modern age, executioners often refrained from carrying out every detail of the medieval punishment, so as to mitigate the victim's suffering. Bodies might be left hanging for anything up to a quarter of an hour before being cut down, so as to ensure death by asphyxiation – or at least insensibility – before they were butchered.

'Observing some signs of life' in Towneley's body, the executioner on Kennington Common reportedly 'struck it several violent blows on the breast'. It is unclear whether this was intended as a *coup de grâce*, or to break the sternum and rib cage, allowing an easier passage of the knife to the heart which, along with the entrails, was to be cut out and shown to the crowd. One account states that Towneley's throat was mercifully slit prior to this operation, while according to another the innards were removed from the still living body, raised to the mob with a cry of 'Gentlemen, behold the heart of a traitor', then thrown onto the fire.[9] The head was severed with a cleaver. Restraint was otherwise exercised in that the carcase was not quartered following decapitation and evisceration. The limbs were instead notionally cut or 'scored' with the knife, but not severed completely. Nevertheless, this refinement of custom did not prevent the executioner from observing the formula of the old ritual and, having made the requisite cuts, he turned to the crowd bidding them, '*Behold the four quarters of a traitor.*'

Morgan's body was the next to be cut down, disembowelled and beheaded. Then, one by one the rest – the accumulated stench of burning viscera pervading the execution ground – until finally the corpse of James Dawson was dealt with. 'Gentlemen, behold the heart of the last traitor,' the executioner roared, before throwing it onto the fire with, '*God save King George!*' The crowd responded with 'a great shout'.[10]

Captain John Farquharson, awaiting trial in the New Surrey Gaol, wrote that 'after every execution the mangled bodies were brought back to the gaol and remained there some days to show the remaining prisoners how they were to be used in their turn.'[11] A week later it was reported that Charles Deacon, 'on a thorough Grief for the Loss of his Brother . . . has fell into a panic Disorder, [from] which it is thought he cannot recover.'[12]

Newspapers claimed that on Kennington Common that day, 'there were present the greatest Number of Spectators ever seen together in the Memory of Man, some Thousands of whom waited in the Rain several Hours to see the Execution.'[13] The immense press may have weakened the platforms provided for onlookers, because when three more prisoners were put to death at the same place and in the same manner three weeks later, 'a Scaffold fell down near the Gallows . . . and several Persons were hurt by the Fall.'[14] A more serious, indeed lethal, collapse would occur on Tower Hill at the execution of Lord Lovat the following year.

*

In some cases, departing from the strict letter of the sentence, executed men's bodies and heads were given to their friends for burial, instead of being kept 'at the King's disposal'.[15] His Majesty retained only six of the nine heads from the first spate of London executions. Towneley's and Fletcher's were 'fix'd on two Poles on Temple Bar'.[16] Horace Walpole remarked that 'people make a trade of letting spying-glasses at a halfpenny a look'[17] and it was reported two days later that 'many Thousands of Spectators have been already to view them.'[18] They provided a profitable distraction for a trio of well-dressed pickpockets, enabling them 'to rob a great many People as they . . . stood gazing at the Heads put up there'. Following a hue and cry the woman and two men were caught by a mob who 'duck'd them severely' in the nearby horse pond on Carey Street.

The heads of Deacon, Sydall, Berwick and Chadwick were 'preserv'd in Spirits, in order to be carried down to Manchester and Carlisle, to be affix'd on Places most proper for the Purpose'.

It was rumoured that Thomas Sydall's was to be displayed on the same Market Cross in Manchester that his father's head had occupied thirty years earlier for his part in the rising of 1715. When he joined the Manchester Regiment to fight for the Prince's cause, the son allegedly 'told his Friends and Relations, that now he would revenge his Father's Death'.[19] About five o'clock on a Thursday morning in September, six weeks after their execution, the pickled heads of Sydall and Deacon were fixed, not on the Market Cross, but close by on the portico of the Cotton Exchange in Market Place, where the display proved as great a popular attraction as did that on Temple Bar. Among the crowd one morning was a black-clad gentleman who 'made a full stop near the Exchange, and looking up at the Heads, pulled off his Hat and made a Bow to them with great Reverence. He afterwards stood some time looking at them.'[20] Dr Thomas Deacon – physician and Nonjuring bishop – had now lost two sons to the insurrection, Lieutenant Robert Deacon of the Manchester Regiment having died in captivity at Kendal the previous January. Charles Deacon had recovered from the trauma of his brother's execution, and remained a prisoner in the New Surrey Gaol.

Following trials at Carlisle, sentence was ordered to be carried out 'in the three principal towns of Cumberland' on the grounds that it 'might have a better effect in the Country than if all the Executions had been confined to one place'. Nineteen were accordingly put to death on Gallows Hill, Harraby, a mile outside Carlisle, the remaining fourteen, divided equally between Brampton and Penrith, met their end on 21 and 28 October, each 'being a market day for that town'.[21] Four sergeants of the Manchester Regiment were among those who perished at Penrith, along with Robert Lyon, Chaplain to Ogilvy's Regiment, who 'read a most infamous Libel at the Gallows, near 20 minutes long and declared that if his Life had been given to him he would still have continued in the same Principles'. All seven men 'died in a very unbecoming manner,' according to a government eyewitness, 'hardened to the greatest degree, and beyond any sense of their crime'. Among the large crowd of spectators 'There [were] several saying they pitied them as men, but rejoiced at their fate as Rebells.'[22] At Brampton, sentence on the other seven was carried out more literally than elsewhere and, following decapitation, 'their Arms and Legs [were] cut off'.[23]

A letter dated 8 November from the High Sheriff of Cumberland to the Secretary of State, Thomas Pelham-Holles, Duke of Newcastle, acknowledged receipt of George Hamilton's head from the County Sheriff of York, and informed his lordship that he had 'caused [it] to be set up on the Scotch gate of the City of Carlisle'.[24] This latest trophy joined those of Major Donald MacDonell of Tirnadris and his kinsman of Kinlochmoidart executed at Gallows Hill three weeks earlier. Greeting visitors from across the border the Scotch Gate faced north. Crow-pecked, the three-month-old heads of John Berwick and Thomas Chadwick still adorned the English Gate, facing south.[25]

*

MacDonell of Tirnadris was a model for the character of Fergus Mac-Ivor in Walter Scott's 1814 novel *Waverley*, its subtitle – *'Tis Sixty Years Since* – alluding to the relatively recent events of the rising. Before being drawn by sledge from Carlisle to his death, Mac-Ivor wryly observes to his English friend, 'This same law of high treason is one of the blessings, Edward, with which your free country has accommodated poor old Scotland – her own jurisprudence, as I have heard, was much milder.' Under the 1707 Act of Union, Scotland had retained her original legal system, a convicted traitor being hanged until dead, and eviscerated post mortem. But after an abortive Jacobite attempt the following year, the full sophistication of English Treason law was introduced north of the border, stipulating that the condemned remain conscious when disembowelled. Despite this legislative convergence no prisoners of the '45 stood trial for High Treason in Scotland, it being feared that juries there might be loath to convict. To that end an Act of Parliament was passed into law in early 1746 empowering the king 'to issue commissions for trying the rebels in any county of the kingdom, in the same manner as if the treasons had been committed in that county'.[26]

Taking his place on the cart below the gibbet, Mac-Ivor's original read aloud a speech pledging loyalty to the Stuart cause that convention entitled him to make, however treasonous. It began with the words: 'As I am now to suffer a publick, cruel & barbarous & in the Eyes of the World an ignominious, shameful Death . . .'[27]

The Beheading of the

l Lords on Great Tower Hill.

PART V:

RECKONINGS

I

A week after the battle of Culloden – but some hours before news of the victory reached London – five men would be marched from the Savoy prison in the Strand to an area at the north-east corner of Hyde Park close to the Tyburn triple tree gallows. It was a place marked on John Rocque's 1746 map of the city with the words 'Where Soldiers are Shot'. The first Jacobite prisoners to suffer judicial execution were formerly the British army's own men: deserters from the first and second regiment of Foot Guards, captured on board a French transport vessel en route to fight against the King in Scotland.

The condemned men were dressed in white, escorted by 'a great Party of . . . Guards under Arms' and followed by 'a prodigious Croud of People'. At the execution site were five freshly dug graves and five coffins. After half an hour of prayer led by the chaplains in attendance, the five were made to kneel, each at the head of his grave, and their caps drawn down over their eyes. The youngest men from the escort had been selected for the firing party and had orders to proceed by signal instead of spoken command. A white handkerchief tied to a halberd was raised to signify 'Make Ready'; a second motion, 'Present'; and a third, 'Fire'. The kneeling men waited, blind in the silence, praying 'with great Fervency'. At the second motion of the handkerchief they heard the collective sound of firelocks cocked four yards away.

The crowd fell silent and only the prayers could be heard, 'invoking God for Mercy', until the handkerchief moved again. 'Their Faces and Breasts were all tore to Pieces by the Balls, and all dead before they fell.'[1]

*

On the day after the battle sergeant majors from each regiment had been ordered to 'visit all the Prisoners taking the names of those who have been in any of the Regts. in our Service'.[2] Once identified they faced military courts martial, charged with desertion and enlisting with the enemy. Found guilty, it was often a mark of the contempt in which such despised wretches were held, that instead of dispatch by firing squad, they were hanged until dead, 'a paper . . . pin'd upon the breast of each with the word Desertion in large letters'.[3] One, formerly a Grenadier in Sowle's 11th Foot, had deserted in Flanders, enlisted with the French and been given a Lieutenant's commission in Lord John Drummond's *Royal Ecossais*. As a particular warning against such treacherous ambition, Duncan Colquhoun was ordered to be 'hanged in his Uniform with a Label on his breast, setting forth who & what he is', likewise in large letters. Furthermore, the corpse was 'to hang till further orders' in its dark blue coat, red waistcoat and silver lace, with two sentries posted 'to prevent [its] being stripped'.[4] A similar example was made of former Sergeant Dunbar, another deserter from the same regiment as Colquhoun. Dunbar was hanged in 'a Suit of laced Cloaths' – the property of Major James Lockhart of Cholmondeley's – that he had looted from the government army's baggage after the battle of Falkirk. 'By the Duke's Order he hung 48 Hours in these Regimentals, a Party of *Kingston*'s Horse guarding the Gibbet.'[5] Conversely, fourteen men who were dispatched at one time, were stripped naked by the executioner as they hung from the gallows and 'suffered to continue exposed for three days'.[6]

A total of thirty deserters were mentioned by name in the Duke's daily orders as being executed at Inverness in April and

May alone. But a roughly equal number, guilty of the same crime, were spared during that period. In a seeming departure from the reputed practice of 'Hangman Hawley' – his predecessor as Commander-in-Chief – there were frequent instances of the Duke's clemency, extended even to serious capital crimes. Eleven deserters, 'condemned for inlisting with the Rebells', were released and allowed to rejoin Guise's Regiment, after the Reverend Mr McBevan, a local minister, 'spoke favourably' of them. The minister also prevailed upon the Duke to pardon several more men that were in custody for similar offences.[7] Some, such as William Beau, James Gullery and Joseph Wilson of Guise's, and William Chisholm of the Scots Fusiliers, were unaccountably spared without civilian intercession, 'HRH having been graciously pleased to pardon' them.[8]

This was not entirely surprising. At the outset of his Scottish campaign, while still in Edinburgh towards the end of January, the Duke of Cumberland had exercised a considerable and – for the military ethos of his time – surprising degree of leniency towards 'Several Crimes & Misdemenners which deserve[d] Severe and Capital punishment'. It suggests an intention to raise and maintain the spirit of his troops, following the shambles that Generals Cope and Hawley had led them into at Prestonpans and Falkirk:

> Being desirous from his great Clemency & goodness as also from a fondness of the Troops . . . he has been graciously Pleased to grant them his pardon relying upon their future Courage & good Conduct to convince the Enemys of their Country that he is placed at the head of Troops whom he has a pride in Commanding, and, whom he is Convinced will Support the King to his Honour and to that which they have so often and so justly acquired.[9]

A balance had to be struck, however, and military discipline under the Duke of Cumberland could be as savage as under any other commander of the time. Two men of Sackville's and one of the Royals each received 500 lashes for stealing meat. A sentence of more than 500 lashes would normally be carried out in instalments, Roger Wey of Wolfe's receiving 200 at the head of each of the army's five brigades for the exacerbated crime of stealing meat and 'Marauding'. Similarly, for pickpocketing, Alex Campbell and Walter Anderson of Sempill's, endured '1000 Lashes each at 5 different times' and stoppage of pay until the two pounds and sixteen shillings stolen from their victim had been reimbursed.[10] A range of punishments was meted out to three men of Loudoun's regiment on 16 May. First, Alexander Campbell was hanged for 'Deserting and Inlisting with the Rebells'. That done, John Campbell – charged with mutiny – was shot at the gallows by a firing squad. The third man, also a mutineer, was spared the death penalty, but the corporal punishment inflicted was unremitting. After Martin McTurner had been 'tied to the Gallows and there receive[d] 1000 lashes with a Catt and 9 Tails', it is astonishing he survived to undergo the second part of his sentence, 'to be Drummed along both lines out of the Army with a halter about his Neck'.[11]

11

THE most comprehensive record of Jacobite prisoners held in Scotland and England during the years 1745–8 documents a total of 3,471 men, women and children.[1]

Surrender of the Carlisle garrison to the Duke of Cumberland on 30 December 1745 yielded the largest number captured in England. Most of the 354 common men and sergeants were subsequently distributed between gaols in the castles at Chester, Lancaster, Lincoln and York. Forty-one officers – guarded by a regiment of foot – were taken directly to London, arriving on 10 February and providing a timely fillip to the capital's morale following news of Hawley's defeat at Falkirk. As they were marched through Southwark to the New Surrey Gaol, 'the People shew'd their Resentment, by hissing and pelting them with Dirt . . . notwithstanding all that the Soldiers could do to prevent it.'[2]

In the immediate aftermath of Culloden about nine hundred captives were held in Scottish prisons, some three hundred of them divided between gaols in Aberdeen, Dumfries, Dundee, Edinburgh, Leith, Musselburgh, Irvine and Stirling. The majority, around six hundred, were confined in Inverness, at first filling gaols and lockups throughout the town, then aboard seven transport ships anchored in the Moray Firth.

Among the Duke of Cumberland's orders during the weeks following the battle was one appointing Captain Stratford Eyre of Battereau's regiment to 'have the Inspection of all the French and Rebel Prisoners as are now or shall for the future be brought in'. He was to 'give directions what to do with them, and in everything relating to such prisoners, application [was] to be made to him'. He was 'to do no other Duty'.[3] It was to this meticulous Anglo-Irish officer that some of the most detailed documentation concerning prisoners of the '45 can be credited.

*

A witness to conditions in the Inverness gaols wrote of manacles 'so tight that . . . hands swell'd and at last broke the skin so that the irons coud not be seen'. The resulting injury was likened to 'a horse sore sadle-spoild which runs a great deall of thick matter and blood'. He described 'the wounded feltring in their gore and blood'; and 'a Frenchman in the agonies of death lying in nastiness up to his stomack . . . a great stone under his head that he might not be choaked with which he l[a]y in'. And he wrote of corpses 'covered quite with pish and dirt, the living standing to the middle in it', the smell of 'their own excraments [mingling] with the stink of the dead bodys that seldom were taken away before they began naturaly to melt by the heat of the weather'.[4]

When fully laden, the seven vessels anchored in the Firth were to take captives to England for trial. It was at first proposed that prisoners captured north of the border be tried either in Carlisle or Newcastle, and by August two hundred and seventy had been marched south and awaited their fate in the cellars of Carlisle Castle. Those concentrated at Inverness were destined by sea for Newcastle.

Horrors continued aboard the transport ships. On the *Thane of Fife* 'every one [was] in the most deplorable condition . . . about 4 score or 100 all confined in the hold, lying or sitting on the bare stones that were ballast, all of them in a most sickly condition, and some dieing every day.'[5] At Kennington Common the following November James Bradshaw would tell a crowd assembled to watch him die of the privations endured in the hold of the *Jane of Leith*, of prisoners unable to lie down but 'obliged to sit on large stones, by which means their legs swell'd as big almost as their bodies'.[6]

Even before Bradshaw's ship sailed eleven of her 109 prisoners were dead, as were eight of the ninety-six on board the *Alexander & James*. Together with the *Thane of Fife*, the *Wallsgrave*, the *Margaret & Mary*, the *Jean of Alloway* and the *Dolphin*, they put to sea on 28 May escorted by two Royal Navy ships, HMS *Winchelsea* and the sloop *Hawk*. By the time this convoy, with its combined cargo of 564 souls, arrived at the mouth of the Tyne on 9 June, five more had died in the hold of the *Alexander & James*.

Appalled at the prospect of having to accommodate a desperate horde of half-starved, probably diseased dependents awaiting justice, the Mayor of Newcastle, Cuthbert Smith, successfully appealed against 'the great inconveniences which must have attended their Tryals in this town, where . . . we have not proper places for their Security'.[7] Even in January he had written to the Secretary of State for the Southern Department, Thomas Pelham-Holles – Duke of Newcastle by inheritance but with no other connection to the town – pleading to be relieved of the few prisoners he then had.[8] On this occasion Mr Smith was able to show authoritative letters from His Grace to Captain Dyve, commander of the *Winchelsea*, ordering the convoy to proceed with its captives to the port of London.

Precise mortality figures of prisoners aboard the transports – before leaving the Moray Firth, *en route* to Newcastle and from thence to London – are unclear because partial records were preserved of deaths on only two of the seven vessels. Anecdotal evidence, however, is graphic. John Farquharson described the *Jane of Leith* crew's 'diversion', when, six or seven times in a day, they would pitch the sick into the sea at the end of a rope, 'as they said to drown the vermine', but drowning lice and man together. 'Then they'd hawll them up upon deck and ty a stone about on the leggs and over board with them.'[9] Another witness on the *Thane of Fife* wrote of a macabre coupling of the sick and the dead, 'tyed together and thrown over'.[10]

Nine days after leaving Newcastle the transports dropped anchor in the eastern reaches of the Thames at Tilbury Fort, the late seventeenth-century bastioned stronghold opposite Gravesend that in one form or another had defended the city of London from seaward attack since the reign of Henry VIII. Three hundred prisoners were disembarked here – the maximum that place could accommodate – and confined in the gunpowder magazines. The rest remained on board the transports, proceeding upriver to anchor at Woolwich, where fifty-seven officers were landed. These men ran the same gauntlet as the Carlisle prisoners on their way to Surrey Gaol, 'exposed to the furry of a tumoultous mob, who neither spared them with their outrageous words, spitles, dirt, and even stones and bricks . . . through all the streets of Southwark'. Conditions in the gaol were little better than on the transports. They lay in shackles, only those having money allowed to 'purchase the liberty of on[e] leg [and be] relived a litle'.[11]

A second convoy, of three transports, set sail from Inverness on 28 July carrying nearly 200 prisoners. The hold of one was weighted with a ballast of 'black earth and small stones' in which Wlliam Jack and his fellow prisoners were 'oblig'd to dig holes to lie in to keep [themselves] warm'.[12] Registered as the *Liberty & Property*, her very name was a shibboleth of the Protestant Hanoverian state that promised 'Preservation of the Religeon, Liberty, and Property of the People'.* The other two transports were named in less partisan manner. The *James & Mary* may have honoured an owner's son and daughter, the *Pamela*, a daughter or wife. No record of the *Pamela* appeared in newspaper notices of sailings or arrivals prior to August 1744 when she had reached Gravesend from Jamaica, probably bearing a cargo of sugar. Defying the taint of slave trade, it is possible that her name was

* *Country Journal or The Craftsman*, 12 February 1743. Paradoxically the colours of Towneley's Manchester Regiment bore the words *Church* and *Country* on one side, *Liberty* and *Property* on the reverse.

dictated by a fanciful current fashion, inspired by the eponymous heroine of Samuel Richardson's phenomenally popular novel, published in 1740 and subtitled *Virtue Rewarded.*

All three transports reached their destinations in early August, the *James & Mary* and *Liberty & Property* at the Nore anchorage in the mouth of the Thames estuary, and the *Pamela* at Woolwich.

III

A logistical problem had presented itself to the civil authorities from the outset: the administrative and procedural complexity – not to mention expense – that bringing more than three thousand individuals to trial would involve. All in theory were to answer a charge of levying war against the King in his realm. Should even half be convicted and suffer the ultimate penalty for High Treason, the most zealous proponents of exemplary retribution would blanch at the forest of gibbets necessary to carry out those sentences.

The expedient arrived at, of lottery, had been first employed in the aftermath of the 1715 Jacobite rising:

> Taking into consideration the great Numbers of Persons detained in Custody . . . and how much it imports the publick Peace of the Kingdom that a speedy Example be made of some of them . . . Prisoners [are] to draw Lots, to the Intent that every Twentieth Man on whom the lot shall fall shall be appointed for Tryal.[1]

The nineteen men from each group of twenty who evaded a fatal ticket and did not stand trial were granted leave to petition the king for mercy and given to understand that so long as they acknowledged their guilt, 'such a Petition [would] be favourably receiv'd'.[2]

The 'Act for the King's Most Gracious General and Free Pardon' extended amnesty even to 'such as had rendered themselves obnoxious to the Law and subject to the highest penalties'. Mercy was bestowed 'in a large and bountiful manner [by the king] not doubting . . . it will raise a due sense of gratitude in all who have been artlessly misled into treasonable practices against his person and government'.[3] Commonly abbreviated to the 'Act of Grace', it came with an 'express Condition'. Pardoned prisoners were to be transported as indentured servants – euphemistically termed 'apprentices' – to plantations in the British Colonies of Virginia, Maryland and the West Indies, 'during the term of their natural lives'.[4] Those in receipt of the King's questionable mercy numbered at least 866 men, women and children.*

An additional consideration – beyond that of practicability – persuaded the authorities to try no more than one in twenty. 'It is to be feared many will be Acquitted for Want of Evidence,' pointed out Treasury Solicitor, John Sharpe. 'There is no Evidence against [a large number of] them but what hath been Collected from amongst the Rebells themselves and it cannot be Expected this Sort of Evidence will be Sufficient to Convict them all.' Better a limited conviction rate than wasting the court's time by trying hundreds impossible to convict.

Only rank and file, or 'common' men, were to be lotted. 'Gentlemen or Men of Estates' – those most likely to be officers – were all to be tried, as were individuals who had 'distinguish'd themselves by any Extraordinary Degree of Guilt'.[5] Exempted from both lotting and from trial were men who volunteered – or might be persuaded – to turn King's Evidence and act as witnesses against their former comrades-in-arms. The process of selecting 'Evidences' had begun in May, before the seven transports left the Moray Firth, when the Judge Advocate of the army, David Bruce, accompanied by Lieutenant Tucker of Blakeney's regiment,

* A total of 936 names appear in the records as being ordered for transportation. However, there is no precise number for those on whom the sentence was actually carried out. Only in one case is there a list of prisoners transported on board a particular ship.

visited each ship in turn. One particularly compliant witness they found was Lord Cromartie's former gardener, who claimed to have been employed by his Lordship enlisting men to the rising. The form of words drawn up by Mr Bruce for him to sign was, in all but its particulars, standard and would be reproduced for all 'Evidences' secured at Inverness:

> [Witness] Depones that he has seen since the Commencement of this Rebellion the persons whose names are mentioned on this and the Two preceding pages, Amounting to Ninety Six in Number, in arms against His majesty King George, (and for the Pretender) and Depones that he is Willing to Give Evidence against them before any Court and Depones he knows them all personally . . . and Declares he Cannot write But Desires Mr Tucker and Mr Bruce to Sign for him, he has put his mark to this on board [the *Jean of Leith*] the Twenty first day of May 1746 Daniel X Fraser his Mark.

Bruce and Tucker found fifteen witnesses prepared to testify against a total of about four hundred and twenty.

Witnesses, when selected, could expect removal from prison or prison ship – and so from the reach of reprisal by those they betrayed – to a 'Messenger's house'. This was a domestic establishment, secured as a private gaol by a court official charged with delivering 'Evidences' as and when required. Such prisoners would, as a matter of course, receive a free pardon. 'A great number of the Rebells,' remarked the Treasury Solicitor, 'must be used as Evidences and consequently pardoned if all the rest are to be Tryed.'[6] Clearly Sharpe perceived it as an evasion of justice by self-confessed 'Rebells', and another argument against indiscriminate trial.

The task of recruiting further 'Evidences', and of lotting or exempting prisoners in London gaols, aboard the transports and at Tilbury, fell to Captain Stratford Eyre. Letters from his employer, Mr Sharpe, could reach him either at the Old Bagnio – a louche establishment on the west side of St James's Street – or in the nearby St James's Coffee House. Throughout late

July, August and September, Eyre was a busy and often exasperated man.

Visiting Tilbury, he was shocked to discover that civilian sympathisers had been making cash donations to the prisoners' welfare: 'three and thirty guineas . . . by one Walkinshawe & by two other Persons unknown'. A prominent Jacobite family, the Walkinshaws numbered ten daughters, the youngest of whom, Clementina, had nursed Charles Edward Stuart through a period of illness near Bannockburn. She would later become his much abused mistress for eight years. Eyre thought it advisable to restrain prisoners at Tilbury from any further communication with visitors 'to prevent their receiving more of these ill Design'd & unnecessary charitys . . . sent with no other view, but to keep up the Spirit of Dissatisfaction'. He pointed out, besides, that 'His Majestie's allowance [of fourpence per day per head for subsistence] is full sufficient & very Equally & Justly Distributed & great care taken of the Prisoners at Tilbury.' And he added, with no apparent irony, that '8 Prisoners dyed since last monday.'[7]

Compiling reliable lists of prisoners was not always straightforward, and Eyre suspected subterfuge to cheat or obstruct justice. Lieutenant Alexander McKenzie of Corrie had been left with the rank and file on one of the transports, while Kenneth McKenzie, 'a private man' had been transferred to the Surrey Gaol where he 'personates the officer'. Eyre's misgivings had been aroused when he found the said Kenneth to be a 'most abject, sickly, illiterate contemptable wretch', unlikely officer material for any army. 'Whether this has been done by mistake or design,' he remarked to Sharpe, 'I can not say but I much suspect the latter for I have the original Lists of the whole, and there's not an officer or Person of Consideration amongst them all, of the name of Kenneth, and there has been strange Jumbling in bringing [the officers] on Shore.'

He even suspected that the dead were evading him. Five had perished already in the New Gaol, but he only had another's word for it. 'Is it not right,' he asked Sharpe, 'to order the keepers of these Prisons to report when any of their Prisoners die [and] immediately that a proper Person may be sent to view and see if it be the Person represented[?]'

The inmates of another prison were a particular cause of concern. In less turbulent times the Marshalsea – a little north of the Surrey Gaol – accommodated only two categories of prisoner: insolvents held captive until discharge of their debts, and mutineers, pirates and other offenders incarcerated by the Admiralty. It was in keeping with the naval authority's jurisdiction over a part of this establishment that it contained many prisoners taken at sea aboard French ships, such as the *Espérance*, the *Bourbon* and the *Soleil*, bringing aid to the insurgency. A small number of men claiming French nationality captured at Carlisle had been brought there also. Most so-called French prisoners were in fact from Ireland. Romantically dubbed 'Wild Geese', they were mercenary troops 'forc'd by the Severity of the Laws against popery, to seek their fortune under a [French] Prince, who wd. employ them'. By January 1747 there were nearly a hundred in the Marshalsea, all claiming prisoner-of-war status by dint of being in the 'French Service', and all awaiting their discharge. Five months earlier there had been only a quarter of that number, but nonetheless a source of irritation to Captain Eyre, who thought there was 'too great a Resort of Company, with them, Continual entertaining and drinking and visitors admitted without the least Caution!' Both inside the prison and at the doors giving onto Borough High Street, 'the Concourse of people is amazing,' he complained, 'as crowded as a fair, and a Recruiting Serjeant could not look for a fuller assembly to beat up for volunteers at.' Fearing the spread of sedition Eyre made recommendations. 'It will be prudent to Remove all the French officers and private men from this populous City (where Priests and Jesuits – foreign ministers' agents – and Papists and Dissaffected who I fear are too, too numerous! . . .) to a Retired place in the Country . . . well look'd to and properly restrain'd from visitors.'

And he concluded his diatribe with increasingly discordant exclamations at his principal annoyance, the high life prisoners of this sort were allowed to lead. 'Here they have perpetual entertaining and drinking, See a Multitude of Company and Persons . . . Dress exceeding gay! live expensively! and all This, for the Honour of France! and to let the unthinking crowd judge from their ostentation of the power and Riches of The Grand Monarch [Louis XV].'

Their behaviour in London was very different from what it had been in Inverness when first captured, and where 'Humility was seen in every Instance'. Eyre seemed personally offended by the change in them on arrival in London. 'From some of these persons I met little less than Insult,' he complained, 'great ill manners!'

Eyre's preoccupation with the so-called French prisoners was partly prompted by a particular grudge originating five years earlier in his native Ireland. A 'sea farring young man' by the name of Thady Teirny had been contracted by the Mayor of Galway to transport sixty convicts to the North American plantations, receiving the 'County allowance' of six pounds per head for the job. But instead of shipping his charges across the Atlantic, he had taken them to a French port 'where he rec'd nine pounds a man for them, to recruit [in] the French army'. He also acquired an officer's commission for himself into the bargain. One of the convicts – a former tenant on Captain Eyre's Galway estate – subsequently deserted from the French service and returned home where the captain had him arrested. It was from this man that he learnt of Teirny's double-dealing, outlawed him and posted a reward for his capture. On the basis of this tenuous hearsay and coincidence – and assuming his quarry to be among the *Royal Ecossais* sent by the French king to fight in Scotland – Eyre scanned every Irishman that came before him and wished enquiries made of prisoners 'confin'd in other parts of Great Britain . . . of the same nation', hoping in vain to apprehend the 'tall, slender black [haired] man, who undoubtedly goes by another name'.[8]

Meanwhile, in the north of England, Crown Solicitor Philip Carteret Webb was carrying out the same official procedures as Eyre: examining prisoners, recruiting 'Evidences', lotting, and setting aside the especially criminal for trial. He was also subject to similar exasperation. Arriving in Carlisle on 1 August, he found it so overcrowded that he was hard pressed to find a bed for the night, let alone beds for his servants and stabling for their horses. The small city – 'Inhabitants from 16 Years and upwards . . . only 359', he was told – had been quite overwhelmed by having to accommodate more than three hundred French prisoners and thirty-eight of their officers. Mr Webb 'soon began to Experience what it was to be in a Rebel Town'. His observations of those claiming privileges as prisoners of war, and refusing to be humbled by defeat, were markedly similar to Captain Eyre's. 'Those French Officers live here at a great Expence, give Balls or Plays to the Towns People almost every Night which . . . make[s] the whole Run of the Town Incline to favour the Rebels.'[9] Moreover, he feared that their presence in Carlisle, 'at full Liberty', might even compromise the forthcoming trials. 'The Influence they have by means of the Expence they live at, prevents many Persons from giving Testimony and . . . when the Tryals come on several of these Officers will appear as Witnesses for the Rebells to prove them formerly in the French Service.'[10]

To prevent this interference with procedure some French officers were transferred to Penrith, and later in the year they would become an annoyance to Lieutenant Colonel Howard, when he escorted seven prisoners, sentenced at Carlisle, to their execution. He was told that the officers had not only supplied meat and drink for the last supper and breakfast of the condemned men, but had also 'ordered Coffins to be made for them, and were at the Expence of buying them'. Howard regarded this as 'the greatest Insolence and highest Insult I know'. He pointed out to Mr Webb that 'they were sent over to make War here' and should not be allowed 'to practice such behaviour . . . in defiance of the Law, and as an Insult to us who were present'.[11]

*

Visiting Tilbury Fort on 2 August Captain Eyre reported that, of nearly three hundred prisoners taken off the first transport from

Inverness in June, two hundred and sixty-eight remained. Twenty-nine had died of fever and forty more he believed 'will be dead in a few days'. He had been there compiling a list of the 'most criminal' – marking the eleven names with a flourished letter 'm' – and of those 'as can be usefull & necessary [as witnesses] in the Prosecutions', marking those twenty-seven names with a cross.[12] Eyre may have had second thoughts because when messengers arrived to take away the 'Evidences' for safe-keeping, they left with only twenty. The Tilbury governor Francis Cayvan reported that six more remained in his custody, willing to 'turn Evidence for his Majesty, [and] in my opinion they know more than all the rest'. Another prisoner, John Mason, had complained that Captain Eyre 'promised to send for him and was surprized he was not in the List'.[13]

The spread of gaol fever among the prisoners remained a concern. After visiting the *Pamela*, 'lately arrived' at Woolwich, Eyre reported that even the guards were 'very Sickly' and many of the prisoners 'in a Dyeing Way'.[14] This was corroborated a week later, when a medical officer was sent to assess their condition. Mr Minshaw had taken the precaution of stuffing his nostrils with 'proper Herbs', but when he peered down into the darkness of the *Pamela*'s hold he was 'saluted with such an Intolerable smell that it was like to Overcome [him]'. Sitting with Thomas Grindley, the ship's commander, on the quarterdeck – some distance from the hatchway – Minshaw watched as fifty-four prisoners were called up one by one to give name, age, place of birth and the regiment or corps in which they had served. Many of them were diseased, 'as appeared by their countenance and their Snail Creep-pace in ascending the ladder, being only just able to crawl up'. Another eighteen were left below, too weak even to negotiate the ladder. There was a brief discussion as to whether they should be hoisted up in a sling to account for themselves to Mr Minshaw but instead 'two of the most hardy of the Guard' volunteered to descend and make a list of the remainder where they lay. They reported that 'the uncleanness of that place, [was] surpassing Imagination & too

Nautious to Describe.' The medical officer's judgement – albeit made at more than arm's length – was that 'Malignant Fever . . . & another Odious Distemper peculiar to Scotchmen, is such a Complication of Disorders, that if not timely Remedied by a Speedy Removal from the Ship (which is very small) is much feared will terminate in a More Dreadful Disorder than any . . . before Mentioned.'

In addition the *Pamela*'s Commander complained of the quality of guards he had been assigned. Because they were not regular army men, and therefore not subject to 'Military punishments for Neglect of Duty', and being 'so harrassed with Watching as to be quite worn out therewith', Mr Grindley feared he was 'in Danger of being Deserted by them all and left alone to Guard the prisoners'.[15] The escape of two of his charges the following month was probably due to low morale among the guards and their lack of discipline, rather than to their being 'Scotch' as Eyre was 'perswaded'.[16]

After examining likely witnesses at Tilbury and at Woolwich, Captain Eyre visited the *James & Mary* and the *Liberty & Property* at the Nore. Although disclosing no details as to the sanitary conditions on these two transports, while there he contracted 'an agueish Disorder & a Feavour' that confined him at Sheerness for three days. His observations – if not a sense of empathy – prompted him to recommend that the *Pamela* and both transports at the Nore be moved from their current moorings and come to anchor near Tilbury Fort, enabling 'the Apothecary who victuals those there, [to] take the same Care of the Rest'. The location would have other benefits. 'They may in Certain numbers at a time, with a proper guard be permitted to go on shore & walk within the Ramparts of Tilbury, which will contribute much to their Recovery & may prevent Infection.'

Care for the prisoners' health was not entirely altruistic, given that Eyre's primary concern was to identify, persuade and, above all, preserve the lives of prosecution witnesses for the ongoing treason trials. 'Some very usefull people are in a Miserable way,' he told Mr Sharpe. 'I assure you, Sir, Some people you'll want, . . . cannot live many days in their present situation & . . . must Inevitably perish.'[17]

Whatever its motive, the strategy of anchoring transports at Tilbury where prisoners could 'be daily landed for air'[18] proved effective because less than a month later, visiting the *Pamela*, he declared, 'there is nothing of Infection (except the Itch) in the Distemper or Sickness amongst them . . . let who will report the Contrary.' He found forty-nine sick men that had been transferred to the hospital ship *Mermaid* 'recovering fast' and some that had seemed starved at Woolwich, 'so surprisingly recovered [he] scarce knew them'. The improvement was, he remarked, in large part due to the 'extraordinary good attendance they have from a Rebel Surgeon, employ'd by the Principal to assist him.' This was probably Kinlochmoidart's brother, the 'chirurgeon', Dr John MacDonald. A prisoner on the *Pamela*, it was to his care that many 'sick of fevers, fluxes, and other distempers'[19] owed their lives, while the apothecary at Gravesend could not be prevailed upon to go on board for fear of himself contracting the infection. The condition of prisoners inside Tilbury Fort meanwhile worsened. 'It is not their victuals that gives occasion for animadversion', Eyre reported, 'but non Attendance of the Doctor.' That, and 'suffering filth & nast to remain . . . since their confinement gathering in their rooms'.[20]

By the time he had completed his examinations there, and on the transports, seventy-five prisoners had been 'set apart for Tryal or further Examination, and for Evidence'. Of those to be tried, three were thought to be 'guilty of many acts of Barbarity'.[21]

Captain Eyre was uncharacteristically moved by the plight of one prisoner on the *Liberty & Property*. Lady Anne Stewart of Burray in Orkney was recently widowed, her husband Sir James having been 'carried . . . to New-Prison, . . . soon after fever'd, and died within a week or two'.[22] Sir James had taken no active part in the rising and his arrest and incarceration were on suspicion of his being a close friend of the Prince. As for his widow, 'I can't Discover any thing against her,' Eyre told Sharpe. 'The Lady's Case . . . is really Deplorable. I wish her in a more agreeable Situation than the poor unfortunate woman is at present.' His chivalry did not extend to her companions, however. 'The other two ladys [Margaret Macdonald of Clanranald and Anne McKinnon] are Jack Rebels,' he declared; 'let them Suffer.'[23] Nonetheless, all three women were soon transferred to more salubrious accommodation in Mr Money's messenger house where a modicum of comfort could be had at a price.

*

Lotting the 355 common men of no use for evidence and undistinguished by any significant degree of villainy – in the powder magazine of Tilbury Fort, on the hospital ship *Mermaid* and aboard the three neighbouring transports – began in early October. A hat containing numbered slips of paper was passed among each group of twenty. Names of the seventeen on whom each twentieth lot had fallen were 'expressed in Red letters' and the word 'Justice' written opposite.

Thinning the trial lists by lottery was not a perfect system for the prosecuting authority. As a hat went round at Carlisle on 9 August, prisoners were told that 'it was to draw for [their] lives'. But when all one hundred and eighty had drawn, Philip Carteret Webb complained that 'of the 9 on whom the Lott fell, only one can be indicted, there being no Evidence against the Rest.'[24] In the event six would be indicted. Three were found guilty but their death sentences commuted to Transportation, although one died in prison before he could be shipped. The other three would be acquitted, one of them 'Ignorant & an Infant under 14'.[25] Mr Webb remarked on the anomaly, that there were prisoners committed only 'on Suspicion, or for Words, or treasonable Practices, the Proof against most of whom, on its being properly sifted, comes out to be Slight and Insufficient . . . when the Crown is shewing so much mercy to 19 out of 20 Rebels who unquestionably deserve to be hanged.'[26]

The lotting procedure continued, with slight variations, elsewhere. Only thirty-six were lotted at Chester Castle and a single roll of paper marked 'To be tried' was drawn by Alexander McLean, an Inverness pedlar, from thirty-five rolls left blank. He was accordingly taken to York with twenty other men who 'on account of their Quality, Estate, or Degree of Guilt' were also to stand trial.[27]

Of the 109 prisoners in York Castle, eight had been set apart as witnesses and twenty-five to be tried. Lotting the remaining seventy-six added four more, raising the number for trial to twenty-nine. Another forty-five, marched from Lincoln and Chester, brought the total to seventy-five. Only one of the four prisoners who drew the 'Justice' lot at York would be executed. On 8 November the unfortunate William Hunter – a sergeant in the Manchester Regiment and a victim of purest chance – went to his death with a dozen other men selected on far less arbitrary grounds than himself.

IV

BEFORE trials could begin in Carlisle and York a Special Commission of Oyer and Terminer – its arcane gravity emphasized by the Norman French phrase meaning 'to hear and to determine', but otherwise an assize court for trying cases of High Treason, felony and other misdemeanours – sat in conclave with a 23-man grand jury to find bills of indictment against the seventy-five accused. On the Sunday before this preliminary hearing, commissioners and jurymen attended holy worship in York Minster. James Ibbetson, chaplain to the Bishop of Lincoln, preached a 'most excellent discourse' upon 'the heinous Nature of Rebellion', intended to encourage his congregation in their deliberations. His opening text was taken from the Book of Numbers, a passage concerning punishment for those of the chosen people who had given allegiance to the enemy and his gods: 'And Moses said unto the Judges of Israel, Slay ye every one his Men that were joined unto Baal-peor.'* The message would have been familiar to audiences of Handel's oratorios, associating the Jews' embattled early history with a paramount necessity to preserve the Protestant faith and British Union. Mr Ibbetson concluded his sermon with a conflation of inaccurate Old Testament quotations:

> Let the King ever rejoice in Thy Strength, O Lord; Let Him be exceeding glad of thy Salvation. Blessed be the Lord His God,

* Numbers 25: 5

which hath delivered up the men that lift up their hands against Him. Even so perish all His Enemies.*

In the days that followed 'the Evidence [presented to the tribunal] was so clear and full, and the Grand Jury proceeded with so much Unanimity and Dispatch' that 'true bills' of indictment were brought against all seventy-five.[1]

Of 382 prisoners being held at Carlisle, 118 were set apart for trial as being men of estate or especial guilt. One hundred and eighty common men were lotted, producing a further nine, bringing the total number to be tried to 127. Of these, forty-one would plead guilty, intending to petition the king for mercy, and thirty-six were acquitted. Of the fifty found guilty and sentenced to death, thirty-three would be executed.

A common condition of reprieve for condemned prisoners was enlistment in the British army, recruits being in great demand by commanders fighting the French and Spanish in outlying theatres of war in the Americas. Documentation suggests that ninety-two were handed over to the army by prison authorities in Carlisle and York for service in the West Indies. Of these, twenty-six under sentence of death at Carlisle, and thirty at York, were granted reprieves at the eleventh hour, subject to enlistment. James Miller of the Manchester Regiment received his on the morning he was to have been executed. Others were probably spared upon the same proviso from the list of condemned at Southwark, although no related documentation survives.

One of the four judges who presided at Carlisle, York and Southwark, Baron of the Exchequer Charles Clarke, kept a notebook in which he summarised proceedings, making occasional terse comments on those passing before him and his colleagues. 'A common fellow', he wrote of Molineux Eaton, and the same of James Miller, adding that Miller was 'of no Consequence one way or other'. He did, however, display compassion, if only on paper. He described Thomas Lawson as 'a poor wretched Mortal',[2]

* Ibbetson cited Psalm 21: 1 and 2 Samuel 18: 28, but the last sentence is to be found in neither.

Simon Longdown, 'a poor silly Fellow',[3] and Thomas Turner, 'a poor boy an object of Mercy'. These three were sentenced to death but reprieved, as were Eaton and Miller. Thomas Hayes, 'a poor miserable Fellow', would be executed on testimony that he had worn 'a sash plad', a white cockade, and once 'took up a Gun & presented at [the witness who] wouldn't fetch him bread'.[4] The court heard evidence that James Brand was a quartermaster in Lord Strathallan's Perthshire Squadron and responsible for distributing subsistence money to government army deserters enlisting in the Prince's service. When captured near Ecclefechan, he was riding a white horse, 'had several pistols' but only one of them loaded, 'a tartan Wastecoat, Dragoon Boots [and a] Broad Sword he took from [a] Dragoon at Preston Pans'. However, his defence council brought two witnesses claiming he had stayed the night of 20 September at a house in Musselburgh, left 'about 5 or 6 o'Clock next morn' and probably missed the fighting. He was 'a bold daring fellow,' wrote Clarke 'but on the whole we thought he lay at Musselburgh the Night before the Battle of Gladesmoor, to avoid the Danger.'[5] Despite this alibi, Brand would be put to death on 18 October.

John Thoris was 'a little deformed Boy', Clarke noted: 'The Pretender ask'd . . . what use he could be of – to which he answer'd "Sir tho' my body is Small my Heart is as big as any Man's you have."'[6] Prosecution council saw no reason to pursue the matter further and he was acquitted.

A 27-year-old curate, and chaplain to the Manchester Regiment, Thomas Coppock was said to have affected a loftier status having been promised the Bishopric of Carlisle after joining the Jacobite army. He appeared at the bar of the court in his gown and cassock. Mary Humphreys, a witness for his defence, testified that he had been pressed into the service by Thomas Sydall, the three Deacon brothers, Thomas Chadwick and two other men who grabbed him as he crossed the inn yard of The Bull with the words, 'Now Coppock, now is the time to make your fortune – a Gold Chain or a hempen Halter!' Then they hustled him away, threatening to kill his companion if she interfered. The defendant's father testified that he had also tried to get his son released, 'but a man drew a penknife & said I was a Rascal'. After what must have been a comparatively lengthy trial given the fullness of Clarke's notes, he was found guilty, and with 'no hesitation in the Jury'.[7] He would not have endeared himself by his comments in court. 'Never mind it my boys', he told his fellow prisoners at the bar, 'for if our Saviour was here, these fellows would condemn him.' And catching sight of one of them weeping as sentence was passed: 'What the devil are you afraid of? We shan't be tried by a Cumberland jury in the next world.'[8]

Coppock's sixteen-year-old brother John also stood trial although the relationship was not mentioned in Clarke's notes. The defence was that he was 'only a Drummer', that he was 'very young', 'not active' in the Jacobite army, had been 'averse to go with them', and had 'hid himself in a Garrett'.[9] He was, as a matter of course, found guilty but the jury 'desire[d] he may be recommended to the Crown to save his Life'. He would eventually be 'Pardoned on condition of enlistment'.[10]

A plea of lunacy was entered in defence of William Hargrave, described as being 'of a distempered brain'.[11] Five or six years earlier 'he went mad', a witness testified, '& was bound in his bed'. Another confirmed he had then been 'carried to a Mad-house', and that he had been seen since, 'at Preston . . . in a Melancholy Way – & going in to [the] same way again'. Mr Baron Clarke appeared to doubt unsoundness of mind, commenting 'he seems a very ordinary Man & no virulence attending his Crime.'[12] He was found guilty but later reprieved and pardoned, also on condition of enlistment.

The Edinburgh watchmaker John McNaughton was one of those common men set apart for trial and alleged to have 'distinguish'd themselves by [an] Extraordinary Degree of Guilt'. A witness from Lee's Regiment testified that, at Prestonpans, McNaughton 'shot at Colonel Gardner – who fell from his Horse – & as he lay on the ground leaning on his Hand . . . struck him twice on the shoulder with his broadsword – & when he lifted up his Hand to defend the blow he made a third stroke at his head.' The same witness added prior design to the charge, claiming the defendant had earlier called out, 'Where is that Bouger Colonel Gardner?' Another Lee's man claimed to have remonstrated with McNaughton over the Colonel's body, 'told him he had killed a better man than ever stood on his Legs,' and received the reply, 'If you speak three words I will kill you too.' When it could be proved to the court's satisfaction that an offence of levying war against the king was compounded by being 'remarkably cruel' to his troops in battle, the guilty verdict required little consideration.[13] The jury also 'made no doubt'[14] as to the culpability of MacDonell of Tirnadris, on the evidence of two government soldiers, that at Prestonpans 'he was against putting a stop to the shedding of blood.'[15] The court may also have taken into account this prisoner's active role at Falkirk, and his leadership of the first hostile action in the rising: the ambush and capture of Captain Scott's column of the 1st Foot at Highbridge, Lochaber.

During the trial of William Home jury members were instructed by Baron Clarke on the limits of their discretion in sentencing. The accused had been advised by his defence council to enter a plea of not guilty, 'not that he pretended to Deny or Excuse his Crime but only that he might have an opportunity of Proving his age which was not fourteen years compleat when he engaged in [the rising] so as to be recommended by the Court or jury to the Kings Mercy.' A witness who had been present at Home's christening duly swore in his defence that he had been born no earlier than November 1731. But evidence was brought against him that, as an Ensign in Balmerino's Life Guards, he had carried the Prince's standard at Falkirk and Culloden. In his summing up, Clarke declared that 'the plea of Youth could not avail where it did appear that the Criminal was endued with Maturity of judgement.' This being the prisoner's case, 'from his being Trusted with a Standard in two pitched Battles', the jury 'ought not to interpose but leave him entirely to the King and such application as his friends should be able to make for him'.[16] He was accordingly found guilty and condemned to death. The style and particulars of Home's petition to the King departed from the formulaic phrasing of other such documents submitted to His Majesty's attention. The supplicant's 'unhappy Departure from his Duty proceeded from no fix'd rebellious Principle,' he declared, 'but from the Levity of Youth'. He had been 'a prey to the Crafty Insinuations of those who were concerned in the Rebellion' and their persuasion had consisted of 'the promises of Lac'd Cloaths and the Carrying [of] a Set of the Rebel Colours'. He added that this battlefield role was all his 'youth & want of Strength rendered him fit to undertake'.[17] William's petition was supported by his distant kinsman, the Earl of Home, and his sentence commuted. He declined an offer of pardon on condition of enlistment in the East India Company's service on account of his health, weakened by gaol fever contracted in Carlisle Castle. Eventually pardoned unconditionally, he was allowed to settle abroad where he rose to the rank of Colonel in the Prussian Army.

The trials at Carlisle began on Friday 12 September and ended a fortnight later on the 26th. Over the thirteen days on which the court sat, the fate of nearly 130 men was decided. Three trials were notable for inordinate length. John Henderson's lasted six hours – twelve witnesses being examined against him, and nine in his favour. Clarke thought him 'a better sort . . . and . . . appeared throughout . . . to have been a very active busy man'. Testimony was heard as to his good character and it was said that 'the rebels . . . forced [him] to take a Cockade & cursed him they would stick him if [he] did not let it remain.' Notwithstanding, the jury 'did not stay a Minute to debate' their guilty verdict.[18] Donald MacDonald of Kinlochmoidart – 'a principal Man in the Pretender's army', whose head would adorn the Scotch Gate[19] – was found guilty 'after an Obstinate Tryal of 8 hours', as was Francis Buchanan of Arnprior 'after a Tryal of 9½ hours'.[20]

A mystery surrounds Buchanan's conviction. He played no active part in the rising, and had been arrested on suspicion only. And yet, arriving in Carlisle, he 'was immediately ordered into a dungeon and to have irons clapt upon him', a level of severity and security surprising even to the officer guarding him. When Captain Thompson made enquiry of the Solicitor General, William Murray, he received the reply: 'Pray, Sir, give yourself no more trouble about that gentleman. I shall take care of him. I have particular orders about him, for HE MUST SUFFER!'[21] A fortnight before the trial Andrew Fletcher, Lord Justice Clerk to the Duke of Newcastle, had written to Phillip Webb concerning Buchanan, that it would be of 'more consequence to His Majesty's Service and for the peace and quiet of the country to get rid of such a person of rank and ability . . . artful and able to poison a whole County, than to convict ninety and nine of the lowest rank of Rebels.'

The sole evidence brought against him was an intercepted unsigned letter said to be in his handwriting. But in Fletcher's opinion the very lack of firm proof appeared to confirm his guilt: 'by his art and interest he had . . . been able to stifle all direct evidence against himself.'[22] On the evening of 22 September, Mr Webb had the satisfaction of personally informing Newcastle of Buchanan's conviction. He added that twenty-three sentences had already been pronounced that morning, and 'the Council for the Prisoners have repeatedly confessed in Court, that the Proceedings were carryed on with the Greatest candour & fairness.'[23] Writing again five days later to report the Carlisle trials ended, Webb was triumphant: 'We have had the good fortune that not one hath Escaped thro' any slip or mistake in the proceeding or one been acquitted contrary to the Opinion of the Court & the King's Council.'[24] Francis Buchanan was duly executed at Carlisle on 18 October.

Trial dates at Southwark, Carlisle and York were staggered to enable judges to travel from one court to another. The circuit was to have included a fourth city but proceedings having been delayed at Carlisle – due to the late arrival of a hundred and forty prisoners, along with 'several Scotch Advocates & writers coming from Scotland to defend [them]' – it was decided that holding trials in Lincoln would be impracticable. Of the eighty-four held there – described by Webb as 'the very scum and refuse of the Rebellion' – twenty-seven were boys under eighteen years of age, twenty were under sixteen, and a number of them 'not above 12 or 13'. Lincoln gaol yielded only twenty-four indictments and these prisoners were accordingly marched to York for trial, 'a great Saving both of Time and Expence'.[25]

Of seventy-five bills of indictment brought by the grand jury in York – following Ibbetson's exemplary sermon at the Minster – Mr Baron Clarke made notes on just sixteen of the subsequent trials conducted in early October. David Ogilvy, 'about 17 – a poor Boy & seems worthy of mercy', was duly reprieved but died later in prison.[26] Another youth, David Wilkie – said to be under 16 – was sentenced to death, 'but the Jury having some doubt [about the evidence] recommended him for Mercy'. His life was spared conditional on enlistment.[27]

It was reported at Captain George Hamilton's trial that after Prestonpans he had threatened to shoot government army prisoners if they refused to join the insurgents. Counter-evidence was produced, but rebutted, that he had tended to the English wounded. Clarke noted only 'Full proof against him but no Circumstance of Cruelty or ill-usage'.[28] He was executed on 1 November regardless, as was William Connolly, a Londonderry man who had deserted from the Royal Scots. He was convicted on the grounds of his alleged advice at Prestonpans 'to kill the redcoats, especially of Lee's regiment, because they would know him again' and also because he had personally 'killed an English soldier'.[29]

When the piper John Ballantine was acquitted, Clarke wrote that he 'shewed such honest and unaffected Signs of Joy on his Delivery as I never saw – he jump'd & danced [at] the Bar with his Irons & couldn't be contained by any means from expressing his Joy and Gratitude.'[30] A newspaper reported that 'he threw up his Bonnet to the very Roof of the Court, and cry'd out, *My Lords and Gentlemen, I thank you, Not Guilty! Not Guilty! Not Guilty! pray God bless King* George *for ever, I'll serve him all the Days of my Life.*' Then he ran out into the Castle Yard, fell to his knees, scooped up water from the gutter in his cupped manacled hands 'and drank his Majesty's Health'.[31] The trial of another piper on the same day had a less happy outcome. James Reid was found guilty of complicity in levying war, but was able to prove that although he 'bore arms sometimes . . . he was originally pressed into the [Prince's] service'.[32] Despite the jury recommending mercy on the grounds 'that he was only a piper',[33] mercy was denied him. Justice Burnett ruled that 'no regiment ever marched without musical instruments such as drums, trumpets and the like; and that a highland regiment never marched without a piper; and therefore [Reid's] bagpipe, in the eye of the law, was an instrument of war.'[34] On 15 November he would sit alone in the sledge dragging him to be hanged, gutted and decapitated, three other men condemned with him having been reprieved.

When the York trials ended on 7 October, seventy of the seventy-five indicted had been convicted and sentenced, five acquitted.[35] Of the seventy death sentences, forty-six were commuted on condition of enlistment or transportation.

V

A distinction should be drawn between the eighteenth-century institution of indentured servitude and the 'chattel slavery' imposed upon thousands of native Africans trafficked to the Americas as enforced labour. Although both categories worked for their masters without pay, one did so usually for a fixed term, while the other toiled until death. An indentured servant had legal and contractual status – albeit that of a prisoner – while the slave's only status was as property, his death in transit viewed as lost or spoiled cargo and the trader entitled to compensation by maritime insurance. The distinction, however, would have seemed a fine one for the shackled captives awaiting shipment from English ports as beneficiaries of 'the King's Mercy'. And there was no distinction at all in the threats made by Captain Benjamin Moodie of the 57th Foot to the hapless young men rounded up on the islands of Westray and North Ronaldsay in Orkney, that as their landlords 'were Rebells and Traitors they were all in the Eye of the Law such also and therefore their certain and unavoidable doom was to be hanged in England or at best to be sent to the plantations as Slaves for Life.'[1]

*

In early September, the Treasury Solicitor John Sharpe offered contracts to two capable individuals – one in the south of England and one in the north – to arrange the transportation to plantations in the West Indies and the North American mainland of prisoners who had escaped trial or sentence of death.

Mr Samuel Smith of Cateaton Street, Cheapside, like many another London merchant, had already contributed to the £6,000 raised by the Lord Mayor's Veterans' Scheme for the relief of 'brave Soldiers, . . . Subalterns, . . . the Maim'd & Wounded' of the government army in Scotland. And having exercised his patriotic generosity on behalf of the defenders of King and Country, Smith lost little time offering his assistance in ridding the kingdom of those who had attempted to subvert it. Just a fortnight after news of the victory at Culloden reached the capital, he had written to Sir Everard Fawkener, the Duke of Cumberland's private secretary, with a proposal, 'for transporting such of those Rebel Villains . . . as His Royal Highness may judge proper, and at the same time requesting the favour of [Sir Everard's] interpositions with His Royal Highness, that I may have the Contract.'[2]

Responding to reports in the London papers 'that a Body of Rebels to the Number of 4000 [were] assembled in Lochaber' well supplied with 'Money and Stores'[3], he wrote again at the end of May suggesting that the rumoured resurgence of Jacobite activity in the west of Scotland might even prove to the government's advantage. 'The Banditti which are gather'd together at Lochaber convinces me that there is a Providential Fatality . . . to put it in HRH's power to root up the very seeds of Rebellion which I'm satisfied can only be done, by clearing the country of every man of them.'[4]

Although he cannot have known it, Smith's suggestion agreed with Cumberland's thinking at this time. 'I believe . . . the only sure remedy for establishing Quiet in this country,' he wrote to the Duke of Newcastle, '[is] the transporting of particular Clans, such as the entire Clan of the Camerons and almost all the Tribes of the M'Donalds . . . for . . . it is my opinion, was there the least Occasion, they would rise again to-morrow.'[5]

When in September Smith was offered a share in the transportation contract, he declared himself honoured to be entrusted with 'the banishment of those fellows who have acted such a Villainous, ungratefull part'. Knowing that the going rate for shipping ordinary convicts to Maryland and Virginia 'in Time of Peace' was £5 per man, he pointed out that 'in Time of War', and for a longer voyage to the West Indies plantations, 'consideration ought to be had to the great difference of Expence in the Freight, Provisions, Men's Wages, Insurance, &c. which Swells the Account above One half.' He therefore offered to undertake the contract at a rate of £6 per man. The government was to provide a military escort to conduct the prisoners safe to the ports of embarkation and also 'to see them secured on board Ship with proper Irons at the Government's expence'. After the voyage, at the ports of destination, Mr Smith's agents were to 'make a proper Disposition of [the prisoners] amongst [his] friends'. These new masters would, he fancied, 'make them usefull Members of Society & in time they may possibly become good Subjects'.[6]

Three times Mayor and twenty years member of Parliament for Liverpool, Alderman Richard Gildart traded in Virginia tobacco and – like many gentlemen designated 'merchants' operating out of that city's flourishing port – in 'Negro' slaves. While the Treasury contract would represent a departure from Mr Gildart's customary line of merchandise, his ships had carried white human cargo before. Thirty years earlier, following the rising of 1715, and in partnership with his father-in-law Sir Thomas Johnson, he had shipped 639 Jacobite prisoners, at a cost of forty shillings each, to the plantations of Jamaica, South Carolina and Virginia.[7] Like Smith, Alderman Gildart reminded his employers that 'in peaceable Times this County gives £5 per head for [the transportation of] Convicts.' But at a time of war with France, and carrying such particularly unruly malefactors, his ships would 'require to be double Mann'd to supply what will be needful for the prisoners & to prevent any Insurrection or Escapes'. He hoped therefore that a rate of five pounds and ten shillings would not be thought too much. He also offered to supply every prisoner with 'Hand Cuffs & Shakles' for an extra five shillings apiece.[8]

Meanwhile, a consortium of six merchants of Chester – being informed that prisoners held in the castle of that city were to be transported to the Colonies – expressed themselves eager to undertake the contract for £5 a head. 'And if any other Merchant shall be willing to undertake the transportation of em at a Less Sum,' they added, 'we do hereby declare ourselves to be willing to transport the said Rebels at as low a price as any other person will do.'[9] This competitive tender having unaccountably been rejected by Mr Sharpe, the contract was divided instead between the two London and Liverpool merchants, albeit strictly at the peacetime rate. The Lords Commissioners of his Majesty's Treasury were 'of opinion that the sum of Five pounds per Man, and no more, should be allowed to Alderman Gildart, & Mr. Smith'.[10] Their Lordships were to be 'at noe more charge for Shackles, Irons or any other accounts after [the prisoners] are put aboard the Contractor's Ships'.[11] Until embarkation the Crown would provide its own chains.

Two pounds ten shillings was to be paid to the contractors for each prisoner shipped, within fourteen days of departure, and the remaining half of the per capita sum at the port of destination, on production of a numbered list of names and an affidavit as to any individual's 'Loss, Death, or Capture' during the voyage. The third of these eventualities would later prove of particular importance to Samuel Smith.

*

It was a matter of concern that such undesirables as were shipped across the Atlantic by Messrs Gildart and Smith might, at some future date, find their way back to the country whose constitution they had attempted to overthrow. The Crown Solicitor proposed a measure to remedy this eventuality. 'Suppose,' Philip Carteret Webb suggested, 'a Law was made for Transporting them, and marking them on the Face with a Hot Iron and making it Felony if they return; without such a Mark, any Law will be ineffectual.'[12]

Samuel Smith also believed it 'absolutely necessary that an act of parliament sh'd be passed to make it Death in case any of the Rebells return'. However, he expressed a surprisingly humane concern regarding the status of those he transported. Smith believed that 'making them Slaves, rather [than] Servants, for Life', might offend public opinion, or, as he put it, give 'umbrage to the nation'. Instead he suggested 'Transported Rebells . . . serve a certain number of years not to exceed fifteen.' He was, he declared, 'glad to forgo the difference of advantage' such an arrangement would entail 'to prevent any [public] uneasiness'.[13] By signing the standard certificate of indenture – round-hand sepia script on vellum – prisoners agreed to 'bind and put themselves as Apprentice and Servant to Samuel Smith or such other person or persons to be nominated . . . to serve them or their Assigns in his majesty's Colonies in America . . . during the Term of their natural Lives.'

However, a memorandum on the reverse of this document outlined the more compassionate compromise. It set a limit to the Indenture of Apprenticeship 'for and during and unto the full End and Term of Seven Years'.[14] At worst, given hard labour, murderous climate and prevalence of fever – especially in the West Indies plantations – seven years might well have exceeded the term of a prisoner's natural life. At best – as one man was told to induce him to sign – should their masters be pleased with their work, they 'would probably give us doun two years of our time, and a gun, a pick and a mattock, and a soot of cloths, and then we was fre[e] to go . . . any place . . . we pleased.'[15] There was, however, a proviso to the indenture memorandum. 'Discharge . . . from his Servitude' after seven years, granted only liberty 'to remain and continue in his majesty's Colonies or Plantations . . . according to the express Condition and terms of his Majesty's Most Gracious Pardon'.[16] That is, for the term of his natural life.

Mr Webb's recommendation of facial branding was not implemented and his fears of miscreants returning proved in the main groundless. Only six transported individuals were ever known to have done so. One was Alexander Stewart, former footman to the Prince. Fortunate in having friends and kinsmen in Virginia who repaid the nine pounds and six shillings of his purchase price, he was enabled covertly to take ship for Scotland, and reached Edinburgh a free man, albeit fugitive, exactly nine months after leaving Liverpool in shackles.

On the last day of April 1747, Stewart had been one of 88 prisoners brought from Carlisle and taken aboard the Liverpool merchant's eponymous ship *Gildart* lying at anchor in the Mersey estuary. A further forty-three Carlisle prisoners were embarked on the *Johnson*, named after Alderman Gildart's late father-in-law. Thirty-four more were marched, under military guard, the seven miles from Chester Castle to the Liverpool foreshore on Saturday 2 May for embarkation that evening, also aboard the *Johnson*. Sixteen of these prisoners were carried out to the anchorage in the ship's yawl. The remaining eighteen were placed in a long boat so overcrowded – and the five crewmen 'not having a sufficient room to row her' – that it had to be towed out into the channel behind the yawl. Most of the prisoners were shackled in pairs. Endeavouring to manoeuvre around the *Johnson's* bows and gain the 'offinside' or seaward facing side of the ship 'where the Ladder was', the yawl lost control of the vessel it was towing. 'The Tyde run so strong and made so fast down,' the impotent longboat crew testified, 'that the . . . Yawl had not force or strength to Tow her clear of the . . . *Johnson*'s Hawser.'[17] Forced up against this heavy anchor rope, pulled taut from the water at an angle by the powerful current, the craft capsized in the darkness. Some of the prisoners were able to cling to the overturned boat, while the crew saved themselves by catching hold of the ship's bobstays. One mercifully unshackled prisoner was rescued clinging to the hawser of the *Griffin* anchored nearby. Eight more were drowned, 'hand-cuffed two and two together, which made it impossible for any of them to save their Lives'.[18]

Alderman Gildart was partially compensated for the loss. Affidavits sworn before the Mayor of Liverpool by his agent and the longboat crew gave full details of the accident, and half of the transportation fee was paid by the Treasury for each of the eight drowned men, despite their never having reached the *Johnson*. What chiefly exercised the Liverpool contractor was that fourteen of the earlier contingent of Carlisle prisoners had been discharged by a warrant from the Duke of Newcastle before the *Gildart* set sail. The Alderman claimed to be 'at a large Expence in providing Provisions, Bedding and Cabbins in the Ships and other necessarys for the . . . Prisoners and . . . at great Expence in keeping a large Ship and a Number of hands in proportion to the Number of Prisoners Contracted to be carried therein.'

He therefore requested two pounds ten shillings for each of the fourteen to cover the expenditure of provisions for them, 'an Extraordinary Expence of £35'.

Samuel Smith suffered a greater commercial loss but with a happier result for his enforced passengers. In early May, his ship, the *Veteran*, carrying 150 prisoners to Antigua, was intercepted, a day's sail from her destination, by the French privateer *Diamond*, captured and escorted to Martinique where the prisoners were set at liberty by that island's French governor. 'Upon hearing of this bad news' Smith applied to the Duke of Newcastle for an order to General Mathew, Governor of the Leeward Islands, to reclaim them. At his own expense he arranged for a ship to take Mathew to Martinique to demand their return, but the French Governor 'refused to deliver them until he had directions from France to that purpose'. The merchant's last recourse for recovery of his cargo was that, in the event of any future cartel – or exchange of prisoners – being agreed with France, his former charges be included, and 'deliver'd to Mr John Chalmers his Agent at Antigua who has Instructions about them'.[19] He supplied the Duke of Newcastle with a list of the 150 names, giving age, occupation, and physical description – ranging from 'dark hair ruddy well set robust' to 'fair hair pock pitted slender' – to aid in their identification. This too proved fruitless. While Smith was happy to confirm that another 600 prisoners, 'all the rest that I had the care of, are safely arrived at Barbadoes, Jamaica, and Virginia', there is no record of the Treasury paying him the outstanding balance of two pounds ten shillings per head for those he had lost to the French.[20] As for the liberated prisoners themselves, an unknown number enlisted in the French colonial army, of whom five were subsequently court-martialled for desertion. All records of others freed from the *Veteran* were destroyed by a volcanic eruption on Martinique later in the century.[21]

*

Charles Deacon recovered from the 'panic Disorder' that had afflicted him following his brother's execution. Reprieved from the sentence of death, and held in the New Surrey Gaol for more than two years, he was at last pardoned and granted the King's mercy. In January 1749, he and seven others were taken to Tooley Street Watergate, placed in a passage yacht and conveyed to Gravesend 'to embark on board a Ship, in order to be transported for Life'. An air of defiant celebration prevailed among the prisoners and 'some of them went off with White and others Blue Ribbands in their Hats.'[22] The voyage to Jamaica lasted three months, during which Charles must have contracted some infection. On 29 April, two days after his arrival, he died.[23]

Sixteen months later, in January 1751, the heads of Thomas Theodorus Deacon and Thomas Sydall were removed from the portico of the Manchester Exchange, 'and privately conveyed away'. It was said to have been done 'without the Knowledge, Desire, or Consent, of any of their Relations'. Disloyal elements were instead blamed, intent on bringing 'a Slur and Imputation upon the Town, and to raise new Commotions and Animosities'. A reward of five guineas was offered by the authorities, and similar premiums by prominent tradesmen, 'for the detecting of any Person concerned in . . . this concerted malice and audacious Act.'[24]

VI

SPACE provided for spectators in Westminster Hall being at a premium during the trial of the 'Rebel Lords' – Balmerino, Cromartie and Kilmarnock – an essential cane or whalebone fashion accessory was discouraged. 'We hear an Order is given out,' reported the *Caledonian Mercury*, 'that all Ladies who come to hear the Trials, do not come in Hoops, in order to make moor Room in the Galleries.'[1] The width of hoop petticoats had increased throughout the first half of the eighteenth century, reaching a maximum of six feet during the 1740s and '50s. 'Hoops [are] of an enormous size', remarked an observer in 1746, ladies in their voluminous skirts 'appearing like so many *blown bladders*'.[2]

It was rumoured that 'Two fine Chairs' had been made and placed either side of the presiding Lord High Steward's throne, 'that on the Right Hand for the Prince of Wales, and on the Left for the Duke of Cumberland'.[3] This extra seating, however, proved superfluous as no member of the royal family attended on any of the three days the trial lasted. The occasion was not lacking in lavish pageantry, however. Ermined members of the House of Peers processed to the Hall, 'two and two', preceded by the 'Peers eldest sons' and 'Peers minors' in like formation, then the York and Windsor Heralds, and four Sergeants-at-Arms with their maces. After the Peers came the Sergeant-at-Arms attending the

Great Seal and Purse Bearer, then the Garter King of Arms, and the Gentleman Usher of the Black Rod, carrying – anomalously – a white staff before Philip, Lord Hardwicke, Lord High Chancellor of Great Britain, the Lord High Steward. Hardwicke's stewardship – its emblem the white staff of office presented to him by Black Rod at the start of proceedings – was a temporary commission for the duration of the trial only.

Indictments were read: that the defining act of High Treason alleged against Balmerino and Kilmarnock – the capture and occupation of the city of Carlisle – had occurred on 10 November 1745, while that against Cromartie – capturing the town of Perth – had taken place on 1 December. The Lieutenant of the Tower was then ordered to bring forth his prisoners, who were led into the Hall by Mr Fowler, Gentleman Gaoler of the Tower, carrying an axe. After making 'three reverences' towards relevant parts of the chamber, the accused knelt at the bar until bidden to rise by the Lord High Steward, while the Gentleman Gaoler stood to their left with the edge of his axe turned – for the time being – away from them.

Further proceedings were abbreviated when Cromartie and Kilmarnock pleaded guilty to the charges against them and subsequently returned to the Tower to await sentence. Lord Balmerino, however, entered a plea of not guilty on the grounds that – contrary to the indictment – he could prove himself to have been 'not within 12 miles' of Carlisle on the date he was said to have participated in capturing the city.* He later joked that he had pleaded not guilty and prolonged the trial 'that so many ladies might not be disappointed of their show'.[4]

'Culprit,' the Clerk of the Crown addressed the prisoner, 'how will your lordship be tried?'

'By God and my peers.'

'God send your lordship a good deliverance,' the Clerk responded.

Six witnesses were called by the Attorney General, each testifying that the prisoner had been seen in arms at Carlisle, 'going

* He was in fact at Longtown, 9 miles from Carlisle.

and coming', during the months of November and December. All were unclear as to specific days of the month. Balmerino occasionally questioned a witness as to the precise dates he was alleged to have been seen in Carlisle.

Finally, a ruling was made by Chief Justice Sir William Lee regarding Balmerino's presence or otherwise in Carlisle precisely on 10 November 1745. 'It is not necessary to prove the overt act to be committed *on the particular day* laid in the indictment: but as evidence may be given of an overt act *before* the day, so it may be *after* the day specified in the indictment; for the day laid is circumstance and form only, and not material in point of proof.'[5]

The prisoner graciously acknowledged his ignorance of the law and apologised for 'giving [their] lordships so much trouble'. He was then removed from the bar, protocol dictating that '[their] lordships' opinions on the question of Guilty or Not Guilty, should be delivered severally in the absence of the prisoner.'

Then each of the 135 Peers present – beginning with the youngest baron and ending with Lord President of the Council, the Duke of Dorset – were asked by the Lord High Steward, 'Is Arthur lord Balmerino Guilty of the high-treason whereof he stands indicted, or Not Guilty?' Each in turn stood up in his place, uncovered his head, clapped his right hand to his breast and answered: 'Guilty, upon my honour'. It then remained for Lord Hardwicke himself to make the verdict unanimous: 'My lords, I am of the opinion that Arthur lord Balmerino is Guilty of the high treason whereof he stands indicted, upon my honour.'

When the three prisoners were next brought to the bar the following morning, this time for judgement – one found guilty by his peers, the others guilty by admission – the Gentleman Gaoler's axe 'was carried with the edge towards them'.[6]

Each was asked 'why judgement of death should not pass upon you, according to law'. Kilmarnock and Cromartie had prepared lengthy speeches extolling their past good conduct, their past loyalty 'to the present happy establishment, both in church and state' and their 'constant attachment to his majesty's interest'. Kilmarnock, with a very fine voice',[7] spoke of his 'present anguish for having ever been concerned in this unnatural rebellion, and . . . undissembled sorrow and remorse for it which must attend me to my last moments'.[8] The appeal of Lord Cromartie would have especially moved the unhooped ladies in the public gallery as he conjured up for them 'an innocent wife', 'an unborn infant', 'eight infant children', an 'eldest son, whose . . . regard to his parent hurried him down the stream of rebellion', offering them as 'pledges to his majesty . . . pledges to your lordships . . . pledges to my country, for mercy: . . . the silent eloquence of their grief and tears . . . the powerful language of innocent nature, supply[ing his own] want of eloquence and persuasion.' But, unlike Kilmarnock, Cromartie was no orator and 'spoke so low, that he was not heard but by those who sat very near him'.[9]

If Balmerino had behaved as convention dictated and made a statement of atonement, loyalty or defiance, the ladies in the public gallery would next have thrilled to the awful frisson attending sentence of death for High Treason, its gruesome particulars barely disguised by judicial formality. Coincidentally, that sentence was at the same moment being exercised with rope, knife and cleaver on the bodies of Colonel Francis Towneley and the other eight officers of the Manchester Regiment not two miles away on the other side of the Thames. But Lord Balmerino again tried the patience of the court when he handed a document to the Clerk of the Crown and requested it be read aloud. The communication, he said, had been delivered to him only an hour before, but contained legal advice calling the entire validity of the last two day's proceedings into question. It argued that the law enabling prisoners accused of committing treason in one county to be tried in another – as though the offences were committed in that county – had been enacted 'after the time that the facts, implying treason, were actually committed'. In short the law was being implemented retrospectively and was therefore null and void. The author, one Nathaniel Williamson, pressed home his advice in postscript: 'If the bill found by the grand jury [in Surrey] has any flaw, so as to make it illegal, all the superstructure falls of course.'[10] Having previously declined benefit of legal counsel, Balmerino now accepted it and the court was adjourned for forty-eight hours while he consulted as to the viability of this line of defence. Horace Walpole remarked that 'the plea would have saved them all; and affected [the] nine rebels who had been hanged [on Kennington Common] that very morning'.[11] Mr Williamson's challenge was never tested in open court however, because the two lawyers assigned him told Balmerino there was nothing in the paper that would be of any use to him. And he again begged their lordships' pardon for the trouble he had given them.

On Friday the Lord High Steward addressed the three guilty men at the bar and pronounced the requisite sentence of death for High Treason. It was a sentence, he declared, 'which the law has appointed for crimes of this magnitude; a sentence full of horror such as the wisdom of our ancestors has ordained, as one guard about the sacred person of the king, and as a fence about this excellent constitution, to be a terror to evil-doers, and a security to them that do well.'

His final duty discharged, Lord Hardwicke had only to dissolve his commission as Steward. Receiving the white staff for the last time from the Gentleman Usher of the Black Rod, he rose to his feet and broke it in two.[12]

*

It was a privilege of noble birth that the sentence for High Treason – with all its degrading horrors – be commuted to beheading as a matter of course, and that this departure from the terms of execution read out in court required no official explanation or justification. Death warrants for Kilmarnock and Balmerino arrived on 11 August, Cromartie having been pardoned at the intercession, it was believed, of Augusta, wife to the Prince of Wales, 'who compassionated his Lady and Children', her highness being 'famed for Sense and Goodness'.

A week later, on the day of execution the two condemned men emerged under escort from the westernmost gate of the Tower to be saluted by a mob 'always ready, [to] huzza for the King and Government, and curse all traytors'.[13] Accompanied by their chaplains and two sheriffs, they walked up the broad avenue fenced to right and left by rows of horse and foot, keeping back the densely packed spectators unable to secure places on the grandstands surrounding the execution site. The solemn procession was led by the Constable of the Tower Hamlets, the knight's marshal's men and tip-staves, and sheriff's officers; and bringing up the rear were the Tower Warders, a guard of 'musqueteers', two hearses and a mourning coach.

Kilmarnock and Balmerino were conducted first to a building conveniently situated on the corner of Catherine Court some twenty or thirty yards from the scaffold, wine and cake being laid out for their refreshment in two separate apartments where each would be sequestered for an hour to make their devotions and condole with friends. The house had been rented for the purpose at a cost of 100 guineas from the Worshipful Company of Mercers.[14] 'The parlour and passage . . . the rails enclosing the way from thence to the scaffold, and the rails about it, were all hung with black at the sheriff's expence.'[15] Balmerino paid a visit to Kilmarnock's apartment to bid him farewell. They discussed whether or not Prince Charles Edward Stuart had signed an order before the battle of Culloden to give no quarter to the Duke of Cumberland's army. That both men – so close to death and at risk of perjuring their immortal souls – vehemently denied the charge would be later held as proof that no such order could have been issued.

Kilmarnock, being the first named in the warrant, was first to mount the sawdust-strewn scaffold. Two coffins lay ready, covered with black cloth and decorated with gilt nails. Copper plates gave the Latin forms of his and Balmerino's name, the date of their decapitation – 'Decollatus 18 die Augusti 1746' – together with their age, 'Aetatis suae 42' and '58' respectively. Enclosed in deal cases were two new axes, handles about three feet long, a pristine blade for each condemned man. The block also was new, hollows scooped and smoothed back and front to accommodate chest and chin, the whole covered in black cloth, and a black cushion to kneel on. The only article of colour was a length of scarlet baize that undertakers were to hold below the block to catch the head as it fell. At Kilmarnock's special request the number assigned to this office was increased from two to four lest the object be fumbled and 'roll about the scaffold, and be thereby mangled and disfigured'.[16] Further protective of his dignity *post mortem*, he also asked that the head be not exposed to the crowd with the customary words: 'Behold the head of a traitor!' The law did not require this to be done and the only reason for the practice was to show the public that execution had in fact taken place. To make the fatal stroke as visible as possible the black baize that hung from the railings around the scaffold was ordered to be removed and 'the Soldiers instantly tore it off and seized it as Plunder.'[17] To improve the spectators' view still more and 'give them a greater satisfaction, the sheriffs directed that every body upon the scaffold should kneel down'.[18]

Kilmarnock had been uneasy when told that the appointed executioner 'was a very good sort of man', and replied that 'a rougher and less sensible temper might perhaps be fitter to be employed' than 'a tender-hearted and compassionate' one.[19] His uneasiness seemed well grounded when the headsman, 'dressed in a blue Coat and scarlet Waistcoat laced with Gold', was introduced to him and promptly burst into tears.[20] He had earlier 'been obliged to use artificial spirits to support and strengthen him' and 'to keep him from fainting'.[21] He still appeared nervous, cautioning Kilmarnock – when he momentarilly laid his hands on the block to steady himself as he knelt – 'to let them fall, lest they should be mangled, or break the blow'.[22] There was a full two-minute pause while his Lordship composed himself before giving the agreed signal. As a white handkerchief dropped from his fingers the blow was a powerful one, producing 'a Cloud of Blood'[23] from the discharging carotid artery – visible from the surrounding grandstands – and severing head from body 'except only a small part of the skin, which was immediately divided by a gentler stroke'.[24]

The second execution was not so deft. When all traces of the first had been removed – Kilmarnock's remains enclosed in his coffin and carried to one of the hearses, bags of fresh sawdust strewn across the bespattered area in front of the block, the executioner having meanwhile 'changed such of his cloaths as appeared bloody' and taken the other axe from its box – Lord Balmerino stepped briskly onto the scaffold. In contrast to his predecessor's mourning clothes, he was dressed in 'a blue coat turned up with red, trimmed with brass buttons . . . the same which he wore at the battle of *Culloden*'. He walked around the perimeter, bowing to the spectators, identifying his hearse and requesting it be brought closer to enable more efficient transfer. He examined the inscription on his coffin, pronouncing it 'right', and referred to the block as his 'pillow of rest'. Next he presented the Captain of the Guard with his snuff box and the executioner with three guineas together with his coat and waistcoat which he took off and placed on the coffin for him. He took the axe from the man's hand, felt the edge and returned it, slapping him heartily on the shoulder for encouragement and bidding him strike – on his signal – with resolution, 'For in that,' he said, 'will consist your kindness.' His Lordship's equanimity was in inverse proportion to the executioner's, and when the signal came, sooner than expected, he was unprepared and brought the blade down with insufficient force to inflict a mortal wound. The partial severing of nerves and tendons caused the head to twist convulsively in the direction from which the blow came, its lower jaw dropping open and clamping shut 'very quick, like anger and gnashing the teeth'.[25] The terrified executioner raised the axe and struck again, but it was only on the third stroke that Balmerino's mauled head fell into the red baize cloth held ready to receive it.

*

Only two more men were ever afterwards beheaded on Tower Hill. The first was a Northumbrian Jacobite, Charles Radcliffe, younger brother of James, 3rd Earl of Derwentwater, who had been executed at the same place for his part in the rising of 1715. Charles was to have suffered similarly at that time but before sentence could be carried out in 1716, he escaped from Newgate Prison and fled to France. Following the death of James's son, Charles styled himself 5th Earl of Derwentwater, despite a bill of attainder denying him the right to pass on or inherit the title. Nevertheless, when he was recaptured in November 1745 aboard the French ship *L'Espérance*, Charles Radcliffe was accorded the privilege, as titular Earl, of imprisonment in the Tower and – when the original thirty-year-old warrant against him was at last implemented on 8 December the following year – both the manner and the place of his brother's death.

The execution of Simon, Lord Lovat four months later, in April 1747, was notable for the large number of collateral casualties attending it. On Postern Row, where the thoroughfare narrowed alongside the Tower moat, the crowd was so tightly packed that when a woman fell to the ground she 'was trod to Death immediately'. Elsewhere a lad of thirteen, knocked down by a guardsman's horse, was reportedly 'bruis'd in such a Manner that his Life is in Danger'. Mrs Carter, a childminder, went to see the execution, leaving a three-year-old infant unattended in bed, near Petticoat Lane, and a fire burning in the grate. The child awoke and ran to the fire, 'but unluckily falling into it, had both its Hands and Face burnt in so terrible a Manner, that it died [the following day] in the greatest Agony, to the inexpressible Grief of its Parents'. But by far the greatest loss of life occurred near Barking Alley on the western side of Tower Hill, when a scaffolding attached to the Ship alehouse, 'in many Stories, and computed to have on it near 1000 Persons, fell entirely down'. Between fifteen and twenty people were killed outright, 'many had their Arms and Legs broke', and a further dozen were to die later of their injuries. Among the dead was a master carpenter – said to have been responsible for erecting the structure – together with his wife and son who had been underneath selling beer when it collapsed, and their daughter 'so much bruised . . . her Recovery is doubted'. A newspaper report deplored 'the avaricious Views of the Proprietors of those Scaffolds, who build them without the least Regard to the Safety of their Fellow-Creatures', but ascribed some responsibility to the spectators, 'whose too fatal Curiosity may incline them unthinkingly to venture their Lives on such Occasions'.[26] The catastrophe happened a couple of hours before Lord Lovat was led to the block, but there is no foundation to the story he went to his death highly amused that those assembled to watch him die had themselves been killed, nor that this originated the expression, 'to laugh one's head off'.

*

On 7 June 1753, a final reckoning was paid by Dr Archibald Cameron, brother of Cameron of Lochiel. Apprehended on his return to Scotland from exile – and suspected of involvement in a conspiracy to kidnap the king, following an abortive attempt the previous November – he was tried and condemned to death for high treason. Lord Chief Justice Sir William Lee pronounced sentence with theatrical relish and practised timing. The delivery was neutral until he reached that portion of the formula dealing with the manner of execution:

'You must be hanged by the neck', he intoned.

Then he paused, before uttering the next words 'with a particular Emphasis', allowing them their full weight of significance and the implication they carried of torture to come:

'*But not till you are dead . . .*'

He stared Cameron full in the face:

'. . . for you must be cut down alive,' he went on, his eyes still fixed on those of the man before him:

'. . . then your bowels must be taken out, and burnt before your face.'

Lee's piercing stare from the bench was, Cameron supposed, 'to see . . . if I was as much frightned at [the words] as he perhaps would have been had he been in my Place'.

The court had heard the prisoner's guilt spoken of, and of his 'having been instrumental in the *Loss of so many Lives*'. As he awaited death Cameron reflected on the culpability of his judges, 'that . . . at their Hands, not at mine, will all the Blood that has been shed on that Account be required'.[27]

View near Loch Rannoch

'A frightful country'

BEFORE Walter Scott 'invented' Scotland – first in verse, then in prose, inviting literary tourists to gaze and swoon at the landscapes of *Waverley* and *The Lady of the Lake* – the Highlands had been 'frightful'. Daniel Defoe wrote in 1726 of a 'mountainous, barren and frightful country', repeating the word for emphasis in the sentence that followed: 'indeed a frightful country full of hideous desert mountains and unpassable, except to the Highlanders who possess the precipices'.[1] Twenty years later, when Michael Hughes arrived at Fort Augustus with the Duke of Cumberland's army in pursuit of those Highlanders, his evaluation of the prospect was no more positive. 'The Mountains hereabout are as high and frightful as the Alps in Italy,' he declared, 'so we had nothing pleasant to behold but the Sky.' Colonel Yorke was also dismissive, conceding such landscape 'worth seeing once in one's life, but not more'.[2] But writing from Inverness to his sister Elizabeth, his response was more nuanced. Were she in Scotland during the Spring, he told her playfully, she would abandon the female vanity of face painting 'and draw nothing but landscapes'. His description of the scenery swung from an aristocratic oppressor's disgust for the 'nasty houses . . . and the more nasty vermin that inhabit 'em', to a sensibility anticipating by ten years the substance of Edmund Burke's remarks on the

Sublime and, by half a century, the Romantic Movement of the early 1800s:

> The variety of prospects, all romantic, that the eye takes in at one glance, is something one is not used to in England, where nature smiles for ever gay; but here the scene is diversified with wide, dreary wastes of barren moor . . . till the eye . . . is at last lost in an innumerable quantity of black mountains whose tops are covered with snow all the year round.

Even the jarring accretions of military occupation – 'the fleet riding at anchor near the shore, and the army encamped in the plain' – could not detract from 'the beauty of the prospect'. Then, as though embarrassed by his betrayal of poetic sensitivity: 'Don't from this think me grown fond of anything I see here,' the Colonel bade his sister, 'for I am further from it than ever.' But he concluded as playfully as he had begun, repeating a word that would later serve to define a generation: 'I won't promise,' he told her, 'that I mayn't grow romantic.'[3]

Romantic landscape fascinates by its obscurity, by what it conceals as much as by what it reveals, stimulating the imagination to speculate what might be around the bend in a path or river, behind a rocky outcrop or tree, beyond a blanket of mist or the haze of extreme distance. It is obscurity which can render such landscape 'frightful', 'awful', and 'sublime'. And it is that very obscurity which is anathema to the military tactician and the cartographer.

'If a country . . . is but little known, a state of warfare generally produces the first improvements in its geography.' Writing in 1785, William Roy uses the term 'geography' in its literal sense of graphic definition or mapping a landscape:

> In the various movements of armies in the field, especially if the theatre of war be extensive, each individual officer has repeated opportunities of contributing . . . more or less towards its

> perfection; and these observations being ultimately collected, a map is sent forth into the world.[4]

Such improvements – albeit 'still defective' – had been made in the wake of military campaigns against the Jacobite risings of 1689, 1715 and 1719. And improvements to the physical landscape, in the form of roads, had been as much to the advantage of the insurgents in the summer of 1745 – enabling them to march rapidly from Lochaber to Perth and onwards to Edinburgh – as to that of the army that had made them.

In Newcastle at the end of December that year, General Hawley, newly appointed Commander-in-Chief of the Army of North Britain, complained that his road-building predecessor, General George Wade, 'won't let me have his map'. Only two, it seems, had been drawn and the other belonged to the King. 'I could wish it was either copied, or printed,' he wrote, 'or that his majesty would please to lend it me: 'tis for the service, or I should not be so bold.' He was about to march into Scotland and without a reliable map, 'I am going in the dark.'[5] It is questionable whether the battle's outcome, some days later, would have been altered – and Hawley's ignorance of the lie of the land on Falkirk Moor much enlightened – by any map then drawn. And if the Lowlands of Scotland were inadequately charted, the area beyond the Great Glen was *terra incognita* by comparison. Defoe had remarked on its wildness and the lack of precise information not only hindering conquest but dictating cartographic style:

> Our geographers seem to be almost as much at a loss in the description of this north part of Scotland, as the Romans were to conquer it; and they are obliged to fill it up with hills and mountains, as they do the inner parts of Africa with lions and elephants, for want of knowing what else to place there.[6]

If accurate mapping was needed for the successful prosecution of a war, it was equally important during the aftermath, as a means of subjugation and control, in order that a country 'so very inaccessible by nature, should be thoroughly explored and laid open, by establishing military posts in its inmost recesses, and carrying roads of communication to its remotest parts'.[7] Overseeing the logistics of this programme in 1747 was the Duke of Cumberland's Quartermaster General. In addition to the role literally associated with that office, of coordinating the cantonment or quartering of troops in the field, Lieutenant General David Watson, a military engineer to the Board of Ordnance, was charged with extending the network of military roads begun by General Wade in 1725. He was also responsible for restoring the decrepit accommodation and defences of Fort Augustus, the smaller forts and barracks of Kiliwhimen, Bernera, Inversnaid and Ruthven, and the conversion of isolated medieval tower houses such as Braemar and Corgarff into 'a Condition fitt to accommodate His Majesty's Forces'. A recent map of Scotland showing locations of more than 480 barracks, forts, camps and posts documented in the army's cantonment register from 1746 to 1755 is testimony to the success of this operation. Coloured spots pepper Lowlands and Highlands, like a virulent rash, reaching as far north as Orkney, where a subaltern and thirty men of Battereau's Regiment had been sent 'with orders to protect His Majesty's peaceable subjects against the Insults of the Disaffected of that Country'.[8]

*

One of the most ambitious, elaborate and time-consuming projects to emerge from Watson's extensive consolidation of Hanoverian power was also the most beautiful: the 'Complete and Accurate Survey of Scotland', also known simply as 'The Great Map'.

The Quartermaster General employed a civilian to undertake the task. William Roy would later rise to a Major General's commission in the army but in the summer of 1747, when summoned to Fort Augustus, he was the twenty-year-old son of a Lanarkshire land-steward, and known to Watson through the somewhat tenuous connection of his brother-in-law's second wife's extended family.

The starting point for the survey was to be a first accurate measurement of Wade's existing military roads. Roy was ordered to 'Measure the roads from Inverness, Fort Augustus, Fort William by Blair & Dunkeld to Perth'. He was to 'carefuly follow the line of the principal Roads . . . every half-mile's distance minutely expressing every variation or Change that happens'.[9] Measurements of each straight length of road were made by trundling a perambulator – a surveyor's wheel, or 'waywiser' – between bends, while the angles of divergence from one length to another were measured by a simple type of theodolite called a 'circumferator', incorporating a compass and sighting mechanism. A slower but more accurate measuring tool was the 66-foot 'Gunter's chain'.

The same methods were used to trace and measure the lines of rivers, edges of lochs and, in time, seacoasts. Precise notes and sketches were made of the features of country surrounding each road, river and body of water: crofters' cottages, perimeter walls of fields and estates, prominent crags, hills and mountains. Watson was emphatic as to the military priorities of the project. 'As the Encampments, Marches, and every possible movement proper for an Army to make in the Field, entirely depend on a just and thorough knowledge of the Country, the greatest care & Exactness should be observed in Examining minutely the Face of that Country.'[10]

But only the angles and compass direction of such landmarks could be calculated using the circumferator. Their distances – the one from another, and from road, river or water – had to rely on practised guesswork, as the laborious application of wheel or chain for any greater precision would have been impossible if a given area was to be surveyed within the practical time constraints of the spring and summer months, during which fieldwork of the survey could continue. The winter months were spent in the Board of Ordnance's Drawing Room in Edinburgh Castle where the calculations, measurements, angles, notes and sketches were collated and the sections of the 'Great Map' itself drawn and painted in watercolour across multiple sheets of paper.

No documentation or correspondence survives from the nine years the survey took to complete. During 1747 and '48, Roy seems to have worked alone, with one, or at most two, untrained assistants. But in 1749, observing how slowly the work was proceeding, Watson recruited five more young map-makers to the project, along with a draughtsman. Paul Sandby had been previously employed by the Quartermaster General executing watercolour drawings and plans of fortifications, and his elder brother Thomas Sandby was similarly occupied, as 'Draughtsman & Designer' to the Duke of Cumberland, at a salary of £100 per annum, but had returned to England with his master in July 1746.

A pen, ink and watercolour wash drawing by the younger Sandby shows William Roy's expanded survey team at work near the River Tummel in Perthshire. A distant figure stands holding a flagged pole at the eastern edge of Loch Rannoch. Another flag bearer is in the foreground, and near to him the surveyor – probably Roy himself – bends over his circumferator mounted on a tripod. In the middle distance, between the surveyor and the farthest flag, two more men are laying out their Gunter's chain. Two other members of the party are attending to the horses, while a woman, and two tartan-clad figures – dress strictures of the Disarming Act notwithstanding – observe the proceedings, either as local guides or in aid of the picturesque.

By 1752 Roy's survey and map of the Highlands was complete. It extended from John o' Groats and Cape Wrath in the north to the Forth in the south-east and the Kintyre Peninsula's tip in the south-west. Fifteen thousand square miles of moors, bogs, mountains and lochs were reduced to a scale of 1:36,000 or 1,000 yards to the inch. Roy was said to have been personally responsible for the extraordinary feat of surveying the entire maddeningly intricate coastline. Architectural features were picked out in red, thin ribbons of brown delineated roads, patches of yellow in stippled parallel rows marked cultivated land, while tiny stalked green circles showed forest, light brown denoted moorland, and light turquoise water, shading darker along the shore. Sandby specialised in mountains. Unlike their formulaic depiction on earlier maps, as separate molehills drawn in profile, Sandby's appear, as though seen from above, as a homogeneous whole, a spectacular, undulating carpet composed of fringed hedges of dashing, clustered pen strokes – called 'hachures' – in brown and graduated shades of grey, thickening to black with the steepness of slopes.

One remarkable topographical anomaly is shown on the coastline ten miles north-east of Inverness: the elongated, angular plan of Fort George, outlined in red on a hook of land curving out into the Moray Firth. At the time the mapping of the Highlands was completed little more than the ravelin giving access to the forty-acre site had been built. The premature inclusion of the entire structure can be seen as the map-maker's tribute to George II, sponsor of the survey.

Plans to rebuild the old Fort George at Inverness during Watson's renovation campaign had been abandoned: the devastation wrought by its Jacobite occupants the previous February, following a two-day siege, was deemed too extensive. In 1750 a precisely drawn plan of the buildings and fortifications showed it to be in large part rubble, 'the Gov[ernor's] House intirely in Ruins . . . Officers Barracks part Blown up . . . Barracks for Soldiers, the walls ruin'd, the Roofs and Floors, Burnt . . . Several parts . . . that the Rebels destroy'd by their Mines [and the] Wall of the Rampart . . . Crack'd & Settl'd in several Parts.'

The new fortress was designed by Lieutenant General William Skinner to the most advanced defensive specifications of the day. Construction was to be overseen by William Adam, Master Mason to the Board of Ordnance and the foremost architect in Scotland. However, following his death in 1748, before a stone was in place, his eldest son John took over, assisted by brothers James and, for a time, Robert – the future architect of the neoclassical revival. It was 'the most considerable fortress and best situated in Great Britain', remarked Lieutenant Colonel Wolfe as work began. It was also the most remote. In 1815 Fort George would be briefly considered a viable alternative in security and isolation to St Helena as a place of exile for Napoleon Bonaparte. It took more than twenty years to build, at a cost rising from Skinner's original scrupulous estimate of £92,673 19s 1½d to a more approximate £210,000 by 1769.

Warned of an anticipated French assault in 1759 upon the yet incomplete stronghold during the Seven Years War, Lord Ligonier, then Commander-in-Chief of the army, declared, 'I shall be extremely glad they would do it, because I look upon that fort to be impregnable against any force that could be sent against it.' The perfect deterrent, Fort George was neither attempted nor attacked, then or since, and its sinister geometry remains pristine: angles, planes and rule-straight lines of rampart, ravelin, glacis and bastion, 'a harmony of pure reason and serene menace'.[11]

*

Although not strictly necessary to the original military purposes of mapping the Highlands, the survey was continued south to cover the Scottish Lowlands. The gentler terrain enabled Roy's team to accomplish this in just three years, with a final season of fieldwork in the summer of 1755. Thereafter, the Seven Years War was to divert the resources of the Department of Ordnance to Europe.

Only the Highlands section of the map was ever finished in 'Fair Copy'. That of the Lowlands, although wondrously detailed, was completed in 'Protracted' – or draft – form only. The whole was mounted in sections on twenty-two brown linen rolls which were later cut up and reconstituted into thirty-eight folding sheets. Pieced together they form a map of mainland Scotland thirty feet high and twenty feet wide. Awe-inspiring though it is as a demonstration of human perseverance, of scientific rigour, and of aesthetic skill, 'The Great Map', when considered only in terms of the practical utility for which it was originally conceived, was arguably entirely futile. It was not published to meet the requirements of pacifying Scotland, nor were portions of it ever reproduced and issued to assist the military patrols on their forays into that country's 'inmost recesses, and . . . remotest parts'.

When Watson died in 1761, the sheets of the 'Fair' and 'Protracted' copies were found to be still among his papers and it is open to question what use would have been made of them had he lived longer. Transferred to the King's Library at Windsor Castle, 'The Great Map' now forms part of the vast 'King's Topographical Collection' in the British Library: '50,000 atlases, maps, plans, prospects and views' amassed during the reign of George III.[12]

Thirty years after work on the 'Complete and Accurate Survey of Scotland' was abandoned in favour of more pressing military concerns, the sixty-year-old Major General William Roy summed up the limitations of his early endeavour:

> Although this work, which is still in manuscript, and in an unfinished state, possesses considerable merit, and perfectly answered the purpose for which it was originally intended; yet, having been carried on with instruments of the common, or even inferior kind, and the sum annually allowed for it being inadequate to the execution of so great a design in the best manner, it is rather to be considered as a magnificent military sketch, than a very accurate map of a country.[13]

The year before writing these words Roy had initiated a system of mapping the whole of Great Britain enabling a degree of accuracy compared to which his painstaking work in Scotland from 1748 to 1755 might be considered no more than a cursory reconnoitre. In the summer of 1784 he established a line between two fixed points on Hounslow Heath, precisely 5.19 miles, or 27,404.7 feet apart.* From either end of this original Base Line, the angles from it to any given landmark could be measured by theodolite. Provided that the same landmark was visible from both ends of the Base Line, its exact distance from each of the two points could also be calculated, by simple triangulation. Each of the other two sides of the triangle springing from the Base

* The accuracy of Roy's original calculation has a disparity of 0.005 miles or 27.9 feet from a modern GPS measurement.

Line would then form the base from which to calculate angles and distances to other landmarks. And so on, until the entire country could be imagined as enveloped in a dense web of interconnected triangles, each point denoting a specific topographical feature and the precise distance from one to another calculated with unprecedented accuracy. The Primary Triangulation of Great Britain began in 1791, a year after William Roy's death. Initiated by the Board of Ordnance in response to the threat of French invasion following the revolution of 1789, it was the basis of the Ordnance Survey that we know today.

IACOBO III
IACOBI II MAGNAE BRIT REGIS
KAROLO EDVARDO
ET HENRICO DECANO PATRVM CARDINALIVM
IACOBI III FILIIS
REGIAE STIRPIS STVARDIAE POSTREMIS
ANNO MDCCCXIX
BEATI MORTVI
QVI IN DOMINO MORIVNTVR

PART VI: ENDINGS

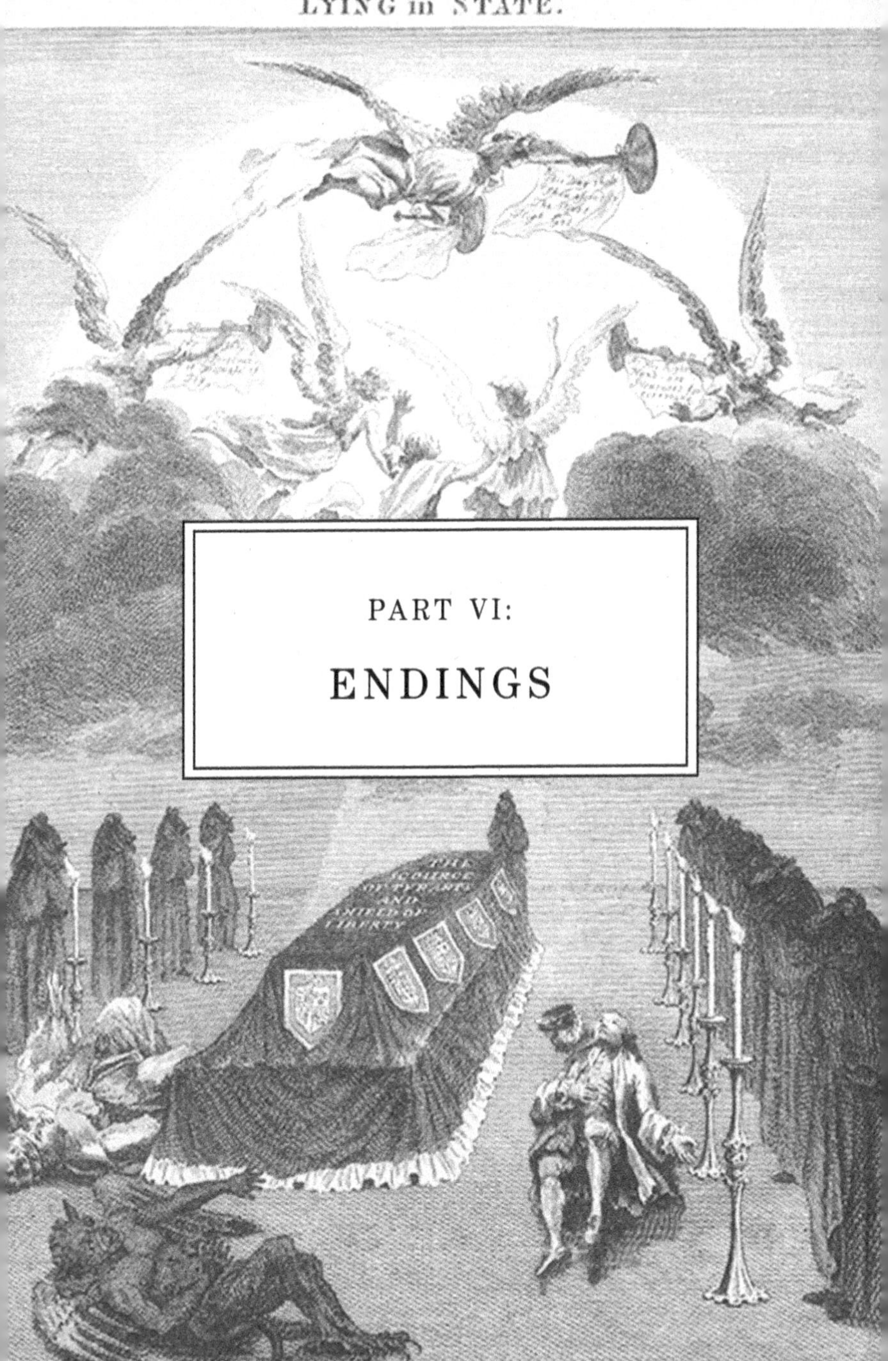

The Remains of His Late Royal Highness, Prince Wm Augustus, Duke of Cumberland (Who departed this Life Octo 31. 1765. in the 45.th Year of his Age)

LYING in STATE.

I

ACCOUNTS vary as to the name of the French privateer that set sail with the Prince from Borrodale on Lochnanuagh on 20 September 1746. Some identified it as the *Bellona* or the *Louini*, while others claimed that it was the *Prince de Conti*, *L'Heureux*, or more prosaically, 'the Happy Frigate'.[1] All agreed that the vessel docked on 29 September at the French port of Roscoff on the north Breton coast.

Arriving in Paris, Charles Edward sequestered himself 'until he got cloathes made', while the ragged garments in which he left Scotland 'were looked upon as so many reliques'. French ladies especially competed for them: 'one had his bonnet, one his Coat, another the old Shoose & Stokens, another his pipe.' One insisted on having his wig, even when told 'it wou'd infect her [as] it was full of Vermine'.[2] He paid his informal respects to the French King at Versailles, shortly after his arrival; then, ten days later, in full pomp: 'His Coat was Rosecoloured Velvet embroidered with Silver and lined with silver Tissue; his Waistcoat was a rich gold Brocade, with a spangled Fringe set on in Scollops. The Cockade in his Hat, and the Buckles of his Shoes were Diamonds; the [order of St] *George* at his Bosom, and the Order of St *Andrew* which he wore also tied by a Piece of green Ribbon to one of the Buttons of his Waistcoat, were prodigiously illustrated with large Brilliants.'[3]

O'Sullivan, who accompanied him throughout his time in Paris, claimed that he first attended the theatre unwillingly and 'out of complaissance' with the wishes of others. 'How can yu imagine,' he asked, 'I can enjoy any pleasure, when I have continually before my eyes, the cruelty wth wch my poor friends are traited in England.' If this was a true reflection of his feelings, his intoxicating reception from the French must soon have dispelled such reservations. 'When [he] came out of his Coach to go into the Opera, there was such Claping of hands, such a Cry of Vivat, such demonstrations of Joy . . . [that] the like was never seen even for their own King.'[4] Inside, 'the Attention of the whole Audience was fixed upon him, regardless of what was presented on the Stage; the Moment of his Entrance into the Box, a general Whisper . . . ran from one Side of the Theatre to the other, and few of the fair Sex but let fall Tears of mingled Pity and Admiration' at the legendary trials he had undergone.[5] 'Oh! the fine Prince,' people whispered as he passed, 'oh! the brave Prince, we are not surpris'd if his own peoples did wonders with him, we wou'd all do the same if we were permitted.' And O'Sullivan was 'most certain they wou'd'. A lady 'of the first rank of the Court' declared that, if there were another expedition to Scotland, she would 'answer in fifteen days time to get four millions of [livres] in the Town of Paris, for his service'.[6]

*

News from Rome in June 1747 that Henry Benedict Stuart, Duke of York, was about to take holy orders and be made, with minimal preliminaries, a Cardinal, came like 'a dagger throw my heart', Charles Edward wrote to his father. Such an ostentatious embrace of the Roman Catholic faith by one brother made the other's succession to a Protestant throne an even more remote possibility than before. It also made the Prince a target. Henry's elevation, and mandatory celibacy, meant that he would never sire legitimate offspring, leaving his elder brother their father's sole heir. From that moment, a single Hanoverian assassin's blade, bullet or bomb could sever the Stuart bloodline at a stroke. He had carried a brace of small pistols concealed about his person ever since his return from Scotland. He now had cause. An unsuccessful attempt on his life was reported in which five masked men fired their pistols into his coach. 'One of the Bullets lodged in the back of Part of the Chaise, just above his Head, another went through his Hat, and a third grazed upon his Breast, without any other Mischief than taking off one of the Buttons of his Coat; the others were so ill directed that they were lost in the Air.'[7]

He would also surround his bed 'with chairs placed on tables, and on the chairs little bells, so that if anyone approached during the night, the bell would be set a-ringing'.[8]

*

Within a month and a half of the battle, it was reported that the conquering hero of Culloden would be honoured with a statue, placed on top of a fifty-foot column, at the centre of Parsonstown, in King's County, Ireland.* The principal town of this so-called plantation county – one of a number confiscated from Irish Gaelic clans by the English Crown and settled by Protestant 'planters' in the sixteenth and seventeenth centuries – was named after the family of its most prominent Anglo-Irish proprietor, Sir Lawrence Parsons. Sir Lawrence was also sponsor and main subscriber to the Cumberland monument. The statue – designed and made by Henry Cheere of London – was cast in lead and represented the Duke, one and a half times life size, 'resplendent in the costume of a Roman emperor, left foot projecting, right arm extended [and holding a truncheon], left hand on hip, and on his head the laurel leaf garland of the victor'.

* Now Birr, County Offaly, Leinster.

Writing a decade after the Battle of Waterloo, the historian Robert Chambers observed: 'Duke William received fully as much public gratitude for ridding Britain of the poor Chevalier, as the great General of modern times received for overthrowing the Usurper of the Continent.'[9]

A fortnight after news of the victory reached London, Parliament awarded Cumberland £25,000 a year, in addition to his civil list annuity of £15,000, 'as a proper Testimony of National Gratitude for his signal Service in extinguishing the Rebellion in Scotland'.[10] His father also granted him the highly desirable sinecure of 'Ranger and Keeper of Windsor Great Park . . . during his Life', enabling him to indulge his enduring passion for blood sports.[11]It was reported in the summer of 1746 that 'Talk of his Royal Highness's going to Flanders this Campaign is dropt' and that instead he would 'reside at his Seat at Windsor Forest for some Time during the Hunting Season'.[12]

But in July of the following year he led an army into the field, at Lauffeld, near Maastricht, and once more against his old adversary Marshal Saxe. As at Fontenoy, the battle ended in honourable defeat, the Duke's forces outnumbered by 20,000 and yet inflicting almost as many casualties upon the enemy as suffered by his own. Towards the end of 1748, the Treaty of Aix-la-Chapelle brought an end to the War of the Austrian Succession that had consumed Europe and other parts of the world for the previous seven years. Still Commander-in-Chief – or Captain General – in peace as in war, Cumberland went on to oversee a reduction of the British Army. Ten infantry regiments were disbanded, leaving three of foot guards and forty-nine line regiments. Three cavalry regiments of horse guards remained and fourteen of dragoons. Overall strength was reduced to 30,000, of which 20,000 were to serve at home and 10,000 in His Majesty's colonies overseas.

Cumberland was again able to devote himself to 'the Diversion of Stag-Hunting' and to the improvement of his Windsor domain.[13] Hundreds of now idle troops were set to work landscaping the Great Park. Five hundred were employed in 1753 to excavate a serpentine lake, one and a half miles long and 300 feet wide, the largest man-made body of water at that time in Britain. An ornamental Chinese junk, called the 'Mandarin Yacht', was launched upon it, together with 'a Pleasure Barge to be rowed in on the same Place'.[14] A watercolour panorama by the Duke's draughtsman Thomas Sandby showed this expanse of Virginia Water in the foreground and – picked out in the distance – a tall white structure, the single vertical stroke in the wide rolling horizontals of the composition. Despite his second defeat by Marshal Saxe, a Portland stone obelisk, topped with an iron finial in the shape of a radiant sun, had been raised to him by order of the king. It was incised on the north face: CULLODEN.

In addition to the indigenous population of red deer, Windsor Park became the destination for an assortment of exotic animals. In 1750 a young lioness, a leopard and a turtle were delivered to the Ranger's Lodge, 'a fine Ostrich' having died on the voyage from Port Mahon, Minorca. They were a gift of the Duke's former comrade-in-arms Major, now Lieutenant Colonel, James Lockhart, his brutal reputation seemingly no bar to advancement. Other creatures followed, most notably, in 1764, a cheetah presented to George III by Sir George Pigot, outgoing Governor General of Madras. Informed that Mogul Emperors had employed cheetahs as hunting animals for hundreds of years, Cumberland was eager to put the animal through its stalking paces and arranged a demonstration in the Royal Paddock, setting the cheetah onto one of the Park's stags. The stag fought off the foreign assailant and Cumberland rewarded its bravery, ordering that particular care be taken of it, and that it should wear a large silver collar to distinguish it from the rest of the herd and spare it further harassment. The celebrated animal painter George Stubbs was commissioned by Pigot to portray the cheetah attended by two Indian servants, the proud stag in the background.[15]

*

The treaty between France, Great Britain and Holland – signed at the Belgian spa town of Aix-la-Chapelle, on 18 September 1748 – introduced an all too brief interlude of peace between the end to the War of the Austrian Succession and the beginning of the Seven Years War in 1756. Even before the final terms of the treaty had been agreed, Charles Edward Stuart had written from Paris to reject, in advance, all agreements detrimental to his status that would be ratified there. 'We regard . . . as null, void, and of no effect,' he pronounced, 'everything that may . . . tend to the acknowledgement of any other person whatsoever as sovereign of the kingdom of Great Britain, besides the person of the most high and most excellent prince, James the Third, our most honoured lord and father, and in default of him, the person of the nearest heir agreeably to the fundamental laws of Great Britain.'[16]

The objection was 'a Thing of Form'. It had been made by both his father and grandfather – James III and II respectively – on the occasion of every European congress defining territorial entitlements held since the Glorious Revolution of 1689, 'and indeed to have omitted it would have been deemed as a Tacit relinquishing [of the Stuart] Claim'.

Besides, there were rumours, 'whispered by several who pretended to be deep in the Secrets of State', that informal approaches had been made by the British government that, were he to renounce forever all claim to the Crown, 'a perpetual yearly Subsidy should be granted him . . . sufficient to support the Dignity of a Prince'. He would even be allowed to retain the title 'Prince' as a branch of the Polish royal line of Sobieski, through his mother, Clementina. He did not hesitate, however, to repudiate such rumours:

> That whatever might be insinuated to the contrary, he would never accept any offers, or enter into any Conditions, for giving up his Claim, which he was determined to maintain by all Means Heaven should put in his Power.

In the meantime he took out a lease on 'an extreme fine *Hotel*' on the Quai des Théatins,* directly opposite the Palais du Louvre and Tuileries, 'on purpose, as he said, to be near the Opera, the Comedy, and other Diversions . . . some one or other of which he . . . very seldom failed of partaking every Evening'. He was now reconciled to such pleasures, the suffering of his friends in Scotland and England notwithstanding.

He took a mistress, his first cousin, Marie Louise de la Tour d'Auvergne, wife of the duc de Montbazon. Their passionate affair was terminated at the insistence of Marie's mother-in-law but not before she had become pregnant. She gave birth to a son, claimed as his own by her husband and baptised Charles Godefroi Sophie Jules Marie de Rohan but dead within six months. There followed a liaison with a Polish-born princess, Maria de Talmont, *née* Jabłonowska, over two decades his senior. She would stay with him for three years, before being supplanted in late 1752 by Clementina Walkinshaw, renewing an earlier association with the Prince at her uncle's home in Bannockburn.

*

Whenever anyone in the Prince's company – whether at the Quai des Théatins, the Opera or the Comedy – turned conversation towards the implications to himself of the peace treaty being negotiated between Britain and France, he sang to drown out what he did not wish to hear 'or found some way of waving making any Reply'.[17]

And when the treaty was signed, those implications were as serious as anticipated. Article XIX guaranteed succession of the kingdom of Great Britain 'to the house of His now-reigning Britannic Majesty [King George II] and to his descendants of both sexes'.[18] But this Article was to have more immediate consequences for the Prince, beyond confirming the increasingly unlikely

* Now the Quai Voltaire.

prospect of his ever succeeding to the British throne. At the insistence of the British negotiators, it included significant terms from another treaty, signed in London thirty years earlier, between France, Britain, Holland and the Holy Roman Empire. Article V of the 1718 Treaty of the Quadruple Alliance referred explicitly to Charles Edward Stuart's father, as 'the person, who during the life of James II, took the title of Prince of Wales, and since his death the title of King of Great Britain'. By its terms Louis XV had agreed 'never to help [the said person] directly or indirectly, by sea or by land, by advice, aid, or assistance of any kind, whether in money, arms, ammunition, Ships, Soldiers, Sailors, or in any other way whatsoever'. Furthermore, the said person was 'to be given and accorded neither asylum nor refuge in any part of [France]'.[19] And those same terms applied also to the putative James III's descendants. Although drafted before Charles Edward Stuart was born, and originally bearing primarily on the standing of his father, Article V was to be 'evoked and renewed' in the 1748 treaty 'as if it were rendered in full'.[20]

All financial, diplomatic and military assistance was to be withdrawn from him by his erstwhile patron and protector, the King of France, with the additional stipulation that he be immediately deported.

During the weeks that followed, the French King used every diplomatic avenue to persuade the Prince to leave France voluntarily. He arranged with the canton of Fribourg in Switzerland that he be received there 'with all the Demonstrations of Respect due to his Birth and Virtues'. A Minister of State, and former French ambassador to Rome, Cardinal PierrePaul Guérin de Tencin, was sent 'to acquaint him with the Necessity there was for his Departure', delivering his message 'in the most tender Terms', but to no avail.[21] On 4 October, Louis' First Gentleman of the Bedchamber, the duc de Gesvres, was sent to the Quai des Théatins to deliver the same message, together with a copy of the relevant terms of the treaty and a personal letter from the King: 'I shall be obliged if the Prince Charles Edward will make this easy for me by definitely quitting all the territories of my

Dominions. I have too good an opinion', Louis added disarmingly, 'of his wisdom and good sense to think he will act against my wishes.'[22] When the unwelcome guest still made no move to leave, Gesvres was sent again a fortnight later and this time the Prince became heated, peremptorily instructing the messenger to remind the King of his obligation to protect him, an obligation, he argued, which predated the Treaty. There were rumours that 'he threatned to kill the first Man that should offer to arrest him, that . . . beginning thus by Murder, he would finish by Suicide'.[23] An appeal was made to the Prince's father, who wrote him a five-page letter from Rome, pleading with him to do as he was told. Like many another fond parent of a wayward child, he suggested his bad behaviour was a result of the bad influence of associates, 'show[ing] plainly that it is not your own way of thinking that you follow but that of others. In Gods Name who can these be, is it possible they can be your sincere friends and at the same time give you such advice. No surely . . .'[24]

Following a third and fourth unsuccessful embassy from his Gentleman of the Bedchamber, the French King put the matter in the hands of a military man: Louis Antoine, duc de Biron, Colonel of the Guards, hero of Fontenoy and future Marshal of France.

Biron made his preparations. The Prince was to be arrested going into the opera house at the Palais Royale on the night of Tuesday 10 December. Mindful of the great popular support he commanded in the city and anticipating a possible riot in his defence, troop numbers deployed in the operation were somewhat disproportionate to the arrest of one man. Twelve hundred of Biron's own Guards regiment surrounded the building. Sergeants of the Guard, 'armed with Cuirasses and Scul-caps', were posted in the passageway leading to the opera house and in the doorways of adjacent buildings, while Sergeants of the Grenadiers, 'as being the most intrepid', would be employed to make the actual arrest. A further two companies of Grenadiers were to wait in a courtyard off the passageway and next to the palace kitchens, with the duc de Biron, 'disguised and in a Coach . . . to see the Success of [his] Enterprise'. Mounted Musketeers would be at hand should their presence prove necessary. In addition, members of the City Watch were to be distributed in all the neighbouring streets, to divert traffic and turn pedestrians away, and more troops posted on the road east of the Palais Royale in the direction it was proposed to conduct the Prince when apprehended. Every eventuality was prepared for. Should the quarry 'throw himself into some House, and there resolve to stand a Siege', hatchets and 'Scaling-Ladders' were provided, and locksmiths in attendance, while a physician and three surgeons were to stand by to dress the wounded.[25]

Despite efforts to maintain secrecy, such a major mobilisation of force inevitably attracted attention, and the Prince received 'several Notes, giving him Advice of the whole Design', all of which he ignored. 'I've heard these reports for some time,' he replied to one of his attendants while walking in the Tuileries on the afternoon of the 10th, 'but I believe there's nothing in them.'[26] That evening, as his coach rattled along the rue Saint-Honoré someone shouted from the pavement, 'Prince! Go back! They are going to arrest you, the Palais-Royale is beset!' But 'Notwithstanding these Advices', he went on. The main attraction to be presented that night by the Académie royale de musique was an opera-ballet in a prologue and three acts by Jean-Philippe Rameau entitled 'The Festivities of Hymen and Cupid, or the Gods of Egypt',* but he would not hear a note of it.

As he alighted from his coach, the military presence in the Place du Palais-Royale – albeit doubled and with fixed bayonets – may not have seemed entirely unusual, given the necessity of controlling enthusiastic crowds whenever he appeared in public. But as he entered the passageway leading to the opera house, the theatre doors were slammed shut in front of him, the barrier closed behind and he was surrounded by Sergeants of Grenadiers dressed in grey to look like servants. 'Two . . . seized him by the Arms behind, two seized his hands, one seized him round the

* *Les Fêtes de l'Hymen et l'Amour, ou Les Dieux d'Egypte* was first performed at Versailles, 15 March 1747, to celebrate the marriage of the Dauphin to Maria Josepha of Saxony.

Middle, and another seized his Legs.'[27] He was then carried through a side gate at the end of the passage and into the kitchen courtyard where a Major of the Guard, the marquis de Vaudreuil – backed by the two Grenadier companies, and watched from his coach by the duc de Biron – formally arrested the Prince, 'in the Name of the King my Master'. According to one correspondent, Vaudreuil had been given 'the Charge of executing this important Commission' by Biron, who, 'either through Shame or Fear', chose to distance himself from it.[28]

The Prisoner was searched and relieved of his sword, his brace of small pistols and a two-bladed penknife. In one account of the arrest a Grenadier 'insolently broke his sword in the scabbard'. He was tied up using ten ells – about thirty-seven feet – of crimson silk cord that Biron had procured as being suitable to bind a person of royal blood. He was placed in a carriage, Vaudreuil next to him and two Captains of the Guard opposite. 'Gentlemen, this is a dirty office you are employed in', he said to them. Then, as the coach set off towards the east, and believing he was to be rendered into the custody of his enemies, 'I suppose I am straight on my way to Hanover.'[29]

Their destination, however, was Philip VI's grim fourteenth-century donjon tower at Vincennes, where he remained a prisoner for the following four days until he agreed to sign a four-article declaration setting out the terms of his expulsion. He was 'to retire . . . from all territories under the domination of the King of France, leaving by the Pont de Beauvoisin', on the border between France and Savoy, en route to Italy. He was on 'no account [to] pass through Paris'. He was 'not [to] stay in Lyon or in any other town of consequence in France' on the way, and finally, he was to be 'accompanied on his journey only by those persons . . . which His Majesty [had] been pleased to approve'.[30] These designated companions were the members of his personal suite who had been arrested with him and spent the intervening four days in the Bastille. The Prince signed the agreement, and on Sunday 15 December he and his party left the outskirts of Paris, taking the road south. But close to the Italian border, he broke the agreement he had signed and took the road instead to Avignon, a French city but under the jurisdiction of the Pope.

*

In London, on 17 January, 1751, every member of both Houses of Parliament received, by the Penny Post, a printed pamphlet: *Constitutional Queries, Earnestly recommended to the serious Consideration of every True Briton*. Although mentioning him neither by name nor title, the object of these concerns was the Duke of Cumberland. Despite a substantial reduction in its size since the treaty of Aix-la-Chapelle, the very idea of a standing army in time of peace was viewed with disquiet as a potential threat to the rights and freedom of the nation – and it had been regarded as such since the oppressive years of military rule under Oliver Cromwell's New Model Army. The Duke's continued tenure as Captain General did nothing to mitigate the perceived threat.

There had been suspicion from some quarters – particularly the adherents of the Prince of Wales – that George II intended transferring the succession from his heir apparent, Frederick Louis, to William Augustus – a growing possibility, as the notoriously bad relations between father and eldest son worsened over the years. Longstanding rivalry between the two brothers was also a factor. The anonymous author implied that the Duke of Cumberland's command of the army could facilitate the king's radical alteration to the constitution by *coup d'état*:

> If a *younger* Son of the Crown should ever be invested with absolute Power over *such* an Army, and at the same Time, . . . make himself Master of the *Fleet*, our Lives and Fortunes might . . . be dependent on his *Will* and *Pleasure*, and the *Right of Succession* have no other Security than his *Want of Ambition*.

The prospect 'of *arbitrary* and tremendous Power' – commonly cited in anti-Papist propaganda – was now raised in warning against a man once lauded as the protector of Religion and Liberty:

> An *Army* . . . usurping a Dominion over *Law* . . . Orders . . . given by *Authority*, to the Troops to execute the Law, to seize and imprison the Persons of the Subjects, upon such Information as *they should think sufficient*, without the Concurrence of the *civil Power*, such Country might . . . be deemed under a direct *military Government* in its rankest Form.

The experiment having already been made in Scotland, it was argued, 'a successful Attempt, in one *Part* of our Country, would . . . furnish Hopes [in the mind of a tyrant] of reducing the *remaining Part* to the like *unconditional* Dominion.'[31]

The pamphlet was condemned in the House of Lords as 'a false, malicious, scandalous, infamous, and seditious libel, containing the most false, audacious, and abominable calumnies and indignities', and 'with intent to instil groundless suspicions and jealousies into the minds of his Majesty's good subjects'.[32] It was likewise denounced in the House of Commons, although Sir Francis Dashwood objected to the word 'false' in the resolution 'as he thought some of the charges in the [pamphlet] not ungrounded'.[33] Rewards of £1,000 were offered for the discovery of the author, £200 for each of the printers and £50 for each of the publishers. Those responsible were never held to account, although the authorship was attributed to John Perceval, 2nd Earl of Egmont, Gentleman of the Bedchamber to the Prince of Wales. The pamphlet was burnt 'by the hands of the common hangman' in New Palace Yard, Westminster, on Friday 25 January at one o'clock in the afternoon.[34]

If the assessment of that shrewd judge of character Horace Walpole was to be relied on, anxiety over the Duke's threat to the constitution was in fact groundless. 'It is uncertain whether his inordinate passion for war proceeded from brutal courage, from love of rule, or from love of blood . . . it is certain it did not proceed from love of glory, nor much from ambition.'[35]

*

During the month he spent in Avignon at the beginning of 1749, the Prince and his rowdy associates and hangers-on introduced the British sport of prize-fighting to the Papal city, and enthusiastically disturbed the peace with carousing, to the embarrassment of both the civil and church authorities. The British government, concerned at his continued residence in France, put pressure on Pope Benedict XIV to have him expelled, and threatened the Papal free port of Civitavecchia with bombardment by the Royal Navy if he remained. He left Avignon at the end of February, travelling incognito to Paris. Here he took up covert residence at the Convent of St Joseph, in the Faubourg Saint-Germain, sheltered by two of its wealthy *dames pensionnaires*, Jacobite friends of the Princess de Talmont. In May he was on the move again, by way of Switzerland to Venice. Expelled from Venice he crossed back over the border and made his way to the château de Lunéville, in Lorraine, then an independent duchy, as a guest of the duc de Lorraine, Stanislas I, former King of Poland. His bewildering peregrinations across Europe in 1749 were to be the pattern of the next fifteen years.

Plans for a further attempt to gain his father's throne seemed never to have been far from his mind. Two years earlier, he had approached Spain for support and gained an offer of arms for another rising in Scotland. But the retreat from Derby must still have rankled as a lost opportunity and nothing short of commitment to an insurrection in England would satisfy him. In 1750 this seemed for a time a realistic possibility. In early June the Prince had procured through an agent 6,000 broadswords and 26,000 muskets to be stored at Antwerp until needed, and when he left Lunéville in September, travelling to Ostend, his 'full powers and commission of Regency [had been] renewed', enabling him to assume the English throne in his father's stead.[36] Something was clearly afoot.

On 16 September he arrived in London, no doubt wearing one of the many disguises he had mastered during his secretive wanderings. The purpose of this dangerous excursion to the heart of the Hanoverian state is obscure. His supporters, it seemed, 'had formed a scheme which was impracticable', he told the English academic William King. But even if 'it had been as feasible as they had represented it to him, . . . no preparation had been made, nor was anything ready to carry it into execution. He was soon convinced that he had been deceived.' The precise nature of the scheme is not known, but it has been suggested that it may have evolved into what became known as the Elibank Plot after its prime mover Alexander Murray of Elibank:

> Two or three thousand picked men were to be assembled [and] on the night fixed for the attempt [10 November 1752] some were to seize [St James's] Palace, and others to summon the Tower to surrender, which, failing compliance, was to be carried by assault, after the gates had been blown in.[37]

The entire Royal Family was to be captured and the King forced to abdicate. While there is no proven connection between this failed conspiracy and the Prince's visit to London two years earlier, his movements during the visit might point in that direction. He had walked the streets, and on one occasion took a stroll around the Tower, closely examining walls and defences, even identifying the most vulnerable gate to the fortress that he calculated might be blown apart by attaching a petard mortar shell to the outside. The disguise he adopted must have been impenetrable because his features were well known and easily recognisable from prints, broadsides and particularly from the plaster busts – said to be 'more like him than any of his pictures' – then on sale in Red Lion Street, Holborn.[38]

He stayed in Essex Street, off the Strand, with the widow of Sir Archibald Primrose, a Jacobite executed at Carlisle in 1746. And it was during these five days that a clandestine ceremony took place at the 'New Church' of St Mary Le Strand, a short walk from Lady Primrose's house. A statement Charles made some years later suggested that it was a principal reason for his visit:

> In order to make my renountiation of the Church of Rome the most authentick, and the less liable afterwards to malitious interpretations, I went to London in the year 1750 and in that capital did then make a solemn abjuration of the Romish religion, and did embrace that of the Church of England as by Law established in the 39 Articles in which I hope to live and die.[39]

This ceremony removed the single legal impediment to his ascending the throne of Great Britain, as laid out in the 1701 Act of Settlement: 'that every person or persons that should be reconciled to, or shall hold communion with the see or Church of Rome, or should profess the popish religion, or marry a papist, should be excluded, and made for ever incapable to inherit, possess or enjoy the crown and government of this realm or exercise any regal power, authority, or jurisdiction within the same.' Emerging onto the Strand following his conversion the Prince's claim on George II's crown was stronger than it had ever been before.

It was a development that the Prime Minister, Henry Pelham, had anticipated two years earlier when terms of the Treaty of Aix-la-Chapelle were being drafted and discussions held regarding a future domicile for the troublesome individual following his expulsion from France. Suggesting that exile in Switzerland was not far enough away, and 'heartily wish[ing] they could get him back to Rome', Pelham still saw a potential danger to the Hanoverian succession, should the current legitimate heir to the throne prove himself obnoxious. 'If *this young gentleman* should declare himself a Protestant, and another, [Frederick Louis, Prince of Wales] should not act suitable to the great and good examples he has had before him, the Lord knows how matters may end.'[40] As it turned out, Pelham need not have concerned himself on the latter account.

*

On 20 March, 1751, following a short illness, Prince Frederick Louis complained of 'an unusual Smell, like that of a dead Corpse', and died abruptly of 'a large Abscess form'd upon the Lungs, which burst'. It was said to have been caused by a contusion from the impact of a cricket ball two years earlier, and which had formed in the interim a 'Bag near six Inches long, down his Side, full of Corruption'. On the same day that the Prince of Wales expired at Leicester House, the Duke of Cumberland 'had the Misfortune to be thrown from his Horse in Windsor Park, but happily received little or no hurt'. The coincidence of contrasting outcomes inspired a chorus widely sung in the streets by supporters of the Prince's faction: 'Oh! that it was but his brother! Oh! that it was but the butcher!'[41]

The late Prince's eldest son, next in line to the throne and future George III, was then thirteen years old and speculation turned on who would assume the duties of sovereign should his grandfather die before George William Frederick reached his majority. The most logical choice, of his uncle Cumberland, revived anxieties expressed in the *Constitutional Queries*. 'The consternation that spread on the apprehension that the Duke would . . . be Regent on the king's death, and have the sole power in the meantime,' declared Horace Walpole, 'was near as strong as what was occasioned by the notice of the rebels being at Derby.'[42]

The King left the appointment of a Regent to Parliament and Cumberland was passed over in favour of Frederick's widow, Augusta, dowager Princess of Wales. Later that year, when the Duke had another, more serious, hunting accident – he 'was taken up speechless . . . grew dangerously ill with a pain in his side, and was given over by the physicians' – his father 'was inexpressibly alarmed, wept over him; and told everybody . . . that the nation would be undone, left to nothing but a woman and children!' But the favoured son recovered and, in the event, there would be no regency, because George II survived until after the young Prince reached his eighteenth birthday. Nevertheless, Cumberland expressed hurt at being passed over, blamed the machinations of Henry Pelham and the Prime Minister's brother the Duke of Newcastle, and spoke privately of 'his own insignificance' and of his name being 'blotted out of the English annals'. He was also convinced that his nephew had been turned against him. In an effort to entertain the child, he had once taken a sword down from the wall of his apartment and drawn it from its scabbard. 'The young Prince turned pale, and trembled, and thought his uncle was going to murder him.' Suspecting that this reaction showed 'in what light he had appeared at his brother's court' – as the Butcher of Culloden – the Duke complained to the boy's mother.[43]

*

In the Summer of 1752 reports from Berlin that the Prince was now a Protestant and 'going publickly to one of the Lutheran Churches every Sunday' was said to have been taken sufficiently seriously by the London government as to entail summoning 'the whole members of the Privie Counsell . . . from their country houses' to a Saturday-night conference exploring the constitutional implications of that intelligence. Further reports that he was married, and to the Princess Royal of Prussia, were unconfirmed.[44]

Although Frederick the Great had in fact balked at giving his daughter in matrimony, he had appeared, in early 1751, to consider offering military support. The Prince's conversion in London may even have been a means of ingratiating himself to this end with one of the most powerful Protestant rulers in Europe. His demands, however – in particular for a force of 12,000 troops – proved unreasonable and nothing came of these discussions.

Attending church in Berlin during August 1752, Charles was accompanied by Clementina Walkinshaw. She had joined him a month or so earlier, the reunion arranged at the Prince's request by John O'Sullivan. They lived together in Ghent, then, secretly in Paris where – by August of the following year – she was said to be 'now . . . big with child' and that 'the Pretender keeps her well. And seems very fond of her.'[45] They moved to Liège – living as the Count and Countess de Johnson – where she gave birth to a daughter in October 1753, baptised Charlotte Stuart. From Liège they went to Basle where, it was reported, 'He treats Miss Walkinshaw very badly and . . . is regarded as the worst of husbands.'[46]

Despite the Walkinshaw family's Jacobite leanings, one of Clementina's nine sisters, Catherine, was a fixture at the Hanoverian court, being housekeeper in the Prince of Wales's residence, Leicester House, and later the Princess Augusta's Woman of the Bedchamber. For this reason, Clementina was viewed with suspicion as a possible spy by Charles Edward's English supporters, and she was widely but unjustly accused of exposing the Elibank Plot. Pressure was put on him to break with her. This, to his credit, he refused to do, declaring it would be 'a cruel and unmanly desertion', even though by his own admission he 'neither honour[ed] nor esteem[ed] her', thinking her 'a woman of low tastes, of no elegance of manners, and for whom [he had] not a particle of affection'.[47]

They were together for eight years, his initial happiness in her company giving way to contempt, then to physical abuse. She claimed that 'he often gave her as many as fifty thrashings with a stick during the day.[48]

*

In September 1752, a daring individual climbed the column in Parsonstown under cover of darkness and removed the truncheon from Cumberland's hand. 'A very large Reward [was] offer'd by Sir Lawrence Parsons for discovering the Villain who took it.'[49] Over the years the monument would suffer further indignity. Weathering opened a crack in one of the legs and, given the material of which it was made, restoration was undertaken by a local plumber. The repair cannot have been entirely successful because in time the statue 'assumed a dangerous lean' towards the western side of the square, 'in the direction of the police barrack'.[50]

In 1757 Britain was again at war with France, and the Duke was able to return to his preferred métier. Commanding an allied army of Hessian, Brunswick and predominantly Hanoverian troops near the town of Hastenbeck, he fought what was to be the final battle of his military career. Heavily outnumbered – yet suffering fewer casualties overall than the French – he believed the day to be lost and ordered a retreat, leaving Hanover unprotected. Convinced of his son's 'sense and capacity and zeal' the king authorised Cumberland to, as he expressed it, 'get me and my country out of these difficulties' and negotiate peace. Cumberland did so, at a congress held in Kloster Zeven, agreeing to disband his army and surrender Hanover to French occupation. On his return to London the King received him 'with extreme coldness' and an interview lasting four minutes. A military defeat might be accepted but not the loss of Hanover. Later in the evening he entered the chamber where his father was playing at cards. 'Here is my son,' the old man said to no one in particular, 'who has ruined me and disgraced himself.' That night the Duke determined 'to resign everything', the post of Captain General of the army and his Colonelcy of the 1st Foot Guards.[51] The King insisted his son attend court as usual, and to visit him each morning, but they remained estranged.

The Duke of Cumberland himself remarked on the irony of losing his father's favour, 'that he had formerly got praise where he did not deserve it', for his victory over a despised Jacobite army, 'and now was blamed where he was not guilty'.[52] The monument in Windsor Great Park would have to wait for more than 70 years – until George IV's brother William came to the throne – for the dedicatory inscription intended by its original sponsor:

THIS OBELISK
RAISED BY THE COMMAND OF
KING GEORGE THE SECOND
COMMEMORATES
THE SERVICES OF HIS SON

WILLIAM DUKE OF CUMBERLAND
THE SUCCESS OF HIS ARMS
AND
THE GRATITUDE OF HIS FATHER.
THIS TABLET WAS INSCRIBED BY
HIS MAJESTY
KING WILLIAM THE FOURTH.

In the three years left to him before his death in 1760, the father could not bring himself to express gratitude, in quite such an emphatic manner, for his son's 'success in arms'.

During the reign of Queen Victoria – last of the Hanoverian dynasty – the name CULLODEN would be chiselled out of the obelisk's north face and CUMBERLAND incised in its place.

*

In the summer of 1760 – the Prince and his unhappy mistress and daughter having been living for two years at the château de Carlsbourg, near Sedan, seat of his uncle, the duc de Bouillon – Clementina left him. She took with her the seven-year-old Charlotte and found refuge at the convent of the Visitation de Ste Marie, in the rue du Bac, Paris. Mother and child were supported by a pension of 12,000 livres from the Prince's father until his death six years later. Thereafter Charlotte's uncle, Henry Benedict, Cardinal Duke of York, continued the stipend but reduced by half.

Charles stayed at Carlsbourg for the next five years, drinking destructively, resentful at losing his daughter and no doubt brooding on the vicissitudes of fortune. In early 1765, three weeks after his father's death, he arrived in Rome where he was greeted by a crowd of supporters recruited by his brother the Cardinal, with cries of '*Viva il Re*!' But although his father had been granted the full obsequies of a king – eight days lying in state dressed in the robes and crown of the royal House of Stuart and bearing orb and sceptre – Pope Clement XIII refused to recognise the son as Charles III, fearing the same reprisals from the Royal Navy as his predecessor. He continued to pay Charles his late father's pension and allowed him to live in the Palazzo Muti, but the royal arms were removed from above the door and the state coach with its royal insignia was confiscated.

*

In August 1760, at the age of 39, the Duke of Cumberland had suffered a stroke which for a time affected one side of his body and caused memory loss, but its only lingering effect was a slight distortion of the mouth. A further attack in 1764 left him 'sensibly more drowsy & inactive than before', and he was also prone to 'imagine he saw absent people & express anger upon their intruding into his presence'. On 30 October 1765, while playing cards at his London home in Upper Grosvenor Street, those present were alarmed by an outburst of 'groundless offence taken at one of the company'. The following morning, despite passing a restless night, he rose as normal, dressed and went to court. That evening a servant noticed some spasmodic movements or 'catchings' in his left arm and he complained of pain in that shoulder. His surgeon was called, who bled him, but within an hour he had died. During an autopsy conducted the following day, the corpse was opened, and although the condition of the internal organs on examination proved to be 'perfectly sound', their disposition in abdomen and thorax indicated the cause and manner of death. The chest cavity was found to be 'remarkably small', its natural volume having been contracted 'by the pressing upwards of the parts contained in the belly.' The Duke's entire abdominal viscera – stomach, liver and intestine – 'together with a vast quantity of fat had by their immense bulk forced up the diaphragm preternaturally high', thereby lessening the area above 'as not to leave sufficient space for the expansion of the lungs'. He had suffered considerable difficulty in breathing for some time. On further dissection, 'There was not found one drop of blood in either of the vesicles of the heart', whereas, when the upper part of the cranium was removed, 'All the bloodvessels of the membranes & substance of the brain were overfilled with blood.'[53]

In the moments before death that arterial blood – already starved of oxygen by the morbidly constricted lungs – had been expelled from the failing heart to the engorged brain and extremities of his massive body swollen by leakage of blood fluid into atrophying tissue. The entire ruined network of grossly distended veins and capillaries was by then so congested as to be incapable of allowing the sluggish stream to flow back into the exhausted heart, vainly contracting to receive it. The cause of death would today be diagnosed as congestive cardiac failure.

*

At the age of fifty-one Charles Edward Stuart married the twenty-year-old Princess Louise Maximilienne de Stolberg-Gedern, by proxy in Paris on 22 March 1772 and then by a Catholic ceremony at Macerata, Italy on Good Friday, 17 April. The couple moved to Florence in 1774, affecting the titles Count and Countess of Albany. The marriage would effectively last no more than eight years and follow a familiar pattern of alcohol-fuelled abuse.

During the last decade of his life the Prince underwent a catastrophic and lingering decline. In October 1776 he was 'very ill in his health from eating and more from excessive drinking'. Despite greatly swollen legs, one of which was 'commonly open, the discharge from which [was] supposed to be necessary for his existence', he refused to stay at home and repaired each night to the theatre where he would sit in a corner of his box, 'in a drowsy posture, . . . frequently obliged by sickness at his stomach to retire to the common and much frequented *corridore* . . . assisted by two servants'. No longer the glamorous cynosure of men and women of fashion, it was reported that 'all the others who attend [the theatre], fly from such a nuisance.'[54] By May 1779 he was described as 'insupportable in stench and temper'.[55] Unsurprisingly, his wife had long since taken consolation in a series of lovers, the latest and most enduring a Piedmontese poet, Count Vittorio Alfieri.

The Prince's marriage reached an inevitable crisis in late November 1780, although 'the intemperance of his behaviour especially when he was heated with wine and stronger liquors [had] been vented against his Wife . . . in the most . . . cruel manner' for some time past.[56] On St Andrew's Day, ever an occasion for greater indulgence than usual, 'he used her extremely ill, and at night committed the most nauseous and filthy indecencies from above and below upon her, tore her hair, and attempted to throttle her.'[57] Her screams roused the household and prevented further violence, but from that night she made plans to separate from him. Within a fortnight she had escaped into a convent with the connivance of her lover. The enraged Prince offered a reward of a thousand Venetian gold pieces to have Alfieri killed. He even accused Sir Horace Mann – British diplomatic representative to the Grand Duke of Tuscany – of bribing Louise with an even greater sum of money 'to administer a potion to render him impotent'.[58]

Four years later he was solaced for the loss of a wife by the return of a daughter. Charlotte Walkinshaw – now thirty and mistress to the Archbishop of Bordeaux – joined him in Florence where she was formally legitimised as his only child and given the title Duchess of Albany. A happier St Andrew's Day was celebrated in 1784 with a gala dinner during which the self-styled Charles III bestowed upon his daughter the Order of the Thistle.[59] She stayed with her father to the end and effected a reconciliation with his brother, enabling them to return to Rome where he once again occupied the Palazzo Muti. On 30 January 1788 he died in the same room in which he had been born. Of the intervening sixty-seven years only fourteen months spanned the legend by which he is remembered. Twenty-four years prepared him for it, forty-one of decline and disappointment led back to where he began.

II

THE Duke of Cumberland's passing was commemorated by a medal. The obverse presented him in heavily jowelled profile, his armoured shoulder decorated by a grotesque mask with flaring nostrils and bristling eyebrows. On the reverse, to either side of a cartouche bearing his birth and death dates in Latin, leant a lionskin-clad Hercules carrying a club and an extinguished, still smoking torch, and a disconsolate Britannia, a scroll at her feet revealing the name CULLODEN. Above the cartouche Fame's trumpet and a sword were crossed, and the whole was surmounted by a laurel crown and a bowl of incense. Embossed around the rim were the words: SWEET WILLS BLOOM IS CLOSD. This referred to a tradition that the flowering plant *Dianthus barbatus* had been popularly named 'Sweet William' in the days of his fame.

The pride of France is *lily* white;
The *rose* in June is Jacobite;
The prickly *thistle* of the Scot
Is northern knighthood's badge and lot;
But, since the Duke's victorious blows,
The *lily, thistle,* and the *rose*
All droop and fade, all die away;
Sweet William only rules the day.
No plant with brighter lustre grows,
Except the laurel on his brows.[1]

Conversely, the common ragwort* – poisonous to cattle – is known in Scotland as 'Stinking Willie'.

On 15 April 1766 – what would have been the Duke's forty-fifth birthday and the eve of the anniversary of Culloden – Captain John Ross of the 31st Foot had the distinction of being the last member elected to the Cumberland Society, and proud possessor of the last Cumberland Society medal ever struck. Thereafter, in accordance with the Society's constitution, the membership list was frozen and its numbers allowed to reduce by mortal wastage.

*

Five years after his death, an equestrian statue of the Duke in gilded lead† was erected in London's Cavendish Square at the expense of his friend and companion in arms, Lieutenant General William Strode, 62nd Foot. It was unveiled on 4 November 1770, 'being the birth-day and landing of King William III of glorious memory'.[2] According to the inscription it had been 'erected In Gratitude For His Private Kindness, In Honor To His Publick Virtue'. The Duke faced north towards Scotland and, unavoidably, the horse's buttocks towards Hanover Square. By 1868, its gilt weathered away, and in a decrepit state, the statue was removed and melted down by order of the 5th Duke of Portland. The monument was recreated in soap by the Korean artist, Meekyoung Shin in 2012, as part of celebrations marking the London Olympics, and allowed to degrade over the four years between that and the following Games in Rio de Janeiro, when it was finally taken down. The plinth remains.

It has been suggested that the Duke's other statue was toppled from its column in Cumberland Square at the centre of Parsonstown in March of 1915 to placate the feelings of a Scottish regiment

* St. James-wort, *Jacobaea vulgaris*.

† Like the Parsonstown statue, it was the creation of Sir Henry Cheere and probably the last, prior to his retirement in March 1770.

stationed at the time in that area, but it is just as likely that the local council decided to take it down before it fell, its 'dangerous lean' impossible to rectify. Economy dictated it be removed in pieces, and tenders – per hundredweight – were invited for the purchase of the lead. Today, only an arm remains on display in the town's library; the head is in Birr Castle, still home to the Parsons family.

A month after the statue's removal a stranger, 'tall, bearded, and decidedly unconventional in appearance' excited the interest of local police, by taking a photograph of the recently vacated column. Suspecting a breach of national security in time of war, Constable Walshe questioned the individual and found him to be Mr George Bernard Shaw, author of *John Bull's Other Island*. His suspicions of espionage allayed, Walshe apologised to the celebrated playwright and 'they parted after amicable interchanges'.[3]

In 1922, following the creation of the Irish Free State, Cumberland Square was renamed to honour the Irish republican hero Robert Emmet, executed for High Treason in 1803. Duke Street, entering the square from the south, and Cumberland Street from the north were renamed at the same time O'Connell Street and Emmet Street respectively. The cracked and weathered 'Cumberland Column', pockmarked in places by small arms fire during the years of insurrection and civil strife, still stands.

*

Following the death of Charles Edward, Cardinal Henry Benedict Stuart styled himself Henry IX of Great Britain but never pursued the claim which had consumed his brother's life. Symbolism alone was sufficient: his coat of arms to the right of the altar in the ancient church of Santa Maria in the Trastevere district of Rome is topped by a crown instead of the customary *galero* or cardinal's red hat.

After Henry Benedict's death in 1807 his executor, Monsignor Angelo Cesarini, presented George Augustus Frederick, Prince of Wales, later Prince Regent, with a number of jewels and other treasures from the late Cardinal's estate, together with papers amassed by the exiled Stuarts between 1716 and 1770. These bequests – now part of the Royal Collection at Windsor – were in part recognition of the £4,000 annual pension awarded by George III to relieve the Cardinal's destitution following Napoleon Bonaparte's invasion of Italy and the confiscation by France of his Frascati estate.

The remains of both brothers and their father lie in the crypt of St Peter's in Rome. Above, and towards the back of the Basilica, a handsome monument, designed by Antonio Canova in white marble, depicts idealised busts of the three in bas-relief profile and a pair of naked androgynous angels flanking a definitively closed door. The Latin inscription acknowledges only father and grandfather as rightful Kings of Great Britain.

IACOBO III
IACOBI II MAGNAE BRIT REGIS FILIO
KAROLO EDVARDO
ET HENRICO DECANO PATRUM CARDINALIVM
IACOBI III FILIIS
REGIAE STIRPIS STVARDIAE POSTREMIS
ANNO M DCCC XIX*

In 1815 the future George IV subscribed 50,000 francs – approximately 200 pounds sterling – towards the completion of this memorial to the 'Last of the Royal Stuart line'. Seven years later, during his celebrated visit to Edinburgh, he would wear the formerly proscribed philibeg, albeit with the addition of 'Buff coloured trowsers like flesh'.[4] He would reclaim his remote lineage with the adoption of £1,355-worth of scarlet plaid that became known as the 'Royal Stuart' tartan. And in doing so he gave irrevocable royal assent to the Highland dress and culture that his great uncle had sought to eradicate.

* James III / son of James II King of Great Britain / Charles Edward / and Henry, Dean of the Cardinal Fathers / Sons of James III / Last of the Royal Stuart line / 1819

NOTES

Abbreviations

BL	British Library
CP	Cumberland Papers, National Archives, Kew (also available at State Papers Online)
NA	National Archives, Kew
NRS	National Records of Scotland
NLS	National Library of Scotland
TS	Treasury Solicitor Papers, National Archives, Kew

'Forbes' refers to Robert Forbes, *The Lyon in Mourning*, ed. Henry Paton, 3 vols (Edinburgh: 1896), unless otherwise specified.

PRELUDE: ADVICES

1 'Two Letters from Magdalen Pringle', in Tayler, p. 39.
2 Duff, p. 204.
3 Ibid.
4 Murray, 'Marches of the Highland army', in Forbes and Chambers, p. 57.
5 Atholl, vol. 3, pp. 18, 21.
6 Ibid., p. 12.
7 [Fielding], pp. 4–5.
8 Charles Edward Stuart to James Edgar 12 June 1745, quoted Cassavetti, p. 230.
9 O'Sullivan, p. 47.

10 Charles Edward Stuart to James Edgar, in Cassavetti, p. 230.
11 Forbes vol. 1, p. 205.
12 Ibid., p. 148.
13 Ibid., p. 289.
14 Ibid., vol. 3, pp. 120–21.
15 Atholl, vol. 3, p. 7.
16 *Memorials of John Murray*, p. 166.
17 Anon., 'A History of the rebellion . . .', in Tayler, p. 35.
18 *Memorials of John Murray*, p. 166.
19 To Sir Alexander Macdonald, 19 Aug 1745: Duff, p. 376.
20 Forbes and Chambers, p. 22.
21 Forbes, vol. 1, p. 292.
22 Home, p. 50 fn.
23 Forbes and Chambers, p. 24.
24 Danby Pickering, *Statutes at Large* (London: 1761), vol. 18, cap. XXXIX, pp. 274–6.
25 *Caledonian Mercury*, 20 Aug 1745.
26 National Museums Scotland, K.2001.332.
27 *Report of the proceedings*, p. 12.
28 *Scots Magazine*, *History of the Rebellion*, p. 5.
29 Johnson and Boswell, p. 30.
30 *Report of the proceedings*, pp. viii–ix.
31 *Scots Magazine*, *History of the Rebellion* p. 5.
32 *Report of the proceedings*, pp. viii–ix.
33 3 September 1745: Atholl, vol. 3, p. 19.
34 Ibid., p. 51.
35 8 Feb 1746: Ibid., p. 198.
36 Ibid., p. 25.
37 *Woodhouselee MS* pp. 20, 17.
38 *Report of the proceedings*, p. 74.
39 Ibid., p. 70.
40 Ibid., p. 73.
41 Ibid., p. 70.
42 Blaikie, *Origins*, p. 341.
43 Campbell, 'Leaves from the diary', p. 537.
44 *Woodhouslee MS*, pp. 29–21.
45 Carlyle, p. 127; Home, pp. 102–3 fn.
46 *Caledonian Mercury*, 18 Sept 1745.
47 Home, p. 67.
48 *Trial of Archibald Stewart*, S 36.
49 Maclaurin, p. 319.
50 Clerk, p. 180.
51 Carlyle, p. 58.

52 *Report of the proceedings*, p. 71.
53 Quoted in Duffy, *The '45*, p. 197.
54 *Woodhouselee MS*, p. 32.
55 *Report of the proceedings*, p. 35.
56 *Woodhouselee MS*, p. 33.

Tactics, Pox & 'Secrets'

1 Bland, p. 67.
2 Quoted in Duffy, *Fight*, p. 131.
3 Charles, vol. 2, p. 49.
4 *Gentleman's Magazine*, October 1745, p. 517.
5 See *Memorials of John Murray*, p. 205.
6 Threadneedle-street, Nov. 28: *Westminster Journal*, 7 December 1745.
7 22–4 October 1745.
8 Carlyle, p. 66.

PART I: ONSLAUGHT

I

1 See Clerk, p. 186; also Riding, pp. 172–4 for a full discussion.
2 *Report of the proceedings*, Appendix XXXI, p. 36.
3 Ibid., p. 37.
4 Allardyce, vol. 1, p. 279.
5 Johnstone, p. 37.
6 Clerk, p. 180.
7 Elcho, p. 250 fn. 3.
8 Clerk, p. 180.
9 Allardyce, vol. 2, p. 607.
10 To Charles Guthrie 25 September 1745: NRS, Dalhousie Muniments, ex GD45/14/859.
11 O'Sullivan, p. 77.
12 *Report of the proceedings*, p. 38.
13 Murray, 'Marches', in Forbes and Chambers, p. 37.
14 Elcho, p. 269.
15 *Report of the proceedings*, p. 48.
16 Elcho, p. 268.
17 Earl of Home to the Duke of Argyle, Lauder, 21 September, 1745, *Report of the proceedings*, Appendix XXXII, p. 39.

18 Blaikie, *Origins*, p. 406.
19 *Report of the proceedings*, p. 14.
20 Henderson, *Edinburgh History*, p. 29.
21 *Report of the proceedings*, p. 67.
22 *Report of the proceedings*, p. 65.
23 O'Sullivan, p. 80 fn.
24 Quoted in Duffy, *Fight*, p. 129.
25 'Murray's Argument against Cope': *Report of the proceedings*, p. 168.
26 *Report of the proceedings*, p. 87.
27 Lockhart, vol. 2, p. 491.
28 Blaikie, *Origins*, p. 407.
29 Ibid.
30 O'Sullivan, p. 80.
31 *Scots Magazine*, September 1745, p. 439.
32 Charles, p. 58.
33 Allardyce, vol. 1, p. 281.
34 Home, p. 118 fn.
35 *Report of the proceedings*, pp. 85–6.
36 *Woodhouselee MS*, pp. 38–9.
37 Boyse, p. 81 fn.
38 *Report of the proceedings*, p. 50.
39 Allardyce, vol. 1, p. 281.
40 Chambers, vol. 1, p. 151.
41 *Report of the proceedings*, Appendix XXIX, p. 30.
42 Ibid., p. 88.
43 *Newcastle Courant*, 21 September 1745.
44 *Report of the proceedings*, Appendix XXIX, p. 30.
45 Ibid., p. 49.
46 Rev. P. Sumner, '13th Dragoons at Prestonpans, 1745', *Journal of Army Historical Research*, vol. 28, 1950, p. 145.
47 *Woodhouselee MS*, p. 38.
48 *Report of the proceedings*, p. 55.
49 Marchant, p. 105.
50 Johnstone, pp. 35–44.
51 Elcho, pp. 273–4.
52 Johnstone, p. 36.
53 Doddridge, p. 187.
54 Marchant, p. 105.
55 Mr Sharpe, Solicitor to the Treasury, to The Duke of Newcastle, 20 September 1746, quoted in Seton and Arnot, vol. 1, p. 133.
56 *Report of the proceedings*, Appendix XXXI, p. 37.

57 Wightman to the Lord President, Newcastle, 26 Sep 1745: Duff, p. 224.
58 *Woodhouselee MS*, pp. 38–9.
59 O'Sullivan, p. 81.
60 Charles, p. 59.
61 *The Dewar MSS*, pp. 226–7.
62 *Report of the proceedings*, p. 56.
63 Ibid., p. 57.
64 Ibid., p. 60.
65 Ibid., Appendix XXXI, p. 37.
66 Duff, p. 225.
67 Carlyle, p. 74.
68 Henderson, *Edinburgh History*, p. 31.
69 Howes, p. 34.
70 Johnstone, p. 37.
71 Henderson, *Edinburgh History*, p. 31.
72 Johnstone, p. 38.
73 Henderson, *Edinburgh History*, p. 31.
74 *General Advertiser*, 1 November 1745.
75 Blaikie, *Origins*, p. 408.
76 Henderson, *Edinburgh History*, p. 31.
77 Forbes, *Gleanings*, pp. 12–13.
78 Elcho, p. 277.
79 Carlyle, p. 74.
80 *Scots Magazine*, 6 September 1745.
81 Howes, p. 34.
82 Duff, p. 224.
83 *Report of the proceedings*, p. 42.
84 Ibid., p. 54.
85 Ibid., p. 84.
86 *Scots Magazine*, 6 September 1745.
87 *Report of the proceedings*, Appendix LXI, pp. 77–8.
88 Bland, Ch. VIII, Art. I, p. 114.
89 *Report of the proceedings*, p. 100.
90 Rev. John Waugh to Dr Bettesworth, 2 October 1745: Mounsey, p. 27.
91 Forbes, vol. 1, pp. 211–12.
92 Elcho, p. 277.
93 Forbes, vol. 1, pp. 211–12.
94 Johnstone, p. 44.
95 24 September 1745; NLS, MS 3733 (Campbell Letters I), f. 25.
96 *London Evening Post*, 19–22 October 1745.
97 *St James's Evening Post*, 26–9 October 1745.

II

1 See Johnstone, p. 75.
2 Henry Fielding, 'The present history of Great Britain', in *True Patriot*, 10 December 1745.
3 Hardwicke, vol.1, p. 419 fn. 1.
4 *True Patriot*, 17 December 1745.
5 CP, Box 8/11, the Duke of Cumberland to Field Marshal Wade, Blackhall, 24 December 1745.
6 Murray, 'Marches', in Forbes and Chambers, p. 72.
7 Forbes, vol. 2, p. 89.
8 Hardwicke, p. 486.
9 Forbes, vol. 2, pp. 88–9.
10 Marchant, p. 222.
11 TS 20/3, No.3, Anonymous Jacobite Journal.
12 Murray, 'Marches', in Forbes and Chambers, p. 72.
13 Quoted in Duffy, *Fight*, p. 263.

III

1 Elcho, Appendix F, pp. 459–60.
2 Duff, p. 270.
3 Elcho, p. 379; see also William Corse to the Lord President Forbes, 15 February 1746: Duff, p. 270.
4 Atholl, vol. 3, p. 146.
5 Duke of Wellington to John Croker, 8 August 1815. *Quarterly Review*, vol. 92 (1853), p. 545.
6 See Atholl, vol. 3, pp. 153–4: Hawley to Duke of Cumberland, Linlithgow, 17 January 1746.
7 Corse to Forbes: Duff, p. 271.
8 Fergusson, p. 134.
9 Mure, vol. 1, p. 75: Mr Miller to Mr Mure, Glasgow, 10 February 1746.
10 James Pringle to Hugh, 3rd Earl of Marchmont: 'Marchmont Correspondence Relating to the '45', *Miscellany of the Scottish History Society*, vol. 5 (Edinburgh: 1933).
11 CP, Box 9/102.
12 Duff, p. 271.
13 Willson, p. 55.
14 See H.M. Chichester's entry on Francis Ligonier in the *Dictionary of National Biography* (Smith, Elder and Co., 1892).
15 Home, p. 167.
16 Lockhart, vol. 2, p. 469.

17 Seton and Arnot, vol. 1, p. 224.
18 Chambers, vol. 2, p. 10.
19 Collins, p. 22.
20 Home, pp. 175–6 fn.
21 Duff, p. 265 fn.
22 'John Daniel's Progress', in Blaikie, *Origins*, p. 195.
23 Chambers, vol. 2, p. 301 n.2.
24 Maxwell, p. 102.
25 Home, p. 174 fn.
26 Graham, p. 50.
27 Johnstone, p. 122.
28 Quoted in Oughton, p. 7.
29 See Atholl, vol. 3, p. 155.
30 Johnstone, p. 122.
31 Chambers, vol. 2, p. 302, n.5.
32 Major General Cholmondeley to Charles Fleetwood Weston Underwood, 21 January 1746: Fraser, *Reports*, p. 440.
33 Chambers, vol. 2, p. 8.
34 Scott, *Tales of a Grandfather*, vol. 5, p. 279.
35 Ray, p. 244.
36 O'Sullivan, p. 118.
37 'An Account of the Battle of Falkerk': NLS, MS 3733 (Campbell Letters I), f.187.
38 Andrew Fletcher, Lord Milton to President Forbes, Edinburgh, 21 January 1746: Warrand, vol. 4, p. 200.
39 Major General Cholmondeley to Charles Fleetwood Weston Underwood, 21 January 1746: Fraser, *Reports*, p. 440.
40 Hughes, pp. 23–4.
41 *Daily Post*, 24 January 1746.
42 Marchant, pp. 314–15.
43 NLS, MS 3736 (Campbell Letters IV), f. 1020.
44 Quoted in Oughton, p. 8.
45 CP, Box 9/110.
46 Ibid., Box 9/102.
47 Duff, p. 268; see also Alexander MacKenzie, *History of the Monros of Fowlis* (Inverness: 1898), p. 130.
48 Chambers, vol. 2, pp. 10–11.
49 Ibid.
50 CP, Box 9/102.
51 Ibid.
52 Andrew Fletcher, Lord Milton to President Forbes, Edinburgh, 21 January 1746: Warrand, vol. 4, p. 200.
53 Mure, vol. 1, p. 76: Mr Miller to Mr Mure, Glasgow, 10 February 1746.

54 'Narrative of John Lord MacLeod': Fraser, *Earls of Chromertie*, vol. 2, p. 392.
55 Blaikie, *Origins*, pp. 198–9.
56 Duff, p. 272, 'Mr Corse to the Lord President', Edinburgh, 15 February 1746.
57 Mr Maule to Duke James, London, 25 January 1746: Atholl, vol. 3, p. 166.
58 Duff, p. 272, 'Mr Corse to the Lord President' Edinburgh, 15 February 1746.
59 CP, Box 9/102.
60 Murray 'Marches': Forbes and Chambers, p. 85.
61 Duff, p. 272.
62 Marchant, p. 314.
63 Cholmondeley to Edward Weston, 21 January 1746: Fraser, *Reports*, p. 441.
64 Marchant, pp. 314.
65 Johnstone, p. 125.
66 Home, p. 173.
67 To William Sotheron, Edinburgh, 20 January 1746: Willson, p. 56.
68 Cholmondeley to Edward Weston, 21 January 1746: Fraser, *Reports*, p. 441.
69 See Forbes, vol. 2, p. 128.
70 Quoted in Oughton, p. 9.
71 Egmont, p. 313.
72 *Newcastle Courant*, 1 Feb 1746.
73 *Gentleman's Magazine*, March 1746, p. 168.
74 Francis Grose, *Military Anecdotes Respecting a History of the English Army*, vol. 1 (London: 1801), pp. 109–10; see also *Gentleman's Magazine* March 1746, p. 168.
75 Chambers, vol. 2, p. 22.
76 NLS, MS 303, 'Order Books of the Commanders-in-Chief'.
77 Marchant, pp. 314–15.
78 Home, pp. 174–5 fn.
79 William Corse: Duff, p. 272.
80 Chambers, vol. 2, p. 302 n. 5.
81 CP/MAIN/9/99: Hawley to the Duke of Cumberland, 17 January 1746.
82 Home, p. 177.
83 Johnstone, p. 106.
84 Duff, p. 267.

Bayonet & Broadsword

1 Anon., *Seasonable considerations on the present war in Scotland, against the rebels* (London: 1746).
2 Hume, p. 6.

3 Published in London, Wednesday 8 January 1746.
4 Bland, pp. 29–30.
5 January 1746, p. 30.
6 13–15 November 1745.
7 Saturday 3 May 1746.
8 *Scots Magazine*, April 1746.
9 [Hamilton], p. 28.
10 Ibid., p. 22.
11 May 1746, p. 244.
12 18 May 1745.
13 Ibid., 5 July 1746.
14 November 1746, p. 524.

PART II: CARNAGE

I

1 Lockhart, vol. 2, p. 518; Maxwell, p. 140; Murray, 'Marches': Forbes and Chambers, p. 120.
2 Murray, *Marches*, p. 96.
3 Ibid., pp. 120–21; Atholl, vol. 3, p. 278.
4 CP, MAIN/13/404, Orders, 14–15 April 1746.
5 Lockhart, vol. 2, p. 510.
6 Elcho, p. 426.
7 O'Sullivan, p. 155.
8 See Elcho, p. 427.
9 Dennistoun, p. 56.
10 Lockhart, vol. 2, p. 508.
11 Murray to William Hamilton of Bangour: Home, Appendix 42, p. 364.
12 Dennistoun, p. 57.
13 Elcho, p. 428.
14 Murray to William Hamilton of Bangour, Home, Appendix 42, pp. 365–6.
15 O'Sullivan, pp. 157–8.
16 Maxwell, p. 146.
17 Andrew Lumisden in Blaikie, *Origins*, p. 416.
18 'March of the Highland army in the years 1745–46 being the Day Book of Captain James Stuart of Lord Ogilvie's Regiment', *Miscellany of the Spalding Club*, vol. 1 (Aberdeen: 1841), p. 343.
19 Colonel Henry Kerr of Graden: Forbes and Chambers, p. 139; Rev. Innes: Forbes, vol. 2, p. 275.

20 Blaikie, *Origins*, p. 211.
21 *A full and authentic history*, pp. 319–20.
22 NRS, GD1/322/1Duke of Cumberland's Order Book.
23 [Hamilton], p. 22.
24 CP, MAIN/14/47.
25 Home, p. 226.
26 NLS, MS 3735, Campbell of Mamore Letters, Donald Campbell of Airds to Archibald Campbell of Stonefield, 22 April 1746'.
27 Hughes, p. 36.
28 CP, MAIN/13/404, Orders 14–15 April 1746.
29 NLS [ref. no.], 'Order of March from the Camp at Nairn, 15th April 1746'; see also Cumberland's Order Book, NRS, GD1/322/1
30 Whitefoord, pp. 76–8.
31 Hughes, p. 37.
32 Hardwicke, p. 522.
33 Marchant, p. 399.
34 NLS, MS 3735, Donald Campbell of Airds to Archibald Campbell of Stonefield, 22 April 1746.
35 Hardwicke, p. 522.
36 [Hamilton], p. 29.
37 *Scots Magazine*, May 1746, pp. 216–18.
38 William Corse to Lord President Forbes, 15 February 1746, Edinburgh: Duff, p. 272.
39 Wilson, p. 62.
40 Blaikie, *Origins*, pp. 213–14.
41 Boyse, p. 146 fn.
42 Dennistoun, pp. 55–6.
43 *A particular account*, p. 14.
44 Dennistoun, p. 61.
45 Maxwell, pp. 148–9.
46 O'Sullivan, pp. 160, 163.
47 [Linn], p. 24.
48 'A Gentleman in the King's army, from Inverness', *Scots Magazine*, May 1746, p. 247.
49 Hughes, p. 39.
50 Act IV, scene iii.
51 Ray, pp. 329–30.
52 O'Sullivan, p. 163.
53 Maxwell, p. 151.
54 Ibid., p. 148; Elcho, p. 429; Dennistoun, p. 65; 'Rev. George Innes' Narrative': Forbes, vol. 2, p. 277.

11

1 'Rev. George Innes' Narrative': Forbes, vol. 2, p. 278.
2 *Newcastle Journal*, quoted Reid, *1745*, p. 161.
3 *A description of the memorable sieges*, p. 401.
4 *Scots Magazine*, April 1746, pp. 187 and 192.
5 Ibid., p. 194.
6 Royal Chelsea Hospital Admissions: NA, WO.120.
7 Forbes, vol. 2, p. 278.
8 Blaikie, *Origins*, p. 214.
9 John Daniel: Blaikie, *Origins*, p. 214; Chambers, vol. 2, p. 95; Forbes, vol. 2, pp. 160, 225.
10 Dennistoun, p. 63.
11 Wilson, p. 65.
12 *Scots Magazine*, May 1746, p. 247.
13 NLS, MS 3735, Donald Campbell of Airds to Archibald Campbell of Stonefield, 22 April 1746.
14 Hardwicke, p. 523.
15 Whitefoord, p. 78.
16 Maxwell, p. 153.
17 Johnstone, p. 188.
18 Hughes, p. 39.
19 *Scots Magazine*, May 1746, p. 247.
20 Hughes, p. 38.
21 *Gentleman's Magazine*, 1745, p. 422; *Old England or the Constitutional Journal*, Saturday 3 August 1745.
22 *George Faulkner: The Dublin Journal*, 28 January–1 February 1746.
23 See Reid, *1745*, p. 160.
24 Hughes, p. 39.
25 Biggs, p. 359.
26 Hughes, pp. 39–40.
27 [Hamilton], p. 17.
28 O'Sullivan, p. 164.
29 *Scots Magazine*, April 1746, pp. 193–4.
30 Maxwell, p. 152.
31 Chambers, vol. 2, p. 316, n.1.
32 Maxwell, p. 152.
33 Elcho, p. 433.
34 *Scots Magazine*, April 1746, p. 193.
35 Hughes, p. 39.
36 Maxwell, p. 152.

37 *Report on the Laing Manuscripts*, p. 367.
38 Forbes, vol. 1, p. 262.
39 Maxwell, p. 152.
40 Johnstone, p. 190.
41 Whitefoord, p. 78.
42 Hardwicke, p. 523.
43 Elcho, pp. 433–4.
44 Wilson, p. 63.
45 Duke of Cumberland to the Duke of Newcastle, Fraser, *Reports*, p. 443.
46 *Gentleman's Magazine*, April 1746, p. 220.
47 Hughes, pp. 39–40.
48 *Scots Magazine*, April 1746, p. 187 fn.
49 *A full and authentic history*, pp. 327–8.
50 *Scots Magazine*, April 1746, p. 192.
51 *A full and authentic history*, pp. 327–8.
52 Wilson, p. 64.
53 *Scots Magazine*, April 1746, p. 193.
54 Henderson, *Edinburgh History*, p. 117.
55 Murray, 'Marches': Forbes and Chambers, p. 124.
56 'Journal of Mr John Cameron, Presbyterian Preacher and Chaplain at Fort-William': Forbes, vol. 1, p. 87.
57 Hughes, p. 40.
58 Service Historique de la Défense Chateau de Vincennes A1 3154 'Relation de la bataille de Culloden': 'D'ailleurs les rangs étoient si fermés [serrés?] que leur que les montagnards avoient Coupés en morceaux ne tomboient pas, et les vivants, les blessés et les morts composient un corps si solide, que les montagnards furent obligés de renoncer à l'esperance de la percer.'
59 [Hamilton], p. 17–18, 20.
60 O'Callaghan, p. 450.
61 See NA, WO 120, Chelsea Hospital Admission Register, and *A full and authentic history*, p. 328.
62 T. Pollard, *Culloden Battlefield: Report on the Archaeological Investigation*, GUARD (2006), p. 33.
63 Captain James Ashe Lee, of Wolfe's: O'Callaghan, p. 450.
64 Murray, 'Marches', in Forbes and Chambers, p. 124.
65 Allardyce, vol. 2, p. 610, 'Extract of Letter from Officer to friend in Edinburgh dated 18th April'.
66 O'Sullivan, p. 164.
67 Hardwicke, p. 523.
68 Whitefoord, p. 78.
69 Graham, pp. 78–9.
70 Duke of Cumberland to the Duke of Newcastle: Fraser, *Reports*, p. 443.
71 Henderson, *Duke of Cumberland*, p. 254.

72 Maxwell, p. 153.
73 Johnstone, p. 190.
74 Chambers, vol. 2, p. 100.
75 Cumberland to Newcastle, Fraser, *Reports*, p. 443.
76 Henderson, *Duke of Cumberland*, p. 256.
77 Johnstone, p. 214.
78 *Newcastle Journal*: quoted Reid, *1745*, p. 168.
79 Henderson, *Duke of Cumberland*, p. 256.
80 O'Sullivan, p. 165
81 Forbes, vol. 1, p. 381.
82 See Pollard, pp. 123–4.
83 Wilson, p. 63.
84 Dennistoun, pp. 64–5.
85 Johnstone, pp. 196–7.
86 MacKenzie, p. 611.
87 Maxwell, p. 154.
88 [Linn], p. 22.
89 Chambers, vol. 2, p. 99.
90 Marchant, p. 397.
91 [Hamilton], p. 18.
92 *Newcastle Courant*, Saturday 19 April 1746, 'Extract of a Letter from Inverness, April 18'.
93 *Scots Magazine*, April 1746, p. 192.
94 [Hamilton], p. 18.
95 Duke of Cumberland to Duke of Newcastle, Blackhall, 30 December 1745 (CP, MAIN/8/161), cited in Riding, p. 324.
96 [Linn], p. 24.
97 NLS, MS 3735, Campbell Letters, f. 566.
98 Duncan Forbes to Major General Campbell: ibid., f. 554.
99 *Scots Magazine*, April 1746, p. 186.
100 Hughes, pp. 42–3.
101 Forbes, vol. 2, p. 310.
102 Ibid., pp. 310–11.
103 Ibid., p. 307.
104 Ibid., vol. 3, p. 56.
105 Ibid., vol. 1, pp. 217–8.
106 *A full and authentic history*, pp. 332–3.
107 Forbes, vol. 1, p. 219. Lady Mackintosh's house was seven or eight miles from Inverness.
108 Chambers, vol. 2, p. 10.
109 *Gentleman's Magazine*, April 1746, p. 219.
110 Forbes, vol. 2, p. 190.
111 Ibid., pp. 190, 298; vol. 3, pp. 53–4.
112 Ray, pp. 334–7.

The Lyon in Mourning

1 Forbes, vol. 2, p. 190.
2 Ibid., vol. 2, pp. 173, 256.
3 Ibid., p. 352.
4 Ibid., p. 356; vol. 3, p. 57.

PART III: AFTERMATH

I

1 Johnstone pp. 198–201.
2 Forbes, vol. 2, p. 303.
3 See e.g. *Plunderingstaferelen na een veldslag*, Musées royaux des Beaux-Arts de Belgique/Koninklijke Musea voor Schone Kunsten van België, Brussels, Inv. 10836.
4 Hans Jakob Christoffel von Grimmelshausen, *The Adventures of Simplicius Simplicissimus*, tr. J.A. Underwood (London: 2018), p. 51.
5 Carlyle, p. 149
6 O'Sullivan, p. 83 fn.
7 Carlyle, p. 74.
8 Chambers vol. 2, p. 24.
9 Graham, p. 53.
10 Chambers, vol. 2, p. 15.
11 Johnstone, p. 133.
12 Henderson, *Edinburgh History*, p. 95.
13 Elcho, p. 272.
14 Boyse, p. 76.
15 Carlyle, p. 74 fn.
16 Doddridge, pp. 194–5.
17 Chambers, vol. 1, p. 171.
18 Henderson, *Edinburgh History*, p. 33.
19 Chambers, vol. 1, p. 290.
20 Ibid., p. 129.
21 Scott, *Tales of a Grandfather*, vol. 3, p. 210.
22 See Lockhart, p. 450; Elcho, p. 273; *Memorials of John Murray*, p. 209; and *Caledonian Mercury*, 27 Sept 1745.
23 Hume, p. 6.
24 Chambers, vol.1, p. 171.
25 *Gentleman's Magazine*, January 1746, p. 42.
26 O'Sullivan, p. 20.

27 Forbes, vol. 1, p. 381.
28 NLS, MS 3736, f. 1020.
29 NLS, MS 3787, Order Book of the Stewart of Appin Clan Regiment, 11 October 1745 to 18 January 1746.
30 *Gentleman's Magazine*, February 1746, p. 61.
31 Chambers, vol. 2, pp. 11, 15; and Lord George Murray to Duke William, 18 January 1746: Atholl, vol. 3, p. 158.
32 NLS, Order Book of Commanders-in-Chief.

II

1 O'Sullivan, p. 83.
2 H.A.L. Howell, 'The Story of the Army Surgeon . . . from 1715 to 1748', *Journal of the Royal Army Medical Corps*, vol. 22 (1914), p. 466.
3 *Memorials of John Murray*, p. 205.
4 Carlyle, p. 74 fn.
5 Chambers, vol. 1, p. 168.
6 Carlyle, p. 75.
7 NA, WO 120.
8 Carlyle, p. 153.
9 David Hume, p. 6.
10 NA, WO 120.
11 O'Sullivan, p. 83.
12 Charles Edward Stuart to his Father, Pinkie House, 21 September 1745: Forbes, vol. 1, p. 215.
13 Royal Collection Trust, RCIN 729154.
14 Chambers, vol. 1, pp. 171–2.
15 Forbes, vol. 2, pp. 88–9.
16 'Letter from a Volunteer Surgeon in the Duke's Army, dated at Clifton, Dec. 21': *London Evening Post*, 24–6 December 1745.
17 Sir Philip Musgrave to Dr Waugh, Barnard Castle, 20 December 1745: Mounsey, p. 135.
18 'Letter from a Volunteer Surgeon', *London Evening Post*, 24–6 December 1745.
19 Ray, pp. 198–9; Mr Nicholson to Dr Waugh (n.d.): Mounsey, p. 137.
20 Marchant, p. 221.
21 Ibid., p. 224.
22 Hughes, p. 17.
23 See Appendix in Home, p. 392.
24 See Atholl, vol. 3, p. 155.
25 Allardyce, vol. 1, p. 298.

26 Chambers, vol. 2, p. 302.
27 Maxwell, p. 105.
28 Elcho, pp. 378–9.
29 Atholl, vol. 3, p. 158.
30 January 1746, p. 43.
31 14 January 1746.
32 Wilson, p. 57.
33 George Murray to Lady Murray, '22 Jan, 9 at night': Atholl, vol. 3, p. 159.
34 Elcho, p. 380.
35 Maxwell, p. 110.
36 *Jacobite Correspondence of the Atholl Family*, Alexander Robertson of Strowan [Struan] to Mr. Thomas Blair in Atholl, p. 165.
37 Elcho, pp. 381.
38 Chambers, vol. 2, p. 25.
39 Hardwicke, p. 494.
40 'Lochgarry's Narrative': Blaikie, *Itinerary*, p. 119.
41 Johnstone, p. 128.
42 *The Operative*, Sunday 24 February 1839.
43 Chambers, vol. 2, p. 24.
44 'Two Letters of 1746': to James Urquhart, writing from Aberdeen, 24 January, in *Miscellany of the Spalding Club*, vol. 4 (Aberdeen: 1849), p. 321.
45 'Extracts from the Diary of the Rev. John Bisset': *Miscellany of the Spalding Club*, vol. 1 (Aberdeen: 1841), pp. 370–71.
46 Stephen Abel Laval, *A compendious history of the Reformation*, vol. 4, appendix, pp. 93–4.
47 Reid, *1745*, pp. 38–41, compiled from Whitefoord, p. 59.
48 Carlyle, pp. 76–7.
49 Seton and Arnot, vol. 1, pp. 274–5.
50 Henderson, *Duke of Cumberland*, p. 262.
51 Cited in Seton and Arnot, vol. 1, pp. 275–6.
52 Henderson, *Duke of Cumberland*, p. 262.
53 *Gentleman's Magazine*, February 1746, p. 61.
54 Marchant, p. 322.
55 Home, pp. 133–9.
56 Collins, pp. 23–4.

III

1 O'Sullivan, p. 84 fn.
2 Chambers, p. 166.

3 Henderson, *Edinburgh History*, p. 32.
4 *Gentleman's Magazine*, April 1746, p. 235.
5 NRS, GD1/322/1, Cumberland's Order Book, 19 April 1745.
6 Ibid., p. 104.
7 Ibid., p. 119.
8 Ibid., p. 107.
9 *Gentleman's Magazine*, May 1746, p. 272.
10 Marchant, p. 395.
11 NRS, GD1/322/1, Cumberland's Order Book.
12 Henderson, *Duke of Cumberland*, p. 260.
13 NRS GD1/322/1, Cumberland's Order Book.
14 Lord Archibald Campbell, *Notes on Swords from the Culloden Battlefield* (London: 1894), p. 13.
15 *Caledonian Mercury*, Thursday 5 June 1746.
16 *Stamford Mercury*, Thursday 19 June 1746.
17 *Caledonian Mercury*, Thursday 5 June 1746.
18 *Stamford Mercury*, Thursday 19 June 1746.
19 Whitefoord, p. 81.
20 *Newcastle Courant*, Saturday 28 June 1746.
21 Forbes, vol. 3, p. 12.
22 Pringle, p. 45.
23 Buchanan, p. 153.
24 Pringle, p. 16.
25 Ibid., p. viii.
26 NRS, GD1/322/1, Cumberland's Order Book, 23 April 1746.
27 Pringle, pp. 46–53.
28 Seton and Arnot, vol. 1, p. 153.
29 NRS, GD1/322/1, Cumberland's Order Book.
30 *Gentleman's Magazine*, April 1746, p. 220.
31 Forbes, vol. 1, p. 381.
32 Ibid., p. 251.
33 Ibid., vol. 2, p. 4.
34 Ibid., vol. 1, p. 218.
35 Ibid., vol. 2, pp. 329–30.
36 Ibid., vol. 1, p. 251–2.
37 Ibid., vol. 2, p. 303.
38 See Anderson, *Culloden Moor*, pp. 129–30.
39 Forbes, vol. 2, pp. 261, 328.
40 Ibid., vol. 3, p. 71.
41 Ibid., vol. 2, p. 230; see also p. 303.
42 Ibid., vol. 3, pp. 2–3.
43 Ibid., vol. 2, pp. 302, 330, and vol. 3, p. 72.
44 Anderson, *Culloden Moor*, pp. 114, 89, 76.

45 Ibid.
46 Charles Edward Stuart to his Father, Pinkie House, 21 September 1745: Forbes, vol. 1, p. 215.
47 Ibid., p. 219.
48 Ibid., vol. 3, p. 12.
49 Anderson, *Culloden Moor*, pp. 34, 88.
50 Chambers, vol. 2, p. 115.
51 'Croy and Dalcross', p. 561 fn.
52 Chambers, vol. 2, p. 116.
53 Anderson, *Culloden Moor*, pp. 89–90.

IV

1 Forbes, vol. 3, p. 74.
2 Forbes, 'Memorandum for His R[oyal] Highness the Duke, Inverness May 20 1746', (CP, 15/101).
3 Forbes, vol. 3, p. 97.
4 Ibid., vol. 2, pp. 301, 330.
5 *Scots Magazine*, August 1746.
6 Albemarle, vol. 1, p. 56.
7 Forbes, vol. 3, p. 74.
8 *Scots Magazine*, July 1746, pp. 339–40.
9 *Statutes at Large*, vol. 6 (1764), cap. XXXIX, pp. 704–10.
10 CP, 14/234.
11 *Scots Magazine*, June 1746, p. 285.
12 To Philip Yorke, 22 May 1746: Hardwicke, pp. 528–9.
13 Ibid.
14 NRS, GD1/322/1, Cumberland's Order Book, 24 May 1746.
15 Idib., 3 June 1746.
16 Hardwicke p. 543, 3 June 1746.
17 June 1746.
18 Whitefoord, p. 79.
19 Forbes, vol. 3, p. 108.
20 *Gentleman's Magazine*, June 1746.
21 NRS, GD1/322/1, Cumberland's Order Book, 29 May 1746.
22 NLS, MS 3735, Campbell of Mamore Letters, Duke of Cumberland to Major General Campbell, 30 May 1746.
23 Hughes, p. 52.
24 NRS, GD1/322/1, Cumberland's Order Book, 29 May 1746.
25 NLS, MS 3735, Campbell of Mamore Letters, Duke of Cumberland to Major General Campbell, 30 May 1746.
26 Albemarle, vol. 1, p. xxx.
27 Ibid., vol. 1, pp. 331–40.

28 Whitefoord, p. 79–80.
29 To Philip Yorke, 3 June 1746: Hardwicke, p. 543.
30 CP, Box 15/190, 'Camerons' Submission'.
31 CP, Box 15/278, Campbell to Sir E. Fawkener, Strontian, 31 May 1746.
32 Albemarle, vol. 1, p. 340.
33 Hardwicke, p. 544.
34 Hughes, p. 54.
35 NRS, GD1/53/9.
36 *Scots Magazine*, June 1746, p. 288.
37 Forbes, vol. 2, p. 308 and fn. 1; vol. 3, p. 57.
38 Ibid, vol. 1, p. 94; Albemarle, vol. 1, p. 333.
39 Forbes, vol. 2, p. 306-7 and vol. 3, p. 57.
40 Hughes, p. 52.
41 Forbes, vol. 2, p. 355.
42 Ibid., vol. 3, p. 120.
43 Ibid., p. 17.
44 Whitefoord, pp. 79–80.
45 Hardwicke, p. 543, 3 June 1746.
46 NRS, GD1/53/92, 'Anecdotes of Captn. Caroline Scott Communicated by MacNeil of Barra & the Revd. M. Ed. MacLuen'.
47 Royal Archives, SP/MAIN/275/26: Desmond Shawe-Taylor, ed., *The First Georgians: Art and Monarchy 1714–1760* (London: 2014), cat. 64, p. 125.
48 Browne, vol. 3, pp. 263–4.
49 Forbes, vol. 1, p. 168.
50 Ibid., pp. 142–3 and 136.
51 Blaikie, *Itinerary*, p. 53, fn.3.
52 Johnson and Boswell, p. 284.
53 Forbes, vol. 3, p. 211.
54 NLS, MS 3736 (Campbell Letters VI), f. 835, 13 July 1746.
55 See *Scots Magazine*, July 1746, p. 341.
56 Earl of Albemarle to the Duke of Newcastle, 15 October 1746: Albemarle, vol. 1, p. 289.
57 Forbes, vol. 1, pp. 280 and 308-10 fn.3.
58 Ibid., p. 280.
59 Johnstone, p. 213.
60 Forbes, vol. 1, p. 311.

Wine, Punch & Patriotism

1 Act I, scene viii.
2 Benjamin Victor to David Garrick, 10 Oct 1745: Victor, vol. 1, p. 118; *Gentleman's Magazine*, October 1745, p. 552.

3 *Stamford Mercury*, 12 December 1745.
4 *General Evening Post* 28 September–1 Oct, 1745.
5 *Gentleman's Magazine*, October 1745, p. 552.
6 Ibid., October 1836, p. 373.
7 *Spectator*, no. 18, 21 March 1710–11.
8 *Gentleman's Magazine*, November 1745, p. 593.
9 *True Patriot*, no. 1, November 1745.
10 Royal College of Physicians, Edinburgh, Pringle Papers, vol. 7, pp. 603–4.
11 Ranby, pp. 46, 52.

PART IV: CELEBRATION

I

1 Hughes, pp. 34–5; see also Forbes, vol. 2, p. 274.
2 *Scots Magazine*, April 1746, p. 194.
3 *Woodhouselee MS*, p. 13.
4 *Scots Magazine*, April 1746, p. 194.
5 *Stamford Mercury*, 10 April 1746.
6 *Caledonian Mercury*, 18 April 1746.
7 *Glasgow Courant*, 21 April 1746.
8 Ibid., 19 April 1746.
9 *London Magazine*, April 1746, p. 256.
10 *George Faulkner: The Dublin Journal*, 19 April 1746.

II

1 *Derby Mercury*, 27 December 1745.
2 *London Courant*, 19 November 1745.
3 *General Advertiser*, 15 November 1745.
4 *London Magazine*, December 1745.
5 *General Advertiser*, January 8 1746.
6 [Fielding].
7 Ibid., p. 46–7.
8 *True Patriot*, no. 1, 5 November 1745.
9 Burney, vol. 4, p. 452.
10 Ibid.
11 *La caduta de' giganti*, libretto.
12 Part I, scene vii.
13 *Derby Mercury*, 27 December 1745, 'Extract of a letter from Brampton, Dec. 25'.

14 *London Gazette Extraordinary*, 2 January 1746.
15 Quoted by Speck, *Butcher*, p. 102.
16 *Ode on the Success of His Royal Highness the Duke of Cumberland*, 1746.
17 *London Evening Post*, 4–7 January 1746.
18 *General Advertiser*, 7 and 15 January 1746.
19 24 January 1746.
20 'Ocassion'd by the present Rebellion', published December 1745.
21 'On the Duke of Cumberland's going to Scotland, to take upon him the Command of the Army against the Rebels', January 30 1746.
22 *General Advertiser*, Saturday 1 February 1746.
23 *Penny London Post*, 3–5 February 1746.
24 *Newcastle Courant*, 18–25 January 1746, 'Extract of a Letter from Sunderland, January 23'.
25 *Newcastle Courant*, 4 January 1746 'Extract of a Letter from Stokesley in Yorkshire, December 27'.
26 *London Evening Post*, 14–16 January 1746, 'Letter from Edinburgh Jan. 7'.
27 *General Advertiser*, 12 February 1746, 'Letter from Edinburgh 1 February'.
28 Surgeon's Hall, Edinburgh, College Minute Book, 25 March 1746.
29 Foundling Museum, Gerald Coke Handel Collection, accession no. 2702, 'Jennens Holdsworth Letters 2,' item 110. f. 1.
30 *Occasional Oratorio*, Part I, soprano air.
31 Rev. Wiliam Harris to Mrs Thomas Harris, Lincoln's Inn, 8 February 1746: Deutsch p. 630.
32 1733, 1738 and 1741 respectively.
33 Chorus and castrato solo, Part II.
34 Bass air, Part III.
35 Chorus, Part III.
36 Forbes vol. 1, p. 293.
37 *General Evening Post*, 14–17 December 1745, 'Letter from a lady in Preston to her friend in town, 14 December 1745'.
38 *St James's Evening Post*, December 1745–February 1746, *passim*.
39 The costume suggested for the character by Benjamin Victor on another occasion: see Victor, vol. 1, p. 120.
40 Britannia Rediviva.

III

1 Sir Godfrey Dalrymple-White, 'The "Cumberland" Society', *Society for Army Historical Research*, Special Publication, vol. 6 (January–March 1927), pp. 164–74.

2 *London Evening Post*, 24–6 April 1746.
3 *Scots Magazine*, April 1746, p. 185.
4 NRS, GD18/3259 Rd. Pringle, Edinburgh, 24 April 1746, to George Clerk of Drumcrief, Dumfries. Pringle's letter puts the round of guns at 'about 3 o'clock'; all other reports an hour earlier.
5 *Caledonian Mercury*, 21 April 1746.
6 *General Advertiser*, 1 May 1746.
7 *Glasgow Courant*, 21–8 April 1746; see also NAS, GD18/3259, Rd. Pringle to George Clerk of Drumcrief.
8 2 Samuel 18: 28; see *Newcastle Courant* 26 April–3 May 1746.
9 Exodus 15: 1, 6, 7.
10 Walpole, *Correspondence*, vol. 19, p. 247, letter to Sir Horace Mann [British Envoy to the Court of Tuscany], 'Arlington Street April 25th [started 24th] 1746'.
11 *Newcastle Courant*, 19 April 1746.
12 Walpole, *Correspondence*, vol. 19, p. 247.
13 *General and St James's Evening Post*, 26 April 1746.
14 *Newcastle Courant*, 26 April 1746.
15 S. Poyntz to Sir E[verard] Faulkener [secretary to Cumberland], St James, 24 April 1746: CP, Box 14/109.
16 *General Advertiser*, 26 April 1746.
17 *General and St James's Evening Post*, 26 April 1746.
18 'Extracts from the Diary of the Rev. John Bisset': *Miscellany of the Spalding Club*, vol. 1 (Aberdeen: 1841), p. 352: 21 Oct. 1745.
19 Carlyle, pp. 59 and 98–9.
20 *General and St James's Evening Post*, 26 April 1746.
21 *General Advertiser*, 26 April 1746.
22 *Gentleman's Magazine*, June 1746, p. 324.
23 *General Advertiser*, 17 May 1746.
24 Ibid., 30 April 1746.
25 Ibid., 29 April 1746.
26 Ibid., 7 May 1746.
27 Ibid., 8 May 1746.
28 CP, 14/114.
29 *General Advertiser*, 30 May 1746.
30 *Newcastle Courant*, Saturday 19 July–Saturday 26 July 1746.
31 *General London Evening Mercury*, 24–6 July 1746.
32 *George Faulkner: The Dublin Journal*, 29 July 1746.
33 Albemarle, vol. 1, p. 194, Magistrates to Lord Justice-Clerk, Aberdeen, 29 August 1746.
34 NLS, MS 17527, ff.45–57 'Aberdeen August 2nd 1746 . . . Copie Precognition anent the Ryot committed by the Soldiers in this Town last night'.

35 Albemarle, vol. 1, p. 194, Magistrates to Lord Justice-Clerk, Aberdeen, 29 August 1746.
36 NLS, MS 17527, ff.45–57, 'Copie Precognition'.
37 Albemarle, vol. 1, pp. 28–9, Lt. Col. Geo. Jackson to Major Roper, Aberdeen 3 Aug 1746.
38 Ibid., Fletcher to the magistrates.
39 Ibid., p. 194, Magistrates to the Earl of Albemarle, 16 August 1746.
40 *Derby Mercury*, Friday 4–Friday 11 July 1746.
41 NA, SP 54/32/24C, Sir Everard Fawkener, Secretary to the Duke of Cumberland, to the magistrates of Montrose, Scotland, Fort Augustus, 19 June 1746.
42 Albemarle, vol. 1, pp. 348–9: Earl of Albemarle to the Duke of Newcastle, 24 December 1746.
43 Quoted in Deutsch, p. 639; advertisement in *General Advertiser*, 2 April 1747 quoted ibid.
44 Quoted ibid., p. 851: letter from Morrell to unknown recipient, *c.*1764.
45 To John Nichols, reprinted in full in Ruth Smith, 'Thomas Morell and His Letter about Handel', *Journal of the Royal Musical Association*, vol. 127, no. 2 (2002), pp. 191–225.
46 *Public Advertiser*, 12 May 1773.
47 Ibid., 18 September 1775.
48 *Lloyd's Evening Post*, 10 February 1779.
49 *Morning Herald and Daily Advertiser*, 28 December 1782.
50 *St James's Chronicle or British Evening Post*, 14 June 1794.
51 *Public Advertiser*, 20 April 1787.
52 *Morning Chronicle*, 23 June 1815.
53 Walpole, *Correspondence*, vol. 19, p. 288, 1 August 1746 to Sir Horace Mann.

'a publick, cruel & barbarous Death'

1 'distrahendo, suspendendo, decolando, eius uiscera concremando ac eius corpus quaterando', NA, MS E372/150, Pipe Roll of 33 Edward I (Michaelmas 1304–5).
2 See *Scots Magazine*, July 1746, p. 325.
3 Treason Act 1351: 25 EDW. III. Stat.5.c.2,3, *Statutes of the Realm*, pp. 319–20.
4 Seton and Arnot, vol. 1, p. 95.
5 *Scots Magazine*, July 1746, pp. 325–6.
6 *Penny London Post or Morning Advertiser*, 25–8 July 1746.
7 *Scots Magazine*, July 1746.
8 Howell, vol. 18, pp. 377–8.

9 Ibid., pp. 351-2 and 377–8.
10 *Scots Magazine*, July 1746, p. 329.
11 Forbes, vol. 3, p. 158.
12 *Westminster Journal or New Weekly Miscellany*, 9 August 1746.
13 *London Evening Post*, 31 July 1746.
14 *Caledonian Mercury*, 28 August 1746.
15 *Scots Magazine*, July 1746, pp. 325–6.
16 *Westminster Journal or New Weekly Miscellany*, 9 August 1746.
17 Walpole, *Correspondence*, vol. 9, p. 46, 16 August 1746.
18 *General Advertiser*, vol. 9, August 1746, p. 464.
19 *Westminster Journal or New Weekly Miscellany*, 9 August 1746.
20 *Derby Mercury*, 26 September 1746.
21 Seton and Arnot, vol. 1, pp. 105–6.
22 NA, G. Howard, SP 36/89/1/19.
23 *Derby Mercury*, 24 Oct 1746.
24 NA, SP 36/89/1/55.
25 They were placed there about 10 o'clock at night on 19 September. See *Old England or the Broadbottom Journal*, Saturday 4 October 1746.
26 'An Act for the More Easy and Speedy Trial of Such Persons as Have Levied, Or Shall Levy War Against His Majesty; and for the Better Ascertaining the Qualifications of Jurors in Trials for High Treason, Or Misprision of Treason, in that Part of Great Britain Called Scotland' (19 Geo. 2. C. 9): Howell, vol. 18, pp. 329–30.
27 NRS, GD1/384/32, 'Major MacDonald's Speech who was executed at Carlile the 18 of October 1746'.

PART V: RECKONINGS

I

1 Bradstreet, pp. 156–7.
2 NRS, GD1/322/1, Duke of Cumberland's Order Book, p. 103, 17 April.
3 NRS, MS303, Order Books of Commanders-in-Chief, Edinburgh, 21 January 1745/6.
4 NRS, GD1/322/1, Duke of Cumberland's Order Book, p. 131, 27 April 1746.
5 Boyse, p. 154.
6 Henderson, *Duke of Cumberland*, p. 263.
7 NRS, GD1/322/1, Duke of Cumberland's Order Book, pp. 114 and 120, 20 and 23 April 1746.

8 Ibid., p. 125, 25 April 1746.
9 NRS, GD103/2/387, 'Brigade order book of the Duke of Cumberland's army'; a contemporary transcript of the Duke of Cumberland's Order Book (NRS, GD1/322/1) for 30 January 1746, pp. 3–4, has 'Corporal' for 'Capital'.
10 NRS, GD1/322/1, Duke of Cumberland's Order Book, pp. 148–95, May 1746.
11 Ibid., p. 171, 16 May 1746.

II

1 See 3 vols of Seton and Arnot. Vol. 1, p. 86 gives 'not less than 2500' in confinement in England at different times during 1746–7.
2 *General Advertiser*, 11 February 1746.
3 NRS, GD1/322/1, Duke of Cumberland's Order Book, pp. 145–6, 4 May 1746.
4 Captain John Farquharson: Forbes, vol. 3, pp. 155–6.
5 Ibid., vol. 2, pp. 312–13.
6 Ibid., vol. 1, p. 49.
7 Quoted in Seton and Arnot, vol. 1, p. 5.
8 Quoted ibid., p. 90.
9 Forbes, vol. 3, p. 157.
10 Ibid., vol.2, p. 315.
11 Ibid., vol. 3, p. 158.
12 Ibid., p. 15.

III

1 NA, TS 20/44/2.
2 Seton and Arnot, vol. 1, pp. 7–8.
3 Ibid., p. 55.
4 Ibid., p. 26.
5 NA, TS 20/44/3.
6 NA, TS 20/44/1, William Sharpe to Duke of Newcastle, 13 June 1746.
7 NA, TS 20/15/11–12, 10 August 1746.
8 NA, TS 20/15/1–24.
9 NA, SP 36/86/1/31, Webb to Sharpe, 2 August 1746.
10 NA, SP 36/86/1/289, Webb to Sharpe, Carlisle, 14 August 1746.
11 NA, SP 36/89/1/22, Howard to Webb, Carlisle, 3 Nov. 1746.

12 NA, TS 20/15/7–8, 6 August 1746.
13 NA, TS 20/8/11–2, letter from F. Cayvan, Gravesend, to Captain Eyre, 19–20 August 1746.
14 NA, TS 20/15/13–14, 15 August 1746.
15 NA, TS 20/80/29, 20 August 1746.
16 NA, TS 20/15/20–21.
17 NA, TS 20/15/33–34 'Saturday morn' [n.d.]
18 Cited in Seton and Arnot, vol. 1, pp. 159–60.
19 Forbes, vol. 3, p. 32.
20 NA, TS 20/15/22-23, 14 September 1746.
21 'Captain Eyre's report', dated 11 October 1746, quoted in Seton and Arnot, vol. 1, pp. 10–11.
22 Forbes, vol. 3, p. 30.
23 NA, TS 20/15/26-27, 7 October 1746.
24 NA, TS 20/38/11–12.
25 Clarke, p. 54.
26 NA, TS 20/38/9–10, Carlisle, 11 August 1746.
27 NA, TS 20/44/7–11, Sharpe to the Duke of Newcastle, 29 July 1746.

IV

1 *Derby Mercury*, 29 August 1746.
2 Clarke, p. 29.
3 Ibid., p. 34.
4 Ibid., p. 21.
5 Ibid., pp. 38–40.
6 Ibid., p. 54.
7 Ibid., p. 29.
8 Mounsey, p. 258.
9 Clarke, p. 32.
10 Seton and Arnot, vol. 2, p. 128.
11 Ibid., p. 277.
12 Clarke, p. 33.
13 *Scots Magazine*, September 1746, p. 437.
14 Clarke, p. 31.
15 *Scots Magazine*, September 1746, p. 440.
16 NRS GD1/384/30.
17 NRS GD1/384/31.
18 Clarke, p. 25.
19 Ibid., p. 51.
20 NA, TS 20/38/15 and NA, SP 36/87/3, Philip Carteret Webb to the Duke of Newcastle, 25 and 22 September 1746.
21 Forbes, vol. 1, p. 52.

22 Albemarle, vol. 2, p. 419.
23 NA, SP 36/87/3, Webb to Newcastle, 22 September 1746.
24 NA, SP 36/87/3/119, Webb to Newcastle, 27 September 1746.
25 NA, SP 36/86/1/284 and 289, Webb to Newcastle, Carlisle, 14 August 1746.
26 See Seton and Arnot, vol. 3, p. 237; also Clarke, p. 57, in which his name appears as 'Ogilby'.
27 See Seton and Arnot, vol. 3, p. 402; also Clarke, p. 59.
28 See Seton and Arnot, vol. 2, p. 275; also Clarke, p. 57.
29 Seton and Arnot, vol. 1, p. 133.
30 Clarke, p. 59.
31 *Derby Mercury*, Friday 10 October 1746.
32 Clarke, p. 57.
33 Quoted in Seton and Arnot, vol. 3, p. 267.
34 *Scots Magazine*, November 1746.
35 NA, SP 36/88/1/138.

V

1 'The Case of Archibald Steuart of Brugh . . .' NRS GB18/3256.
2 CP, Box 15/263, Samuel Smith to Fawkener, 30 May 1746.
3 *General Advertiser*, 29–31 May 1746.
4 CP, Box 15/263, Samuel Smith to Fawkener, 30 May 1746.
5 5 June 1746, quoted in Seton and Arnot, vol. 1, p. 5.
6 CP, Box 15/263, Samuel Smith to Fawkener, 11 September 1746.
7 See A.C. Wardle, 'Sir Thomas Johnson and the Jacobite Rebels', *Transactions of the Historic Society of Lancashire and Cheshire*, vol. 91 (1939), pp. 125–42.
8 NA, TS 18/1.
9 NA, TS 20/47/1–5.
10 NA, TS 20/25/56.
11 NA, TS 20/18/2.
12 NA, SP 36/87/1/148.
13 NA, TS 20/35/9, 18 November 1746.
14 NRS, GD103/2/383/1–2.
15 Forbes, vol. 2, pp. 240–41.
16 NRS, GD103/2/383/2.
17 NA, TI 328/36-7.
18 *Scots Magazine*, May 1747.
19 NA, SP 36/106/2/145, 27 April 1748.
20 To Sharpe, 22 October 1747: NA, SP 36/102/129; see also *Caledonian Mercury*, 9 April 1747.
21 See Dobson, p. 126.

22 *Newcastle Courant*, 14 January 1749.
23 *Derby Mercury*, 23 June 1749.
24 'Extract of a Letter from Manchester, Jan. 24': *Aberdeen Press and Journal*, 12 February 1751.

VI

1 31 July 1746.
2 Mary Granville Delany, *The Autobiography and Correspondence of Mrs Delany*, ed. Mary Chauncey Wolsey (Boston: 1879), p. 339, cited in Kimberly Chrisman, 'Unhoop the Fair Sex: The Campaign Against the Hoop Petticoat in Eighteenth-Century England', *Eighteenth Century Studies*, vol. 30, no. 1 (Fall 1996), p. 16.
3 *General Advertiser*, 28 July 1746.
4 Walpole, *Correspondence*, vol. 19, p. 285, to Horace Mann, 1 August 1746.
5 Howell, vol. 18, pp. 485–6.
6 *Scots Magazine*, August 1746, p. 376.
7 Walpole, *Correspondence*, vol. 19, p. 285 to Horace Mann, 1 August 1746.
8 Howell, vol. 18, pp. 491–4.
9 Walpole, *Correspondence*, vol. 19, p. 285, to Horace Mann, 1 August 1746.
10 Howell, vol. 18, pp. 491–4.
11 Walpole, *Correspondence*, vol. 19, p. 287, to Horace Mann, 1 August 1746.
12 Howell, vol. 18, p. 502.
13 Bradstreet, pp. 160–61.
14 *Newcastle Courant*, 16 August 1746.
15 *Gentleman's Magazine*, August 1746.
16 Howell, vol. 18, pp. 509–10.
17 Bradstreet, p. 161.
18 Howell, vol. 18, p. 520.
19 Ibid., p. 509.
20 Bradstreet, p. 162.
21 Howell, vol. 18, p. 513; *Gentleman's Magazine*, August 1746, p. 392.
22 Ibid.
23 Bradstreet, p. 163.
24 *Gentleman's Magazine*, August 1746, p. 393.
25 Ibid.
26 *Newcastle Courant*, 11–18 April 1747.

27 'Copy of what Dr Archibald Cameron intended to be delivered to the Sheriff of Middlesex, at the Place of Execution': *A full and authentic history*, p. 368.

'a frightful country'

1 Defoe, p. 672.
2 Hardwicke, vol. 1, p. 541, Yorke to the Lord Chancellor, Fort Augustus, 26 May 1746.
3 Ibid., Yorke to Hon. Elizabeth Yorke (afterwards Lady Anson), Inverness, 22 May 1746.
4 Roy, pp. 386–7.
5 'dated at Newcastle, on the 29th of December 1745', quoted in Chalmers, vol. 2, pp. 60–1 fn. i.
6 Defoe, p. 663.
7 Roy, pp. 386–7.
8 *Cantonment Register*, p. 42, 17 July 1747.
9 Quoted in Hewitt, p. 20.
10 Quoted in Anderson and Fleet, p. 119.
11 MacIvor, p. 412.
12 Hewitt, p. 39.
13 Roy, pp. 386–7.

PART VI: ENDINGS

I

1 For a full discussion see Blaikie, *Itinerary*, Additional Note 7, pp. 102–3.
2 O'Sullivan, p. 208.
3 *An authentic account*, p. 10.
4 O'Sullivan, p. 209.
5 *An authentic account*, p. 51.
6 O'Sullivan, p. 209.
7 Goring, p. 29.
8 MS Journal of Lord Elcho, quoted by Ewald, vol.2, p. 230.
9 Chambers, vol. 2, p. 123.
10 *Derby Mercury*, 9 May 1746.
11 *Newcastle Courant*, 12 July 1746.
12 *Penny London Post or Morning Advertiser*, 30 July–1 August 1746.

13 *Westminster Journal*, 9 Aug 1746; *Public Advertiser*, 8 December 1752.
14 *Derby Mercury*, 12 Jan 1753; *Oxford Journal*, 11 August 1753.
15 See Paul O'Keeffe, https://artuk.org/discover/stories/george-stubbs-cheetah-and-stag-with-two-indians(accessed 20 August 2020).
16 16 July 1748, quoted in David Daiches, *Charles Edward Stuart: The Life and Times of Bonnie Prince Charlie* (London: 1973), p. 268.
17 *An authentic account*, pp. 37–41.
18 Broglie, p. 325.
19 *Traité entre le roy . . . 1718.*
20 Broglie, p. 325.
21 *An authentic account*, p. 45.
22 Quoted Casavetti, p. 266–7.
23 *Copy of a letter from a French lady at Paris*, p. 5.
24 Lochaber Archive Centre, Fort William: 'Copy of the Chevalie[r]'s Letter to his Son P[rince] E[dwar]d', included in 'Copy of a Letter from France, concerning the Adventures [of Prince Charles Edward]'.
25 *Copy of a letter*, pp. 9–11.
26 Lochaber Archive Centre, Fort William, 'Copy of a Letter from France, concerning the Adventures [of Prince Charles Edward]'.
27 *Copy of a letter*, p. 13
28 *An authentic account*, p. 62
29 Lochaber Archive Centre, Fort William, 'Copy of a Letter from France, concerning the Adventures [of Prince Charles Edward]'.
30 quoted Casavetti, pp. 269–70.
31 *Constitutional queries.*
32 *Scots Magazine*, January 1751.
33 Walpole, *Memoirs*, vol. 1, p. 6.
34 *Scots Magazine*, January 1751.
35 Walpole, *Memoirs*, vol. 1, p. 68, fn. 5.
36 Petrie, p. 178.
37 Ibid., p. 187.
38 King, p. 197.
39 'Draft Proclamation of 1759', quoted in Petrie, p. 180.
40 Henry Pelham to the Duke of Newcastle, 29 July–9 August 1748: Coxe, vol. 1, p. 462.
41 Ibid, vol. 2, p. 169; see also Walpole, *Memoirs*, vol. 1, p. 55.
42 Ibid.
43 Ibid., pp. 71–2.
44 Forbes, vol. 3, pp. 128–9.

45 Lang, p. 213.
46 MS Journal of Lord Elcho, quoted by Cassavetti, p. 280.
47 Ewald, vol. 2, p. 222.
48 MS Journal of Lord Elcho, quoted by Ewald, vol. 2, p. 230.
49 *General Advertiser*, Dublin, 19 Sept 1752.
50 *Leinster Reporter*, 6 February 1915.
51 Walpole, *Memoirs*, vol. 2, pp. 282–3.
52 Chambers, vol. 2, p. 123.
53 Royal College of Physicians, Edinburgh, Pringle Papers Vol. 7 pp. 601–8, 'The Duke of Cumberland's Autopsy'.
54 12 October 1776: Walpole, *Correspondence*, vol. 24, p. 244.
55 25 May 1779: ibid., vol. 24, p. 480.
56 NA, GD1/264/1, Florence, 12 December 1780, Horace Mann to the Earl of Hillsborough.
57 12 December 1780: Walpole, *Correspondence*, vol. 25, pp. 100–101.
58 NA, GD1/264/1, Florence, 12 December 1780, Horace Mann to the Earl of Hillsborough.
59 See Cassavetti, p. 292.

II

1 *Stamford Mercury*, 14 August 1746.
2 *Oxford Magazine or Universal Museum*, vol. 5, November 1770, p. 195; see also John Stewart, *Critical observations on the buildings and improvements of London* (London: 1771).
3 *Liverpool Echo*, 16 April 1915, and *Leinster Reporter*, 17 April 1915.
4 NRS GD157/2548/3, Harriet Scott to her daughter Anne.

SELECT BIBLIOGRAPHY

Primary Sources

A description of the memorable sieges and battles in the North of England . . . chiefly contained in the Memoirs of General Fairfax, and James Earl of Derby; to which is added . . . an impartial history of the Rebellions . . . 1715, and 1745 (Bolton: 1786)

A full and authentic history of the Rebellion 1745 and 1746 . . . by an impartial hand (London: 1755)

Albemarle, William, 2nd Earl of, *The Albemarle Papers: being the Correspondence of William Anne, Second Earl of Albemarle, Commander in Chief in Scotland, 1746–1747*, ed. Charles Sandford Terry, 2 vols (Aberdeen: 1902)

Allardyce, James, ed., *Historical Papers Relating to the Jacobite Period, 1699–1750*, 2 vols (Aberdeen: 1895–6)

An authentic account of the conduct of the Young Chevalier: from his first arrival in Paris, after his defeat at Culloden, to the conclusion of the Peace at Aix-la-Chapelle . . . in a letter from a gentleman residing at Paris, to his friend in London, 2nd edn (London: 1749)

A particular account of the Battle of Culloden . . . in a letter from an officer of the Highland Army to his friend at London (London: 1749)

Atholl, John, 7th Duke of, ed., *Chronicles of the Atholl and Tullibardine Families*, 5 vols (Edinburgh: 1908)

Biggs, William, *The military history of Europe, &c: from the commencement of the war with Spain in 1739, to the treaty of Aix-la-Chapelle in 1748: containing all the transactions of that *war both by sea and land: also comprehending a concise and impartial history of the rebellion in Scotland* (London: 1755)

Blaikie, W.B., *Origins of the 'Forty-Five and Other Papers Relating to that Rising* (Edinburgh: 1916)

Bland, Humphrey, *A treatice of military discipline; in which is laid down and explained the duty of the officer and soldier, thro' the several branches of the service*, 5th edn (London: 1743)

Boyse, Samuel, *Historical review of the transactions of Europe . . . to which is added an impartial history of the late Rebellion* (Reading: 1747)

Bradstreet, Dudley, *The life and uncommon adventures of Capt. Dudley Bradstreet* (Dublin, 1755)

Britannia Rediviva: or Courage and Liberty, an Allegorical Masque as it is Performed at the New Wells, Clerkenwell, The Music composed by Mr John Dunn (London: 1746)

Buchanan, John, *Regimental Practice: An Eighteenth Century Medical Diary and Manual*, ed. Paul Kopperman (Farnham and Burlington, VT: 2012)

Burney, Charles, *A general history of music from the earliest ages to the present period*, vol. 4 (London: 1789)

Burton, John, *A genuine and true journal of the most miraculous escape of the Young Chevalier, from the Battle of Culloden, to his landing in France* (London: 1749)

Campbell, John, 'Leaves from the diary of John Campbell, an Edinburgh banker in 1745', *Miscellany*, Scottish History Society, First Series, vol. 15 (Edinburgh: 1893)

Cantonment Register of the British Army in Scotland, 1746–52, transcribed and published by Stennis Historical Society (Version 1.2, 13 January 2019, https://sites.google.com/site/stennishs/downloads, accessed 20 August 2020)

Carlyle, Alexander, *Anecdotes and Characters of the Times*, ed. James Kinsley (London: 1973)

Charles, George, *History of the Transactions in Scotland, in the Years 1715–16, and 1745–46*, vol. 2 (Leith: 1817)

Clarke, Charles, *Transcript of Baron Clarke's Note-Book,* transcr. Kenneth Smith, Carlisle Library, Local Studies Dept., Local Studies 1BC 9072 Jacobite Rebellion

Clerk, John, *Memoirs of the Life of Sir John Clerk of Penicuik*, ed. John M. Gray (Edinburgh: 1892)

Constitutional queries earnestly recommended to the serious consideration of every true Briton [London: 1751]

Copy of a letter from a French lady at Paris. Giving a particular account of the manner in which Prince Edward was arrested (London: 1749)

Coxe, William, *Memoirs of the Administration of the Right Honourable Henry Pelham*, 2 vols (London: 1829)

'Croy and Dalcross, County of Inverness', *Old Statistical Account*, vol. 11, 1794

Defoe, Daniel, *A Tour through the Whole Island of Great Britain* (Harmondsworth: 1986)

Dennistoun, James, ed., *Memoirs of Sir Robert Strange and Andrew Lumisden*, 2 vols (London: 1855)

Deutsch, Otto Erich, *Handel: A Documentary Biography* (London: 1955)

The Dewar Manuscripts, Collected Originally in Gaelic by John Dewar for George Douglas, VIIIth Duke of Argyll . . ., ed. John Mackechnie, vol. 1 (Glasgow: 1964)

Doddridge, Philip, *Some Remarkable Passages of the Life of Colonel James Gardiner* (London: 1747)

Duff, H.R., ed., *Culloden Papers comprising an extensive and interesting correspondence from the year 1625 to 1748* (London: 1815)

Egmont, John, First Earl of, *Manuscripts of the Earl of Egmont, Diary of the First Earl of Egmont (Viscount Percival)*, vol. 3, 1730–1747, Historical Manuscripts Commission (London: 1923)

Elcho, David, Lord, *A short account of the affairs of Scotland in the years 1744, 1745, 1746*, ed. Evan Charteris (Edinburgh: 1907)

[Fielding, Henry,] *The History of the Present Rebellion in Scotland* (London: 1745)

Forbes, J. Macbeth, *Jacobite Gleanings from State Manuscripts, Short Sketches of Jacobites, The Transportations in 1745* (Edinburgh and London: 1903)

Forbes, Robert, *The Lyon in Mourning: or a collection of speeches letters journals etc, relative to the affairs of Prince Charles Edward Stuart by the Rev. Robert Forbes*, ed. Henry Paton, 3 vols (Edinburgh: 1896)

Forbes, Robert, and Robert Chambers, eds. *Jacobite Memoirs of the Rebellion of 1745* (Edinburgh: 1834) [includes Lord George Murray, 'Marches of the Highland army']

Fraser, Sir William, *The Earls of Chromertie, Their Kindred, Country, and Correspondence*, 2 vols (Edinburgh: 1776)

Fraser, Sir William, Reports on the Manuscripts of the Earl of Eglinton, Sir J. Stirling Maxwell, Bart., C.S.H. Drummond Moray, Esq., C.F.

Weston Underwood, Esq., and G. Wingfield Digby, Esq, Royal Commission on Historical Manuscripts (London: 1885)

Goring, Henry, *A letter from H— G—g, Esq. . . . to a particular friend* (London: 1750)

Graham, D[ougal], *An impartial history of the rise, progress, and extinction of the late rebellion in Britain . . . 1745 and 1746*, 8th edn (Glasgow: 1808)

[Hamilton, Daniel], 'Observations on Mr Home's Account of the Battle of Culloden' (Exeter: 1802)

Hardwicke, Philip, Earl of, *Life and Correspondence of Philip Yorke, Earl of Hardwicke*, 3 vols (Cambridge: 1913)

Henderson, Andrew, *The Edinburgh History of the Late Rebellion*, 4th edn with additions (London: 1748)

Henderson, Andrew, *The Life of William Augustus, Duke of Cumberland* (London: 1766)

Home, John, *The History of the Rebellion in the Year 1745* (London: 1802)

Howell, T.B., ed., *A Complete Collection of State Trials and Proceedings*, vol. 18, 1743–53 (London: 1813)

Howes, Audrey, ed., 'An account of Prestonpans, 1745', *Journal of the Society for Army Historical Research*, vol. 80 (2002), pp. 32–5.

Hughes, Michael, *A plain narrative and authentic journal of the late Rebellion*, 2nd edn (London: 1747)

Hume, David, *A true account of the behaviour and conduct of Archibald Stewart, Esq., late Lord Provost of Edinburgh* (London: 1748)

Jacobite Correspondence of the Atholl Family During the Rebellion . . . From the Originals in the possession of James Erskine of Aberdona, Esq. (Edinburgh: 1840)

Johnson, Samuel, and James Boswell, *A Journey to the Western Islands of Scotland* and *The Journal of a Tour to the Hebrides*, ed. R.W. Chapman (London: 1970)

Johnstone, James, *Memoirs of the Rebellion in 1745 and 1746*, 2nd edn (London: 1821)

King, William, *Political and Literary Anecdotes of his own Times* 2nd edn (London: 1819)

[Linn, Edward] W.H. Anderson, 'The Battle of Culloden . . . as described in a letter from a Soldier of the Royal army to his Wife', *Journal of the Society of Army Historical Research*, vol. 1 (1921–2), pp. 21ff.

Lockhart, George, *The Lockhart Papers*, 2 vols (London: 1817)

MacKenzie, Alexander, *History of the MacKenzies with Genealogies of the Principal Families of the Name* (Inverness: 1894)

Maclaurin, Colin, 'Colin Maclaurin's Journal of the "Forty-five"', ed. Bruce A. Hedman, *Miscellany XIII*, Scottish History Society, Fifth Series, vol. 14 (Edinburgh: 2004)

Maclean, John, 'A journall of the travells and marches of John Maclean in his Highness's army 1745', transcr. in Iain Gordon Brown and Hugh Cheape, *Witness to Rebellion: John Maclean's Journal of the 'Forty-Five and the Penicuick Drawings* (East Linton: 1996)

Marchant, John, *The history of the present rebellion* (London: 1746)

Maxwell of Kirkconnell, James, *Narrative of Charles Prince of Wales' Expedition to Scotland in the Year 1745* (Edinburgh: 1861)

Memorials of John Murray of Broughton sometime secretary to Prince Charles Edward 1740–1747, ed. Robert Fitzroy Bell (Edinburgh: 1898)

Mure, William, *Selections from the Family Papers Preserved at Caldwell*, Part II, vol. I (Glasgow: 1854)

O'Sullivan, John William, *1745 and After*, ed. Alastair and Henrietta Tayler (London: 1938)

Oughton, James Adolphus, *By Dint of Labour and Perseverance*, ed. Stephen Wood, Society of Army Historical Research (London: 1997)

Pringle, John, *Observations on the diseases of the army in camp and garrison*, 2nd edition (London: 1753)

Ranby, John, *The method of treating gunshot wounds*, 3rd edn (London: 1781)

Ray, James, *A compleat history of the Rebellion* (York: 1749)

Report of the proceedings and opinion of the Board of General Officers, on their examination into the conduct, behaviour, and proceedings of Lieutenant-General Sir John Cope (Dublin: 1749)

Report on the Laing Manuscripts Preserved in the University of Edinburgh, vol. 2, Historical Manuscripts Commission (London: 1925)

Roy, William, 'An account of the measurement of a base on Hounslow-Heath', *Philosophical Transactions of the Royal Society*, vol. 75 (1785), pp.385–480.

Ruffhead, Owen, *The statutes at large, from the third year of King George II to the twentieth year of King George II*, vol. 6 (London: 1763)

Scots Magazine, *The history of the Rebellion in 1745 and 1746, extracted from the Scots Magazine; with an Appendix containing an account of the trials of the rebels . . .* (Aberdeen: 1755)

Scott, Walter, *Waverley; or 'Tis Sixty Years Since*, 3 vols (Edinburgh: 1814) [Penguin edition details TBC]

Scott, Walter, *Tales of a Grandfather*, vols 3 and 5 (London: 1836)

Statutes of the Realm printed by command of His Majesty King George the Third in pursuance of an address of the House of Commons of Great Britain from original records and authentic manuscripts, vol. 1 (London: 1810, repr. 1963)

Trial of Archibald Stewart . . . for neglect of duty and misbehaviour in the execution of his office, as Lord Provost of Edinburgh (Edinburgh: 1747)

Tayler, Henrietta, ed., *A Jacobite Miscellany: Eight Original Papers on the Rising of 1745–6* (Oxford: 1948)

Traité entre le roy, l'empereur et le roy de la Grande Bretagne, pour la pacification de l'Europe: conclu à Londres . . . 1718 (Paris: 1719)

Victor, Benjamin, *Original letters, dramatic pieces, and poems*, 3 vols (London: 1776)

Walpole, Horace, *Horace Walpole's Correspondence*, ed. W.S. Lewis, 48 vols (New Haven and London: 1937–83)

Walpole, Horace, *Memoirs of King George II*, ed. John Brooke, 3 vols. (New Haven and London: 1985)

Warrand, Duncan, ed., *More Culloden Papers*, 5 vols (Inverness: 1927–30)

Willson, Beckles, *The Life and Letters of James Wolfe* (London: 1909)

Whitefoord, Charles, and Caleb Whitefoord, *The Whitefoord Papers: being the correspondence and other manuscripts of Colonel Charles Whitefoord and Caleb Whitefoord from 1738 to 1810*, ed. W.A.S. Hewins (Oxford: 1898)

Woodhouselee Manuscript. A narrative of events in Edinburgh and district during the Jacobite occupation, September to November 1745 (London and Edinburgh: 1907)

Secondary Sources

Anderson, Carolyn, and Christopher Fleet, *Scotland: Defending the Nation* (Edinburgh: 2018)

Anderson, Peter, *Culloden Moor*, rev. edn (Stirling: 1920)

Blaikie, W.B., *Itinerary of Prince Charles Edward Stuart from his Landing in Scotland July 1745 to his Departure in September 1746* (Edinburgh: 1897)

Black, Jeremy, *Culloden and the '45* (Stroud: 2010)

Bowditch, Lyndsey, Andrew MacKillop and Tony Pollard, *Cùil Lodair/Culloden*, National Trust for Scotland (Edinburgh: 2009)

Broglie, [Albert, 4th] duc de, *La paix d'Aix-la-Chapelle* (Paris: 1892)

Browne, James, *History of the Highlands and of the Highland Clans*, vol. 3 (Glasgow: 1840)

Campbell, John Gregorson, *Superstitions of the Highlands and Islands of Scotland Collected Entirely from Oral Sources* (Glasgow: 1900)

Cassavetti, Eileen, *The Lion and the Lilies: The Stuarts and France* (London: 1977)

Chalmers, George, *Caledonia: or, an account, historic and topographic, of North Britain, from the most ancient to the present times*, vol. 2 (London: 1810)

Chambers, Robert, *History of the Rebellion in Scotland in 1745, 1746*, 2 vols (London: 1827)

Charteris, Evan, *William Augustus Duke of Cumberland: His Early Life and Times (1721–1748)* (London: 1913)

Collins, Varnum Lansing, *President Witherspoon* (Princeton: 1925)

Daniels, Stephen, and John Bonehill, *Paul Sandby: Picturing Britain* (London: 2009)

Devine, T.M., *The Scottish Nation: 1700–2000* (London: 1999)

Dobson, David, *Scottish Emigration to Colonial America 1606–1785* (Athens, GA: 2004)

Duffy, Christopher, *The '45: Bonnie Prince Charlie and the Untold Story of the Jacobite Rising* (London: 2003)

Duffy, Christopher, *Fight for a Throne: The Jacobite '45 Reconsidered* (Solihull: 2015)

Ewald, Alex[ander] Charles, *The Life and Times of Prince Charles Stuart, Count of Albany, commonly called the Young Pretender, from the State Papers and other sources*, 2 vols (London: 1875)

Fergusson, Sir James, *John Fergusson 1727–1750: An Ayrshire Family and the Forty-Five* (London: 1948)

Forsyth, David, ed., *Bonnie Prince Charlie and the Jacobites*, National Museum of Scotland (Edinburgh: 2017)

Hewitt, Rachel, *Map of a Nation: A Biography of the Ordnance Survey* (London: 2010)

Horrock, Hilary, ed., *Glenfinnan Monument*, National Trust for Scotland (Edinburgh: 2006)

Howley Hayes Architects, *The Cumberland Column, Birr, Co. Offaly Conservation Report* (Dublin: 2009)

Lang, Andrew, *Pickle the Spy, or The Incognito of Prince Charles* (London: 1897)

Livingstone, Alastair, Christian Aikman and Betty Stuart Hart, eds., *No Quarter Given: The Muster Roll of Prince Charles Edward Stuart's Army, 1745–46* (Glasgow: 2001)

MacIvor, Iain, 'Fort George, Inverness-Shire, Part I', *Country Life*, 12 August 1976, pp. 410–13.

Maclachlan, A.N. Campbell, *William Augustus, Duke of Cumberland: Being a Sketch of His Military Life and Character, Chiefly as Exhibited in the General Orders of H.R.H., 1745–1747* (London: 1876)

McLynn, Frank, *Bonnie Prince Charlie: Charles Edward Stuart* (London, 1988)

McLynn, Frank, *The Jacobite Army in England 1745* (Edinburgh: 1998)

Mounsey, G.G., *Authentic Account of the Occupation of Carlisle in October 1745, by Prince Charles Edward Stuart* (London: 1856)

O'Callaghan, John Cornelius, *A History of the Irish Brigades in the Service of France* (Glasgow: 1885)

Petrie, Sir Charles, 'The Elibank Plot, 1752–3' *Transactions of the Royal Historical Society*, vol. 14, 1931, pp.175–96

Pittock, Murray G.H., *Jacobitism*, British History in Perspective (London: 1998)

Pollard, Tony, ed., *Culloden: The History and Archaeology of the Last Clan Battle* (Barnsley: 2009)

Prebble, John, *Culloden* (London: 1961)

Reid, Stuart, *Like Hungry Wolves: Culloden Moor 16 April 1746* (London: 1994)

Reid, Stuart, *1745: A Military History of the Last Jacobite Rising* (Staplehurst: 1996)

Riding, Jacqueline, *Jacobites: A New History of the '45 Rebellion* (London: 2016)

Seton, Bruce Gordon, and Jean Gordon Arnot, eds., *The Prisoners of the '45*, 3 vols (Edinburgh: 1928)

Seward, Desmond, *The King over the Water: A Complete History of the Jacobites* (Edinburgh: 2019)

Speck, W.A., *The Butcher: The Duke of Cumberland and the Suppression of the '45* (Cardiff: 1981)

Speck, W.A., 'Prince William Augustus, Duke of Cumberland', *ODNB* online, 2008

Woosnam-Savage, R.C., ed., *1745: Charles Edward Stuart and the Jacobites* (Edinburgh: 1995)

Archive Sources

Bibliothèque Historique de la Ville de Paris
British Library (BL)
Carlisle Library, Local Studies Department
Foundling Museum, London, Gerald Coke Handel Collection
Highland Archive Service, Inverness
Lochaber Archive Centre, Fort William
National Archives, Kew (NA)
National Museums Scotland
National Records of Scotland (NRS)
National Library of Scotland (NLS)
National War Museum of Scotland
Royal College of Physicians, Edinburgh
Service Historique de la Défense Chateau de Vincennes, Paris
Surgeons' Hall, Edinburgh

Newspapers and Journals

Modern journals

Journal of the Royal Army Medical Corps
Journal of the Royal Musical Association
Journal of the Society for Army Historical Research
Transactions of the Historic Society of Lancashire and Cheshire

Contemporary newspapers, etc.

Aberdeen Press and Journal

Caledonian Mercury
Daily Post
Derby Mercury
Eighteenth-Century Studies
General Advertiser
General Evening Post
General London Evening Mercury
General and St James's Evening Post
Gentleman's Magazine
George Faulkner: The Dublin Journal
Glasgow Courant
Leinster Reporter
Liverpool Echo
London Evening Post
London Gazette
London Magazine
Lloyd's Evening Post
Morning Chronicle
Morning Herald and Daily Advertiser
Newcastle Courant
Newcastle Journal
The Operative
Oxford Magazine or Universal Museum
Penny London Post
Public Advertiser
St James's Evening Post
Scots Magazine
Spectator
Stamford Mercury
True Patriot
Westminster Journal or New Weekly Miscellany

ACKNOWLEDGEMENTS

I am grateful to the Society of Authors for the award of a travel grant that enabled me to visit Inverness and the battlefield of Culloden, and to the military archives in Paris.

Thanks, as ever, to the staff of the wonderful London Library, the British Library, the National Library of Scotland, the National War Museum's library, Edinburgh Castle, the Fellows Library of the Surgeons' Hall, and the library of the Royal College of Physicians, Edinburgh. Thanks to the Local Studies Department of Carlisle Library, the Highland Archive Service, Inverness, the Lochaber Archive Service, Fort William, the Bibliotheque Historique de la Ville de Paris, and the Service Historique de la Defence, Chateau de Vincennes, Paris. I am particularly indebted to the National Archives at Kew and to National Records Scotland, in Edinburgh. Especial thanks also for the time given me in the storerooms of the Royal Armouries, Leeds, by Mark Murray-Flutter, Senior Curator of Firearms, and Robert Woosnam-Savage, Curator of Armour and Edged Weapons.

Thanks to Julie Lawson, Senior Curator of the Scottish National Portrait Gallery, for drawing my attention to the possible implications of Henry Benedict Stuart's ordination for his elder brother's safety and wellbeing; to John Clark Ch.M., FRCS for providing a diagnosis and cause of death based on the Duke of Cumberland's autopsy report; and to Malcolm Hicks for explaining the characteristics of Pindaric verse. Stuart Allan, Curator of Military History at the National Museum of Scotland, and Jacqueline Riding, author of *Jacobites: A New History of the 1745 Rebellion*, gave me early encouragement and confidence in the viability of my offering another treatment of the subject. Membership of the 1745 Association introduced me to a circle of people who generously shared their enthusiasm and knowledge of Jacobite history during annual Gatherings at Shap, London and Edinburgh. They included Stephen Lord, David McNaughton, Michael J. Nevin, Glen MacDonald, and the late and greatly missed Brian Whiting.

Thanks to Carys and Julian McCarthy for their warm and vinous hospitality in New Malden, and to Ian and Helen Wood, for theirs in Portobello, Edinburgh. Ian S. Wood has also been a boundless fund of Scottish history and informative conversation over pints, pies and late-night drams.

I was still at work on the book – checking revised proofs – while being prepared and marked up for full knee replacement surgery at Broadgreen Hospital, Liverpool. Proofreading continued in the recovery ward, and concluded while convalescing at home. I am sincerely grateful for the consummate care and skill of my surgeon, Mr John S. Davidson, anaesthetist Dr Laura Dagg and the rest of the surgical and nursing team that brought the procedure to a happy outcome.

Thanks to my agent Bill Hamilton, to Stuart Williams my publisher at The Bodley Head, to my scholarly copy-editor Henry Howard, and to my meticulous and patient proof-reader Fiona Brown. Jörg Hensgan and Lauren Howard saw the book through to production with their customary thoroughness, patience, and good humour. A special thanks, also, to Stephen Parker for the most apposite jacket design I could have wished for.

Will Sulkin has now been my editor and valued friend for thirty years. His ever insightful contribution to this and previous books has been unfailing, his encouragement unstinting, his constructive criticism unerring. The interruption of our working lunches – so readily and eagerly arranged prior to any London visit – has been a minor but no less keenly felt privation of Covid 19. I look forward to once again raising a glass, eating and talking together face to face – be it in Bow Street or Fitzrovia – and resuming the good times of those last three decades.

My thanks and love go to my Civil Partner, Sian Hughes, who has lived with this book for the past four years and driven us the length and breadth of Scotland during its composition.

Sadly, the book was not completed in time to be shared with my brothers. It is belatedly dedicated to them both.

LIST OF ILLUSTRATIONS

AFTERMATH: Culloden Battlefield © Chronicle / Alamy Stock Photo

Wine, Punch & Patriotism: The Laughing Audience, Engraving by William Hogarth © World History Archive / Alamy Stock Photo

CELEBRATION: The True Contrast. Reproduced with permission from the National Library of Scotland. (Creative Commons Attribution (CC-BY) 4.0 International Licence)

A Public, Cruel & Barbarous Death: The new and complete Newgate calendar; or, villany displayed in all its branches . . . Containing . . . narratives . . . of the various executions and other exemplary punishments . . . in England, Wales, Scotland and Ireland, from the year 1700 to the present time / by William Jackson. Public Domain Mark

RECKONINGS: The Tower of London: Execution © Granger Historical Picture Archive / Alamy Stock Photo

A Frightful Country: 'View near Loch Rannoch' by Paul Sandby © British Library Board. All Rights Reserved / Bridgeman Images

ENDINGS (p.312): Monument to the Stuarts, built by Antonio Canova © DEA / ICAS94 / Contributor via Getty images

ENDINGS (p.313): The Pope, the devil and the Young Pretender lie prostrate near the coffin of the Duke of Cumberland lined with two rows of lit candles and mourning figures. Engraving by WW. after J.C., 1765. Credit: Wellcome Collection. Attribution 4.0 International (CC BY 4.0)

INDEX